BURMA/MYANMAR – WHERE NOW?

T0079700

ASIA INSIGHTS

A series aimed at increasing an understanding of contemporary Asia among policy-makers, NGOs, businesses, journalists and other members of the general public as well as scholars and students.

1. *Ideas, Society and Politics in Northeast Asia and Northern Europe: Worlds Apart, Learning From Each Other*, edited by Ras Tind Nielsen and Geir Helgesen

2. *The Shanghai Cooperation Organization and Eurasian Geopolitics: New Directions, Perspectives, and Challenges*, edited by Michael Fredholm

3. *Burma/Myanmar – Where Now?* edited by Mikael Gravers and Flemming Ytzen

4. *Dialogue with North Korea? Preconditions for Talking Human Rights With the Hermit Kingdom*, by Geir Helgesen and Hatla Thelle

5. *After the Great East Japan Earthquake: Political and Policy Change in Post-Fukushima Japan*, edited by Dominic Al-Badri and Gijs Berends

6. *Walking a Tightrope: Defending Human Rights in China*, by Gert Holmgaard Nielsen

NIAS Press is the autonomous publishing arm of NIAS – Nordic Institute of Asian Studies, a research institute located at the University of Copenhagen. NIAS is partially funded by the governments of Denmark, Finland, Iceland, Norway and Sweden via the Nordic Council of Ministers, and works to encourage and support Asian studies in the Nordic countries. In so doing, NIAS has been publishing books since 1969, with more than two hundred titles produced in the past few years.

UNIVERSITY OF COPENHAGEN

Nordic Council of Ministers

BURMA ☆ MYANMAR
WHERE NOW?

Edited by

Mikael Gravers and Flemming Ytzen

with the special assistance of Marie Ditlevsen

Burma/Myanmar – Where Now?
Edited by Mikael Gravers and Flemming Ytzen

Nordic Institute of Asian Studies
Asia Insights series, no. 3

First published in 2014 by NIAS Press
NIAS – Nordic Institute of Asian Studies
Øster Farimagsgade 5, 1353 Copenhagen K, Denmark
Tel: +45 3532 9501 • Fax: +45 3532 9549
E-mail: books@nias.ku.dk • Online: www.niaspress.dk

A CIP catalogue record for this book is available from the British Library

ISBN: 978-87-7694-112-3 (hbk)
ISBN: 978-87-7694-113-0 (pbk)

Typeset in Arno Pro 12/14.4 and Frutiger 11/13.2
Typesetting by NIAS Press

Printed and bound in Great Britain by
Marston Book Services Limited, Oxfordshire

Cover illustrations – front: monks protesting against the military regime during the
Saffron Revolution, 2007 (David Høgsholt); back: child from the delta, symbolizing
the Burmese people's curiosity yet uncertainty towards their future (Marie Ditlevsen)

Contents

Preface   vii
Contributors   ix
Abbreviations   xiii

Introduction (Mikael Gravers and Flemming Ytzen)   1
Dark realities, glimmers of hope (David Høgsholt)   3
The Gathering Pace of Change   19

Part 1: Order and change
Preserving order amid change and developing change amid order
    (Flemming Ytzen)   25
        Apropros fear • Different media culture, different pressure from above •
        Broadcast media still heavily controlled • Human rights in Burma
Local actors (Flemming Ytzen and Mikael Gravers)   46
        The 8888 generation
Towards a new state in Myanmar (Michael Lidauer)   72
Development of civil society (Charles Petrie and Ashley South)   87
        Defining civil society
The Kyi to the Great Game East (Bertil Lintner)   95
        China tolerates the United States in Burma, up to a point
International actors (Josine Legêne and Flemming Ytzen)   109
Social issues (Marie Ditlevsen)   121
        The situation of women

Part 2: Challenges to unity
The colonial legacy (Mikael Gravers)   143
        Myanmar Citizenship Law 1982
Ethnic diversity, multiple conflicts (Mikael Gravers)   149
        Non-Burman ethnic groups • Natives and foreigners • Ethnic nationalities –
        main political organizations and armed groups • Kachin Independence Army
Ethno-nationalism and violence in Burma/Myanmar – the long Karen
        struggle for autonomy (Mikael Gravers)   173
        Who Are the Karen? • Key dates for the Karen
The Karen in Myanmar's southeast – great hopes and many unresolved issues
        (Tim Schroeder & Alan Saw U)   198
        'If they come again … '

Coming home! (Lian H. Sakhong)   217
Peace-building in Myanmar (Charles Petrie and Ashley South)   223
Update on the peace process (Ashley South)   250
    Casualties of war
The struggle for peace in northern Myanmar (Wai Moe)   262
    Who are the Kachin?
The religious dimension (Mikael Gravers and Marie Ditlevsen)   279
Religion, identity and separatism – the case of the Kachin (Mandy
    Sadan)   284
    Aung San Suu Kyi: Translating Buddhist concepts into democracy
Politically engaged Buddhism – spiritual politics or nationalist medium?
    (Mikael Gravers)   293
Contending approaches to communal violence in Rakhine State (Ardeth
    Maung Thawnghmung)   323

Part 3: Economy, development and environment
Economic fundamentals, ongoing challenges (Marie Ditlevsen)   341
    *The Myitsone entanglement • Local actors in the economy • Crony capitalists
    • What does political change in Burma offer migrant workers in Thailand?*
Burma's economy and the struggle for reform (Sean Turnell)   369
    Foreign investors • Investment issues
Development challenges and environmental issues (Marie Ditlevsen)   387
    Cyclone Nargis
Foreign aid to Myanmar (Marie Ditlevsen)   399
Opportunities and challenges for donors and INGOs operating in Myanmar
    (Jonas Nøddekær and Marie Ditlevsen)   406

Part 4: The way ahead
Whither Burma? (Mikael Gravers and Flemming Ytzen)   417

    Historical landmarks   422
    List of organizations   425
    Further reading   428
    Index   431

Preface

This book has been written in response to *and as a guide to understanding* the rapidly changing situation in Myanmar/Burma. It is partly written by journalists, partly by academics – all with knowledge of and experience in the country. The overarching theme is the current reform process, peace-building and democratization as well as prospects for the future.

Most of the chapters are brief, and the contributors have been allowed to write in their own style. We do not pretend to cover all relevant subjects of the complex history and present situation in Myanmar. Nor has it been easy to draw these diverse contributions together into a completely coherent volume. However, we trust that the book will stimulate new questions and help its readers search for more information via the many cross-references and Further Reading section.

Why read this book

There are at least six very good reasons for browsing – and, better still, *reading* – this book. It will help you to:

- obtain facts about Burma before you do business, carry out research, work as an NGO, visit as a tourist or are involved in other endeavours in the country;
- learn about some of the main actors and their intentions;
- know at least something about the country's history as well as its ethnic and religious diversity;
- gain an appreciation of the present situation and its complexity;
- know how and where to learn more; and
- face up to the discrepancy between the current optimism and the many stumbling blocks.

Acknowledgements

Every book is an endeavour undertaken by more individuals than just its author(s) but this has been especially so with this volume. Many people made direct contributions to the final text, some bigger than others, but in particular we wish to single out the contribution of Marie Ditlevsen who did not only contribute with material from her own research area but acted also as a tenacious research assistant providing other text for the volume where this was needed.

Though reaching out to readers far beyond the realm of academia, this is a volume prepared to academic standards. We thank those who improved the text by their criticism and comments in the peer review process.

We are grateful for the grant from Politiken-Fonden, which enabled us to acquire a collection of excellent photos taken by David Høgsholt. Our thanks, too, to all the people who contributed or helped with photos for the volume: Burma Campaign UK, Nils Carstensen, Cheng Ruisheng, DanChurchAid, Marie Ditlevsen, the Environmental Protection Agency, Hongwai Fan, the Free Burma Rangers, Jialiang Gao, the Government of Thailand, Mikael Gravers, Jessica Harriden, David Høgsholt, Htoo Tay Zar, International Media Support, the Karen National Union, Kyoko Kusakabe, Joachim Ladefoged, Jonas Leegaard, Sarah Meier, Min Aung Hlaing, Sonny Nyein, Anders Østergaard, Ruth Pearson, Evangelos Petratos, Daniel Sakhong, Lian Sakhong, Sam Spector, Ardeth Thawnghmung, *The Irrawaddy*, the U.N. Office on Drugs and Crime, the U.S. State Department, Vinai Boonlue, Wagaung, Barbara Walton and Flemming Ytzen.

Last but not least, we are grateful for the intensive and meticulous editorial work done by Gerald Jackson, Editor in Chief of NIAS Press. Due to his painstaking work on the heterogeneous collection of articles, we managed to compile a relatively coherent volume on the complex transition process in Myanmar/Burma.

Mikael Gravers and Flemming Ytzen
Copenhagen, June 2014

Contributors

Marie Ditlevsen was recently a project associate engaged in corporate social responsibility issues in Yangon. Previously working for the Danish consultancy firm COWI, her 2013 thesis explores the influence that political changes in Myanmar have had on the strengthening of civil society there.

Mikael Gravers is Associate Professor in Anthropology at Aarhus University. He has conducted fieldwork in Thailand and Burma since 1970, working among Buddhist and Christian Karen and in Buddhist monasteries. The author of *Nationalism as Political Paranoia* and editor of *Exploring Ethnic Diversity in Burma*, he has long published on ethnicity, nationalism, Buddhism and politics as well as on nature, culture and environmental protection.

Jessica Harriden holds a PhD from the University of Queensland. Author of *The Authority of Influence: Women and Power in Burmese History*, her research interests include gender-power relations and ethnic identity in twentieth-century and contemporary Burma.

David Høgsholt is an award-winning Danish photographer based in Shanghai. Focusing on social issues and human rights stories, he has worked for publications such as *The New Yorker, Time, Stern*, the *New York Times* and *National Geographic*.

Kyoko Kusakabe is an Associate Professor in Gender and Development Studies at the Asian Institute of Technology in Thailand. Co-author of *Thailand's Hidden Workforce: Burmese Women Factory Workers*, her recent research is on gender issues in labour migration, mobility and border studies.

Josine Legêne recently graduated in international studies from Aarhus University, her thesis exploring the transformation of Myanmar's relations with the outside world. She now works on the global balance of power and relations between global leaders in Asia and the West.

Michael Lidauer is a social anthropologist pursuing a PhD in political science at Goethe University, Frankfurt. With a background in democratization and civilian peace building and a particular focus on electoral processes, he has researched these issues in Myanmar since 2010. He also works as consultant for international organizations and is associated with the Peace Research Institute Frankfurt.

Bertil Lintner is a Swedish journalist and author living in Thailand. He has covered Burma for more than three decades, mainly for the now defunct *Far Eastern Economic Review* and more recently for Asia Times Online, and has written seven books about the country, including *Burma in Revolt: Opium and Insurgency Since 1948*, *Outrage: Burma's Struggle for Democracy*, and *The Rise and Fall of the Communist Party of Burma*.

Wai Moe is a reporter for the *New York Times* on Myanmar issues and a freelance writer for other publications. Before joining the *Times* in 2012, he worked with *The Irrawaddy* magazine. He spent five years in jail as a prisoner of conscience in the 1990s.

Jonas Nøddekær is Development Director at DanChurchAid (DCA, Folkekirkens Nødhjælp), one of Denmark's largest humanitarian and development organizations. With wide experience in this work, from 2010 to 2013 he was based in Yangon and led DCA's programmes in Myanmar and Thailand. He is chairperson for The Border Consortuim, which has the overall responsibility for nine refugee camps located along the Thailand–Myanmar border.

Ruth Pearson is a feminist economist who has researched and written widely on women, work, migration, development and globalization as well as exploring a broad range of other issues like corporate responsibility and voluntary codes of conduct. Co-author of *Thailand's Hidden Workforce: Burmese Women Factory Workers*, she is Emeritus Professor of International Development at the University of Leeds.

Charles Petrie is a former UN Assistant Secretary-General who currently is Coordinator of the Myanmar Peace Support Initiative. With close to 30 years' experience in conflict and famine situations, working in countries like Sudan, Rwanda, Afghanistan and Myanmar at critical times in their modern history, he was recently awarded an OBE for services to international peace, security and human rights.

Anna Roberts is Executive Director at Burma Campaign UK (an NGO working for human rights, democracy and development in Burma), where she has worked since 2001, interacting with government ministers and officials from across Europe and with the international media.

Mandy Sadan is Reader in the History of South East Asia at SOAS, University of London and Associate Dean (Research) in the Faculty of Arts & Humanities. Researching and publishing on the cultural politics of Kachin ethno-nationalism for nearly two decades, her *Being and Becoming Kachin: Histories Beyond the State in the Borderworlds of Burma* was recently published.

Lian H. Sakhong, Director of the Burma Centre for Ethnic Studies, has long been active promoting the situation of Burma's ethnic nationalities and his own Chin people. Awarded the Martin Luther King Prize in 2007, he is the author of several books in English, Burmese and Chin, including *In Search of Chin Identity: A Study in Religion, Politics and Ethnic Identity in Burma*.

Alan Saw U is the co-founder/programme coordinator of the Karen Development Network, which empowers local populations to participate in the peace-building process. He has been involved in initiating peace negotiations between the Karen National Union and successive Burma/Myanmar governments since 1989.

Tim Paul Schroeder has been in Myanmar since 2006, working as a programme coordinator for INGOs and as a consultant for aid agencies and local organizations including the Myanmar Peace Support Initiative. Much of his work and advocacy there is focused on humanitarian aid, peace building and conflict transformation.

Ashley South is an independent writer and consultant specializing in ethnic politics, humanitarian and peace and conflict issues in Burma/Myanmar and Southeast Asia. Now also a senior adviser to the Myanmar Peace Support Initiative, he is author of *Ethnic Politics in Burma: States of Conflict*. Fuller details are available at: www.ashleysouth.co.uk.

Ardeth Maung Thawnghmung is Professor of Political Science at the University of Massachusetts Lowell. Her areas of expertise include political economy, ethnic politics, and Myanmar/Southeast Asian politics, and has been a recipient of numerous awards and research fellowships.

She has published extensively on Myanmar's political economy and ethnic politics.

Sean Turnell, formerly at the Reserve Bank of Australia and now based at Macquarie University in Sydney, is author of *Fiery Dragons: Banks, Moneylenders and Microfinance in Burma* and has written widely on Myanmar's economy and financial sector for the past two decades. A regular commentator on the country in the international press, he also advises a number of key stakeholders inside Myanmar and around the globe.

Flemming Ytzen is a Danish journalist who has covered East and Southeast Asia for more than three decades, working at the Danish daily, *Politiken*, since 1994. He also appears on Danish television as a regular East Asia analyst and commentator, and teaches and gives public lectures on Asian affairs as well. Some of his (Danish-language) commentaries can be found at http://flemmingytzen.com.

Additional contributions

AR	Anna Roberts
AS	Ashley South
CP	Charles Petrie
FY	Flemming Ytzen
JH	Jessica Harriden
JL	Josine Legêne
JN	Jonas Nøddekær
KK	Kyoko Kusakabe
MD	Marie Ditlevsen
MG	Mikael Gravers
MS	Mandy Sadan
NP	NIAS Press
RP	Ruth Pearson

Abbreviations

*Acronyms for only the most frequently appearing organizations appear here.
See Appendix 2 for a list of all organizations and their acronyms.*

ASSK	Aung San Suu Kyi
BGF	Border Guard Force
CBO	community-based organization (vs NGO, see p. 86)
DASSK	*Daw* Aung San Suu Kyi
EAG	ethnic armed group
GONGO	government-organized NGO
IDP	internally displaced people (i.e. forced to flee their homes but remaining within the country's borders)
KIA/KIO	Kachine Independence Army/~Organization
KNU	Karen National Union
n.d.	no date
NGO	non-government organization (vs CBO, see p. 86)
NLD	National League for Democracy
NSAG	non-state armed group
PMG	People's Militia Group
USDP	Union Solidarity and Development Party

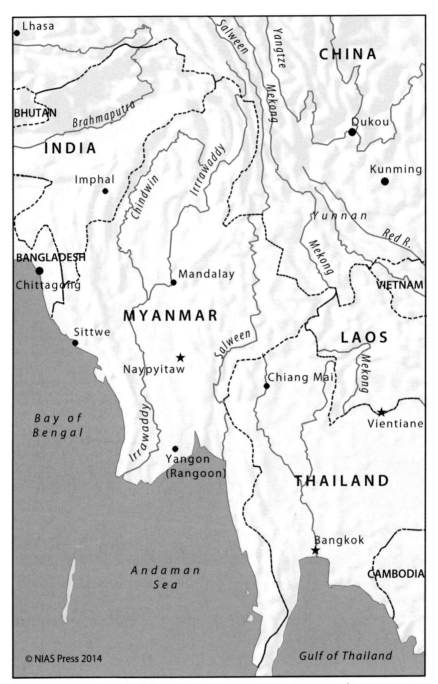

Map 1: Physical environs (relief background © Mountain High Maps)

Burma/Myanmar straddles important mountain and river systems linking India, China and mainland Southeast Asia.

Introduction

Mikael Gravers and Flemming Ytzen

In 2010, the world suddenly had to take a new look at Burma/Myanmar. A new parliament was elected and Daw Aung San Suu Kyi was freed from her long period of house arrest. Myanmar had changed from a military dictatorship with totalitarian tendencies into a democratic state – or had it?

Burma's national hero, and the father of Aung San Suu Kyi, said the following about 'true democracy' in May 1947, two month before he was assassinated:

> Only when the 'State' is there by the people's consent, only when the 'State' identifies itself with the people interests in theory as well as

Images of Aung San are ubiquitous in Myanmar as here at a Yangon newspaper stand (photo: International Media Support)

practice there can be true democracy. Any other kind of democracy is sham. Only true democracy can work for the real good of the people, real equality of status and opportunity for every one irrespective of class, race or religion or sex. [...] True democracy must be our basis if we want to draw up a constitution with the people as the real sovereign and the people's interests as the primary consideration.[1]

These words are still highly relevant, and democracy is not merely an elected parliament but must enter all social institutions.

Myanmar may not become a fully-fledged liberal democracy following Western models in the near future, and it needs years to establish a non-authoritarian tradition with the rule of law, rights and human security. As will be evident from the chapters in this book, the country has to come to terms with its ethnic and religious diversity and to maintain the ongoing dialogue and peace in order to accommodate this diversity and secure some local autonomy and justice.

If the reader thinks that we focus too much on political problems and violence, please remember that in Myanmar you will also encounter a population both extremely kind and positive and living in a very beautiful country with a magnificent cultural heritage – subjects that could fill several volumes.

Please note that in this volume we use both names, *Myanmar* and *Burma*. Burma was the old British colonial name, retained at independence in 1948. Since 1989, Myanmar has been the official name of the country but internationally and especially among some exile groups Burma is still common. *Bamah* (Burma) derives from the oral or colloquial form of *Mranma,* the written name of the dominant Bamar (Burman) ethnic group (or Myanmar in its modern form). But already before independence, the name was expanded to refer to the country as a whole, not just the Bamar. Today, it is argued that the name Myanmar is more inclusive of the country's minorities. However, the ethnic nationalities resent being categorized as Myanmar.

---

1. Cited in J. Silverstein (ed.), *The Political Legacy of Aung San.* Ithaca: Cornell University Southeast Asia Program, 1993 (revised edition), p. 153.

Dark realities, glimmers of hope

David Høgsholt

Shanghai-based photographer David Høgsholt has twice won the World Press Photo Contest and received several other photojournalism awards as well. Focusing on social issues and human rights stories, often opting for a long-term project approach, he has visited Myanmar regularly for almost a decade. Here, he has covered cyclones, elections, political repression, the situation of HIV victims and the military's ongoing war against the Kachin. We are happy he agreed to contribute to this volume.

✍ FY

Monks protesting against the military regime on 26 September 2007, walking on Pansodan Road in Yangon towards Sule Pagoda. Allegedly one was killed and five injured at the beginning of this march by Swedagon Pagoda. When the demonstrators reached Sule Pagoda, soldiers were blocking the roads. After praying and chanting for a while in front of the soldiers, the protesters moved away.

3

Scene from the Saffron Revolution, September 2007. Soldiers pass through Sule Pagoda to close it down before protesting monks can reach it. Sule Pagoda is the second most important temple in Yangon and of major symbolic importance due to its location next to City Hall, where most of the killings in the 1988 uprising took place. The day after this photo was taken, military and riot police prevented monks from entering the pagoda and nearby the Japanese photojournalist Kenji Nagai was fatally shot. Police and soldiers also sealed off Shwedagon Pagoda, the most holy pagoda in the country, and the starting point of most of the demonstrations.

Youngsters playing football in a Yangon street.

People praying at the Shwedagon temple complex in central Yangon, the former capital's most famous religious site.

City life. Decrepit residential building in a Yangon street.

Some Burmese live the good life. Wedding in Yangon.

A day labourer earning two to three dollars a day porters charcoal on the bank of the Yangon River. People work hard, but for decades their living standards deteriorated as a direct result of the failed policies of the military junta. The regime's economic policies resulted in double-digit inflation and devastated wages and salaries. An average Burmese lives on not much more than a few dollars per day. The minimum wage buys 8-10 times fewer basic commodities like rice, salt, sugar and cooking oil than it did 20 years ago, says a local economist.

People push-starting a bus in Myaynigone district, Yangon, in May 2010. The country is one of Asia's poorest with a huge gap between the majority of its people and the tiny elite of high-ranking army officers and their cronies.

Expectations of a better life in the immediate future.

A man takes a swim in the Yangon River near the Botataung Jetties in Yangon while an on-looking boatman smokes a cigarette, June 2007. Myanmar is one of Asia's poorest countries, though it has not been always like this. Fifty years ago it was amongst the richest in Asia and some say that living standards have decreased ever since the military coup in 1962.

An unidentified sick man lies on the pavement a short distance from a health clinic in Yangon, June 2007. A World Health Organization survey in 2000 placed Myanmar's health system as second worst in the world. Another survey showed the country was amongst the fifteen biggest military spenders in the world. The regime spent less than five dollars a year per citizen on healthcare, a situation that has barely improved since 2011.

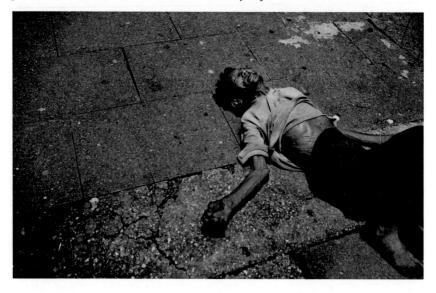

Children, some of them young novice monks and nuns, attend a free school run by a nunnery in a suburb of Yangon, February 2010. School is supposed to be free but teachers are underpaid and this fuels corruption in the educational system. Gifts and donations are expected and thus the poorest families cannot even afford to send their children to government schools.

Caretakers and patients wash clothes and cook outside a shelter for HIV/AIDS patients in Yangon, April 2012. The shelter is run by NLD activists, its founder and leader Phyu Phyu Thin elected to parliament in the 2012 by-elections. After years of harassment by the junta, recent reforms and openness have made Phyu Phyu Thin's work easier. Most of the funding come from local civil society and international donors. No money comes from the government. Phyu Phyu Thin shelters people with HIV while they enrol in some of the very few HIV treatment programmes in the country.

The restaurant at Mount Pleasant was supposedly the favourite dining place in Naypyidaw of the former military regime's top general, Than Shwe. The regime built Naypyidaw as its new capital and moved there in 2005–06.

Motherhood with limited means – mother and baby in an IDP camp in Majayang, in KIA-controlled territory, Kachin State.

Youthful hope and a glimpse into the future.

Khin Mya Mya (left) and fellow patient, Hla Hla Win, comfort each other at a shelter run by a monastery in Yangon. 28-year-old Khin Mya Mya contracted HIV after her husband left her with two children, driving her to work as a sex worker. As the disease took over her body Khin Mya Mya ended up living in a railway station begging for food from passers-by. A monk found her there and brought her to the shelter. Also having TB, she needed to fight that disease before starting the HIV treatment. With a diet of mainly pastry and sweet tea, she had a hard time eating enough and died before she could even start her treatment.

Village life, Kachin State.

A newly arrived male patient in a leprosy colony two hours outside of Yangon, June 2010. This man was living homeless in Yangon when found by another patient from the colony and brought to its health centre. The c. 60 patients living in the colony received the equivalent of 20 cents per day from the regime. This was supposed to cover medicine, food and all other life necessities but barely covered one seventh of the price of a person's daily rice needs.

Detachment of KIA soldiers near Laiza.

Young KIA soldier on guard.

Seconds earlier, a grenade fired by government troops hit this area in Kachin State.

Wounded KIA soldier awaits treatment. He was hit when the village of Namsangyang was shelled by government forces.

Several land-mine victims seek refuge in the KIA headquarter in Laiza.

Maji Tu Ja was a local peasant from the Kachin hill country. Also a KIA militia man, he was killed by mortar shells on 27 December 2012 during the Tatmadaw's big Christmas offensive against the KIA. His wife has just been informed about his death.

15

Camouflage clothing and ammunition gathered in a Kachin Village

Funeral of a Kachin villager killed during the December 2012 offensive.

Church service held in Laiza, December 2012, about the time of the big Tatmadaw offensive against the rebel Kachin.

Kachin villagers near Laiza, December 2012.

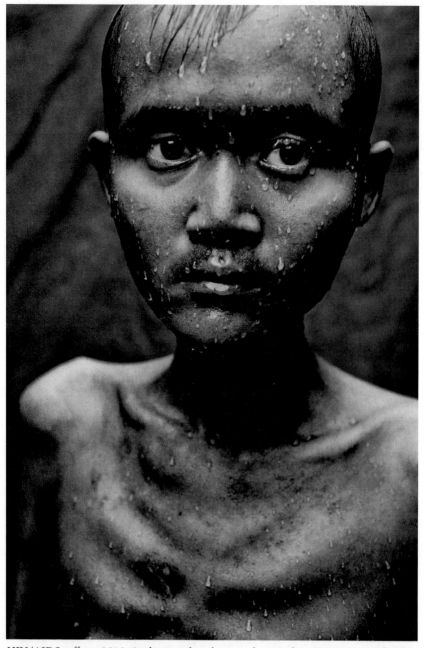

HIV/AIDS sufferer, 2010. At the time this photograph was taken, Myanmar was battling one of Asia's worst HIV epidemics and one of the world's most neglected. The UN estimated that 15,000–20,000 people living with HIV were dying annually in the country due to lack of access to urgent lifesaving anti-retroviral therapy. Official attitudes to the epidemic have changed since 2011 and international NGOs are now allowed to help alleviate the problem.

The Gathering Pace of Change

2005–06   Capital moves from Yangon to Naypyidaw.

2007   Saffron Revolution: monks demonstrate after increase in the price of oil and public transportation. Many are killed.

2008   Controversial new constitution is approved in popular referendum.

Cyclone Nargis devastates the Irrawaddy delta region, killing 130,000 people or more.

2009   Aung San Suu Kyi (ASSK) begins talks with military leaders.

2010   New electoral laws are passed, including provision for a junta-picked electoral commission.

NLD splits after majority votes to boycott upcoming election; breakaway National Democratic Force formed.

First election in 20 years, resoundingly won by military-backed USDP.

Monks demonstrate in Yangon during the Saffron Revolution (photo still taken from the award-winning documentary by Anders Østergaard, 'Burma VJ', reproduced by permission of the director)

ASSK released from house arrest.

Conflicts in (esp. Kachin, Shan and Karen) ethnic areas continue/reignite after ceasefires collapse.

2011   Thein Sein sworn in as president of a new, nominally civilian government.

Beginning of political and economic reforms.

Thein Sein meets with ASSK.

Thein Sein suspends construction of controversial Myitsone dam.

Some political prisoners freed; legalization of trade unions and demonstrations.

NLD rejoins political process; ASSK announces she will stand for parliament.

Visit by U.S. Secretary of State Hilary Clinton, meeting both Thein Sein and ASSK.

Truce deal with Shan rebels; military ordered to halt operations against Kachin.

Less censorship of the news and media, access to international media and websites.

President Thein Sein meets with U.S. Secretary of State Hillary Clinton, Naypyidaw, 2011 (photo courtesy U.S. State Department)

2012
Ceasefire signed with Karen rebels but sporadic conflict in Kachin State.

NLD is the big winner in by-elections with ASSK elected to parliament.

Outbreak of violence between Rakhine Buddhists and Rohingya Muslims.

Pre-publication censorship abolished.

Procession of official visits by foreign dignitaries, including U.S. President Obama.

General easing of sanctions; offers of aid by foreign donors.

2013
Army breaks ceasefire with Kachin rebels but new peace is brokered by Chinese.

Anti-Muslim violence spreads outside Rakhine State to the centre of the country.

First private daily newspapers in 50 years are published.

Thein Sein undertakes to free all political prisoners by year-end; some are freed.

Controversial Tamanthi Dam project on the Chindwin River is cancelled by India.

NLD announces it will contest the 2015 elections even if ASSK is barred from running for president.

2014
Thein Sein says he backs a constitutional amendment allowing 'any citizen' to become president but, when later urged to continue in the post, shows willingness to consider the idea.

The country's first census since 1983 is carried out.

Aung San Suu Kyi begins a national campaign pushing for constitutional reform prior to the 2015 elections but lacks parliamentary support for a change.

Negotiations for a nationwide ceasefire gather pace but sporadic fighting continues, especially in Kachin and northern Shan States.

Serious anti-Muslim riots break out in Mandalay.

PART ONE

Order and change

NLD supporters in Yangon celebrate their by-election victories (photo: Flemming Ytzen)

Since 2010, Myanmar's reforms have impressed the outside world and raised expectations among large segments of its population. The government has released hundreds of political prisoners, shortened blacklists, relaxed press censorship, drafted new laws, and held the first (relatively free) elections since 1990.

But the government's reforms are far from transparent and have serious shortcomings in the handling of conflicts with minority groups such as Kachins and Rohingyas. Nor has the government revealed a clear path to relinquishing military rule and making a proper transition to a wider and deeper democracy.

The section focuses on Myanmar as a country, how it is constituted and the dynamics shaping the ongoing change. Not least, it describes events that followed the opening-up of the country beginning with the dialogue between a top general turned president, Thein Sein, and the country's most popular politician, Aung San Suu Kyi. As this book went into print in July 2014, the process is still developing with few clear conclusions to be drawn.

Preserving order amid change and developing change amid order

Flemming Ytzen

As the former military rulers of Burma/Myanmar began to surprise the outside world with reforms that earlier had seemed unthinkable, uncertainties remain in the country's difficult minefield of politics, economics and special interests. This chapter describes some of the events during that crucial period.

From the start it all seemed surreal. After half a century of brutal, repressive rule an iron-fisted military dictatorship in Southeast Asia began to emerge as something seemingly more civilian, tolerant and conciliatory. No longer responding with force to a chaotic 'people's revolt' as in 1988, but allowing gradual liberalization, the change gave space for cautious optimism among its citizens and the outside world.

During the winter months of 2011–12, internal political developments in and around the country's political landscape began to change, although perhaps more in appearance than in substance. A dialogue during the late summer and autumn of 2011 between President Thein Sein, a high-ranking former general, and the leader of the country's democracy movement, Nobel laureate Daw Aung San Suu Kyi, initiated a thaw between the quasi-civilian government and the country's most popular political party since 1989, the National League for Democracy (NLD).

The formal transition from outright military dictatorship to a softer form of authoritarianism embracing democratic experiments began with carefully staged elections in November 2010, when the junta known as the State Peace and Development Council made way for civilian politicians, a majority of whom had a background in the military. Could such an election – despite all its flaws – pave the way for a less intrusive and more tolerant form of rule in Burma/Myanmar?

Surprise, surprise ...

To the astonishment of millions of Burmese, changes were announced from a podium. On 31 March 2011, in Thein Sein' inauguration speech, he called for workers' rights and an end to corruption; he welcomed international expertise; and, most startling, the president stated that the country's numerous ethnic groups had been subjected to a 'hell of untold miseries' suggesting that it was his intention to end the conflicts that have made Burma/Myanmar host to the world's longest-running civil war. And as the Presidential adviser Nay Zin Latt later told a reporter, 'We do not want an Arab Spring here'.

After an exchange of secret messages, Thein Sein met Suu Kyi in August 2011. When she returned home from the meeting, she told Tin Oo, the deputy leader of the NLD, that she 'could work with the president'. Once the process of confidence building had started, Thein Sein cleared the way for Suu Kyi's supporters in the NLD to register as a political party and for former political prisoners to run for office.

During their August 2011 meeting, Thein Sein and Suu Kyi worked out the plan in which she would run for election. That plan turned out to be critical for reforms that have developed since, even if Suu Kyi and the NLD have very little real legislative power and no executive power.

Bringing the enemy home

As part of the political opening, the Naypyidaw government began to demonstrate a willingness to enter into dialogue with individuals and media groups who had actively opposed the regime for decades. During the early months of 2012, journalists and editors from opposition media such as the New Delhi -based Mizzima, the Oslo-based Democratic Voice of Burma and the Chiang Mai -based *Irrawaddy* were allowed into the country and met with government officials and cabinet members for interviews.

One such notable interaction between a long time critic of the regime and a cabinet member took place in March 2012, when the founder-editor of *Irrawaddy Magazine*, Aung Zaw, was granted a visa and visited Naypyidaw where he met Upper House Speaker Khin Aung Myint.

The interview was published on the magazine's website on 26 March 2012 and demonstrated, at least rhetorically, a reformist political line in the thinking of the Naypyidaw government as the mentioning of such issues as corruption and representative government – unthinkable during the reign of the previous military strongman, Than Shwe – were brought up during the interview. Khin Aung Myint, a former major general, told his visitor that existing anti-corruption legislation 'is out-of date and proposed amendments had already been approved by the Lower House, and would be submitted to the Union Parliament during the next session'.

On the opposition leader Daw Aung San Suu Kyi, the Upper House Speaker said:

> She's a knowledgeable and educated person with both a good international as well as national image. If she's in the Parliament, our capacity will increase, and new ideas will come out. But how she will participate is up to her.

As a member of the National Defence and Security Council, an 11-member government body with the power to declare states of emergency and approve the commander-in-chief of The Defence Services, the Upper House Speaker said that 'even although the council is approved by the Constitution, it cannot be involved in every issue of state affairs'.

The obvious question arose: could the dialogue between Suu Kyi and Thein Sein pave the way for a more institutionalized form of democracy even with the limitations imposed by the military?

One Friday morning ...

During the last week of March 2012, several hundred media people (among them this writer) descended upon Yangon, the former capital, to cover the by-elections scheduled for 1 April in the expectation that this event would bring democracy icon Daw Aung San Suu Kyi into the legal political sphere after having spent years in prison, solitary confinement and house arrest since 1989.

Expectations among election observers, the media and diplomats were high, when on Friday, 30 March, 'The Lady' emerged from a week of convalescence still feeling 'delicate' but hopeful that the election would help lay 'a foundation stone for the future of democracy', as she explained during a news conference on the lawn of her lakeside residence in Yangon.

The then 66-year-old Nobel laureate said that government officials were involved in some of the irregularities and that these had gone 'beyond what is acceptable for democratic elections [...] but, still, we are determined to go forward because we think this is what our people want'.

Since emerging to lead the country's struggle for democracy, political freedom and human rights in 1988, the daughter of the nation's independence hero Aung San had spent more than 15 years under house arrest. For much of that time, she was separated from her husband and children who lived abroad, and her supporters had been locked up and tortured.

Asked if she could forgive the regime, she said: 'This is politics. We are working toward a certain aim. We are not working for personal reasons, and I don't think forgiveness comes into it at all […]. All we should do is to find out what we can best do to bring about national reconciliation'.

The Lady's illness only days before the by-election demonstrated the fragility of the reform process with its very personalized foundation, as it is built around the confidence between her and Thein Sein. Both were born in 1945. Suu Kyi had surgery in 2003 to remove what her physician Dr Tin Myo Win described as noncancerous growths. Thein Sein uses a pacemaker.

The last time her party competed in elections, in 1990, she was under house arrest, and yet the NLD won an overwhelming majority of votes and seats. The junta at the time refused to hand over power.

Voting day …

During the press conference, Suu Kyi made a point of her ambitions to try to change the country's political landscape from the inside after years as a dissident. A handful of opposition members in Parliament can still be powerful, she said:

> Even one voice can be heard loudly all over the world in this day and age. An election alone is not going to change our country. It is the people – the change in the spirit of the people, which will change our nation. I mean a revolution that will help our people to overcome fear, to overcome poverty, to overcome indifference and to take the fate of their country into their own hands.

On 1 April 2012, more than six million Burmese were eligible to go to the polls to elect less than 7% of the nation's parliamentary seats. The vote marked a symbolic turning point by bringing 'The Lady' and her fellow NLD candidates into parliament for the first time since emerging to lead the nation's struggle for democracy nearly a quarter century earlier. But with a parliament overwhelmingly dominated by the ruling party, and with 25% of legislative seats allotted to the army, Suu Kyi and her opposition colleagues were under pressure to demonstrate results. Was the democracy icon being used to uphold the status quo under a different brand?

Presidential advisor Ko Ko Hlaing defended the government against the criticisms of exiled opposition groups, who claimed that the new administration is like 'pouring old wine into a new bottle'.

'It is true that we have some officials who were leaders of the ex-regime', Ko Ko Hlaing told this writer and other visiting media. 'But our setting and policy is changing. The landscape is changing. Now we have a Constitution, and will move forward in accordance with it. Like in dramas, one actor can act different characters based on the role and so his performance can change', he added.

... with celebrations

The scenes throughout the evening of 1 April outside the NLD head-quarters in Yangon said it all. Myanmar's main opposition party was on course for a huge victory in that day's historic by-elections. With intervals of ten minutes news of yet another unfeasibly good result was posted up on a digital display screen facing the street, provoking even more ecstatic cheering from the huge crowd gathered outside. These were extraordinary scenes in a country that just a year earlier was cowed by a feared military dictatorship.

The election was called to fill 48 vacancies in a parliament of a total of 660 seats. The by-elections were held for 37 seats of the Lower House, 6 seats for the Upper House and 2 for regional bodies. Elections for three of the seats, in the northern Kachin State, had been postponed. Over the following days the government confirmed the NLD's landslide. The party contested 44 of the 45 seats on offer to the federal parliament in Naypyidaw. These were the first elections that it had taken part in since 1990, and it won 43 of the seats. The government's single win came in a constituency where the NLD candidate was disqualified.

Despite heavy restrictions – the NLD was not allowed to use flags and posters, and speeches had to be pre-approved by the authorities and could not last more than 15 minutes – the result surpassed the party's most optimistic expectations. In some seats they seem to have won over 90% of the vote, including in a constituency on the edge of the capital, where hardly a vote was cast against Suu Kyi.

Support for the Union Solidarity and Development Party (USDP), the civilian party-organization set up by the army in the late 1980s, was all but wiped out in these constituencies. The party could not even win a seat in the government's own backyard: four were up for grabs in Naypyidaw, where presumably half the voters are government employees. They had been promised extra economic benefits to support the USDP but voted for the NLD.

The previous vote, in late 2010, was heavily rigged in favour of the USDP, which won most of the seats, perhaps only because the NLD boycotted the poll. If the by-election results had been repeated at the national level, the USDP would probably have been annihilated and reduced to a parliamentary rump of its unelected military MPs.

Looking towards 2015

Can the experience of the 2012 elections be expanded and transform the country's politics? The military and the government must be aware that to win the 2015 elections they will either have to resort to vote-rigging and intimidation, which would draw sharp responses of both voters and the international community, or find a way to undermine support for the NLD. The alternative is to resort to military power, through a coup or other intervention in the name of national security, to secure their hold on power.

The NLD's presence in parliament will allow it to call attention to pressing national issues as part of the mainstream political process. Daw Aung San Suu Kyi has said that her party's priorities will be to push for peace in ethnic minority areas, institute rule of law and support amendments to the constitution. But the amendment of the constitution will be very difficult with the few seats held by the NLD. Even with the support of other opposition parties, the party will find it very difficult to secure the necessary 75% of parliament needed to initiate changes.

Nobody doubts the immense popularity of Suu Kyi, and this could lead to an election result in 2015, where the NLD will emerge as the dominant party (the party secured almost 60% of the vote and over 80% of the seats in May 1990) so the popular backing has endured.

However, the stability of the transition to a more representative form of government and its continued success depend on ensuring the broadest possible participation and acceptance from as many segments of society

NLD supporters in Yangon celebrate their by-election victories (photo: Flemming Ytzen)

as possible. An NLD landslide victory risks marginalizing three important constituencies in the legislatures: the old political elite in the form of the USDP; the ethnic political parties; and the non-NLD democratic parties.

As mentioned above, the USDP won only one seat in the 2012 by-elections and only because the NLD candidate was barred from standing. Several of the seats were in ethnic areas, only one of which was won by an ethnic party. And no other democratic party came even close to winning a seat. The risks in such a situation are clear. If the post-2015 legislatures fail to represent the true political and ethnic diversity of the country, continued conflict looms.

Of even greater concern would be a marginalization of ethnic political parties. This would revive memories of how first-past-the-post elections marginalized minority parties in the parliamentary era (1948–62) and favoured large, centrally based parties among the Burman majority.

It could also threaten the ethnic peace process, which is predicated on convincing ethnic armed groups that they can effectively pursue their objectives in the legislatures rather than through armed struggle. But in many areas, ethnic parties will find it a challenge to win against the NLD, particularly in the many mixed-ethnicity constituencies where the vote will split along ethnic lines.

Switching to a more proportional system for the Lower House will require amendments of the constitution. For the provision in question, this would entail a 75% vote in favour in the legislature, followed by a simple majority in a national referendum. In the case of the upper house, a proportional system based on 14 multi-member constituencies corresponding to the states and regions appears not to be ruled out.

The NLD is seemingly opposed to the introduction of a proportional system, and a few ethnic parties have reservations, particularly those that have strong majorities in their areas; meanwhile, many other parties appear favourable towards the idea. However, it is not clear whether there is any willingness within the military bloc to open up the issue of changing the constitution, because it risks also opening up the question of their continued right to 25% of legislative seats. Moreover, at least some military representatives would have to vote in favour of the measure in order to obtain the constitutionally mandated majority.

Another possibility would be for the NLD to form an alliance with some other parties – most importantly ethnic parties, but also some non-ethnic democratic parties – which would agree not to field candidates to compete against each other in certain constituencies. This would reassure those parties that a NLD victory, which many would not be opposed to in principle, would not come at their own expense.

A third option would be for the NLD to take steps to reassure other parties and their constituents that an NLD victory will not represent a threat to their interests. The NLD would need to engage in bridge building with other political forces, particularly the old guard.

The 2015 elections will be a major test of whether the current transition can survive the emergence of a new politics. It will be necessary for the NLD to ensure that its expected electoral success in 2015 does not come at the expense of the broad representation needed to reflect the country's diversity and ensure an inclusive and stable transition.

Censorship abolished, partly

Further progress developed during 2012–13. In August 2012, Naypyidaw announced that it would no longer censor private publications in a move towards greater media freedom in a country where military governments have tried to control the flow of information for decades. Like the liberalization process itself, the government had scaled back censorship gradually. In June 2011, articles dealing with entertainment, health, children and sports were taken off the list of subjects requiring prior censorship. In December of the same year, economics, crime and legal affairs were removed. The only two topics that remained on the list, religion and politics, were freed from censorship in 2013. As of January 2014, censorship of Internet had been abolished.

Even so, laws that have been used by the military government to jail dissidents were still in force during 2013. Among the most repressive laws in the country is the Electronic Transactions Law, which carries a prison sentence of up to 15 years for distributing information in digital form that is deemed detrimental to the interest of or lowering the dignity of any organization or any person.

Critics argue that the trickles of reform that allowed Suu Kyi to travel abroad during the summer and fall of 2012 and have prompted both the United States and European Union to suspend or end most of the remaining sanctions, are little more than cosmetic changes. Admittedly, by the end of 2013 there was no rule of law and no independent judiciary. The new media law retains curbs on press freedom; legislation on the right to peaceful assembly is flawed; the constitution guarantees perpetual, indirect military control. Still, the reforms, by many critics seen as incomplete and flawed, have had an enormous international effect.

Without doubt the political isolation imposed by western countries had an impact. It seems likely that China's increasing assertiveness in the region made the country's military and financial establishment nervous. Partly due to strict American sanctions and soft sanctions from the EU, the military understood that if they were to entice the West to play a balancing role, they would have to improve their human rights record.

Impacts were real in the field of human rights. During 2012, the country's first nominally civilian government in half a century released almost 700 activists, monks and artists, relaxed media censorship, legalized the right to unionize and, perhaps more importantly, distanced itself from the former junta's long-time international backer and financer, China.

Out of the shadow

What made Thein Sein and his associates take steps that moved the country out of the shadow of their former patron, Than Shwe? Since his takeover in 1992, Than Shwe had refused to enter into substantial dialogue with the opposition and had only allowed Suu Kyi limited freedom to speak to their supporters and meet with diplomats and foreign media.

Some observers noted that as Than Shwe aged, he confronted growing worries about his future. By 2010, he told visitors that he had what the U.S. Embassy in a cable released by WikiLeaks called a strong desire not to appear before an international tribunal.

Moreover, it was beginning to seem likely that if a prosecution materialized the top military man would not be the only target; the UN had concluded that state violence originated in the executive, military and judiciary at all levels. So in January of 2011, at the age of 77, Than Shwe appointed his successor, Thein Sein. Since then, Than Shwe has not been seen in public.

During the final months of 2012, the parliament in Naypyidaw began to appear like more than just a rubberstamp legislature. The NLD began to use parliamentary committees to scrutinize ministries and policies, which has emboldened members of the ruling, military-supported party, the USDP, too. In the weeks after the Land Investigations Committee began work, MPs from several parties began to collect evidence about land grabs by military officers and their cronies.

Daw Aung San Suu Kyi has been given her own parliamentary committee to preside over, for 'rule of law and stability', meaning that the NLD is beginning to exert influence out of proportion to its numbers. And just as the NLD wants to use parliament to challenge the executive, so too apparently does the speaker and top USDP member, Shwe Mann.

By the end of 2012, speculation arose that Shwe Mann's next move would be to introduce a system of proportional representation to replace the present winner-takes-all system. That could be the USDP's best bet for hanging on to any vestiges of power after the next elections. If the 2012 by-election results are repeated nationally in 2015, the NLD will wipe the USDP from the map. Under proportional representation, the USDP would probably hang onto some seats, and the smaller parties would also keep a few.

It is parliament who elects the president, and although Suu Kyi would be by far the country's most popular candidate, the constitution bans her from running, because she married a foreigner. However, there is a possibly the constitution could be revised. In that case Shwe Mann could play a central role in persuading parliamentary members of the

USDP to vote for change as the USDP leadership was handed over to him from Thein Sein in May 2013, the constitution not allowing the President to hold political functions.

Shwe Mann is presenting himself as a reformist leader. In a startling admission of the Burmese government's past failings he held a speech in Parliament (9 February 2012) in which he called on parliament members to pass laws that modernize the government: he presented a blistering critique of the failures of the government and told lawmakers not to dwell on the past, but to bring about reforms and 'modern concepts'. Furthermore, he said government employees across the country in almost all departments routinely take bribes and 'grease money' and charge for normal services and documents 'because of low salaries'. Salaries and bonuses for government employees are too low and encourage corruption, he said.

The USDP holds the overwhelming majority of the seats in parliament, more than 60%. But if the party fragments, it is likely to break up into several smaller groups, leaving the military with the largest single bloc and potentially giving it effective veto power over planned reforms. The party's members are a mix of former military men, ministers, civil servants and businessmen. Its main purpose has been to ensure the military's continued dominance but, aside from that, it has no real ideology to hold its constituents together. Shwe Mann may find it necessary to redefine his political agenda, possibly seeking an alliance with Suu Kyi and the NLD.

What will happen in the military?

Speculations on future alliances aside, the country's most dominant and powerful institution is still the military. The constitution grants the military a quarter of the seats in parliament and the right to nominate the most important of the country's two vice presidents.

Although public figures in Myanmar are politically diverse, nearly everyone now claims to be a reformer. This even applies to individuals from more conservative military backgrounds. Ultimately, national stability will remain a key requisite to further liberalization and the consolidation of a more representative form of government.

It is imperative for the continued reconciliation that Thein Sein and his associates demonstrate an ability to provide stability and attract aid, investment and trade. In doing so, diplomatic and political recognition and the increased presence of multinational corporations, primarily from Western countries, can facilitate sustained economic growth and thereby foster an emergent middle class and a high-performing economy in which incomes start to go up.

More than the ballot?

The crucial question is if the country is undertaking more than cosmetic changes in the mode of the 'electoral authoritarianism', known from Russia and Cambodia. The country's constitution has a number of serious flaws that would mean that a more genuine form of democracy would not necessarily emerge, even if the NLD wins a majority of seats in the 2015 election.

Approaching this crucial event, the NLD will press for reform of the constitution and a reform of the federal system. There is the possibility that the parliament can become a forum for dialogue on possible amendments to the constitution and a venue where discussions can unfold about the future of the country.

The country has now a climate of relative freedom – something that has not existed in the last half century – where civil-society groups and organizations have been formed and people are debating seriously about democratic institutions. The provision in the constitution that legitimates a military take-over in a state of emergency with the Commander-in-Chief taking political power needs to be abolished and there needs to be a plan for transition away from the degree of military domination that currently remains in the system. Secondly, the electoral system needs to be revised. If the current first-past-the-post system is retained without amendment, it raises the prospect that the NLD will sweep most of the seats in 2015.

Democratization processes in East and South East Asia have by and large been relatively peaceful over the past three decades. Taiwan and South Korea managed the transition from military rule to democracy in a relatively benign way in the late 1980s; Indonesia followed suit in 1998–2000, whereas Cambodia, Malaysia and Singapore stand out as hybrid models combining authoritarianism and the ballot box. Burma appears to place itself somewhere between the two categories but many uncertainties remain.

IN FOCUS

Apropos fear

'It is not power that corrupts but fear. Fear of losing power corrupts those who wield it and fear of the scourge of power corrupts those who are subject to it.' (Aung San Suu Kyi, *Freedom from Fear*, p. 180)

One of the main reasons why the generals continued their rule and only relinquished power after implementing a constitution based on 'disciplined democracy' was the impact of fear – fear of losing power, fear of revenge. Fear generates profound mistrust, which is a major obstacle to a political deal between the opposition, the ethnic armed groups and the

Line-up of Tatmadaw top brass pre-2010: the second general from the left is Thein Sein, later to be called 'the reformist president', and partially visible on the left is Shwe Mann, now Speaker of the House of Representatives (photographer/copyright holder not identified)

government/military. This mistrust is evident in an important article,[1] published in 2012, in which Kyaw Yin Hlaing cites senior government officials and officers: 'We simply did not trust the leaders of the pro-democracy groups. They were hostile to us. [...] A leading member of the NLD, Kyi Maung, talked about indicting some military leaders at a Nuremberg-style tribunal' (ibid.: 200).

In public, the generals would say they feared the fragmentation of the nation and state. In private, they had a profound fear for their livelihoods *and* lives. For instance, there was a fear that regional commanders ac-cumulated too much power and grabbed the local resources. However, they also feared their own peers. 'If we acted like liberals when Senior General Than Shwe was the head of the state, we could have ended up in jail' (ibid. 201) – as happened in 2004 to General Khin Nyunt, who, before his arrest, had not only been no. 3 in both SLORC and later the SPDC but also head of the intelligence services. He was feared and hated by the other officers, on whom he collected information, but was also a pragmatist who saw the need for a dialogue with the democratic opposi-tion. Neither the fear nor his powerful position was enough to save him.

Than Shwe would dismiss officers whom he thought supported Aung San Suu Kyi, and he is said to hate her. However, his fear of ending up like General Ne Win (who died under house arrest) may also have been in the rationale of the transition to quasi-civilian rule since 2011. More research on how the generals were thinking is underway and is immensely important in order to understand the military rule and its rationale. Certainly, it is obvious today that there are differences of opin-ion within the military about how they should continue to safeguard the unity of the army and the nation.

✍ MG

---

1. Kyaw Yin Hlaing: 'Understanding Recent Political Changes in Myanmar'. *Contemporary Southeast Asia*, vol. 34(2), 2012: 197–216.

Different media culture, different pressure from above

In August 2012, the government officially ended all prepublication censorship of the media, a move that was seen as one more landmark in the
country's reform process. During half a century of military rule Burma
had one of the most tightly controlled media in Asia. Prepublication
censorship was a pillar of the junta's Orwellian system, carried out by the
Press Scrutiny and Registration Department. But since 2012 the media
rules have gradually been relaxed, as newspaper editors are no longer
required to submit articles for prepublication censorship. Controls appear to have been eased even on more sensitive topics, such as ethnic
conflicts.

*A vibrant market for printed media still exists in Myanmar (photo: International Media
Support)*

However, journalists have been warned that by no means does this end restrictions on press freedom. Two elements of repressive legislation remain: the Printers and Publishers Registration Act, dating from the start of military rule in 1962, and the 2004 Electronic Transactions Law. Under the first, publications can lose their licences if they supposedly harm the reputation of a government department and threaten peace and security. And it carries a seven-year jail sentence for failing to register. Under the 2004 law, a person can be imprisoned for up to 15 years for distributing via the Internet information that the courts deem harmful to the state.

Recently, Reporters Without Borders elevated the country 18 places to number 151 in its 2013 Press Freedom Index, just behind Iraq and Singapore.

In the era prior to the military coup of 1962 Burma had a vibrant print media. Daily papers in Burmese, English, Chinese and Indian languages flourished. But it all came to a bleak end in 1964 under General Ne Win's rule, and for the next five decades the military regime became known for spying on, censoring, jailing, torturing and seizing equipment of journalists deemed to oppose the state.

Among the newcomers in the Burmese media market are Mizzima and Irradaddy, both digital media run for years by opposition activists in India and Thailand. They now have offices in the former capital Yangon. For more than a decade, these two have published hard-hitting coverage of military corruption and Myanmar's dismal human rights record, and many have seen their arrival as proof of the regime's tolerance.

But the Press Law of 2013 has brought growing concern about backsliding into former ways of control. The new law bears an unsettling resemblance to the draconian 1962 media law. New provisions include a six-month jail sentence for licence violations and a ban on criticizing the military-drafted constitution. Furthermore, the government has established a committee staffed with members of the military and the Information and Home Affairs ministries to oversee journalists.

About 70% of the country's print media is based in Yangon, much of it controlled by ex-military officials or their relatives, leaving little coverage in rural areas, where most Burmese live.

At the offices of the House of Media & Entertainment multimedia group, founders U Zaw Thet Htwe and comedian Maung Thura 'Zarganar', both former political prisoners, say that overt intimidation is being replaced by overly vague guidelines that can be used as authorities see fit. The guidelines issued in August 2012 warned against articles with 'destructive' views of state policy, or any that might 'frighten the public'.

✎ FY

However restricted the local press has been in its coverage over the decades, the country has been closely scrutinized by international news media, not least since 1988 and the advent of 'The Lady'. One of the earlier foreign journalists to interview Aung San Suu Kyi was Flemming Ytzen in March 1998 (photo: Joachim Ladefoged)

Broadcast media still heavily controlled

Interview with Khin Maung Win, Deputy Executive Director and Deputy Chief Editor of the Democratic Voice of Burma, on the media (October 2013)

" Freedom of print media is remarkable. There are over 10 private daily newspapers in addition to hundreds of weekly and monthly journals. The government abolished the pre-censorship system in 2012. Journalists and writers are seemingly free to write what they want. In general, freedom in print media is much higher even than in some of the [other] ASEAN member [countries].

However there is a controversial development going on regarding a proposed bill, which requires a licence for publishers. Most journalists view this licence system as a control mechanism imposing a heavy self-censorship system, because publishers may not dare to publish some sensitive issues. This bill is still being debated, and we need to see the final outcome of it.

Broadcast media is still heavily controlled by the government. Technically there are so-called private commercial broadcasters, but they all are 'cronies', and the ways in which they get their licences are controversial. No new license has been issued to private entities under the present government. New licenses have to wait until a new broadcast law is passed. Current private broadcasters are mostly broadcasting entertainment for commercial interests and do not provide really newsworthy programmes. The government claims that it will transform state media to 'public service media', but there is still a long way to go for existing media to become high quality public service broadcasters as known from Western countries.

There are still draconian laws, which can effectively restrict the flow of information. These laws include, but are not limited to the Electronics Act, Video Law, the Unlawful Association Act and the Official Secret Acts. These laws should be abolished or amended to pave the way for free flow of information and to safeguard, not to downgrade, freedom of expression. In addition, other good laws should be promulgated to safeguard freedom.

Despite these obstacles, press freedom in Burma is generally on the right track. We had zero freedom for many years, and now we have something better, and that something can become more in the future. What is important to note here is that the impossible is becoming more and more possible in the media sector in line with democratic changes.

✍ FY

Human rights in Burma

As late as 2010, Myanmar was castigated for having one of the world's worst human rights records. Much international attention has been paid to the political liberalization that has occurred since President Thein Sein came to power in 2011 but serious human rights concerns still persist.

President Thein Sein has received high praise for the reforms that began in 2011. There is no doubt that there have been dramatic changes in Burma but the fact that Burma still has one of the worst human rights records in the world must raise serious concerns about whether President Thein Sein and his government are genuine in their stated goal of reform towards democracy.

The reform process has seen major developments, including the release of hundreds of political prisoners, greater political freedom and increased civil liberties, particularly in the major cities, and ceasefire agreements with most of the armed ethnic groups. Yet at the same time we have also witnessed increased conflict and human rights abuses, and

Refugees from eastern Burma fleeing Burmese Army (photo courtesy Free Burma Rangers)

the changes so far have not included any legal or constitutional reforms that reduce the power of the government or military.

Even the positive changes raise questions when examined in detail. On the issue of political prisoners, the majority of those released have only been released conditionally, which means that they face being returned to jail to serve their original sentence if they are arrested again for political activities. They have not been pardoned or received any compensation. Hundreds of political prisoners remain in jail and new arrests are happening at an alarming rate. Virtually all repressive laws remain in place. These hardly seem to be the actions of a government engaged in a process of reconciliation towards respect for human rights and democracy.

Of the reforms that have been made, they often fall far short of international standards and in practice do not guarantee freedoms. For example, the 'Law Relating to Peaceful Assembly and Peaceful Procession' is now being used to stop protests and arrest peaceful activists.

The relaxation of censorship has been rightly praised but it is a relaxation in the application of censorship laws rather than the abolition of censorship. The new draft media law supposed to grant media freedom has been criticized as an attempt to bring in new censorship laws.

And while there may be a new openness to talk about problems, there is no recognition or acknowledgement of past crimes or human rights abuses or any process of justice or accountability.

Women in Burma, particularly in ethnic areas, continue to be subjected to rape and sexual abuse, including gang rape, by the Burmese Army. These attacks are committed with complete impunity. A recent report by the Women's League of Burma, a network of women's organizations representing different ethnic areas in Burma, highlights more than 100 cases where Burmese Army soldiers have raped ethnic women and girls. Of these cases, almost 40% were brutal gang-rapes.[1]

Conflict has actually increased since Thein Sein became president, with ceasefires being broken in Shan State and Kachin State. During these conflicts the Burmese Army has targeted civilians, committing horrific human rights abuses, including rape, torture, executions, arson, mortar bombing of civilian villages, women being bayonetted, looting, forced

---

1. Women's League of Burma, 'Same Impunity, Same Pattern: Report of Systematic Sexual Violence in Burma's Ethnic Areas', 14 January 2014: http://womenofburma.org/same-impunity-same-pattern-report-of-systematic-sexual-violence-in-burmas-ethnic-areas/.

labour, arbitrary detention, beatings, and use of child soldiers. At least a quarter of a million people have been displaced by conflict, human rights abuses and violence since Thein Sein became president. Human Rights Watch reported evidence of state involvement in war crimes and crimes against humanity against the Rohingya in Rakhine State.

The constitution remains a fundamental problem and helps explain why conflict has increased. The constitution, drafted and brought into force under military dictatorship, fails to provide rights and autonomy for Burma's ethnic groups. While ceasefires have been agreed with many armed ethnic groups, there is still no commitment to a political solution to address the rights and aspirations of Burma's ethnic groups and no genuine dialogue process to make the constitution democratic.

The sheer scale of continuing serious human rights abuses and the lack of any political dialogue process, or new freedoms enshrined in law, calls into question whether the current process is a genuine transition to democracy, or part of a carefully planned strategy, beginning with the new constitution, to manage the change necessary to end sanctions and international pressure while retaining political and economic control.

Understanding the vision and goals behind the current reform process is key for the international community to shape their policy and approach to Burma and to securing lasting peace and human rights.

If the government's vision for Burma is that which is laid out in constitution, then the transition seems to be not to democracy but towards some form of continued authoritarian rule, with a modernized economy.

To view the continued widespread human rights abuses as regrettable but understandable difficulties in a transition from dictatorship to democracy is to make a dangerous assumption. If, as seems probable, Thein Sein's desired outcome is to make the minimum number of concessions in order to enjoy the benefits of international trade while maintaining political and economic power, then a much more robust and challenging approach is needed to move beyond the current limited reforms.

To ignore or underplay human rights abuses in Burma – abuses so serious that they could be classified as war crimes, crimes against humanity and ethnic cleansing – does not only betray the victims but also risks undermining the possibility of real reform that would deliver peace, justice and human rights.

✍ AR

Local actors

Flemming Ytzen and Mikael Gravers

As with any country, power in Myanmar/Burma is held, shaped and exercised by a complex network of individuals and institutions. This chapter focuses on a few of the key local actors inside the country while the following chapter will examine some of the formal structures of power.

Behind the structures of power

Over the past century, the people of Myanmar/Burma have experienced British colonial rule, wartime occupation by the Japanese, independence and a faltering parliamentary democracy, and military coups followed by one-party rule or outright dictatorship. The period has also been punctuated by recurrent popular uprisings, each of them brutally suppressed. Finally, in early 2011, an unapologetically authoritarian military junta handed over formal power to a quasi-civilian government ruling, and trying to reform, a semi-federal state (for fuller details of which, see the following chapter). Just why the generals relinquished power is discussed below, as is the extent that the military has indeed ceded power.

The new legislative assemblies and other political structures are important in the country but its people also put great emphasis on personalized as well as institutional forms of power, status and prestige. Moreover, the political culture is also imbued with two contrasting Burmese concepts of power – *ana* (order) and *awza* (influence). For decades this dichotomy has been symbolized by the clash between the military regime (its formal authority based on the exercise of power) and Aung San Suu Kyi (whose broad influence has drawn on a moral authority).[1] Other factors are also

---

1. For a fuller examination of *ana* and *awza* in Burmese political culture and Aung San Suu Kyi's use of Buddhist concepts, see Houtman (1999), esp. pp. 157–176, and Harriden (2012), esp. pp. 20–21 and 219–229.

important here, not least patron–client relationships and hence 'tea-money' (discussed below).

Politicians and other personalities

The popular focus of events in Myanmar/Burma has long been the struggle between the military and the 'Lady'. However, one effect of political liberalization since 2011 has been the widening of the arena for public discourse. There is, then, a much broader circle of local actors influencing developments in the country today than there was just three years ago.

Thein Sein

President Thein Sein (b. 20 April 1945) was born and raised in a small village in southern Myanmar in the western part of the vast Irrawaddy River delta, about 40 km south of Pathein. He attended the prestigious Defence Services Academy and graduated in 1968.

He is said to have commanded various army units around the country. In 1992–95 he served as a general staff officer in the country's War Office (Defence Department), and by 1997 he had been promoted to brigadier general while he headed an army unit in eastern Shan state. By 2001 he was back at the War Office as adjutant general of the army.

Thein Sein's appointment as adjutant general marked his entry into government service in the State Peace and Development Council (SPDC), which was the 'government' in Burma from 1988 to 2011. In 2003 he was appointed second secretary of the SPDC, and a year later he became first secretary. In April 2007 he became acting prime minister for ailing Prime Minister Soe Win, and he formally took office upon Soe Win's death in October. Thein Sein concurrently served as head of the government's emergency-response agency and was reportedly shocked by how poorly officials handled relief efforts during the Cyclone Nargis disaster in 2008, which killed approximately 140,000 people.

In 2010 he resigned from the military to lead the military's political party, the Union Solidarity and Development Party (USDP – see below) as it contested seats in multiparty parliamentary elections held in November. Predictably, the USDP swept to victory, with Thein Sein himself winning a seat. The new legislature met early in 2011 and elected him president of the country's first nominally civilian government in half

Thein Sein (photograph from 2009, courtesy of the Government of Thailand)

a century. He took office on 30 March, and his government embarked on an agenda of political and social reforms, including relaxing press restrictions, releasing political prisoners, and concluding cease-fire accords with rebel ethnic groups. Most notably, the civil liberties of Aung San Suu Kyi were restored. Furthermore, his government sought to end diplomatic isolation and began implementing reforms aimed at ending years of economic stagnation.

In his first interview with a foreign journalist in January 2012, the president stressed the need for peace and stability and highlighted the inclusive nature of the reform process but was unapologetic about engaging with the military in this.

> The reform measures are being undertaken based on the wishes of the people [who want] to see our country have peace and stability as well as economic development. ... People would like to see peace and stability and that is why we have had engagement with the ethnic armed groups. ... When a system needs to be changed, it cannot be done overnight. Some countries that have tried to change overnight have deteriorated. That is why we laid down a seven-step road map and have taken step-by-step measures. You can see we are a democratically elected government. The military is no longer involved in the executive body. Even if you look at our parliament, one-fourth is reserved for the military.

We cannot leave the military behind because we require the military's participation in our country's development.[2]

Despite his reformist image, Thein Sein is not universally admired or trusted (see for instance Anna Roberts' assessment of the current human rights situation, p. 43). However, it is clear that there are limits to his presidential power. For instance, despite his apparent efforts, he failed to rein in the Tatmadaw during recent fighting in Kachin State (see p. 262ff.). It is not forgotten either that he was acting prime minister during the 2007 Saffron Revolution and its violent suppression. He also had a command during the crushing of the 1988 uprising that left thousands of civilians dead. In a September 2012 speech to the U.N. General Assembly, Thein Sein acknowledged the authoritarian nature of the junta he once belonged to, at the same time congratulating Aung San Suu Kyi 'for the honors she has received in this country in recognition of her efforts for democracy'.

Aung San Suu Kyi

Daw Aung San Suu Kyi (b. 19 June 1945) was two years old when her father, Aung San, then the de facto leader of what would shortly become independent Burma, was assassinated. She attended schools in Burma until 1960, when her mother was appointed ambassador to India. She later attended the University of Oxford, where she met her future husband, the British Tibet scholar, Michael Aris. She and Aris had two children and lived a quiet life until 1988, when she returned to her native country to nurse her dying mother, leaving her husband and sons behind. There the mass slaughter of protesters against the brutal rule of military strongman Ne Win led her to begin a nonviolent struggle for democracy (see p. 69).[3]

While working to build up her political party, the National League for Democracy (NLD), she was placed under house arrest in her childhood home in Yangon. The military offered to free her if she agreed to leave the country, but she refused to do so until the country was returned to civilian government and political prisoners were freed.

The NLD won more than 80% of the parliamentary seats contested in the election of May 1990 but the results of that election were ignored

---

2. 'Burma's president gives his first foreign interview', *Washington Post*, 19 January 2012.
3. On her story, see Popham (2011).

by the military government. Only in 2010 did the military government formally annul the results of the 1990 election. In 1991 Aung San Suu Kyi was awarded the Nobel Peace Prize but, as she was still in house arrest, her son, Alexander Aris, accepted the award in her place.

Aung San Suu Kyi was freed from house arrest in July 1995, although restrictions were placed on her ability to travel outside Yangon. The following year she attended the NLD party congress, but the military government continued to harass both her and her party. In 1998 she announced the formation of a representative committee that she declared was the country's legitimate ruling parliament. Michael Aris died in London on 27 March 1999, his wife choosing not to travel to his deathbed because she was convinced the regime would block her return to Yangon.

The junta once again placed Aung San Suu Kyi under house arrest from September 2000 to May 2002, ostensibly for having violated restrictions by attempting to travel outside Yangon. Following clashes between the NLD and pro-government demonstrators in 2003,[4] the government returned her to house arrest. Calls for her release continued throughout the international community in the face of her sentence's annual renewal, and in 2009 a United Nations body declared her detention illegal under the country's own law.

The military government enacted a series of new election laws in March 2010, one prohibited individuals from any participation in elections if they had been married to a foreign national. Aung San Suu Kyi was released from house arrest six days after the November 2010 election.

Government restrictions on Aung San Suu Kyi's activities were relaxed during 2011. She was allowed to meet freely with associates and others in Yangon and by midyear she was able to travel outside the city. In August in the capital Naypyidaw, she met with Thein Sein, who had become the civilian president in March. More meetings followed and led to a process of apparent reconciliation.

---

4. In May 2003, in what has been seen as an assassination attempt, Aung San Suu Kyi and her motorcade were attacked near Depayin in Northern Burma. An estimated 3,000–5,000 USDA supporters and members of its armed wing, the Shwan-ar Shin ('Peoples Force'), lined the roads and attacked her supporters with clubs and iron rods. Four NLD members were killed and 64 jailed (including Daw Aung San Suu Kyi who was wounded). Numerous local NLD supporters are also believed to have been killed.

Aung San Suu Kyi, on campaign in 2012 by-elections (photo courtesy of Htoo Tay Zar)

In advance of parliamentary by-elections scheduled for April 2012, the NLD was officially re-legitimized. In January 2012, Aung San Suu Kyi announced that she was seeking election to a constituency in Yangon, and her bid to run for office was approved by the government in February. She easily won her seat in the 1 April by-elections and was sworn into office on 2 May.

Later that month she travelled to Bangkok – her first foreign trip in 24 years and the start of an extensive programme of international engagements that continues to the present day. In June as part of a trip to Europe, Aung San Suu Kyi was finally able to deliver her Nobel acceptance speech in Oslo, two decades after being awarded the peace prize.

Although Aung San Suu Kyi continues to be a democratic icon both within the country and globally, her image is being tested by the realities of an active political engagement with the current Myanmar government, the Tatmadaw, ethnic groups and many other actors both at home and abroad. For instance, her ambiguous position on the situation of the Rohingya has been criticized by human rights groups (see p. 336), eyebrows are raised at her recent cooperation with the military and some question the value of her parliamentary activities. Speaking to the *New York Times* in 2012,[5] she addressed these and many other issues in a forthright manner.

> [On the conflicts in Rakhine State] I've always spoken out against human rights abuses but not against a particular community. That I'm totally against and I know that people want me to [do], they want strong and colorful condemnation, which I won't do, because I don't think it helps. [...]

> [On the military] We've been open about the fact that we want to amend the constitution to make it more democratic in spirit as well as in practice. We'd like to do this with the cooperation of the military. We can only do this with the cooperation of the army itself. [...]

> [On her work in parliament] The legislature has turned out to be more workable than I would have imagined, in a democratic way.

Whether or not Aung San Suu Kyi will be able to stand for president in the 2015 elections is discussed elsewhere in this volume (e.g. on p. 84). However, she is quite clear about her ambitions here. For instance, in the above interview with the *New York Times*, she also stated: 'I must say that the leader of every political party must aspire to be the head of state; otherwise he or she would be letting the party down.'

Shwe Mann

Thura Shwe Mann (b. 11 July 1947) has been Speaker of the House of Representatives (Pyithu Hluttaw, lower house of the Burmese parliament) since 2011. Previously he was a leading figure in the military junta that ruled Burma until 2011, serving as joint chief of staff of the country's armed forces. He was the third highest-ranking member of the State Peace and Development Council after Than Shwe and Maung Aye, and was, rather than Thein Sein, widely expected to become president after the 2010 elections.

Shwe Mann graduated in 1969 from the Defence Services Academy. He was promoted to major in 1988. He reportedly earned the honoritic title 'Thura' for his bravery in fighting the Karen National Liberation Army in 1989. He joined the Ministry of Defence in 2001, becoming joint chief-of-staff. In 2003, he was promoted to general. He is reported

---

5.   Bill Keller: 'A Conversation with Daw Aung San Suu Kyi', New York Times, 30 September 2012.

Shwe Mann during 2011 meeting with Hilary Clinton (photo courtesy US State Department)

to have led a secret 2008 trip to North Korea, reaching an agreement on missile technology cooperation.

On 31 January 2011, Shwe Mann was elected Speaker of the Pyithu Hluttaw and since then has been a key player in the country's ongoing political transition. On 13 June 2013, he stated that he is not ruling out a coalition government with the opposition party of Aung San Suu Kyi after crucial elections in 2015 'if it's in the national interest'. He made the comments to the Associated Press during a visit to Washington with a multi-party delegation of Burmese lawmakers, one of them from Suu Kyi's National League for Democracy. 'I believe time will decide on this matter. But the important thing here is to have confidence between Aung San Suu Kyi and us', he said.

In 2013, Shwe Mann replaced Thein Sein as head of the Union Solidarity and Development Party, which dominates the legislature. Although he has insisted that he and Thein Sein are not vying for power, Shwe Mann has been openly critical of the president's performance, for instance on the peace process. Here, there has been a convergence of interests between Shwe Mann and Suu Kyi, both concerned to preserve parliamentary oversight of such matters.[6]

---

6.   For a fuller portrait of Shwe Mann, see *The Irrawaddy*, 25 October 2013.

Than Shwe (photograph from 2010, courtesy of the Government of Thailand)

Than Shwe

Senior General Than Shwe (b. 2 February 1933) graduated from the Officer Training School in 1953 and gradually worked his way up through the ranks, being promoted to lieutenant general in 1987 and became deputy minister of defence in July 1988 just weeks before the 8888 democracy uprising. Following the 18 September military coup and crushing of the uprising, Than Shwe became vice chairman of the State Law and Order Restoration Council (SLORC), then headed by General Saw Maung. In 1990 he became army commander in chief and vice commander in chief of the Tatmadaw. After the resignation of Saw Maung in 1992, he elevated himself to the rank of senior general and became both Tatmadaw commander in chief and head of SLORC (from 1997 the State Peace and Development Council, of which he was chairman).

During the period up to 2011, Than Shwe consolidated the political and economic power of the military by such means as forming the Union Solidarity and Development Association (USDP – the forerunner of the Union Solidarity and Development Party – see below) in 1993, pushing through a new constitution in 2008 on the basis of which the USDP won the subsequent general election of 2010, and founding the military-owned Myanmar Economic Corporation in 1997.

In early 2011, he officially resigned as head of state in favour of his hand-picked successor, Thein Sein. Apart from the president, Than Shwe managed to place many others of his protégées in important positions and remains a powerful background figure commanding a very powerful personal network. Apparently he still receives important official documents and probably influences and gives advice to his network of supporters among the officers.

Although Than Shwe has been seen as a hardliner and an opponent of democratization, nonetheless the current reformist government has its roots in the period of his rule. Just why he pushed for a return to a quasi-civilian government is debated. Possibly Than Shwe had no wish to end as humiliated as his predecessor, General Ne Win, who died under house arrest. He is also a brilliant tactician in 'divide and rule' games; the present political arrangements have created multiple centres of power, the Tatmadaw continues to be both independent and a dominant player and much of the focus has been taken away from his person.

Min Aung Hlaing

Senior General Min Aung Hlaing (b. 1956), who succeeded Than Shwe as Tatmadaw commander-in-chief in March 2011, has a reputation as a hardliner who has defended the military's continued role in national politics and is said to have worked to thwart aspects of President Thein Sein's reformist and peace agenda. For instance, when Thein Sein apparently ordered the army to stop its military actions in Kachin State in 2012, his command was ignored by the Tatmadaw.

Min Aung Hlaing's military career touched on significant developments in the later period of Than Shwe's rule. As head of the Triangle Regional Command from 2002, he became a key player in dealing with two ceasefire groups, the United Wa State Army and National Democratic Alliance Army. In 2008, he was promoted to oversee military affairs in Karenni and Shan States and in that role he pressured ceasefire groups to convert into Border Guard Forces under Tatmadaw control. When the Myanmar National Democratic Alliance Army rejected this demand, Min Aung Hlaing oversaw the 2009 Tatmadaw attack on the semi-autonomous Kokang region, leading to widespread abuses and the flight of over 30,000 refugees into China prompting fury in Beijing. During the Saffron Revolution in 2007, Min Aung Hlaing is said to be among those who supported the brutal crackdown on the monk-led protests.

Senior General Min Aung Hlaing 🖒 Like

41,143 likes · 2,389 talking about this

Despite a non-nonsense image, Min Aung Hlaing has an active presence on Facebook

Not only is Min Aung Hlaing a rising star in Burmese politics but also the constitution gives him as Tatmadaw commander-in-chief a pivotal position. In a 'state of emergency', the commander-in-chief 'has the right to take over and exercise state sovereign power' via the military-dominated National Defence and Security Council, of which he is a member (see also p. 77). His position is also probably bolstered by having had dealings with Chinese President Xi Jinping on military cooperation going back several years.

Ashin Wirathu

U Wirathu (b. 10 July 1968) is an abbot of the Mesoeyin monastery in Mandalay. He is a leading monk in the 969 (Buddha, Dhamma, Sangha) nationalist movement. In 2003 he was jailed for 25 years after organizing anti-Muslim riots causing more than 10 deaths in Kyaukse and Mandalay. He was released after an amnesty in 2012. His movement claims to protect Buddhism as well as the (Burman) nation, race and language from Muslim conquest. He has widespread support in Burma although many monks are against the violence that his rhetoric seems to have provoked.

He is critical of Daw Aung San Suu Kyi: 'She doesn't know about Burma and its nature. All she knows is to stage revolution and attack government. So, if she becomes president, the governance would be in chaos', he claimed recently. Thus, as candidate for president in 2015,

U Wirathu supports Shwe Mann, the present Speaker of Parliament's lower house (see above). U Wirathu is said to be a skilled teacher in Pali, the liturgical language of Theravada Buddhism, but otherwise he has little knowledge of the world and is said to be politically naive. However, he is also an able communicator and skilled at using social media like YouTube, often with provocative rhetoric aimed at compromising Aung San Suu Kyi. (See also p. 314ff.)

TIME magazine's portrayal of Wirathu and militant Buddhism was not well received in Myanmar

Political parties

In recent years, the country has seen an explosive growth in the number of political parties contending for power both at national and regional level. Even though most observers focus on the governing USDP and opposition NLD, collectively the multitude of ethnic parties are also significant actors.

Union Solidarity and Development Party (USDP)

The Union Solidarity and Development Party (USDP) registered in June 2010 as a political party and is the successor to the Union Solidarity and Development Association (USDA, see below). During the 2010 election, the USDP recruited party members by offering low-interest loans, particularly in central Burma. The plausible aim of forming the USDP was to increase the army's representation in the new parliament by 20–30% in addition to the 25% already reserved for the military.

In the 2010 general election, the USDP won 883 seats out of the total of 1,154 seats, 259 of 325 seats in the lower house (Pyithu Hluttaw), 29 of 168 seats in the upper house (Amyotha Hluttaw), and 495 of 661 seats in the various Regional and State Hluttaw. At the national level, the party was the only one to contest every electoral seat apart from the 29 seats set aside for ethnic groups.

At the party's first national congress in October 2012, the country's president, Thein Sein, was re-elected as party chairman. However, constitutional issues with this dual role saw the chairmanship pass to the Pyithu Hluttaw Speaker, Shwe Mann.

The forerunner of the party was the Union Solidarity and Development Association (USDA), a mass organization founded in September 1993 by the State Law and Order Restoration Council (SLORC) and dissolved in July 2010. At the time of the USDA's transformation into the USDP, all members under the age of 25 were excluded, the remaining members transferred to the USDP together with all USDA assets.

Although the USDP did not explicitly link the party with the USDA at the time of its registration, during the following months USDP statements, actions and members made it explicitly clear that the USDP was born out of the former junta's mass organization. The USDP had inherited the USDA's membership, policies and resources as well as its physical clout and threatening reputation as a violent branch of the SPDC.

Reliable data on the USDA and USDP are scarce. Some sources mention that the USDA had a membership of over 24 million and was used by the regime to garner public support for its policies by holding mass rallies and conducting rural development and educational projects. It offered lucrative government contracts for running public utility services. It had its own paramilitary force known as Swan-Arr-Shin that had been used for violence against demonstrators or the opposition. The USDA reportedly engineered the massacre at Depayin in May 2003, when the convoy of Aung San Suu Kyi was attacked, resulting in an unspecified number of NLD casualties.

The USDA held more than 50% of the seats in the national convention that took more than 14 years to draft the new constitution.

National League for Democracy (NLD)

The National League for Democracy was formed in the aftermath of the 8888 Uprising, a series of protests in favour of democracy that took place in 1988 and was ended soon after the military took control of the country in a coup (see p. 69). In the 1990 election, the party won 392 out of 492 contested seats, compared to 10 seats won by the governing National Unity Party. The result was eventually annulled by the ruling junta on the grounds of the need for a new constitution (more details on p. 73).

The NLD boycotted the election held in November 2010 because many of its most prominent members were barred from running for office. New electoral laws based on the 2008 constitution were written in such a way that the party would have had to expel these members in order to be allowed to run.

However, the elevation of Thein Sein to the presidency and his subsequent rapprochement with Aung San Suu Kyi transformed the fortunes of the party. On 18 November 2011, following a meeting of its leaders, the NLD announced its intention to re-register as a political party in order to take part in by-elections necessitated by the promotion of parliamentarians to ministerial rank. Subsequently, on 1 April 2012, the NLD won 43 of the 44 seats it contested, reinforcing the concerns of some about the current first-past-the-post electoral system (see below, also the discussion from p. 82).

At the NLD's first-ever party congress in March 2013, a new central committee of 120 members was elected with the press invited in to observe the counting. The party also invited the armed forces' political party, the Union Solidarity and Development Party, to observe proceedings.

The party advocates a non-violent movement towards multi-party democracy and supports human rights, including broad-based freedom of speech, the rule of law and national reconciliation. In a speech on 13 March 2012, Suu Kyi demanded, in addition to the above, independence of the judiciary, full freedom for the media, and increasing social benefits to include legal aid. She also called for amendments to the constitution of 2008, which was drafted with significant input from the armed forces. She stated that its mandatory granting of 25% of seats in parliament to appointed military representatives is undemocratic.

Questions remain whether the army-drafted 2008 constitution will be changed before the 2015 elections. It is an electoral college drawn from both houses of parliament that elects the president and, although

Aung San Suu Kyi would be by far the country's most popular candidate, the constitution written by the generals bans her from running because she married a foreigner and her family members are foreign citizens. Thein Sein has promised to form a committee to look into changes and has said that he would accept Suu Kyi's bid for the presidency if she does run. But changes will require the support of at least 75% of parliament, still largely constituted of former generals.

Other political parties

Apart from the USDP and NLD, more than fifty political parties dot the fragmented political landscape of Myanmar/Burma, many of them of ethnic origin.[7] Two parties, both nationally based, are of historical interest but they have little real influence today – the National Unity Party (NUP) and National Democratic Force (NDF).

The National Unity Party (NUP) was formed by the military junta and members of Ne Win's Burma Socialist Programme Party to contest the 1990 general election for the government. However, the party was heavily defeated by the NLD. In the following general election in 2010, the party functioned as the main opposition party challenging the new junta-backed USDP but won only 63 out of 996 seats contested. In the 2012 by-elections, the party also fared poorly. Although still active, it is seen as representing the Ne Win old guard and some big business interests, and risks annihilation in the 2015 elections.

The National Democratic Force (NDF), also known as the United Democratic Front, was formed by NLD members who opposed their party's boycott of the 2010 general elections and who thus chose to contest the election under a new party. The NDF was only the third party to do so on a nationwide basis (the other two being the USDP and NUP). Winning only a few seats, the party has been in decline ever since with some of its elected members splitting to form a new party or defecting back to the NLD.

The remaining parties currently represented at the national or regional level are all ethnically based. These are the:

- All Mon Region Democracy Party
- Chin National Party

---

7. An updated list of parties is maintained by ALTSEAN-BURMA (the Alternative Asean Network on Burma) at http://www.altsean.org/Research/Parliament%20Watch/Parties.php.

- Pa-O National Organization
- Phloung-Sgaw (Karen) Democratic Party
- Rakhine Nationalities Development Party
- Rakhine State National Force of Myanmar
- Shan Nationalities Democratic Party
- Wa National Unity Party

A further 30–40 ethnically based parties (e.g. the new Karen National Party) are currently active but at present have no seats in either the national parliament (*Pyidaungsu Hluttaw*) or the State/Regional *hluttaws*.

The ethnic parties are not as well represented (at least at the national level) as assumed population numbers suggest they could be. The superior organization and resources of the USDP and NLD may be a factor here, also the fact that these small, local parties often split the ethnic vote in their electorates.

Although there has been a push towards a voting system based on proportional representation (PR) instead of the current first-past-the-post system, this is opposed by Aung San Suu Kyi and the NLD. Moreover, few ethnic parties would succeed in national or regional elections under such a proportional system, being small and locally based. The emerging political process has thus seen a number of ethnic political groupings emerge onto the public scene. For instance, in June 2013, formation was announced of an umbrella grouping, the Federated Union Party. This brings together 15 different ethnic parties, one of their purposes being to safeguard ethnic representation if PR is introduced for the 2015 election.[8]

The military (Tatmadaw)

Although the military handed over formal power to a quasi-civilian government in early 2011, the extent that the military has indeed ceded real power is disputed. Many argue that the Tatmadaw (or its proxies) still controls most political developments in Myanmar; at best, other actors like Aung San Suu Kyi and the NLD can only hope to influence events. Another view, however, is that power is currently shared in Myanmar by a tripartite alliance between the Tatmadaw, reformist ex-generals like

8. See p. 30 and the following chapter by Michael Lidauer (esp. p. 82) for a fuller discussion of the PR issue.

Sign outside a Tatmadaw base in Yangon – the military is implacable in its defence of the Union (photo: Flemming Ytzen)

Thein Sein and Shwe Mann, and the opposition (essentially Aung San Suu Kyi and the NLD), with the ethnic minorities effectively excluded from this triangle.

Whichever interpretation is argued, no one disputes that under the present constitution the military retains significant entrenched powers. Examples are the military-dominated National Defence and Security Council, which in a 'state of emergency' can take control of the state, and the requirement that constitutional changes must be approved by 75% of parliamentarians – only possible with military agreement; the reservation of 25% of seats for the military and filling of many other seats by ex-military members ensures this.[9] In addition, even in sheer numbers, the Tatmadaw is a significant force with about 400,000 personnel (up from 180,000 in 1988). It is no surprise, then, that it continues to play a leading role in the country's development.

This leading role is no historical accident. The Tatmadaw has its roots in the anti-colonial nationalist force formed by Aung San. This trained in Japan and at first was allied to the Japanese when they invaded British Burma in 1942. However, Aung San and his Burma National Army were hugely disappointed by the brutal Japanese regime, turning against it and helping the return of the British army in 1945. After independence

---

9. For fuller details, see p. 78.

in 1948 and the installation of a civilian-led government led by U Nu, the military played an important role. Indeed, General Ne Win was even asked to form a caretaker government in 1958 due to a split in the ruling Anti-Fascist People's Freedom League (AFPFL). Power was returned to U Nu in 1960 after fresh elections but in 1962 Ne Win seized power in a military coup; thereafter, the military ruled the country in one way or another until 2011. One reason for the coup was a perception within the military that, due to ethnic groups exercising their right to secede or achieving this by means of outright insurrection, the Union of Burma was about to fragment.[10]

The Tatmadaw has been proud of this heritage and has educated its officers to view it as the sole institution protecting the union. Over the years, the military became infused with a strong nationalist ideology of a homogeneous nation in a unitary state. During the rule of Than Shwe's State Peace and Development Council (SPDC), this ideology was expressed as the Three Main National Causes – essentially, to preserve the nation, national solidarity and national sovereignty. Hence a slogan often seen on billboards at the time was 'uplifting the patriotic spirit, and uplifting the morale and morality of the nation'. The core of this ideology was 'One Nation/Race, One Language, One Religion' (i.e Buddhism) – a culturally hegemonic construction with little room for a non-Burman identity.

Before the new constitution came into force in 2010, the military managed to transfer enormous economic resources into private ownership, much of these in the hands of two military-owned companies (Union of Myanmar Economic Holdings and the Myanmar Economic Corporation) that have long been the main economic players in Burma (see also p. 382). Furthermore, the constitution granted a general amnesty to all people involved in the actions/decisions of the SPDC and its forerunner, the State Law and Order Restoration Council (SLORC).

An ongoing issue with the military is corruption (or 'tea money' as it is locally known), a problem shared with government officials (see below).

---

10. On the historical role of the army and its organization, see Callahan (2003) and Selth (2002). On the changes, see Callahan (2012). On nationalism, see Rogers (2010) and Gravers (1999).

Other actors

Most if not all of the actors described above either exercise real power (*ana*) or have the potential to do so. In addition, a number of actors have significant influence (*awze*) over events, chief among them the bureaucracy, the Buddhist sangha and so-called crony capitalists.

Non-state armed groups

Although the Burmese state has reasonably secure control of the country's cities, towns and rural Burman heartland, elsewhere its grip is less secure; for decades it only made its presence felt via armed incursions by the Tatmadaw. Until the 1970s, large parts of the country were controlled by various communist or ethnic insurgent groups ruling often extensive 'liberated zones'. These have since largely vanished due to the demise of the Burma Communist Party, the co-option of armed groups into cease-fire agreements and full-scale attacks on the remaining insurgents and their ethnic communities by the Tatmadaw. Even so, significant parts of Myanmar today are controlled or affected by a multitude of non-state armed groups (NSAGs), some aligned or at peace with the government, others still in varying degrees of conflict.

In many cases, these groups have not only had a military role but also they have provided a rudimentary state apparatus in areas like education, health and local administration. At the same time, they have taxed the villages under their control, fed upon any cross-border trade and engaged in such lucrative enterprises as smuggling, drug production and the plundering of natural resources.

Although most actors (including the Tatmadaw leadership) now realise that continued armed struggle does not lead to freedom, stability or prosperity, there are numerous barriers to current attempts to draw the NSAGs into a conclusive peace process. If peace means the expansion of the Burmese state to all parts of the country, this threatens the local political and economic interests of the NSAGs. Moreover, most groups object strongly to elements of the 2008 constitution (even though this did bring limited local autonomy in the form of seven ethnically based States). Rather, they look towards a more federal future for the country, one that includes a federal army of which they could form part.

An additional factor in this complex situation is the failure of these armed groups to unite in a sustainable alliance working in their interests.

All too often, a mix of political and personal disagreements has caused such organizations to fragment and dissolve. At the local level as well, there has been conflict both between different ethnic groups and between factions within individual communities.[11]

Government officials

Public servants are expected to play an important role in the reform process, both politically and economically. However, in order for this to happen, the bureaucracy itself needs to be reformed. This will not be simple, Alex M. Mutebi has argued. 'The Myanmar bureaucracy can almost be said to be a synonym for inflexibility, lethargy, anachronism, shadiness, unresponsiveness and interference.' For decades it has had a military-controlled, top-down structure, among other things leading to poor organization, mismanaged and undertrained staff, weak accountability mechanisms, and badly implemented public services. Moreover, the military personnel controlling its upper levels have not learnt or been interested in mastering the bureaucratic and administrative tools needed to run a country. Nor has it helped that a parallel military administrative structure exists that renders the civil bureaucracy both redundant and powerless. The result has been the growth of a huge army of officials that is all pervasive but weak and over-extended, and is over-politicized but not master of its destiny. Finally, there is the issue of corruption, which is endemic in the bureaucracy (and military) and acts as a huge brake on the country's development. Unfortunately, the giving of such 'tea money' is difficult to separate from the gifts exchanged in the patron–client networks that are so prevalent in Burmese society.[12]

As a result of this situation, the public administration has had (and still has) a very limited number of people with the required skills to lead the reform process. This means that a small number of individuals are faced with the enormous challenges of reforming the economy and pursuing peace processes with ethnic minorities. After the political changes, the responsibility of the bureaucracy is slowly being transferred to civil servants who are unconnected to the Tatmadaw. However, as is the case with the government itself, the military is still a dominating force.

---

11. For a fuller treatment of NSAGs, see the chapter on peace-building (from p. 223).
12. While much of this assessment dates from the SPDC era – see esp. Mutebi (2005): 140–143 (quote from p. 154) – much said about that time also applies to today's public administration. For more recent issues covered in this section, see ERIA (2013), esp. pp. 1–3.

The condition of the Myanmar bureaucracy is not unique for developing countries, and in particular not for those under military rule for decades. However, with Myanmar changing and developing at a rapid pace, it is necessary for the bureaucracy to adapt and keep up with these developments. Capacity building of the bureaucracy will be crucial for the effective implementation of reforms.

The Sangha

Buddhism has a long history in Myanmar, dating back about two thousand years. Practised by about 89% of the population, it is an integral part of Burmese society. This status is officially recognized, with the 2008 constitution assigning Buddhism a 'special position'. What especially distinguishes Burmese Buddhism is the size and engagement of the Sangha, the monastic community of ordained monks or nuns. For instance, monasteries play an important role in the schooling of many (especially poor) Burmese children and they offer other services (e.g. health clinics) not provided by the state. Indeed, with more than 400,000 monks and 40,000 nuns, the Sangha constitutes a civil force of roughly the same size as the army.

Monks outside a monastery in Bago performing their daily morning ritual of collecting alms (photo: Sarah Meier)

Mindful of its potential power, successive governments have sought to harness Buddhism to their own purposes or otherwise tame the Sangha. In 1980, the Ne Win regime established the State Sangha Maha Nayaka Committee (SSMNC) as a government-appointed body of high-ranking monks to oversee and regulate the Sangha. This did not forestall monastic involvement in the 8888 Movement in 1988 let alone the fully fledged monastic revolt (Saffron Revolution) in 2007 and the current involvement of some monks in nationalistic organizations and anti-Muslim activities. Meantime, in the political mainstream, Aung San Suu Kyi has been effective in her integration of Buddhist ideals into her public profile and the NLD's political programme.

Even so, there is widespread unease within the Sangha about monastic involvement in politics, hence support for a SSMNC directive in September 2013 banning the formation of monastic networks in support of the Buddhist '969' nationalist movement and prohibiting the linking of the 969 emblem to the Buddhist religion.[13]

Business interests

During the decades of military rule, the Tatmadaw became increasingly engaged in business affairs and implicated in rampant corruption. This happened due to the Tatmadaw acting in its own right via military-owned companies, because of the private economic activities of military officers or as a result of patron–client relationships between officers and business people. Although the economy is now being rapidly liberalized, much of it remains in the hands of (or is influenced by) military business interests and so-called crony capitalists (for fuller details, see p. 362).

The often hidden influence of these business interests and lack of a level playing field for newcomers are especially of concern to foreign investors. Hence, in September 2013 an international business risks report warned against a tangled web of cronyism and corruption that awaits foreign telecom companies investing in the development of Burma's mobile telephone network. There is also increasing mention of the issue in the international media, for instance the *New York Times* in December warning foreign investors against enabling a transition from a military dictatorship to military-run crony capitalism.

---

13. The Sangha and Buddhism more generally feature throughout this volume (see especially p. 279ff. and p. 293ff.).

References

Callahan, Mary P. (2003). *Making Enemies. War and State Building in Burma.* Ithaca, NY: Cornell University Press.

——— (2012). 'The Generals Loosen Their Grip'. *Journal of Democracy*, Vol. 23,4, October: 120–131.

ERIA (2013). Economic Research Institute for ASEAN and East Asia, Policy Brief no. 2013-02, June.

Gravers, M. (1999). *Nationalism as Political Paranoia in Burma.* Richmond, Surrey: Curzon Press.

Harriden, Jessica (2012). *The Authority of Influence: Women and Power in Burmese History.* Copenhagen: NIAS Press.

Houtman, Gustaaf (1999). *Mental culture in Burmese crisis politics: Aung San Suu Kyi and the National League for Democracy.* Tokyo: Institute for the Study of Languages and Cultures of Asia and Africa, Tokyo University of Foreign Studies.

Mutebi, Alex M. (2005). '"Muddling Through" Past Legacies: Myanmar's Civil Bureaucracy and the Need for Reform', in Kyaw Yin Hlaing, Robert H. Taylor and Tin Maung Maung Than (eds) (2005): *Myanmar – Beyond Politics to Societal Imperatives.* Singapore: Institute of South East Asian Studies.

Popham, Peter (2011) *The Lady and the Peacock: The Life of Aung San Suu Kyi of Burma.* London: Random House (Rider Books).

Rogers, Benedict (2010). *Than Shwe. Unmasking Burma's Tyrant.* Chiang Mai: Silkworm Books.

Selth, Andrew (2002). *Burma's Armed Forces: Power without Glory.* Norwalk, CT: Eastbridge.

The 8888 generation

*The historical significance of the Four Eight Movement – the 8888 Genera-
tion, as it is also termed – goes way beyond the fateful events on that August
day in 1988.*

After months of countrywide protests by students against the regime's
sudden cancellation of certain currency denominations that wiped out
people's savings, on the morning of 8 August 1988, protesters took to

*Aung San Suu Kyi's first public appearance. Her speech to hundreds of thousands of people
at the Shwedagon Pagoda on 26 August 1988 is remembered as the moment when Aung San
Suu Kyi came to the forefront of popular protests against one-party rule in 1988. But in fact
her first public appearance was two days earlier on the 24th when she mounted a makeshift
platform outside Yangon General Hospital together with the famous film actress, Khin
Thida Htun, and Maung Thaw Ka, a well-known writer. It was the latter who, together
with two fellow intellectuals, had eventually persuaded General Aung San's daughter that
she could not remain silent when the country was in upheaval. The rest is history. (Photo:
Sonny Nyein, courtesy The Irrawaddy – see http://www.irrawaddy.org/feature/magazine-
feature/tribute-maung-thaw-ka.html for a fuller account.)*

the streets and marched toward the city centre in Yangon/Rangoon. The confrontation and the subsequent clashes between demonstrators and soldiers lasted for days; the protests were brutally crushed by the military rulers. The precise number of deaths is unknown, but has been estimated to be around 3,000 people, mostly students. Among many other demands, the protesters were asking for the replacement of one-party rule with a multiparty system.

Much of the country's present-day politics started with the 8888 uprising. It led to the resignation of General Ne Win, who had taken power in a coup in 1962 and ruled the country ever since, and the demise of his Burma Socialist Programme Party, which was largely composed of ex-military officers and was the vehicle through which he built his one-party rule. Ne Win's resignation did not lead to the hoped-for democratic reforms but instead resulted in another military coup in September 1988 and installation of a new government, the State Law and Order Restoration Council, SLORC.

That August uprising also marked the entry of Aung San Suu Kyi into politics. Then on a visit home from England to look after her ailing mother, she was drawn to the protests and, as the daughter of General Aung San who had fought for freedom from British rule, she was almost immediately hailed as its leader.

The 8888 movement culminated in the 1990 elections, the first free elections in three decades that were swept by the National League for Democracy (NLD) led by Aung San Suu Kyi, although the result was not honoured.[1]

One of the best-known members of the group is Min Ko Naing, who was the unofficial leader of the underground student union at the time of the 1988 uprising. Originally named Paw U Tun, his nom-de-guerre Min Ko Naing means 'conqueror of kings', and he has won numerous human-rights awards for his non-violent campaign for democracy.

He was arrested a year after the 1988 protests, and spent 15 years in jail, finally being released in November 2004. He was re-arrested several times and in 2007 a court sentenced him to 65 years in prison. In January 2012 he was released once more and allowed to travel abroad.

---

1. For a particularly fine account of the events of 1988, see Bertil Lintner: *Outrage: Burma's Struggle for Democracy.* Hong Kong: Review Publishing Company Limited, 1989.

Min Ko Naing (photo: Flemming Ytzen)

He visited Denmark in April of that year and gave an interview to the newspaper *Politiken*.

Among other statements, Min Ko Naing advised the Danish and other European governments to ensure that the scheduled 2015 elections will be held according to internationally acclaimed standards for free and fair elections. He also offered words of caution to foreign investors, not least about dealing with the country's crony capitalists:

> Investments in Myanmar are welcome, but any business corporation should carefully consider its local partners. All major corporations are owned or controlled by a small clique, closely tied to the former junta and the present military establishment. If money has to come flowing in now, a series of unresolved problems has to be addressed. We need to be clear about who benefits from foreign investment and trade with the outside world. We need transparency.

✍ FY

Towards a new state in Myanmar

Michael Lidauer

Introduction

The state in Myanmar has gone through several incarnations since pre-colonial times.[1] After decades of military rule (1958–60, 1962–74, 1988–2010) and/or one-party-regime (1974–88), the 2008 Constitution of the Republic of the Union of Myanmar establishes the basis for new governmental institutions and new modes of governance. This constitution – the third for the country following those from 1947 and 1974[2] – has been heavily criticized by democracy activists and opposition parties inside the country and by the international community for not meeting basic international standards for democratic governance. The strong role of the military, in particular the provision for reserved seats in the legislature, has been especially criticized. In fact, the question whether to accept the new constitution as a preliminary framework – that could provide a transitional pathway, opening a window of opportunity for opposition forces to re-engage in politics – was a question of principle for political parties prior to the 2010 elections. These elections were held on the basis of the new constitution. Several parties split over this question, some deciding on a boycott while splinter groups or newly founded parties decided to contest the polls.

Yet, the new constitution and all associated questions have to be viewed in historical context. Public protests in 1988 had brought about the end of General Ne Win's regime and the coming to power of the military State Law and Order Restoration Council (SLORC), later renamed the State Peace and Development Council (SPDC). The protestors had

---

1. For historical accounts of these transformations until today, see for example Taylor (2009).
2. For a comparison of the three constitutions by a legal practitioner from Myanmar, see *The New Light of Myanmar*, 27 October 2013, Volume XXI, Number 194, online: <http://issuu.com/npedaily/docs/27.oct_.13_nlm>, accessed on 28 October 2013.

demanded free multi-party elections. These polls were held in 1990 and led to the victory of the newly founded National League for Democracy (NLD) led by Daw Aung San Suu Kyi. However, immediately prior to the polls, SLORC announced that it would only hand over power to a civilian government after a new constitution had been written.[3] This process lasted for two decades. A national convention was installed to draft the new constitution, but was suspended in the mid-1990s, and only reconvened after the proclamation of the 'Roadmap to Democracy' in 2004.[4] The seven-step roadmap – vague in its formulation, not establishing a clear timeline, and not convincing many outsiders about its earnest intentions – foresaw the completion of the new constitution, the holding of general elections, and the transfer of power to a new government. Following the plan of the roadmap, a national referendum was held in May 2008 only few weeks after Cyclone Nargis had devastated the country. According to the results of the referendum the new constitution was overwhelmingly accepted, but many witnesses spoke of intimidation and undue influence by the authorities.[5]

Unwilling to adopt this new framework and holding on to the 'stolen' election results of 1990, the NLD, under Aung San Suu Kyi, and some other parties decided to boycott the 2010 elections. Their principle of non-collaboration with the military elite and the condemnation of the new constitution were also upheld. The international community largely followed the same principles and from the outset condemned the electoral process, which was allegedly marred with fraud. However, President Thein Sein's unexpected launch of political and economic reforms during his first year in office changed national and international perspectives about the ongoing transition. The unforeseen by-elections of 2012, in which Aung San Suu Kyi and the NLD were convinced to participate and during which the national election administration tried to run a more transparent process than in 2010, served as a 'rite-de-passage' for the country.[6] The NLD won 43 out of the 45 seats in competition; Suu Kyi became a member of parliament, and the chair of the parliamentary 'Rule of Law and Peace and Stability Committee';

---

3. Tonkin (2007).
4. Online: <http://www.ibiblio.org/obl/docs/KMWroadmap104.htm>, accessed on 19 October 2011.
5. Fink (2009): 109ff; cf. Taylor (2009): 487–506.
6. Lidauer (2012).

and the international community began to re-engage with Myanmar, most visibly with the alteration, suspension and ultimately end of most sanctions against the military junta. However, the question of the just-ness of the 2008 constitution remains and is part of the ongoing political discourse ahead of the next general elections expected in late 2015.

The new state – separation of powers and electoral system

The 2008 constitution shapes a hybrid system of government that bor-rows many features usually found in presidential systems. The Union Government is headed by the President and includes the two Vice-Presidents, the Ministers of the Union, and the Attorney General of the Union. The constitution vests considerable powers in the office of the President, in particular through its powers of appointment. The President appoints the ministers – three of whom (Defence, Home Affairs and Border Affairs) upon nomination by the Commander-in-Chief of the armed forces – and other members of the executive. The parliament has to formally approve the appointment of the Ministers of the Union, the Attorney General and the Auditor-General of the Union (but not their deputies or other governmental positions specified in the constitution).

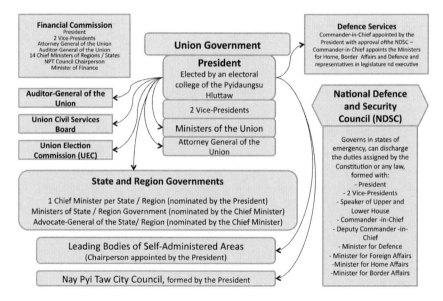

Separation of powers in Myanmar – executive authority (based on 2008 constitution)

The parliament cannot object to appointments 'unless it can clearly be proved that the person concerned does not meet the qualifications'. The President himself is not directly elected, but by an electoral college of the Pyidaungsu Hluttaw (the bicameral National Assembly) including military appointees. Once elected for a term of five years, the President does not need to have the backing of a parliamentary majority, and the incumbent can only be removed through an impeachment process.

Symmetrically to the executive, the parliament also has a fixed term of five years and cannot be dissolved by the President. The 2008 constitution foresees a bi-cameral National Assembly, the Pyidaungsu Hluttaw, consisting of the Amyotha Hluttaw (House of Nationalities or Upper House) and the Pyithu Hluttaw (House of Representatives or Lower House). Each house has a Speaker and a Deputy Speaker who are responsible to convene and supervise *hluttaw* sessions and the work of parliamentary committees. Both speakers of the Upper and Lower Houses act as Speaker of the full Pyidaungsu Hluttaw, each for half of the legislative period. The constitution also foresees degrees of decentralization with the establishment of 14 sub-national assemblies in seven Regions and seven States, and with the establishment of six smaller self-administered areas (see below).

The electoral system largely derives from constitutional provisions. Like other former British colonies, Myanmar has inherited a first-past-the-post (FPTP) system based on single-member constituencies. FPTP usually favours large nationwide influential parties as well as parties with a strong support base in particular constituencies, and tends to disenfranchise smaller parties and parties with a scattered support base. This system determined the outcome of the 1990 polls, which saw the NLD emerge as the overwhelming winner, and enabled the then newly founded Union Solidarity and Development Party (USDP) to establish an almost one-party rule in 2010 when the NLD boycotted the elections. It also led to the NLD succeeding in sweeping the 2012 by-elections, opening the door to a possible transfer of power in 2015 if the FPTP system remains. These swings highlight the potential winner-takes-all effect of FPTP. The potential for such radical electoral changes is exacerbated by the fact that almost all state institutions proceed directly or indirectly from the same general elections, taking the above-mentioned presidential appointments into account. As a consequence, the whole

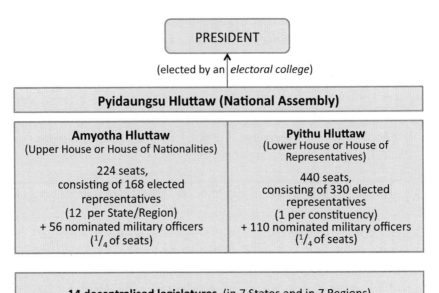

Separation of powers in Myanmar – legislature (based on 2008 constitution)

governance structure of the country is at stake in one single election every five years.

Looking at the judiciary, the 2008 constitution establishes a Supreme Court, High Courts of the Regions and States, courts of self-administered areas and lower-level administrative units, as well as a Constitutional Tribunal and a Court-Martial responsible for members of the Tatmadaw (armed forces). The Supreme Court is headed by the Chief Justice of the Union who is nominated by the President and approved by the Pyidaungsu Hluttaw similar to Union Ministers and the Attorney General. While the constitution foresees a procedure of direct petition to the Supreme Court for the protection of fundamental rights, it appears that this procedure is too remote and expensive for ordinary citizens. It is also disconnected from the process in lower courts, and therefore could not serve to infuse the whole judicial system. In addition, it seems that this procedure cannot serve to protect electoral rights, since the decisions of the Union Election Commission (UEC) are not subject to appeal.[7]

---

7.   EEM (2012: 12).

Courts-Martial	Supreme Court	Constitutional Tribunal
adjudicating court for Defence Serives personnel	Court of final appeal; headed by the Chief Justice of the Union (nominated by the President, approved by the Pyidaungsu Hluttaw; a minimum of 7 and a maximum of 11 judges	9 judges (3 each are nominated by the President, the Speaker of the Upper House and the Speaker of the Lower House); from these, the President nominates the Chairperson who is approved by the Pyidaungsu Hluttaw

14 High Courts of States/Regions
Headed by Chief Justices who are nominated by the President in coordination with the Chief Justice of the Union and the Chief Minister of the Region/State concerned, approved by the State/Region Hluttaw concerned; a minimum of 3 and a maximum of 7 judges
District Courts and Township courts
Under the jurisdiction of the High Court of the State/Region

Separation of powers in Myanmar – judiciary (based on 2008 constitution)

The military remains an important political and economic actor, both based on its self-conception as protector of the country's unity since independence and the position of power gained and maintained over the last five decades. The 2008 constitution states in its basic principles that the 'Defence Services [are] to be able to participate in the National [sic] political leadership role of the State' and gives substantial power to the Tatmadaw in the governance of the country. This role is realised among others through a close consultative relationship between the President and the Commander-in-Chief in the appointment procedures of governmental officials, and through strong military powers in a state of emergency. The military can intervene in case of danger for life and property of people in particular parts of the country, and the Commander-in-Chief 'has the right to take over and exercise state sovereign power [...] if there arises a state of emergency that could cause disintegration of the Union, disintegration of national solidarity and loss of sovereign power or attempts therefore by wrongful forcible means such as insurgency or violence.' In states of emergency, the National Defence and Security Council[8] can suspend the constitution and take over the governance of

8. The National Defence and Security Council consists of the President, the two Vice-Presidents, the Speaker of the Pyithu Hluttaw, the Speaker of the Amyotha Hluttaw, the Commander-in-Chief of the Defence Services, the Deputy Commander-in-Chief of the Defence Services, the Minister for Defence, the Minister for Foreign Affairs, the Minister for Home Affairs, and the Minister for Border Affairs.

the country, or of parts of the country, until a new government is elected and a new administration is formed. The President can also transfer executive, legislative and judicial powers temporarily to the Commander-in-Chief. Most prominently, however, the constitution reserves 25% of seats in the houses of the Pyidaungsu Hluttaw and in each of the Region/State assemblies for members of the army. The logic of the constitution is therefore not one of democratic control of the security sector but rather of an inbuilt role of the security sector in governance.[9] All major executive personnel of the new state, starting with President Thein Sein, have been members of the Tatmadaw. While the senior military leadership seems to support the course of reforms, the army remains a 'black box', and its position towards future reforms or eventual radical changes to government following elections is not foreseen.

Questions of decentralization

In 1931, the British colonial administration counted 135 ethnic groups based on differentiation by language. The SLORC maintained this figure, although others today speak of a number below a hundred. Population figures are currently uncertain and will only become clearer when the results of the 2014 census are fully published. As the census deals with religious, ethnic and other forms of identity, these data are politically highly sensitive and have the potential to cause political turmoil. After decades of highly centralized rule, the 'lack of state strength and penetration are key factors that continue to influence the country's transition'.[10] Beyond the grip of the SLORC/SPDC and previous regimes, local authority was at least partly embodied by customary leaders, non-state political actors or non-state armed groups, but also religious and other civil-society organizations have provided services that the state could not provide, including in the areas of health and education.[11] At the same time, requests for some kind of 'ethnic' autonomy or decentralization from largely 'Burman' central governments reach back to before the country's independence.

The 2008 constitution established a multi-tier administrative structure that forms a unitary framework, despite the fact that the creation

---

9. DRI (2013): 9f.
10. Nixon et al (2013): 7. Well-researched and detailed information on local governance in Myanmar is still rare. A valuable exception is the MDRI/TAF report, Nixon et al. (2013), which also serves as reference for this sub-section.
11. Lorch (2007).

of decentralized legislature could suggest dimensions of federalism. At the sub-national level, the territory comprises 14 administrative units (seven Regions and seven States), each with a Region/State assembly. The rationale behind this division is based on the assumption that Regions are predominantly inhabited by ethnic Burmans and States predominantly by the name-giving national minorities (Chin, Kachin, Kayah, Shan, Kayin, Mon, Rakhine and Shan). Otherwise, there is no institutional difference between Regions and States. In addition to the States, the 2008 constitution allows for self-administered areas for 'National races with [a] suitable population.'[12]

The constitution makes one step towards decentralization in creating the directly elected Region and State assemblies, yet the executive power at sub-national level remains in the hands of the central government. This is illustrated in particular by the nomination of Region/State Chief Ministers by the President, and by the reliance of the Regions and States on officers of the General Administration Department (GAD), a department of the military-led Ministry of Home Affairs, for their administration. The Chief Ministers participate in the Region/State *hluttaws* to which they are elected or appointed but they are accountable only to the President, not to their assemblies. Military influence is also given through the structure of the Ministry of Border Affairs. However, the actual impact on decentralized governance of military representatives in Region/State legislatures and executives is currently unclear.

The potential new political space in Regions/States has to date only been explored in limited ways. Schedule Two of the 2008 constitution lists eight sectors of governance over which the decentralized government has legislative powers,[13] but the specified responsibilities are narrow and exclude such major areas as health and education. Many significant departments and ministries remain centralized, although reforms are ongoing in Naypyidaw to give more autonomy to Regions and States. Some Region/State governmental departments have to report to their local government and some have to report to government at Union

12. The self-administered areas comprise five self-administered zones (Naga, Danu, Pa-O, Pa Laung and Kokang) with 2–3 townships each, and one self-administered division (Wa) with six townships. All self-administered areas are governed by a Leading Council with a Chair; the Tatamadaw is integrated into these councils.

13. Finance and Planning; Economy; Agriculture and Livestock Breeding; Energy, Electricity, Mining and Forestry; Industry; Transport, Communication and Construction; Social Sector; and Management.

Map 2: Regional administration

Note that the Bamar heartland is divided into Regions whereas the minority areas on Myanmar's margins are denoted as States.

level, or have to do so for certain areas of their responsibilities. Thus the independence of the administration in Regions and States remains ambiguous. The restricted decentralization of political power is further limited by administrative and fiscal weaknesses. However, it appears that public interest and awareness in sub-national dimensions of governance are increasing, not only among minorities and 'ethnic parties' but also among localized factions of other parties, civil-society organizations and the media. This underlines the need for a more comprehensive policy on decentralization. Further attention will also have to be drawn to local governance beyond Region/State level where a new law governing ward and village tract administration was enacted in early 2012. For the first time this allows direct elections of local leaders.[14]

Elite contestations and demands for constitutional reform

While it remains clear that decision-making is still highly centralized and characterized by top-down hierarchies with little room for accountability and participation, the emergence of the new state also brings about new contestations at the elite level. The development of the Pyidaungsu Hluttaw is one of the most surprising elements of the ongoing transition. Prior to the inauguration of the new government, the composition of the parliamentary chambers at Union level[15] offered little expectation that parliament might become a powerful institution, let alone a real debating house. Yet, observations during the first half of the ongoing legislative period have shown that there are continuing debates between the USPD majority and the minority of non-USDP MPs. Members of Parliament do not always vote along party lines, and the military MPs do not always vote as one block.[16] The Speaker of the Lower House, Thura Shwe Mann, has not only promoted this development, but he has also challenged the office of the President by demanding stronger roles for the parliament.[17] This contestation has already led to the resignation of the Constitutional Tribunal over a dispute about the status of parliamentary committees in September 2012, and has continued since then, also with

14. Kempel (2012).
15. For the composition of the Pyidaungsu Hluttaw in detail, see MCM Book Publishing (2013).
16. See Kean (2014) for fuller details.
17. The relationship between the two is even more delicate due to the fact that Shwe Mann held a higher-ranking military position than Thein Sein in the SPDC regime (see p. 47 and p. 52).

the effect of delaying some attempts at reforms by the President. On his side, President Thein Sein has undertaken government reshuffles on several occasions to strengthen his course of reforms. It is said that he has no high ambitions for a second term.

The capacities of MPs, however, are still not very well developed, and requirements to pass vast numbers of new bills are a great challenge for the legislature. One political issue still unresolved is the question of the electoral system, which impacts the future composition of the parliamentary houses. The subject of a possible electoral system change from FPTP to a proportional system (PR) was already discussed after the 1990 elections but re-surfaced after the 2012 by-elections when smaller political parties approached the Union Election Commission and President U Thein Sein on this issue. The question whether the electoral system can be changed without constitutional amendments was brought before the Constitutional Tribunal by the UEC Chairman in summer 2012, but no response was received prior to the Tribunal's resignation. In October 2013, the UEC Chairman reminded the parliament of this open question, emphasizing that the Union Election Commission cannot decide over the electoral system and that the issue would need to be addressed in good time if any change should be implemented prior to 2015. In June 2014, the question finally reached the parliament and the Amyotha Hluttaw agreed to discuss a proposal for the introduction of PR. The NLD and ethnic parties with local strongholds are in favour of keeping FPTP, while the USDP and smaller parties without strong local support bases favour a change.[18] With the results of the 2012 by-elections in mind, it is surprising that the topic was not already dealt with earlier by the USDP. The question of electoral system choice has the potential to be part of a political deal when it comes to constitutional amendments.

As outlined in the introduction, demands for constitutional reform, or for another constitution altogether, have accompanied the emerging new state since before its inception. For many observers, however, the motion to formally review the constitution in parliament came as a surprise when it was proposed by senior USDP MPs in March 2013. On 25 July, a Constitutional Review Committee with 109 members was installed; its composition reflected that of the Pyidaungsu Hluttaw

---

18. The question was hotly debated in Naypyidaw at the time of writing, including by Thura Shwe Mann and Daw Aung San Suu Kyi who both reached out to 'ethnic' MPs to win their support and find an agreement.

Parliamentary complex in Naypyidaw (photo: Marie Ditlevsen)

and had a USDP majority. Despite hopes for intensified public debates on the part of opposition parties and civil-society organizations, the Committee decided to operate quietly but was open to receive recommendations from inside and outside parliament. Thousands of individual proposals were compiled in a report by the end of January 2014 and have subsequently been dealt with by a follow-up committee, the 31-member Constitutional Amendment Implementation Committee. This committee studies the clustered proposals in detail and gives recommendations to parliament about constitutional amendments. In parallel, the NLD launched a public information campaign about the 2008 constitution and a discussion process with ethnic parties about possible amendments. In May 2014, having not received a positive response on her repeated demands for a quadripartite elite meeting between the President, the Speaker, Commander-in-Chief Senior General Min Aung Hlaing and herself, Aung San Suu Kyi started to take a more confrontational stance with the organization of mass rallies, backed by the 88 Student Generation.

Some ethnic parties and formerly armed non-state actors still hold the position that a new constitution should be rewritten altogether. Meanwhile, many leading opposition figures agree that article 436 – which establishes the conditions to change substantial parts of the constitution, prescribing a 75% majority in parliament followed by a national referendum – should be amended as a priority. One of the most important issues for ethnic parties is the direct election of State Chief Ministers rather than their appointment by the President. Other major issues at stake are the constitutionally enshrined emergency powers of the military, the quota for military representation in the legislatures, and the restrictions on presidential candidates that currently would not allow Daw Aung San Suu Kyi to stand in 2015. At the time of writing, it appeared unlikely that the Constitutional Amendment Implementation Committee will recommend changing the relevant article, 59(f). In October 2013, Thura Shwe Mann openly said he is in favour of changing the constitution to allow Suu Kyi to run, even though he has repeatedly declared his interest to become the next president himself. Presidential aspirations are also anticipated for Senior General Min Aung Hlaing. However, even if many in the USDP and the military follow their leaders' unlikely guidance on this issue, the difficulties to change the constitution will not go away easily as any substantial amendment will formally require the above-mentioned 75% majority in parliament and a referendum – unless the political will for compromise leads to the unexpected finding of a legal loophole. Although unlikely, Aung San Suu Kyi's right to stand could become a trading element in exchange for an electoral system change that could secure the USDP's political survival.

Constitutional amendment debates have been overshadowed by continued fighting in Kachin and northern Shan States, by the crisis in Rakhine State and the growing anxiety about anti-Muslim violence, and by the negotiations for a national ceasefire accord, possibly to be followed by a structured political dialogue – of which constitutional reforms would again form a part, discussed by more stakeholders than in parliament. Given the demands for more political participation in the new state not only from the NLD but also from many ethnic parties and leaders, all elites will need endurance and creativity to deal with the political challenges ahead, as well as good will and belief in the cause of democratic reforms for the process not to derail in electoral competition.

Author's Note

This contribution builds upon a shorter version in German, Michael Lidauer, 'Wird die Verfassung der Vielfalt gerecht? – Verfassungsreformen und Wahlsystem', in Ute Köster, Phuong Le Trong and Christina Grein (eds): *Handbuch Myanmar*. Berlin: Horlemann, 2014, 143–152. A more in-depth analysis of the electoral framework can be found in Michael Lidauer and Gilles Saphy, 'Elections and the Reform Agenda', in Melissa Crouch and Tim Lindsey (eds): *Law, Society and Transition in Myanmar*. Oxford: Hart, 2014.

References

Democracy Reporting International (DRI) (2013): 'Pluralism in Democratic Constitutions'. Research Report, April 2013. Online: <http://www.democracy-reporting.org/files/dri_research_report_pluralism_in_constitutions.pdf>, accessed on 22 July 2013.

EU Election Expert Mission to Myanmar (EU EEM) (2012): 'Final Report'. Yangon and Brussels. Unpublished document.

Fink, Christina (2009): *Living Silence in Burma. Surviving under Military Rule.* 2nd edition. Silkworm Books, Chiang Mai & Zed Books, London & New York.

Kean, Thomas (2014): 'Myanmar's Parliament: From Scorn to Significance' in Nick Cheesman , Nicholas Farrelly and Trevor Wilson (eds): *Debating Democratisation in Myanmar*. Singapore: Institute of Southeast Asian Studies.

Kempel, Susanne (2013): 'Local Governance: Monitoring and analysis of village tract administration election processes and results'. Draft concept note, 9 April 2013.

Lidauer, Michael (2012): 'Democratic Dawn? Civil Society and Elections in Myanmar 2010–2012'. *Journal of Current Southeast Asian Affairs*, Vol 31, No 12, 87–114.

Lorch, Jasmin (2007): 'Myanmar's Civil Society – a Patch for the National Education System? The Emergence of Civil Society in Areas of StateWeakness'. *Südostasien aktuell*, 26, 3, 54–88.

MCM Book Publishing (ed.) (2013): *The Parliaments of Myanmar. Pyithu Hluttaw (House of Representatives), Amyotha Hluttaw (House of Nationalities).* Yangon: Zin Yadanar Saw Publishing House.

Nixon, Hamish, Cindy Joelene, Kyi Par Chit Saw, Thet Aung Lynn, Matthew Arnold: *State and Region Governments in Myanmar*. Myanmar Development Research Institute (MDRI) and The Asia Foundation, September 2013.

Taylor, Robert (2009): *The State in Myanmar*. London: Hurst & Company.

Tonkin, Derek (2007): 'The 1990 Elections in Myanmar: Broken Promises or a Failure of Communication?' *Contemporary Southeast Asia*, 29, 1, 33–54.

Defining civil society

'Civil society' is a contested concept: there are many definitions of the term, used in different ideological traditions. Furthermore, the sector itself may be contested (i.e. with multiple civil-society actors who compete for material and/or political resources). This chapter uses a non-prescriptive definition of civil society – actors, voluntary associations and networks operating in the space between the family/clan, the state in its various incarnations, and the for-profit market. This includes but is not limited to non-government organizations (NGOs) and community-based organizations (CBOs – see below). Local civil society in Myanmar includes village-level associations and networks whose members conceive of and undertake their work in 'traditional' ways that differ from the western 'rational-bureaucratic' approach (see note 3 on p. 88). It is debatable whether organizations closely associated with state and non-state actors (so-called 'GONGOs' and 'NSAG-GONGOs') should be considered part of civil society.

The terms ('local/national') NGO and CBO are often used interchangeably. However, there are important conceptual and practical differences between the two types of organization. A CBO is used here to mean a grassroots membership organization – based in the community and locally managed – with its members as its main beneficiaries. CBOs usually exist in just one community or a group of adjacent communities. In contrast, NGOs are service providers that work for social, non-profit ends (for the benefit of the community). Staff may be local, national or international but not necessarily drawn from among the beneficiaries. Although NGOs often employ participatory, 'grassroots' approaches, they usually work in broader thematic and geographic areas than do CBOs.

✍ CP/AS

Development of civil society in Myanmar

Charles Petrie and Ashley South

The peace process currently underway in Myanmar represents the best oppor-tunity in half a century to resolve ethnic and state–society conflicts. Critical to the success of this peace process will be the role that is played by various actors in the country's civil society. In this chapter, the nature of civil society in Myanmar is examined. In a subsequent chapter on peace-building in Myanmar, the ac-tual engagement of these various actors in the peace process will be explored in greater detail.

An important aspect of the recent violence and ethnic hatred in parts of Rakhine State and central Myanmar (described elsewhere in this volume – see especially p. 323ff.) has been the role played by various political actors at the local and national levels, often in competition with each other. Not only do these events indicate that there are spoilers on the sidelines, working to undermine the reform process by using local tensions to provoke violence but also it is important to acknowledge the potentially 'dark side of civil society' (an issue we shall return to later in this chapter).

Contestation and evolution of civil society

A contest for power within and over Myanmar's civil-society sector is not a new phenomenon. For half a century, the state has sought to penetrate and suppress, and/or mobilize, the country's diverse social groups, while members of Myanmar's diverse ethnic nationalities (including the Burman majority) have sought to carve out spheres of autonomy – both for the intrinsic value of civil-society work (in providing services, promoting democratization, etc.) and to contest a dictatorial and often brutal state authority – in ways which in many cases reflect ethnic and religious divisions in society.

Following the military takeover of 1958, and especially after the 1962 coup d'etat, the government began extending its control over previously autonomous aspects of social life.[1] Many civil-society networks could no longer operate independently, and opposition to the military regime was eliminated, driven underground or forced into open revolt. The existence of renewed armed opposition to the military government provided a pretext for the further extension of state control, and suppression of diverse social groups deemed antipathetic to the modernizing state-socialist project. The military regime's suppression of non-Burman cultural and political identities, epitomized by the banning of minority languages from state schools, drove a new wave of disaffected ethnic-minority citizens into rebellion.[2]

By 1980, even the previously independent *Sangha* (monkhood) – members of which played key roles in Myanmar's struggle for independence – had been brought under at least partial state control. Nevertheless, Myanmar's 250,000 monks and novices retained a prestige and influence that extended across all strata of society. Among the few institutions in Myanmar not directly controlled by the state, the Sangha – and Christian networks – remained among the potentially most powerful sectors of civil society, especially in ethnic minority areas.[3]

Popular participation may be mobilized either for (or against) an authoritarian regime, and it seemed for a few weeks in the summer of 1988 that 'people's power' might prevail in Myanmar, as it had two

---

1. Kyaw Yin Hlaing (2007).
2. According to David Steinberg, 'civil society died under the BSPP; perhaps, more accurately, it was murdered' (Steinberg 1999: 8). Under the 1974 constitution, all political activity beyond the strict control of the state was outlawed (Taylor 1987: 303–09).
3. The Anglican, Baptist, Catholic and other churches in Myanmar have well over two million members. Although most of their activities are religious-pastoral, the churches devote considerable energy and resources (including some international funds) to education, social welfare and community development projects, also in armed conflict-affected areas. These are significant, countrywide organizations, the majority of whose members come from minority communities. However, they also face considerable skills and capacity constraints. Many Buddhist voluntary associations exist, too. Although many senior monks have been co-opted by the military regime, the Sangha still has great potential as a catalyst in civil and political affairs. However, Buddhist and other traditional networks tend to be localized and centred on individual monks who may not conceptualize or present their aims in a manner readily intelligible to western agencies. Such non-formal approaches are therefore often 'invisible' to western (and western-trained) staff (South 2008).

years previously in the Philippines. The failure of the 1988 'Democracy Uprising' in Myanmar, like that of the May–June 1989 'Democracy Spring' in China, was in part due to the suppressed nature of civil society in these states. Under the rule of the State Law and Order Restoration Council (SLORC), which came to power in 1988, state–society relations were further centralized and attempts were made to penetrate and mobilize the country's diverse social groups. Particularly following the ascension of General Than Shwe in 1992, social control was reinforced by the reformation of local militias, the indoctrination of civil servants, and the major new drive by the SLORC to develop a state- controlled mass organization. In addition to new GONGOs (organizations closely associated with state and non-state actors), these included the military-backed Union Solidarity and Development Association (USDA), a mass organization (many members of which were coerced into joining) that was established in September 1993 along the lines of the pro-military GOLKAR party in Indonesia. The USDA was transformed into the USD Party to contest the 2010 elections.[4] The USDA and pro-government militias were heavily involved in the brutal suppression of the Sangha-led 'saffron revolution' in September 2007 (see p. 293ff.).

The following year, the Irrawaddy Delta and parts of Yangon Division were devastated by Cyclone Nargis, a huge natural disaster that struck on 2–3 May 2008 (see p. 397). Following the cyclone, in the absence of an effective government or international response, local communities took the initiative in responding to the unprecedented humanitarian crisis. In Yangon and across the Delta, monks helped to clear debris, undertook emergency rescues and repairs, and provided shelter to the destitute. This was a politically significant development, given the government's violent suppression of the monks' uprising the previous year. Furthermore, a broad array of formal and informal local associations and citizens, including several prominent celebrities and business networks, participated in an impressive range of relief activities. Church and other civil-society organizations mobilized to deliver assistance, including money and material donated by international organizations.[5]

---

4. Callahan 2003: 8; see also p. 57. The USDA/USDP's objectives include upholding the regime's 'Three National Causes' (non-disintegration of the union, non-disintegration of national solidarity and perpetuation of national solidarity) and reaffirming the Myanmar Army's self-appointed state- and nation-building role.

5. South (2012).

Emergency food relief after Cyclone Nargis, August 2008 (photo: Nils Carstensen, courtesy Dan-ChurchAid)

Mapping civil society in Myanmar today

Since the 1990s, civil society in Myanmar has gradually re-emerged.[6] Until 2011, many of the more dynamic sectors of Myanmar civil society were situated among ethnic groups. The re-emergence of civil society within and sometimes between often highly conflict-affected communities was partly a result of the previous round of ceasefires in the 1990s. The space for civil and political society has again expanded dramatically since mid-2011 when the new government took power in Myanmar.[7]

In brief, then, the civil-society sector can be mapped as follows. A more detailed overview (but one oriented towards mapping peace-building activities) is found in our later chapter (from p. 223). In addition, the general point can be made that, although the peace process in Myanmar is heavily dominated by men, women activists play more prominent roles in civil society, particularly among ethnic-nationality communities.

6.   Lorch (2006).
7.   In a significant development for civil-socity organizations, a new law was passed by parliament in June 2014 that provides voluntary registration procedures for local and international NGOs. It also replaces the draconian laws enacted by the military regime shortly after it seized power in 1988 that effectively banned NGOs not closely tied to the regime. (MD)

Urban/Burman areas

Over the past decade, urban civil society in Myanmar has grown and also become more politicized. Since mid-2011, there has been a huge increase in civil-society activism. While not exclusively identified with the majority community, activism is nevertheless focused particularly around Burman intellectual classes aiming to promote democracy in their country.

Those working to 'build democracy from below' have established a number of predominantly Burman-staffed national NGOs, with significant achievements made in areas like education and community development. Several of these organizations grew substantially in response to Cyclone Nargis and some are now well established. The trend towards a more politically engaged civil society was magnified by the decision of the National League for Democracy (NLD) to enhance its political prospects by engaging in social work.

Ethnic actors in government-controlled areas

Before the socio-political opening of the past two years, the roles and scope of civil-society action in government-controlled areas were severely restricted. Nevertheless, provided they worked with great caution and had powerful patrons, Christian (mostly ethnic minority) civil-society groups enjoyed considerable space and were able to maintain strong international connections while remaining mostly disconnected from Burman-majority civil society. Over the past two years, ethnic-nationality civil-society actors in Myanmar have enjoyed more space for action. The dynamics of this fast-changing situation vary, according to the context of particular conflict and peace processes. Civil society in many ethnic communities is often faith-based or involves other more traditional types of association. Though maybe invisible to Western observers, this indigenous civil society constitutes the heart of the communities in question, being a great reservoir of 'human capital' and strategic capacity for change.

The borderlands; areas of ongoing armed conflict

Over the past two decades, a veritable 'aid industry' has grown up along the Thai border. Here, a number of civil-society groups have flourished, staffed by dedicated Myanmar personnel as well as long-term foreign actors. However, as the peace process gains ground (with the important caveat of recent heavy fighting in Kachin areas), the old distinction between areas of ongoing conflict and ceasefire and government-controlled areas is beginning to break down. Not only are vulnerable, armed conflict-affected communities in remote areas increasingly accessible from inside the country; the political narrative is also shifting more and more *into* Myanmar. Many border-based groups are adapting to this change but others find it threatening, especially those advocacy groups that became used to controlling the political agenda, framing the ethnic conflict for international consumption, and channelling donor funds to their own conflict-affected client populations. The dilemmas and issues thus arising raise important questions about the nature of civil society (see our follow-up chapter, p. 223ff.).

Refugee and diaspora communities

As well as the millions of mainly ethnic minority people internally displaced within Myanmar or living as refugees in the borderlands (discussed above), a further 2–3 million migrant workers and their dependents live in Thailand where they have become part of the 'grey' and 'black' economies. (Their situation is explored in greater detail later in this volume – see p. 364.) As noted for the borderlands, many activist and exile groups in Thailand and beyond have sought to play constructive roles in the peace process while others feel more threatened by the changes in Myanmar, and have positioned themselves as 'spoilers'.

A refugee camp at Mannerplaw in eastern Burma (photo courtesy of Free Burma Rangers)

Strategic roles of civil society

As warned by others,[8] it is important to acknowledge the potentially 'dark side of civil society': the sector may have significant discontents ('uncivil society'). Civil society is not inherently progressive, but can be both reactionary and repressive or at least unaccountable. Indeed, civil society in Myanmar tends to be dominated by (local) elites, and as such may reproduce the inequalities of society at large.[9] Nevertheless, civil-society networks are essential for the achievement of 'bottom-up' social and political transition in Myanmar, and for conflict resolution at both the national and local levels. In order for democratic change to be sustainable, the country's diverse social and ethnic communities must enjoy a sense of ownership in any transitional process, and equip themselves to fill the power vacuum that may emerge, either as a result of abrupt shifts in national politics, or of a more gradual withdrawal of the military from state and local power. The ability of people to organize, and re-assume control over aspects of their lives, which since the 1960s have been abrogated by the military (including insurgent armies), will depend on such grassroots mobilization, and practices of local governance.

At the local level, the development of civil-society networks and 'human capital' establishes patterns of empowerment, trust and participation that can gradually change structures of governance on the part of local authorities (including ceasefire groups). The creation of 'social capital' and the related concepts of reciprocity and 'political trust', through voluntary cooperation in the mutually accountable activities of civil society, is one of the hallmarks of citizen engagement in liberal democracy. In the Burmese context, this is related to a shift in power relations, from 'power over' (the mode of military government, reflected in much of the wider society) to an empowering, innately democratic 'power with' form of participatory social organization.[10] Elements of re-emergent civil society in Myanmar reflect the countries' authoritarian traditions and recent history. Furthermore, Myanmar civil society remains 'segmented' among ethnic lines. Nevertheless, there are reasons

---

8. Alagappa (2004) and, in the case of Myanmar, Lorch (2006).
9. See also South (2012).
10. As noted elsewhere, one way of achieving this transition may be through implementing codes of conduct and supporting the work of local ceasefire- and peace-monitoring networks.

for hope regarding the dynamic engagement of citizens in processes of peace and democratization.

Authors' Note

As with our later chapter on peace-building (see p. 223), this chapter is based on material from the background paper 'Mapping of Myanmar Peacebuilding Civil Society', which was prepared by the authors for a meeting of the Civil Society Dialogue Network focused on the evolving peace processes in Myanmar and held in Brussels on 7 March 2013 (more details at http://www.eplo.org/civil-society-dialogue-network. html). Part of this extracted material is updated from South 2008. For a survey of civil society in Myanmar, see Kyaw Yin Hlaing 2007.

References

Alagappa, Muthiah (ed.) (2004) *Civil Society and Political Change in Asia: Expanding and Contracting Democratic Space*. Stanford, CA: Stanford University Press.

Callahan, Mary (2003) *Making Enemies: War and State Building in Burma*. Ithaca, NY: Cornell University Press.

Kyaw Yin Hlaing (2007) 'Associational Life in Myanmar: Past and Present', in N Ganesan and Kyaw Yin Hlaing (eds), *Myanmar: State, Society and Ethnicity*. Singapore: Institute for Southeast Asian Studies, 2007.

Lorch, Jasmine (2006) 'Civil Society under Authoritarian Rule: The Case of Myanmar'. *SÜDOSTASIEN/aktuell – Journal of Current Southeast Asian Affairs*, 2006: 2.

South, Ashley (2008) 'Civil Society in Burma: The Development of Democracy Amidst Conflict'. Washington, DC: East–West Center, Policy Studies, No. 51.

— (2012) 'The Politics of Protection in Burma', *Critical Asian Studies*, 44: 2: 175–204.

Steinberg, David (1999) 'A Void in Myanmar: Civil Society in Burma', in Burma Centre Netherlands and Transnational Institute (eds), *Strengthening Civil Society: Possibilities and Dilemmas for International NGOs*. Chiang Mai: Silkworm Books.

Taylor, Robert (1987) *The State in Burma*. London: C. Hurst & Company.

The Kyi to the Great Game East

Bertil Lintner

The release of Aung San Suu Kyi has given the Burmese military the kind of international attention it has long desired. The question remains whether democratic concern is the real reason driving the world's attention.

It would be naïve to believe that recent policy changes in Burma, its charm offensive with the West – and the West's warm response to the overtures – are driven by a sudden democratic awakening among the country's ruling military elite. Nor are Western powers, despite their rhetoric and posturing, placing progress on democracy and human rights at the top of their policy priorities. There is hypocrisy on both sides – and the main issue of concern (which, however, neither side would acknowledge publicly) is without doubt China's economic and strategic push south through Burma to the Indian Ocean and the rest of Southeast Asia.

When Burma established diplomatic and military ties with North Korea, more alarm bells began to ring in Washington. It became imperative for the United States to change its policy of isolation in favour of engagement with Burma's military regime. The Burmese generals, on their part, were eager to lessen their economic and political dependence on China, but realised that they could do that only if political 'reforms' were implemented, leading to a certain degree of liberalization of the country's rigid and repressive political system.

While paying lip service to democracy and human rights, the West has welcomed the 'new Burma' with open arms, especially after the new president, ex-general Thein Sein, announced on 30 September 2011 that his government had suspended a US$ 3.6 billion joint-venture hydroelectric dam project with China that threatened environmental damage in the country's northern Kachin State. The dam, located at Myitsone where the Mali Hka and Nmai Hka rivers converge to form the Irrawaddy, would have flooded more than 600 square kilometres, an area bigger than Singapore, and 90% of the electricity was scheduled for export to China. Once online, the dam and its huge reservoir would have done grave harm to the Irrawaddy, the nation's economic and cultural artery.

A massive popular movement against the dam was gaining momentum and an escalation of anti-Chinese tensions could have led to riots even more serious then in 1967 when angry mobs ransacked businesses and homes owned by ethnic Chinese in Rangoon, then the national capital.

Perhaps not surprisingly, a January 2010 diplomatic cable from the US embassy in Rangoon made public by Wikileaks revealed the movement had received American support. The cable, which was signed by then US charge d'affaires Larry Dinger, stated that 'an unusual aspect of this case is the role grassroots organizations have played in opposing the dam, which speaks to the growing strength of civil society groups in Kachin State, including recipients of embassy small grants'.

US interest in Burma began in earnest, and in a completely different context, in August and September 1988, when the country saw the most massive and widespread pro-democracy demonstrations in recent Asian history. Strikes and protests were held in virtually every city, town, and major village throughout the country against a stifling military dictatorship that had held Burma in an iron grip since the army seized power in 1962 and abolished the country's democratic constitution. Aung San Suu Kyi, the daughter of Burma's independence hero Aung San, happened to be in the country at that time (she then lived in England) and people turned to her for leadership. She soon emerged as the main leader of the country's pro-democracy movement.

But the government did not fall. It retreated into the background, and on 18 September 1988, the military moved in, not to seize power – which it already had – but to shore up a regime overwhelmed by popular protest. The result was a brutal massacre. Thousands of marchers were mowed down by machine-gun fire, protesters were shot in custody, and the prisons were filled with people of all ages and from all walks of life.

Not surprisingly, Western countries, led by the United States, condemned the carnage. Later, sanctions were imposed on the regime, but they were always half-hearted and had little if any effect in terms of foreign trade because Burma's neighbours were not interested in any human-rights motivated embargoes. Still, sanctions turned Burma into an international outcast and prevented it from having full access to UN funding and international monetary institutions.

China, which long had coveted Burma's forests, rich mineral and natural gas deposits as well as its hydroelectric power potential, took the most advantage of the situation. In fact, China had already made its intentions clear in 2 September 1985 edition of *Beijing Review*, an officially sanctioned news magazine and a mouthpiece of the government. An article titled 'Opening to the Southwest: An Expert Opinion', written by Pan Qi, a former vice minister of communications, outlined the possibilities of finding an outlet for trade for China's landlocked southern

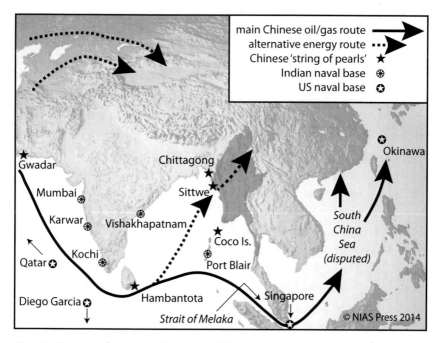

Map 3: Myanmar/Burma at the nexus of Asian energy security issues (relief background © Mountain High Maps)

China has sought to safeguard its energy supplies through the Indian Ocean region with a network of friendly ports (its so-called 'string of pearls') but choke points and security concerns in Southeast and East Asia have encouraged Beijing to find overland solutions.

provinces of Yunnan and Sichuan through Burma to the Indian Ocean. It also mentioned the Burmese railheads of Myitkyina and Lashio in the north and northeast, and the Irrawaddy River as possible conduits for Chinese exports.

It was the first time that the Chinese outlined their new designs for Burma, and why the country was so important to them economically. Until then, China had supported the Communist Party of Burma and other insurgent groups, but after the death of Mao Zedong in 1976 and Deng Xiaoping's ascendance to power, Beijing's foreign policy shifted from supporting revolutionary movements in the region to promoting trade. This was the first time this new policy towards Burma was announced, albeit rather discreetly, by the Chinese authorities.

The first border trade agreement between Burma and China was signed in early August 1988, days before the uprising gained momentum and spread across the country. After the movement had been crushed and sanctions were put in place, China moved in and rapidly became Burma's most important foreign trade partner. It helped Burma upgrade its antiquated infrastructure – and supplied massive amounts of military hardware. In the decade after the massacres, China exported more than US$ 1.4 billion worth of military equipment to Burma. It also helped Burma upgrade its naval facilities in the Indian Ocean. In return, the junta gave Beijing access to signals intelligence from key oil shipment sea lanes collected by the Burmese Navy, using equipment supplied by China. The strategic balance of power in the region was being upset in China's favour. Not only the United States but, especially, India was watching these developments with increasing concern.

But the real resource play came later, and in spades. A plan to build oil and gas pipelines was approved by China's National Development and Reform Commission in April 2007. In November 2008, China and Burma agreed to build a US$1.5 billion oil pipeline and US$1.04 billion natural gas pipeline. In March 2009, China and Burma finally signed an agreement to build that natural gas pipeline, and in June 2009 an agreement to build the crude oil pipeline. The inauguration ceremony marking the start of construction was held on 31 October 2009, on Maday Island on Burma's western coast. The gas pipeline from the Bay of Bengal to Kunming, in China's Yunnan province, will be supplemented with an oil pipeline designed to allow Chinese ships carrying fuel imports from the Middle

Deng Xiaoping and Ne Win, Rangoon, 26 January 1978 (photograph courtesy of Cheng Ruisheng)

East to skirt the congested Malacca Strait. And in September 2010, China agreed to provide Burma with US$4.2 billion worth of interest-free loans over a 30-year period to help fund hydropower projects, road and railway construction, and information technology development.

Western sanctions did not cause Burma's economic – and strategic – push into 'the hands of the Chinese', as many foreign observers have argued. But Western policies certainly made it easier for China to implement its designs for Burma. This has, in return, caused the West to rethink its Burma policy. US strategic concerns were outlined as early as June 1997 in a *Los Angeles Times* article by Marvin Ott, an American security expert and former CIA analyst. 'Washington can and should remain outspokenly critical of abuses in [Burma]. But there are security and other national interests to be served ... it is time to think seriously about alternatives', Ott concluded.

But the turn took some doing. The revelation in the early 2000s that Burma and North Korea had established a strategic partnership eventually tipped the balance in Washington. North Korea was providing Burma with tunnelling expertise, heavy weapons, radar and air defence systems, and – it is alleged by Western and Asian intelligence agencies – even missile-related technology. It was high time to shift tracks and start to 'engage' the Burmese leadership, which anyway seemed bent on clinging on to power at any cost, no matter the consequences.

The November 2010 election in Burma that brought Thein Sein's government to power may have been blatantly rigged and fraudulent but it was just the opportunity that Washington needed. Burma suddenly had a new face and a country run by a constitution, not a junta. It was the perfect time for Burma's generals to launch its charm offensive in the West, and for the United States and other Western countries to begin the process of détente – and of pulling Burma from its uncomfortable Chinese embrace and close relationship with North Korea.

In early December 2011, US Secretary of State Hillary Clinton paid a high-profile visit to Burma, the first such trip by a top-ranking Washington official in more than 50 years. Hardly by coincidence, Clinton visited South Korea before continuing on to Burma. For more than a year prior to the visit, it had been known in security circles that the United States wanted South Korea to lure Burma away from its military cooperation with North Korea. The much richer South would be able to provide more useful assistance to Burma than the North, the argument went.

At the same time, many staunchly nationalistic Burmese military officers were becoming increasingly dissatisfied with their country's heavy dependence on China as well as uncontrolled immigration by Chinese nationals into the north of the country. The first blow against China came in October 2004, when the then-prime minister and former intelligence chief Lt.-Gen. Khin Nyunt was ousted. The Chinese at first refused to believe that their man in Burma, Khin Nyunt, had been pushed out. How could the generals dare to move against a figure so key to the relationship?

Nevertheless, both sides managed to smooth over the incident and bilateral relations appeared to be returning to normal. Then, in 2009, Burmese troops moved into the Kokang area in the northeast, pushing more than 30,000 refugees – both Chinese nationals and local, ethnic Chinese – across the border back into China. Still, China did not get the message – until 30 September 2011, when Thein Sein announced that the China-sponsored, hydroelectric power project in the far north of the country had been suspended.

The newly forged friendship between Burma and the United States has prompted China to start searching for new ways to salvage the relationship. In 2012, academic-style journals in China run several articles analysing what went wrong with Beijing's Burma policy and what could and should be done to rectify it. One proposed measure has been to launch a public relations campaign in Burma aimed at overhauling China's current negative image in the country.

But it may be too little, too late. In order to understand Burma's policy shift it is instructive to look deeper into what was discussed in inner circles in the military in the early 2000s. Then condemned and pressured by the international community, the ruling military junta announced in August 2003 a seven-step 'Roadmap to Discipline-Flourishing Democracy'. That plan called for the drafting of a new constitution, general elections, and convention of a new parliament that would 'elect state leaders' charged with building 'a modern, developed and democratic nation'.

The 'roadmap' was made public, but at the same time a confidential 'master plan' which outlined ways and means to deal with both the international community, especially the US, and domestic opposition was also drawn up. The authors of that plan are not known but an internal military document written by Lt.-Col. Aung Kyaw Hla, who is identified as a researcher at the country's prestigious Defence Services Academy, was completed and circulated as early as in August 2004 – not by coincidence, less than two months before Lt.-Gen. Khin Nyunt, 'China's man', was ousted.

The Burmese-language document, received and reviewed by this writer, outlines the thinking and strategy behind the master plan. It is, however, unclear whether 'Aung Kyaw Hla' is a particular person, or a codename used by a military think-tank. Anecdotal evidence suggests the latter. Entitled 'A Study of Myanmar [Burma]–US Relations', the main thesis of the 346-page dossier is that Burma's recent reliance on China as a diplomatic ally and economic patron has created a 'national emergency' that threatens the country's independence. According to the dossier, Burma must normalize relations with the West after implementing the roadmap and electing a government so that the regime can deal with the outside world on more acceptable terms.

Aung Kyaw Hla goes on to argue that although human rights are a concern in the West, the US would be willing to modify its policy to suit 'strategic interests'. Although the author does not specify those interests, it is clear from the thesis that he is thinking of common ground with the US vis-à-vis China. The author cites Vietnam and Indonesia under former dictator Suharto as examples of US foreign policy flexibility in weighing strategic interests against democratization.

If bilateral relations with the US were improved, the master plan suggests, Burma would also get access to badly needed funds from the World Bank, the International Monetary Fund and other global financial institutions – or exactly what did happen in 2011 and 2012. The country would then emerge from 'regionalism', where it currently depends on the goodwill and trade of its immediate neighbours, including China, and enter a new era of 'globalization', Aung Kyaw Hla argues.

The master plan is acutely aware of the problems that must be addressed before Burma can lessen its reliance on China and become a trusted partner with the West. The main issue at the time of writing was the detention of pro-democracy icon Suu Kyi, who Aung Kyaw Hla wrote was a key 'focal point': 'Whenever she is under detention pressure increases, but when she is not, there is less pressure.' While the report implies that Suu Kyi's release would improve ties with the West, the plan's ultimate aim – which it spells out clearly – is to 'crush' the opposition.

The dossier concludes that the regime cannot compete with the media and non-governmental organizations run by Burmese exiles, but if US politicians and lawmakers were invited to visit the country they could help to sway international opinion in the regime's favour. Over the years leading up to the recent policy shifts, many Americans, including some congressmen, visited Burma and often left less critical of the regime than they were previously. In the end, it seems that Burma has successfully managed to engage the US rather than vice versa.

As a result, relations with the United States are improving rapidly, exactly along the lines suggested by Aung Kyaw Hla in 2004; both China and North Korea were high on the agenda when Clinton visited Burma in December 2011. On a visit to Canberra, Australia, in November of the same year, President Barack Obama stated that 'with my visit to the region, I am making it clear that the United States is stepping up its commitment to the entire Asia-Pacific region'. The United States is a Pacific power, Obama said, and 'we are here to stay'. But he was quick to add: 'The notion that we fear China is mistaken. The notion that we are looking to exclude China is mistaken.'

That statement was about as convincing as Thein Sein's assurance that he had suspended the Myitsone dam project in the north because he was concerned about 'the wishes of the people'. The two old adversaries, Burma and the United States, are beginning to end up on the same side of the fence in the struggle for power and influence in Southeast Asia. Frictions, and perhaps even hostility, can certainly be expected in future relations between China and Burma – and Burma will no longer be seen by the United States and elsewhere in the West as a pariah state that has to be condemned and isolated.

To strengthen its position vis-à-vis China, Burma has also turned to its partners in the Association of Southeast Asian Nations (ASEAN), which it is chairing in 2014. Even more significantly, when Gen. Min Aung Hlaing, who was appointed commander-in-chief of Burma's military in March 2011, went on his first foreign trip in mid-November, he did not go to China – but instead to China's traditional enemy, Vietnam. Burma and Vietnam share the same fear of their common, powerful northern neighbour, so it is reasonable to assume that Min Aung Hlaing had a lot to discuss with his Vietnamese hosts.

Burma is also striving to improve its often-strained relations with India. Immediately after the 1988 pro-democracy uprising in Burma, India sympathized with the Aung San Suu Kyi -led opposition. Rajiv Gandhi, India's prime minister at the time, came out in open support of the movement, and New Delhi implemented policies that gave shelter to Burmese refugees and allowed dissidents to operate freely from Indian territory. This, of course, was not for entirely altruistic reasons: the policy was viewed widely as India's way of countering China's influence in Burma.

India began to re-evaluate that strategy around 1993, out of concern that its policies had achieved little except to push Burma closer to Beijing. Even then it was obvious to policymakers that the opposition would not assume power anytime soon. The result was a dramatic shift in policy aimed at patching up relations with Burma's ruling generals. In turn, Burma signalled to India to take greater interest in improving bilateral relations to lessen its heavy dependence on China.

India's interests in Burma are obvious. Apart from serving as a link to lucrative markets and trading partners in Southeast Asia, New Delhi wants to ensure that ethnic insurgents in India's northeast are deprived of sanctuaries and supply lines through its eastern neighbour – and to keep Chinese influence there at bay. India's rapidly expanding economy also needs energy, and New Delhi has shown strong interest in importing more oil and gas from Burma.

India also has plans to build a 1,200 MW hydroelectric power station on the Chindwin River, across from India's northeastern region, and is involved in several other infrastructure projects inside Burma, including major road construction projects, which will form part of a vision to connect the north-eastern Indian state of Manipur with Southeast Asia – through Burma. In short, India is busy opening its west–east corridor through Burma to protect its own economic as well as strategic interests.

To open the way, India has taken a number of initiatives to rid its rebellious states in the northeast – Assam, Nagaland and Manipur – of insurgents and establish permanent peace in the region. That task was made easier when Sheikh Hasina's pro-Indian Awami League government took over in Bangladesh in December 2008. Her predecessor, Khaleda Zia and the Bangladesh National Party, provided sanctuaries for insurgents who moved about freely in the capital Dhaka and the port city of Chittagong, where Indian rebel groups had received many illicit shipments of arms from China, Thailand and Singapore.

In late November 2009, Bangladesh arrested the United Liberation Front of Asom (ULFA) Chairman Arabinda Rajkhowa and its Deputy Commander-in-Chief Raju Barua along with eight other Assamese militants and handed them over to India. In September 2010, Rajkumar Meghen, better known as Sana Yaima, the leader of Manipur's United National Liberation Front (UNLF), was arrested in Dhaka and bundled off to India. At about the same time, the main arms procurer of the Naga rebels and a frequent visitor to China, Anthony Shimray, was apprehended at Kathmandu airport in Nepal and ended up in Indian custody.

While these arrests have been significant from a strategic perspective, India knows that simply detaining ethnic insurgent leaders will not be enough to achieve peace in the restive region. There are also widespread grievances among the local population that will need to be addressed before there is lasting peace and stability along India's Burmese frontier.

New Delhi's new 'Look East' Burma policy and its anti-China aspect are even clearer in the Indian Ocean, the origin of the pipelines from the sea to Yunnan. Building such a conduit for crucial energy supplies in a foreign country would be risky without substantial political influence and an extensive signals intelligence near the sea lanes along which the fuel is transported, either through Burma or the Malacca Strait.

India has not taken lightly the prospect of another major player in a maritime area that it considers its own lake. This concern provides a new aspect to the age-old strategic rivalry between India and China – and another reason for India to counter China's influence over Burma.

Predictably, the Obama administration has expressed its support for India's 'Look East' policy. On 23 November 2010, US deputy national security advisor for strategic communication Ben Rhodes said: 'The President very much welcomes India's Look East approach. We believe that just as the United States, as a Pacific Ocean power, is going to be deeply engaged in the future of East Asia, so should India as an Indian Ocean power and as an Asian nation.'

In January 2011, a US naval ship visited India's Andaman Islands to conduct search and rescue operations, shipwreck salvaging and naval vessel repair exercises with their Indian counterparts. According to local press reports, the commander of the US vessel, Derek Peterson, 'lauded the cooperation' of the Indian Navy and said he was impressed with its capabilities.

That strategic exchange followed on a March 2010 visit by the USS Patriot at Port Blair, the capital of the Andaman and Nicobar Islands. The news site of the Commander of the US 7th Fleet reported from that US naval visit that 'Patriot Sailors will train with the Indian Navy; special emphasis will be put on damage-control and mine countermeasures training'.

Indian naval officers interviewed in Port Blair by this writer in January 2011 said that there was nothing more to the US naval visit than basic joint training exercises. But it is hard to imagine that routine exercises were the main purpose of the US naval visits. Burma – and even more so China – likely watched the US-Indian naval cooperation with some trepidation.

The recent anti-Chinese stance taken by Burma's new government, therefore, was music to the ears of India's security planners. India rolled out the red carpet for Thein Sein when he arrived in New Delhi on a three-day state visit on 14 October 2011. In a joint statement, the then

Indian prime minister, Manmohan Singh, welcomed Thein Sein's 'ongoing efforts at political, economic and social reform'.

In the 19th century, Arthur Conolly, an intelligence officer of the British colonial army, coined the expression 'the Great Game' to describe the strategic rivalry between the then British and Russian Empires for supremacy in Central Asia. More than any other objective in the competition, the Russians sought access to the Indian Ocean. Another 'Great Game' involving India, China and the US is now playing out in Asia on the eastern fringes of the Indian subcontinent, and that game, coupled with pure economic interests, will decide Burma's future political development – not any newly awakened interest in 'democracy'.

For Aung San Suu Kyi, the transition from an imprisoned popular icon to an elected member of the Lower House of the Myanmar Parliament has not been easy. She wears the uneasy crown of being the daughter of Myanmar's independence hero Aung San – who was assassinated in July 1947, half a year before the British left the country – with the world looking at her expectantly. How will she handle Myanmar's role in the region? How will she handle relations with India, the US, China and Japan? No one really knows because Suu Kyi has never had a chance to lead the country, and she has been cut off from the outside world for years. To the disappointment – and alacrity – of many, she has been strangely silent about the sufferings of the people in Myanmar's minority areas, where the military continues to terrorize civilians, and where thousands of refugees have sought shelter near the Chinese border. At the same time, it would be unfair to say that she does not recognize these problems. Suu Kyi is critical of foreign mediation efforts in the civil war because they emphasize on development over constitutional reform and the rights for Myanmar's ethnic minorities. The question is: How can that be achieved under the terms of the present, undemocratic constitution and without the full support of the still powerful military? To her credit, that may be exactly why Suu Kyi decided to take part in the 1 April 2012 by-election.

China tolerates the United States in Burma, up to a point

Developments since November 2010 have clearly demonstrated the importance of Burma as a nexus in Southeast Asia. In the context of President Barack Obama's so-called 'pivot' to Asia, it may seem that the political opening of Burma will bring the country into the role of becoming a brick in a perceived American-led 'containment' of a rising China. The realities, however, are more complex and filled with dilemmas.

In a short span of time, China has become the largest buyer of raw materials on the globe, and Burma's importance as a supplier in this chain cannot be overstated. A stronger American and European involvement in Burma's economy will not alter this picture. Nor will a stronger voice of the Burmese opposition in the country's decision-making process necessarily mean a lessening of China's influence. Aung San Suu Kyi has repeatedly stressed that 'friendship' with China is important to her country (read: 'I recognize the mutual economic dependence that is the core of our relationship with China').

Since President Thein Sein decided to suspend the construction of the Myitsone Dam, China has embarked on a massive 'charm offensive' in Kachin State. It will require a sustained and expensive effort of Chinese 'soft power' vis-à-vis both government institutions and the emerging civil society in Burma to ensure that Chinese investments in the country do not further contribute to widespread and public anti-Chinese sentiments. As the Myitsone case demonstrates, it will no longer be sufficient for China to ensure that a regime favourable to them will continue to govern. If modest reforms are implemented successfully, the risk of a 1988 style uprising which would threaten China's interests, will diminish, as it lessens internal Burmese pressure for anti-regime and anti-Chinese activities.

The optimistic scenario for future Sino–Burmese relations holds that both sides recognize the need for tranquillity along their mutual border, which eventually may serve to enforce and secure a more lasting peace with armed groups in the region. Indisputably, the political transition in Burma since 2011 has been a top-down affair, which distinguishes it from the so-called 'Arab Spring', or for that matter the 'people power' revolutions in Indonesia in 1998 or the Philippines in 1986. This top-down approach to reform may marginalize ethnic groupings which for decades have opposed successive rulers in Yangon/Naypyidaw, but the likely scenario is that any Burmese government in the future will do whatever necessary to push for an inclusion into the accepted (and to a wide extent controlled) civil society framework.

The American 'pivot' towards East Asia may either evaporate or be enhanced over time, but Burma is not a central issue in Sino–American relations, nor is the rivalry between Washington and Beijing a zero-sum game. As developments in security matters in Northeast Asia/Korea have demonstrated, China does not see it to be in its interest to 'push' America out of Asia.

China has not called for the exclusion of the US from having a political role in Burma, and China will accept a limited American influence in Burma as long as the country does not open up for U.S. bases and/or the exchange of military intelligence. In this respect, Vietnam is a far bigger worry for China than Burma, because of the South China Sea dispute. Burma's long tradition for neutrality vis-à-vis major powers will prevent the country from slipping into one or the other's 'camp'.

China's key interest in Burma is to secure stability and a political order, which can facilitate China's continued economic involvement. In case of a worsening of Sino–Burmese relations, it is unlikely that any Western power, or India for that matter can replace China as an economic player in Burma. China is too close and too big an investor for that to happen. A country may be able to choose it's friends and allies, but it cannot choose its neighbours. And with its growing economic clout, regionally as well as globally, China has come to Burma as an economic giant to stay.

China is too big to be contained and wants the US to improve its relations with Burma to the extent that China will no longer be criticized for its mixed record with successive regimes in Burma. Furthermore, China wants Western investments to improve the Burmese economy to an extent that this also creates an improved foundation for continued Chinese economic involvement.

✍ FY

International actors

Josine Legêne and Flemming Ytzen

China

China has been Myanmar's closest ally since independence and continues to be the most influent international actor on Myanmar. Chinese economic interest in Myanmar has grown and increasingly become linked with Chinese political and security interests. In the context of Western sanctions since 1988 the economic ties between China and Myanmar have been politicized. In the absence of economic and political influence from the West, China has been the main supporter of Myanmar in the form of development assistance, military, economic and technical cooperation.[1]

Burma/Myanmar was the first non-Communist country to recognize the People's Republic of China (PRC) after its foundation in 1949. Myanmar (then Burma) and the PRC formally established diplomatic relations on 8 June 1950. China and Myanmar signed a treaty of friendship and mutual non-aggression and promulgated a Joint Declaration on 29 June 1954, officially basing their relations on the 'Five Principles of Peaceful Co-existence'. However, the expulsion of Chinese communities from Myanmar after 1967 generated hostility in both countries, but relations began to improve during the 1980s. With China's reform-and-opening policy, beginning in 1979, China reduced support for the Communist Party of Burma and on 5 August 1988 China signed a trade agreement, legalizing cross-border trading, and began supplying considerable military aid. Following the pro-democracy uprising and the military coup in September 1988 the new military rulers sought to cultivate a strong relationship with China to bolster their State Law and

---

1. Steinberg (2012): 162.

Order Restoration Council (SLORC); in turn, China's influence grew rapidly after the USA and EU condemned Myanmar.

The Chinese support gave the military regime in Myanmar the confidence to resist political pressure from Western countries concerning human rights issues and demands for improving the human rights situation and initiation of a democratic transition.[2] China never condemned Myanmar for the military's brutal violence against civilians and the pro-democracy movement in 1988, and in return the SLORC defended the Chinese government's crackdown on protesters on Tiananmen Square in 1989. The two countries have thus maintained a strong military and political cooperation.[3]

Trade between China and Myanmar consists of conventional trade, border trade and smuggling. This has greatly increased since 1988 when the two countries signed a cross-border trade agreement that gave China access to markets and resources within Myanmar.[4]

Industrialization and economic growth in China have created a high demand for alternative sources of imported energy, first and foremost oil and gas. This has affected the relationship with Myanmar, because the country plays a major role as a supplier of energy to China. In 2030 China may consume as much oil as all EU member states together, meaning that securing supplies has become a core issue in China's energy policy, and thus also a critical issue of its national security.[5]

Myanmar has implemented a 30-year Hydroelectric Power Strategic Plan with dam projects on main rivers throughout the country. This is considered a national priority in Myanmar, and China is the leading country to invest in and construct these projects. Some Chinese dam projects, however, are carried out in geographically sensitive or politically controversial areas and have been criticized by international organizations and human rights groups for not paying respect to local areas and ethnic groups.[6]

In return for Myanmar's cooperation concerning energy resources, China has provided military support to Myanmar.[7] Furthermore, the

---

2. Myint (2000): 126.
3. Ibid.: 121.
4. Ibid.: 121; Steinberg and Fan (2012): 208.
5. Steinberg and Fan (2012): 163.
6. Ibid.: 187, 196.
7. Ibid.: 163.

numerous projects that China is involved with in Myanmar – such as construction of highways, railways and ports – has made Myanmar increasingly reliant on China. However, Myanmar also uses its fortunate possession of rich oil and gas resources as a trump card in its diplomacy towards China. Cooperation in the area of oil and gas serve as a stabilizer of the relationship between China and Myanmar, as the construction of pipelines will create an interdependence in a long-term perspective.[8]

Notwithstanding increased Western engagement with Myanmar, rising local xenophobia and the shock announcement by President Thein Sein in late 2011 to suspend construction work on the Myitsone Dam, a key Chinese project, these developments are unlikely to mean a lessening of China's influence in the country (see p. 107, also the Myitsone issue on p. 357).

India

India has long had strong cultural and spiritual people-to-people exchanges with Myanmar, a country many in India view as a 'civilizational' neighbour. As the Asia's largest democracy and one of Myanmar's closest neighbours, India has to keep pace with the rising expectations of Myanmar's pro-democratic forces, while consolidating and expanding ties with the ruling military and/or civilian elites in Naypyidaw. Although India supported Myanmar's pro-democracy resistance in the 1990s, it later built diplomatic and commercial ties with the country's military government in a diplomatic shift from idealism to realism.

India is concerned with China's growing influence in Asia and also its major influence in Myanmar. Since 1990 India has provided some assistance to the military junta (SLORC/SPDC) in Myanmar in an effort to balance against the Chinese influence.[9] However, after clashes between Muslims and Buddhists in Myanmar's Rakhine state and central regions, radical groups have threatened to target Buddhist installations in India. The outburst of Buddhist nationalism in Myanmar is thus no longer an internal affair and could have long-term implications for security in wider South and Southeast Asia, including Myanmar's neighbours on the Indian subcontinent. India has indicated that it will tighten security

---

8.   Ibid.: 175, 177.
9.   Steinberg (2010): 160.

to prevent violence from spilling over into its religiously mixed regions, including the already restive northeastern states.

Opposition leader Aung San Suu Kyi is both emotionally and politically closely tied to India, having spent some years of her childhood and youth in the country. She has advocated a greater role for India in Myanmar's new political order.

The recent easing of Western economic and financial sanctions as a reward for political reforms in Myanmar opens the way for India to play a more proactive role. At the same time, New Delhi will give priority to securing its own economic and commercial interests, including oil and gas exploration.

With the rising business interest of Western countries and rapprochement with the United States, India will push more vigorously to expand its economic interests in Myanmar. The two countries have recently agreed to strengthen communication and coordination to accelerate bilateral exchanges in areas including trade, culture and security in pursuit of a more comprehensive relationship. However, the lack of connectivity and poor railroad links in border areas of Myanmar and India's contiguous northeastern region poses a challenge for making Myanmar a land bridge between South and Southeast Asia. India's 'Look East' policy aims to fill this infrastructural gap, including by building roads to connect the two countries, and has been a widely welcomed move.

Japan

The Japanese occupation of British Burma during World War II was arguably the trigger for the country's eventual independence and in the decades that followed Japanese official development assistance played a major role in the country's economy.[10] In 1988 Japan, as most other foreign countries, showed sympathy for the democratic movement in Myanmar. However, in 1989 Japan recognized SLORC and normalized its ties with the country. Following this Japan engaged with Myanmar in trade, investment and ODA.[11] Japan has kept a two-track policy on Myanmar urging democratic transition and protection of human rights, while providing economic support to the military regime.[12] The

---

10. Seekins (2007): viii.
11. Myint (2000): 115.
12. Ibid.: 120.

Japan's economic interest in Myanmar is not recent. In 1943, a summit for (puppet)leaders from the 'Greater East Asia Co-Prosperity Sphere' was held in Tokyo. Ba Maw, the premier of Japanese-occupied Burma is first on the left.

Japanese called this a 'quiet dialogue' or 'sunshine policy'.[13] However, it was criticized by the international community, by the opposition in Myanmar, and also by Japanese democracy and human rights groups.[14] Today Japan is still engaged in Myanmar with regards to development programmes and economic support. Japan is expressing interest in investing even more in Myanmar and the business opportunities that await there. Japan also has strategic geopolitical interests in Myanmar and has expressed concern over Chinese influence.

After having received opposition leader Aung San Suu Kyi in Tokyo in April 2013, Japan's Prime Minister Shinzo Abe paid a visit to Myanmar only a month later, the first such trip by a Japanese prime minister in 36 years. Accompanied by 40 Japanese corporate executives, Japan's motive was clear: to help secure a new market for Japanese companies through boosting trade and investment ties with Myanmar. In January of that year, Japan wrote off a considerable portion of Myanmar's debts to Japan and significantly expanded its aid programme to the country. Abe promised a further US$ 400 million in new loans, wrote off even more of Myanmar's debt, and proposed bilateral cooperation on defence

---

13. Seekins (2007): 94.
14. Ibid.: 97, 115, 137.

and security. He went to inspect the future site of the Thilawa Special Economic Zone near Yangon, the development of which is being promoted as a showcase for Japanese investment, aid and goodwill.

Most media reports attribute the recent surge in aid and investment by Japan to the liberalization that has been occurring in Myanmar. But Japan is reacting less to the reforms overseen by Thein Sein's government than to the shift in US policy on Myanmar. The desire to invest in Southeast Asia has always been a key aspect of Japan's economic diplomacy. While Burma was under direct military rule, the Japanese government was under pressure from the US to withhold aid. Now that there are only few restrictions on commercial ties with Myanmar, both the Japanese government and the private sector are rushing in to make up for lost time to create a foothold for investment in Myanmar.

ASEAN

Myanmar was invited to join ASEAN at its inception in 1967 but the Ne Win regime declined. After decades of isolation, Myanmar became an observer to ASEAN in 1995 and was accorded full membership status in July 1997. The admission of Myanmar into ASEAN was a major change in the relationship between Myanmar and the other Southeast Asian nations; it was now up to ASEAN as a group to play a mediating role in the reconciliation. ASEAN has traditionally kept a non-intervention approach to Myanmar but, incrementally in recent years, ASEAN has adopted a so-called constructive engagement policy. This has been seen as a gradual move away from the policy of non-interference, and it is now commonly recognized in ASEAN that non-interference is not absolute.[15] ASEAN can work is a mediator as it links Myanmar to many other external actors through good relations to the EU, Japan, the US, China, Australia and New Zealand, which Myanmar also benefits from.

Thailand

Thailand has traditionally had an ambiguous and multi-faceted relationship with Myanmar. The border area between the two countries is home to large Shan and Karen ethnic refugee groups, and Thailand and Myanmar also share long-term ties of trade across the border. During

---

15. Chalermpalanupap (2010): 156.

past decades, several hundred thousands of Burmese refugees have fled to Thailand or to refugee camps along the border.

Thailand now relies on Myanmar for much of its gas supply (which is Thailand's main source of electricity). Its neighbour is also the source of a significant part of its labour force and a key partner helping on security needs, particularly with regards to drugs suppression. Without Myanmar's cooperation, Thailand would face power blackouts, rising wages and a more menacing drugs scourge. For its part, Myanmar has shelved its nuclear weapons programme and has gained from workers' remittances from Thailand as well as from Thai aid, loans, investment deals and capacity-building programmes.

Thailand also no longer officially supports its old 'buffer' policy of aiding, abetting and sheltering ethnic minorities such as the Shan and Karen. In fact, there is now a consensus in Thailand over its Myanmar policy. All Thai governments, whether under former Prime Minister Yingluck Shinawatra (deposed in May 2014) or her predecessor Abhisit Vejjajiva (2008–11), have pursued cooperation and collaboration on all matters of bilateral trade and development with Myanmar.

Currently, the big deal in Myanmar–Thai relations is the Dawei mega-project. This multi-billion-dollar deal began in 2008 when the Thai construction conglomerate Ital–Thai Development was awarded a concession to develop 250 square kilometres of land centring on Dawei. The project has languished, but the Yingluck Shinawatra government appears poised to undertake investments with public funds that may benefit ITD and re-invigorate the project.[16]

Mainland Southeast Asia connects Northeast, South and Southeast Asia, straddling more than 3 billion people. Alone it constitutes a subregional market of more than 350 million consumers when southern China and Vietnam are included. The Thai–Myanmar nexus is its centre of gravity. Ongoing infrastructure development on the mainland

---

16. Regarding Ital–Thai pulling out see this note from the Irrawaddy November 19: 'Thailand's largest construction company, Italian-Thai Development, will cease its operations in the Dawei Special Economic Zone this week to make way for "due diligence assessments," according to a Burma government representative, who also refuted earlier reports that Ital-Thai had lost its 75-year concession for the project. "It is not true that Myanmar government wants ITD out," Set Aung, adviser to the President's Office, wrote in an email to the *Bangkok Post*. "However, ITD has to stop all its work to have due diligence assessments conducted on these projects. Without due diligence assessment, no other investor will be able to participate in any projects related to the Dawei SEZ development."'

is increasingly connecting land routes in myriad directions, east–west and north–south.

European actors

The European Union established an arms embargo on Burma/Myanmar following the military's crackdown on the pro-democracy movement in 1988. As a response to the worsening of the human rights situation and possibly inspired by remarks on the need for sanctions by the Nobel Laureate Aung San Suu Kyi, the EU adopted a Common Position on Burma/Myanmar 1996/635/CFSP in October 1996. This position reaffirmed the following measures that had already been adopted in 1990 and confirmed in a Declaration by the General Affairs Council on 29 July 1991:

- expulsion of all military personnel attached to the diplomatic representations of Burma/Myanmar in Member States of the European Union and withdrawal of all military personnel attached to diplomatic representations of the Member States of the European Union in Burma/Myanmar;

- an embargo on arms, munitions and military equipment and suspension of non-humanitarian aid or development programmes. Exceptions could be made for projects and programmes in support of human rights and democracy as well as those concentrating on poverty alleviation and, in particular, the provision of basic needs for the poorest section of the population, in the context of decentralized cooperation through local civilian authorities and non-governmental organizations.

This embargo covered weapons designed to kill and their ammunition, weapon platforms, non-weapon platforms and ancillary equipment. The embargo also covered spare parts, repairs, maintenance and transfer of military technology. Contracts entered into prior to the date the embargo came into force were not affected by this common position.

In April 2000, the Council agreed on Council Regulation (EC) No 1081/2000 that supplemented the Common Position by adding a ban on the export from the EU of any equipment that might be used for internal repression or terrorism.

The arms embargo was extended and amended by Common Position 757/2001/CFSP until 29 April 2002. Since then the embargo has remained in force through regular motions including on 12 April 2011 by Council Decision 2011/239/CFSP until 30 April 2012. In April and May 2012, the EU passed a number of resolutions, including Council Decision 2012/225/CFSP, suspending certain sanctions on the Burmese government, but maintaining the arms embargo until 30 April 2013. In response to the political developments in Burma in April 2013 the EU lifted all sanctions against Burma, except for the arms embargo, which was extended until 30 April 2014.

United States

The United States was quick to recognize the first government of the independent Burma/Myanmar and provided economic assistance to the country, while at the same time giving covert support to Chinese Kuomintang (KMT) forces inside the country. This secret aid was terminated in 1953–54 when most KMT forces were repatriated to Taiwan.

In 1950 the British Commonwealth agreed to lend Burma £ 6 million, but instead the U Nu government turned to the US and received aid from the Technical Cooperation Administration (TCA) in September.

American aid to Burma, mainly in foodstuffs, was resumed in 1956 but later halted by General Ne Win. Training of Burmese military officers in the US reached about 1,000 personnel by 1962, when Ne Win seized power in a coup d'etat. In September 1966, Ne Win paid a state visit to the US and met with President Lyndon B. Johnson.

The relationship between the US and Myanmar was at its worst after the unrest following the military coup in 1988. At this point the US lowered the level of its representation to chargé d'affaires, halted all non-humanitarian aid and opposed the granting of loans from the World Bank and International Monetary Fund.[17] In 1990 the US cut off economic and military aid and downgraded diplomatic relations after the ruling junta refused to recognize the results of the country's first elections in 30 years, which Aung San Suu Kyi's National League for Democracy (NLD) won by a landslide. That year, the US Congress passed the Customs and Trade Act, which empowered the US President to restrict trade to a country if that country failed to comply with certain conditions. In the middle of the 1990s there was a boycott of businesses and companies that invested or traded with Myanmar. This was known

---

17. Myint (2000): 105.

as the *selective purchasing laws.* In May 1997 several American companies exited Myanmar due to increased criticism from human rights groups, consumers and shareholders. Following this the US imposed broad sanctions against Myanmar in several policy acts.[18]

On 28 July 2003 the US implemented even tougher sanctions against Myanmar via the Burmese Freedom and Democracy Act (BFDA). The aim of the BFDA was *[T]o sanction the ruling Burmese military junta, to strengthen Burma's democratic forces and support and recognize the National League of Democracy as the legitimate representative of the Burmese people, and for other purposes* (U.S. Public Law 2003). The BFDA included trade sanctions and bans on all activities of support to the military regime as well as a freeze of all assets in the US belonging to the regime. Furthermore, there was a visa ban and an instruction to vote against all extensions of loans by financial institutions and any other financial or technical assistance to Myanmar.

The BFDA stated that the US should use all appropriate forums and occasions to encourage other countries to put the same restrictions on the military regime and the businesses supporting it and at the same time express recognition of the democratic movement and support the political opposition including NLD and Aung San Suu Kyi. It was stated, that the termination of the sanctions in the BFDA could only be decided by the President in the case of a wish expressed from a democratically elected government in Myanmar.

In the first visit by a US Secretary of State since 1955, Hillary Clinton came to Myanmar in November–December 2011, meeting with President Thein Sein in Naypyidaw and later the democracy icon Aung San Suu Kyi in Yangon. On 13 January 2012, the Secretary of State announced that the US would exchange ambassadors with Burma after a landmark Burmese political prisoner amnesty and the spring of 2012 she announced plans for a 'targeted easing' of sanctions to allow American dollars to enter the country, but companies could not move ahead until the sanctions were formally suspended. In July 2012, the United States formally eased sanctions on Myanmar.

Despite officially welcoming President Thein Sein's reforms, the US will not allow investment in military entities owned by Myanmar's armed forces or its Ministry of Defence, and Congress has bolstered its ability

---

18. Ibid.: 107.

to place sanctions on 'those who undermine the reform process, engage in human rights abuses, contribute to ethnic conflict or participate in military trade with North Korea'. The United States will continue to block businesses or individuals from making transactions with any 'specially designated nationals' or businesses that they control – allowing Washington, for example, to stop money from flowing to groups disrupting the reform process. President Obama also created a new power for the government to impose 'blocking sanctions' on any individual threatening peace in Myanmar. Businesses with more than US$ 500,000 in investment in the country will need to file an annual report with the State Department, with details on workers' rights, land acquisitions and any payments of more than US$ 10,000 to government entities, including Myanmar's state-owned enterprises. American companies and people will be allowed to invest in the state-owned Myanmar Oil and Gas Enterprise, but any investors will need to notify the State Department within 60 days.

United Nations

Burma/Myanmar has been the subject of critical UN attention for many decades, especially since the events of 1988–90. Although the General Assembly has passed a long list of resolutions criticizing the military regime or calling on it to improve the situation in the country, tougher measures enacted by the Security Council have generally been vetoed by China or Russia. UN Special Rapporteurs for human rights have existed since 1992 for Myanmar but some would argue that their role and work have been overstated.

References

Camroux, David and Renaud Egreteau (2010). 'Normative Europe Meets the Burmese Garrison State Processes, Policies, Blockages and Future Possibilities', in Nick Cheesman, Monique Skidmore and Trevor Wilson (eds), *Ruling Myanmar From Cyclone Nargis to National Elections*. Singapore: ISEAS Publishing, pp. 267–93.

Chalermpalanupap (2010). 'ASEAN's Policy of Enhanced Interactions', in Lex Rieffel (ed.), *Myanmar/Burma Inside Challenges, Outside Interests*. Washington DC: Brookings Institution Press, pp. 150–65.

Holliday, Ian (2011). *Burma Redux Global Justice and the Quest for Political Reform in Myanmar*. New York: Columbia University Press.

Myint, Maung (2000). *The International Response to the Democracy Movement in Burma since 1962.* Stockholm: Center for Pacific Asia Studies, Stockholm University.

Seekins, Donald M. (2007). *Burma and Japan Since 1940: From 'Co-Prosperity' to 'Quiet Dialogue'.* Copenhagen: NIAS Press .

Steinberg, David I. (2010). *Burma/Myanmar What everyone needs to know.* Oxford University Press.

—— (2012). 'On China–Myanmar Relations', *Journal of Current Southeast Asian Affairs* 31(1): 3–6.

Steinberg, David I. and Hongwei Fan (2012). *Modern China–Myanmar Relations Dilemmas of Mutual Dependence.* Copenhagen: NIAS Press.

Day labourers in Myanmar work for as little as two dollars a day (photo: Jonas Leegaard, courtesy DanChurchAid)

Social issues

Marie Ditlevsen

The political changes that Myanmar is currently experiencing are creating a positive development towards improved living conditions for its people. The new quasi-civilian government has allocated resources from the military budget to be spent on welfare,[1] but the pace of development is slow and in 2014 Myanmar still struggles with a backlog of social issues that may hamper the overall development of the country. In the following chapter some of the most important social issues will be discussed.

The people of Myanmar

Myanmar has a population of about 58 million people, with estimates varying from 55 million (Danish Ministry of Foreign Affairs) to 60.4 million (Burmese Ministry of Health). In March–April 2014 a nationwide census was conducted, prompting disputes over ethnic identity in many areas. The final results will be announced at the beginning of 2015. The majority of the population (some 70%) still lives in rural areas of the country,[2] while most urban dwellers live in the former capital, Yangon (c. 6 million people). The new capital, Naypyidaw, only has about one million inhabitants.[3]

Myanmar's population is divided into a rich mixture of different ethnic groups (for fuller details, see p. 155ff.). This ethnic diversity is partly a result of British colonial rule, the country being mapped in a manner that split ethnic groups between Myanmar and neighbouring countries – a situation that may partly explain the ongoing conflicts

1. Forbes, 'Health Care in Myanmar': http://www.forbes.com/sites/benjaminshobert/2013/08/19/healthcare-in-myanmar/
2. WHO Country Cooperation Strategy 2008–2011, Myanmar: http://www.who.int/countryfocus/cooperation_strategy/ccs_mmr_en.pdf
3. Index Mundi: http://www.indexmundi.com/burma/

Whether suburban youth in the city or villagers in the countryside, most people in Myanmar continue to wear the longyi *(photo: Marie Ditlevsen)*

and challenges in uniting the country. The hill tribes (minority ethnic groups) inhabiting the mountainous areas were especially affected. With lives once quite separate from the rest of Myanmar, they were suddenly sundered from their kin by arbitrary colonial borders and joined with a lowland population whose culture, religion and traditions they did not necessarily share.[4]

Officially, there are 135 ethnic groups in Myanmar, though traditionally this number has been boiled down to eight major groups: Kachin, Kayah (Karennis), Kayin (Karens), Chin, Bamar (Burmans), Mon, Rakhine (Arakanese) and Shan. The largest ethnic group is the Bamar, who make up two-thirds of the population. The Bamar live in the central lowland along with the Mon, Kayin and Rakhine, while the other groups mainly live in the mountainous border areas. The country's official language is Burmese but the ethnic minorities also have their own languages.[5]

The people of Myanmar are characterized by the traditional *longyi* (a piece of cloth tied at the waist), which many, even young people,

---

4.   Fink (2009): 12.

5.   Ibid.: 8–9.

Girl with thanaka paste on her face (photo: Marie Ditlevsen)

continue to wear. The *longyis* vary in colour and pattern depending on which region or state they come from. Another characteristic is the old habit (mostly maintained by men) of chewing betel nut, which colours the teeth and lips red. Also very common is the use of *thanaka*, a paste from a certain kind of wood that people apply to their face to protect it against the sun, to moisturize it, or just to look good. All of these characteristics apply for both men and women.[6]

From the large number of pagodas, churches, mosques, temples, etc., decorating the country it is easy to tell that religion plays a very important role in the culture and everyday-life of Myanmar. The majority of the population are Buddhist (89%), while the rest are Christian (4%), Muslim (4%), Hindu (2%) and Animists/spirit worshippers (1%).[7] (The religious dimension is described in greater detail elsewhere, see especially p. 279ff.)

According to Index Mundi, the population growth rate was 1.07 in 2012 and on average a woman gives birth to 2.23 children.[8] Compared to other developing countries this is considered a low-growth rate, and

6. Ditlevsen (2013).
7. Index Mundi: http://www.indexmundi.com/burma/religions.html
8. Index Mundi: http://www.indexmundi.com/burma/

the Burmese government has therefore not made any attempts to control the fertility rate through policies like the Chinese one-child policy. However, in the case of Rakhine State, a two-child policy applied to the Muslim Rohingya minority was introduced in 2005. The policy may now be enforced despite opposition from the NLD leader, Aung San Suu Kyi.[9] This official discrimination against the Rohingya minority has been met with strong condemnation from the international community.[10]

Social structures

Myanmar, a country rich on natural resources including teak forests, gems (jade in particular), oil and rice, used to be one of the wealthiest countries in Southeast Asia. The country was once the world's largest exporter of rice and during a long period of time the Ayeyarwady Delta was termed 'the rice bowl of Asia'. But despite this former wealth, the country has today evolved into being among the poorest countries in Southeast Asia and is categorized as a Least Developed Country (LDC).[11]

Some of the main reasons for this economic downturn are attributed to poor governance and mismanagement of the country's natural resources. Furthermore, the economic situation has been aggravated by sanctions including trade restrictions imposed on Myanmar by a number of countries. Today, 25% of the population live below the poverty line and the majority of these people live in rural areas.[12]

The highest incidences of poverty are found in Chin (73%), Rakhine (44%) and Shan States (33%) and in Ayeyarwady Region (32%). However, according to the UNDP, as Myanmar gradually moved from dictatorship towards a marked-oriented economy from 2005 to 2010, the country experienced a positive development with overall poverty indicators dropping by about 6%.[13] In spite of this positive downward

---

9.   Irrawaddy News, 21 June 2013: http://www.irrawaddy.org/archives/38086
10. Life News, 13 June 2013: http://www.lifenews.com/2013/06/13/world-leaders-condemn-myanmars-two-child-policy-ignore-chinas-one-child-policy/
11. Fink (2009): 1; Taylor (2009): 458.
12. WHO Country Cooperation Strategy 2008-2011, Myanmar: http://www.who.int/countryfocus/cooperation_strategy/ccs_mmr_en.pdf
13. UNDP Poverty Profile, 2009–2010: http://www.mm.undp.org/ihlca/01_Poverty_Profile/PDFs/03%20Poverty%20Profile_Poverty%20and%20Inequality.pdf

Once 'the rice bowl of Asia', the Ayeyarwady Delta is marked by high levels of poverty (photo: Marie Ditlevsen)

trend, c. 75% of the population lacks access to electricity[14] and, according to the World Bank, the average per-capita income is between US$ 800 and 1,000 a year. Overall, these measures place Myanmar among the world's bottom-ranking countries for the quality of life (149th out of 186 countries).[15]

The wealth of the individual people is unequally distributed. While the vast majority of the population has been affected by the weakened economy, a minor group appears to have been unaffected and a few so-called 'cronies' even managed to become extremely rich during the time of military rule. The term 'cronies' (or 'oligarchs' or 'tycoons') usually refers to high-ranking business people who enjoyed patronage and economic benefits during the time of the former military regime. These business people, who were closely connected to the military government, grew rich in industries such as construction, rubber, mining and logging. According to the *Irrawaddy News*, the cronies are currently benefitting significantly from the very often unofficial jade sales in Kachin State, a condition that may be hampering Myanmar's economic development.[16]

14. The World Bank, News: http://www.worldbank.org/en/news/feature/2013/09/24/bringing-more-electricity-for-people-of-myanmar

15. Irrawaddy News Magazine, 23 August 2013: http://www.irrawaddy.org/archives/42684

16. Irrawaddy News Magazine, 30 September 2013: http://www.irrawaddy.org/archives/44901

Some people are thriving in the new Myanmar and part of the construction boom is in luxury apartments (photo: David Høgsholt)

The *World Ultra Wealth Report* states that currently there are 40 individuals in Myanmar who have assets worth US$ 30 million or more.[17]

It is not unlikely that these 'cronies' will be the first to benefit from the rapid economic growth that the country is experiencing. President Thein Sein seems to be aware of, and concerned about, the risk that this group of wealthy people, previously connected to the military regime, will end up dominating the economy. Foreign actors like the United States are similarly concerned that such a development could hamper the chances for a healthy middle class to develop.[18] Although the U.S. has gradually lifted some sanctions on Myanmar, a number of cronies remain on its sanctions list. (For more information about these tycoons, see p. 362.)

Health – of the system and the people

Myanmar's health care system is suffering badly from almost half a century of neglect. Health care was not a priority for the military government and, having spent roughly only 2% of its GDP in this area, Myanmar was (and

17. Irrawaddy News Magazine, 23 August 2013: http://www.irrawaddy.org/archives/42684
18. Irrawaddy News Magazine, 31 July 2013: http://www.irrawaddy.org/archives/10435

continues to be) among the countries that spend the lowest amount of money on health care.[19] Although the country is experiencing economic growth, the health-care system is improving at a very slow pace (in 2013 the percentage increased to 3.9%).

This situation is expected to change, as the government is planning to reallocate a significant amount of money from the military to the health-care budget.[20] But in spite of this, the situation does not appear be changing yet, because the government is currently facing a budget deficit and as a consequence it does not plan to boost its allocation of funds for health care substantially within the next year.[21]

When the funds are finally being allocated, expectedly in the fiscal year of 2015, the question is to what extent *and how* an increase in expenditure will benefit the population. The first challenge will be to ensure that any additional funds are not eaten up by administration nor entangled in corruption. Secondly, it will be a logistical challenge to reach the rural population, of whom c. 70% are living in the most remote and difficult-to-access areas, and ensure that they will benefit from the extra funds.

As a consequence of the neglect of the health care system, combined with the challenges in accessing remote rural areas, local (often faith-based) civil-society groups have been responsible of local health care. This also includes monasteries and churches. This local, unofficial health-care system, based on traditional civil-society groups, still plays an important role.[22]

Two diseases that people in Myanmar suffer from in particular are tuberculosis (TB) and malaria. According to the World Health Organization, 'Myanmar is one of the world's 22 high-TB-burden countries, with a TB prevalence rate three times higher than the global average and one of the highest in Asia'. In 2010 there were an estimated 180,000 new TB cases in Myanmar, of which a large proportion were

19. Karen News, 28 June 2013: http://karennews.org/2013/06/burmas-healthcare-system-in-critical-condition.html/

20. Forbes, 'Health Care in Myanmar': http://www.forbes.com/sites/benjaminshobert/2013/08/19/healthcare-in-myanmar/ ; Myanmar Ministry of Health – 'Myanmar Health Care System': http://www.moh.gov.mm/file/MYANMAR%20HEALTH%20CARE%20SYSTEM.pdf

21. Irrawaddy News Magazine, 10 January 2014: http://www.irrawaddy.org/burma/burma-govt-health-education-budgets-likely-remain-low-2014.html

22. Ditlevsen (2013).

Relatives of a Burmese woman who died from HIV/AIDS-related complications minutes earlier grieve outside a hospital in Yangon, September 2012 (photo: David Høgsholt)

resistant to treatment. Furthermore, TB is very often the cause of death for people initially suffering from HIV/AIDS.[23]

However, according to WHO, 'Malaria is the leading cause of reported morbidity and mortality in the country'. Despite the fact that the prevention and treatment of malaria has improved, there is still a long way to go, especially now that a new strain of malaria, resistant to treatment, has emerged in the eastern parts of the country.[24] An important challenge is the fact that the majority of the population lives in these rural, malaria-endemic areas, and as a result of the remoteness these people very often rely on traditional medicines and healers. Apart from TB and malaria, HIV/AIDS also constitutes a serious obstacle for the Myanmar people. This health issue is discussed in detail below.

HIV/AIDS – now officially on the agenda

An area of concern, neglected and kept under wraps during military rule, is the prevalence of HIV/AIDS. The people of Myanmar infected or affected by the disease are benefitting from the political changes, firstly

---

23. WHO Country Cooperation Strategy 2008-2011, Myanmar: http://www.who.int/countryfocus/cooperation_strategy/ccs_mmr_en.pdf

24. DFID Report on Healthcare Programmes in Burma, 25 July 2013: http://reliefweb.int/sites/reliefweb.int/files/resources/16-July-2014-ICAI-Burma-Health-Report-FINAL.pdf

because the government is now willing to publish the true percentage of people living with the disease, thus creating a stronger basis to approach the issue, and secondly because INGOs specialized in HIV/AIDS now have the opportunity to access the areas in need and support national and local HIV/AIDS organizations.

A project president of a local NGO working with HIV/AIDS expressed that 'HIV issues were very sensitive, and before 2005 the prevalence rate, provided by the government and Ministry of Health, was manipulated. Until recently the government didn't like what the NGOs were doing. It was shameful for the face of the country' (Ditlevsen, 2013). In line with the political changes, the Myanmar government now intended to change these conditions. Furthermore, Myanmar is now increasing its HIV/AIDS budget and in October 2012 'the government announced that, for the first time ever, Myanmar will dedicate funds to acquire antiretroviral drugs'.[25] While these funds may not be sufficient to control the disease, it is nevertheless a remarkable development.

According to UNAIDS, in Myanmar it is estimated that around 200,000 people are living with HIV, and that HIV prevalence is around 0.6%.[26] It is important to note, however, that the continued sensitivity of the Burmese context may obscure the accurate number of people affected, as there is likewise inconsistency with regard to the number of people living in Myanmar (see p. 121).

HIV/AIDS is mainly concentrated within three groups of people: sex workers, men having sex with men and drug addicts using contaminated syringes, etc.[27] According to the progress report, there has been a considerable decrease in the prevalence of people infected during the past couple of years. However, the coverage of people receiving treatment remains low, and it is estimated that around 120,000 people are in need of treatment. It is expected that NGOs, including INGOs and international donors, will play a key role in combating the HIV/AIDS epidemic, particularly through the establishment of partnerships with the government and relevant ministries (the Ministry of Health especially) on the one hand and the private sector and civilians on the other hand.

25. UNAIDS, Feature Story, 26 October 2012: http://www.unaids.org/en/resources/press-centre/featurestories/2012/october/20121026myanmarvp/

26. See http://www.unaids.org/en/regionscountries/countries/myanmar/.

27. Global AIDS Response Progress Report 2012: http://www.unaids.org/en/dataanalysis/knowyourresponse/countryprogressreports/2012countries/ce_MM_Narrative_Report.pdf.

From the end of the 1990s there were only a few INGOs working to control the disease, including the Burnet Institute and the International HIV/AIDS Alliance, which 'helped strengthen local organisations working in the field of HIV/AIDS'.[28] Today, the number of international as well as national NGOs working within this field has increased dramatically. However, certain restrictions, rules and administrative structures with links to the past military system still remain, and this may hamper the establishment of projects. In particular the 'township level', which constitutes the middle administrative level (between the states/regions and villages), is in some cases considered a major obstacle. Operation in the rural areas is only possible after having obtained permission from the township authorities responsible of the areas. Obtaining this permission may be a cumbersome and time-consuming process, and the success will often depend on personal relations to the authority in charge.[29]

Another challenge, which is also emphasized in the AIDS Response Progress Report, is that 'laws which criminalize behaviour of groups who are most at risk (sex workers, men who have sex with men and people who use drugs) remain in place'. This statement confirms the suspicion that old laws and regulations still in force (some even dating back to colonialism before 1948) may obstruct the process of eliminating stigmatization and discrimination related to HIV/AIDS.

In October 2012, the democracy icon and NLD leader, Aung San Suu Kyi, was granted the position as ambassador of UNAIDS, an appointment that most likely will speed up the process of eliminating stigmatization and discrimination, and possibly lead to abolition of the old laws and regulations.[30] According to the project president, quoted above, this is an important development for his organization: '[A]fter Aung San Suu Kyi became the ambassador of UNAIDS it is better for our HIV activities. Through Aung San Suu Kyi, sex workers, who are not working legally, can gain a louder voice'.[31] Hence, Aung San Suu Kyi's position as UNAIDS ambassador appears to have improved the chances of the HIV/AIDS issue becoming officially acknowledged.

---

28. Kramer (2012): 37.
29. Ditlevsen (2013).
30. UNAIDS Press Release, 20 November 2012: http://www.unaids.org/en/resources/presscentre/pressreleaseandstatementarchive/2012/november/20121120prasskgwa/
31. Ditlevsen (2013).

Education

As with the health care system, the education system has suffered during the past almost half a century of military rule. During and after colonialism, Myanmar had a well-functioning school system, a high literacy rate and a similarly high level of English (Fink, 2009: 189). After the 1962 military coup the quality of education started to decline. Firstly, during military rule there was a reallocation of money from education to military expenditure with funding of the education system dropping to only 1–2% of the country's GDP.[32] This meant that the school buildings deteriorated, the number of teachers dropped dramatically and educational material became outdated. Secondly, the student uprisings in 1988 (and later in 1996 and 1998) sparked by political dissatisfaction, resulted in the government closing down a large number of schools and universities; these remained closed for several years following the uprisings. During this period, public education was very often taken care of by monasteries (and churches), which offered free education. Based on donations to the temples, the monasteries were able to hire teachers to teach Buddhism as well as the required government curriculum (Fink, 2009: 189).

Another change taking place in the wake of the 1962 military coup affected the school curriculum. Education about the history and culture of the ethnic minorities as well as the tense relationship between the minorities and the Burman majority was gradually downgraded to be a minor and very simplified part of the curriculum. Instead, the main focus was on the historical and cultural background of the Burmans, and the relationship between the Burmans/government and the ethnic minorities was presented as one of unity. Thus, the national curriculum became biased, aiming to create a strong sense of Burman nationalism and highlighting the success of the government. Teachers were required to follow this curriculum. According to the *Irrawaddy News Magazine*, some teachers who did not agree with the curriculum would develop certain signs (nodding and winking) to signal to students if the information appeared incorrect.[33]

---

32. UNDP, Myanmar, IHLCA Report on Education: http://www.mm.undp.org/ihlca/01_Poverty_Profile/PDFs/09%20Poverty%20Profile_Education.pdf
33. Irrawaddy News Magazine, 16 September 2013: http://www.irrawaddy.org/archives/44007

School children in the Delta region (photo: Marie Ditlevsen)

Today, after the military government has been replaced by a so-called quasi-civilian government, the quality of education has once again become an area of priority. The government has now increased expenditure on education from 1–2 to 5%, which amounts to about an increase of 340 million dollars to one billion dollars.[34]

In 2012, the relatively high percentage of students enrolled became clear, even in rural areas of the country. A case study, carried out in six villages connected to Mawlamyinegym Township in the Ayeyarwady Delta, proved that the majority of children received government support to attend school, either in their own or in a neighbouring village (Ditlevsen, 2013). This was also the case for families living below the poverty line. However, most of the children were only able to make it to 5th or 6th grade (the length of primary school), after which they started working for their families in the villages. Hence, the education system may now have the capacity to send all children to (primary) school but the standard of schooling is not necessarily sufficient to make the children qualified enough to continue on to secondary school or high school.

---

34. Ibid.

The issue of low quality is similarly found in the higher education system, which is also an area highly prioritized by the government. During a policy dialogue, held in Naypyidaw on 3 July 2013, the Deputy Union Minister of Education stated:

> The government sees investment in education as the most profitable for the people, and is committed to holistic education sector reform, giving priority to higher education, and following an inclusive and equitable approach, empowering people to make educated choices and take full advantage of the socio-economic benefits that Myanmar foresees.[35]

This statement, the last part of it in particular, is very positive and radically different from statements expressed under the former military government.

The objective of the current government is to provide the universities with the resources required to offer education of a high quality, thus enabling the universities to reach out to the outside world and participate in the international education system. Since the country started opening up, foreign universities and certain INGOs are standing in line to contribute to a speeding-up of this process, and hence also allowing themselves to have a share of the potential new 'market of education' in Myanmar.[36] If the positive economic and social development continues, today's Myanmar looks to offer an attractive and possibly flourishing market for university partners, foreign students and investors to enter.

However, despite the fact that the quality of the school system has improved since the reopening of the universities, there is still a long way to go. While the government may have increased the expenditure on education to 5%, the budget deficit previously mentioned is resulting in the government not boosting the education system substantially – as is the case with the health-care sector.[37]

---

35. News from UNESCO Bangkok, 4 July 2013: http://www.unescobkk.org/news/article/empowering-higher-education-in-myanmar-a-vision-for-myanmars-universities/

36. New York Times, Asia Pacific, 'Myanmar's educators reach out to the world': http://www.nytimes.com/2013/05/06/world/asia/Myanmar-educators-reach-out-to-the-world.html?_r=3&

37. Irrawaddy News Magazine, 10 January 2014: http://www.irrawaddy.org/burma/burma-govt-health-education-budgets-likely-remain-low-2014.html/attachment/7-burmese-soldiers-on-parade-2

References

Ditlevsen, Marie (2013). 'Strengthening Civil Society in Myanmar – the influence of political reforms'. Master's thesis, International Development Studies and Communication, Roskilde University (RUC).

Fink, Christina (2009). *Living Silence in Burma – surviving under military rule.* Second edition. Silkworm Books, Chiang Mai, Thailand and Zed Books, London, New York.

Kramer, Tom (2011). *Civil Society gaining ground – opportunities for change and development in Burma.* Amsterdam, Netherlands: Transnational Institute – Burma Center Netherlands; Drikkerij Primavera Quint.

Taylor, Robert H. (2009). *The State in Myanmar.* London: Hurst Publishers Ltd.

Villager selling fruit, Ngapali Beach (photo: Jessica Harriden)

The situation of women

Throughout Myanmar/Burma's history, women have performed important roles during periods of political and social upheaval. Centuries before Aung San Suu Kyi emerged as an iconic opposition leader in 1988, powerful queens like Bana Thau, Shin Bo Me, Setkya Dewi and Supayalat exercised great influence from behind the throne or played more direct roles in the affairs of the realm. In the first half of the twentieth century, during the nationalist struggle against British colonial rule, women advocated for political representation and a number of female politicians, educators and writers gained prominence as political and social commentators. Despite these examples of female influence, not to mention women's pivotal roles in the family and local economy, cultural attitudes about male superiority and decades of military rule have contributed to a male-dominated political climate in which there is limited acknowledgement of women's leadership capabilities. Elites who claim that women enjoy equal rights and high status ignore widespread evidence of socioeconomic inequality that disadvantages women. Women today face significant challenges, but as the socio-political environment becomes more open and (potentially) inclusive, they are working collectively to engage with policymakers and other actors to promote gender equality. The government has also begun to consult with women's organizations on key issues including gender-based violence.

The former SLORC established the Myanmar National Committee for Women's Affairs in 1996 and ratified the Convention on the Elimination of All Forms of Discrimination against Women (CEDAW) in 1997. The Myanmar Women's Affairs Federation was founded in 2003, but it was difficult for independent women's organizations to operate under military rule. The Women's League of Burma (WLB) was formed in 1999 as an umbrella organization of multi-ethnic and ethnic women's organizations based in exile. In 2008, the Gender Equality Network (GEN) and Women's Organizations Network (WON) were formed inside Myanmar/Burma. The WLB, WON and GEN share

Myanmar's women are slowly gaining more influence and power. In this Delta village, they are now far more strongly represented in the village committee (photo: Marie Ditlevsen)

goals of furthering women's rights and empowerment through capacity building, advocacy and research. Programmes focus on eliminating gender-based violence, promoting peace and increasing women's political participation and leadership. The gap between inside and outside women's groups has hindered cooperation in the past, but in September 2013 the WLB and WON jointly organized the inaugural Myanmar Women's Forum. Over 400 delegates attended with many calling for increased legal protection for women and women's involvement in peace processes and political leadership.

There are now more female parliamentarians than at any other time in Myanmar/Burmese history. Women hold 28 out of 653 seats in the Union Assembly (4.3%) and 4 out of 200 ministerial and deputy ministerial positions (2.0%). In 2012, Dr Daw Myat Myat Ohn Khin was appointed Minister for Social Welfare, Relief and Resettlement (MSWRR). Yet the Inter-Parliamentary Union recently ranked Myanmar at 138 out of 149 countries for female parliamentary representation.[1] Women's or-

---

1. 'Women in national parliaments: Situation as of 1st May 2014', Inter-Parliamentary Union, accessed on 1 July 2014, http://www.ipu.org/wmn-e/classif.htm.

ganizations have sought to raise awareness about women's political rights and leadership potential through engagement with male-dominated political parties and government ministries. Successes include GEN's collaboration with the MSWRR on the ten-year National Strategic Plan for the Advancement of Women, launched in 2013. Current debate about female political representation reflects entrenched and divergent views about women's participation in public life. While the WLB has long advocated for 30% of parliamentary seats to be filled by women,[2] others do not favour a quota system. Aung San Suu Kyi believes that politicians should be elected on the basis of their qualifications and ability, not gender, although the NLD does prioritize female candidates (as well as youth and ethnic minorities). The Constitution presents a challenge for those seeking to increase women's political representation, since it reserves 25% of National Assembly seats for appointed military personnel. Female activists argue that constitutional reform is necessary to further women's political rights. In October 2013 the government announced that women can now, for the first time in more than half a century, join the army – provided that they meet certain requirements. In a country where power has long rested with the military, this invitation offers (some) women an opportunity to gain more power. Yet gender discrimination is still evident, since males can enter the Defence Services Academy training programme after completing 10th standard in high school, whereas females will be admitted only after graduating from university.[3]

Women MPs and others have called for greater legal reform to protect women's rights to substantive equality. Many civil-society groups vehemently oppose the Myanmar Interfaith Marriage Bill, however, which seeks to prevent Buddhist women from marrying non-Buddhist men in the name of preserving race and religion. Women's organizations argue that the proposed law violates women's rights, for example by requiring Buddhist women to gain permission from authorities to marry outside their religion.[4] The MSWRR has involved women's groups in drafting the Anti Violence Against Women Law, a challenging process since the

---

2. Ei Ei Tow Lwin, 'Myanmar women's group calls for more female MPs', *Myanmar Times*, 24 December 2012.

3. Samantha Michaels, 'The Ladies', *The Irrawaddy*, 21, 1 (January 2014): 42–49.

4. Thin Lei Win, 'Myanmar women's rights groups oppose Interfaith Marriage Act', *Women News Network*, 7 May 2014: http://womennewsnetwork.net/2014/05/07/myanmar-womens-rights-groups-oppose-interfaith-marriage-act/.

new law conflicts with some traditional family laws and customs and requires defining terms such as rape and sexual violence. Gender-based violence remains an issue in areas of armed conflict, with activist groups reporting increases in military rape in Kachin and Shan States (for more information, see especially p. 43ff. and p. 260ff.).[5] Female activists have called on the government to end violence against women and provide justice for victims, but the WLB believes that authorities are reluctant to admit their role in condoning military violence. Government officials state that the issue of sexual violence is being discussed as part of the peace process.[6]

Many women have been affected by displacement and violence in areas of military conflict, but only a few women – including Karen National Union (KNU) General Secretary Naw Zipporah Sein – are involved in formal peace negotiations. Other women have been invited to attend peace talks as observers or involved in informal support roles 'around the peace table'.[7] Activists argue that women should participate at all levels and stages of the peace process, but current approaches involve limited consultation and fail to utilize women's considerable experience in peace-building at local and international levels.[8]

Women's economic empowerment is critical for national development, but gender wage gaps, land displacement and economic migration adversely affect women, limiting their access to social services and increasing their vulnerability to trafficking. Other barriers to women's economic advancement include gendered division of labour, limited access to capital, lack of awareness about women's rights and gender discrimination in the workplace. Cultural beliefs about gendered roles and behaviour also limit women's economic opportunities: women, unlike men, are expected to prioritize family over work commitments. Expansion of large-scale production, trade and investment will reduce

---

5. Zoya Phan, 'Time to End Sexual Violence in Burma', *Democratic Voice of Burma*, 17 September 2013, http://www.dvb.no/analysis/time-to-end-sexual-violence-in-burma-myanmar-rape-women-rights/32559.
6. Samantha Michaels, 'Burma Support Withheld on UN Pledge to End Sexual Violence', *The Irrawaddy*, 26 September 2013, http://www.irrawaddy.org/z_border/burma-support-withheld-un-pledge-end-sexual-violence.html.
7. Ja Nan Lahtaw and Nang Raw, *Myanmar's Current Peace Processes: A New Role for Women?* (Centre for Humanitarian Dialogue, December 2012).
8. Jenny Hedström, *Where are the Women? Negotiations for Peace in Burma* (Stockholm: Swedish Burma Committee, May 2013).

Women on a Sittwe beach, Rakhine State (photo: Ardeth Thawnghmung)

the earning potential of many women who are small-scale producers and traders. Local women-led initiatives, including the creation of workers' unions and the provision of microloans and free legal advice to villagers,[9] must therefore be reinforced by political will, legal transparency and employer accountability.

In the future, there will be a need to further strengthen links between women's networks and to increase funding, institutional support and training to enhance women's leadership and negotiation skills as well as their economic opportunities. Women's organizations could benefit from greater engagement with government, community and business leaders as well as the media to promote women's issues and gender equality through policy reform, advocacy and education. Equally importantly, those seeking involvement with Myanmar/Burma could benefit from women's perspectives and knowledge on issues as wide-ranging as diplomacy, environmental management and financial systems.

✍ JH

9. Stephen Campbell, 'Interview with Myanmar labour activist Su Su Nway', *New Mandala*, 11 February 2013, http://asiapacific.anu.edu.au/newmandala/2013/02/11/interview-with-myanmar-labour-activist-su-su-nway/; Ei Thae Thae Naing, 'With a little help from her friends', *Myanmar Times*, 10 June 2013, http://www.mmtimes.com/index.php/special-features/167-the-modern-woman/7089-with-a-little-help-from-her-friends.html; Soe Lin Aung, 'Women and gender in Dawei', *New Mandala*, 5 September 2012, http://asiapacific.anu.edu.au/newmandala/2012/09/05/women-and-gender-in-dawei/.

PART TWO

Challenges to unity

Rohingya children in Sittwe, Rakhine State, 2009 (photo: Ardeth Thawnghmung)

A clear impression from the reportage and analysis found in Part 1 of this volume is a marked improvement in the pace and tenor of change in Burma since the installation of a quasi-civilian government in 2011. The country's outlook is brighter, reform is in the air and initiatives that were once unthinkable or forbidden are now suddenly open to consideration.

Three years after the inauguration of President Thein Sein, however, some of the early optimism about the country's future has started to fade. Burma is a multi-ethnic and multi-religious society but for many decades it has also been a land whose peoples often have been at war with each other. In particular, ever since independence in 1948, the country has suffered from prolonged conflict between the state/army and ethnic armed organizations. These ancient divisions have neither healed nor gone away.

Part 2 examines these challenges to unity in greater detail. It will examine the ethnic situation in general and the peace process in particular before delving into the decades-long Karen struggle for autonomy/independence and the ongoing conflict in Kachen State. Finally, it will consider the worsening religious situation in the country and examine the recent outbreak of ethno-religious communal violence in Rakhine State.

The colonial legacy

Mikael Gravers

Britain annexed Burma in three Anglo–Burman wars, in 1824–26, 1852 and 1885. The conquest aimed at accessing Burma's formidable natural resources of teak wood, oil, gems and other minerals as well as limiting French political influence in Southeast Asia. Burma was integrated into the Empire as a part of India (and, initially, the East India Company) until 1935–37. In 1937, Burma was given its own legislative council but with a British Governor still in control.[1] With the Japanese invasion of 1942, the British were largely driven out of Burma. Although they returned in 1945, their main role quickly became one of managing the transition to independence. However, with only a small political and administrative elite, the Burmese were ill prepared to take over the administration.

Colonial rule had an enormous impact upon Burmese society and self-identification; the reverberations continue to the present day. An appreciation of this era is thus crucial for an understanding of developments since independence in 1948.

The final annexation of Upper Burma in 1885 completed the total humiliation of the Burmese and their culture. King Thibaw and his family were deported to India and where he died in exile.[2] They were taken to the ferry in an ox cart while the crown jewels and thrones were taken to London. The palace in Mandalay was plundered and renamed Fort Dufferin (after the Viceroy of India), and temples were turned into officers' clubs and bars. Soldiers entered monasteries with their boots on, an act of deep disrespect to Buddhists. None of this behaviour was new; the famous Shwedagon Pagoda had been used as a British garrison and fort during the war in 1852.

1.　The term Burman is used for the ethnic Burman (or Bamar), and Burmese as a general notion.
2.　Queen Supayalat was allowed to return to Burma with her daughters in 1919. She died in 1925 in Rangoon where she had a grand funeral and was buried in a royal tomb near the Shwedagon Pagoda.

Death and devastation at Minhla, after its capture by the British, November 1885 (photo: Willoughby Wallace Hooper, 1837–1912)

After 1885 the British 'pacified' Burma, brutally suppressed several insurrections and instituted a new order. All officials were appointed by the British and, unlike earlier Burmese kings, the colonial rulers did not support the Buddhist monastic order (*sangha*). Royal power and Buddhist spiritual power had been intertwined and the core of Burman self-identification based on Buddhist cosmology (see p. 173ff. and p. 293ff.). Buddhist monasteries also organized schools (as they do today) and provided basic knowledge to much of the population. Thus the British (and Christian) secular schools were from the beginning seen as an attack on Burman culture and identity. Conversion to Christianity was seen as adoption of a foreign identity, and the colonizers' habit of taking Burman mistresses was strongly disapproved of as an attempt to destroy Burman race and culture. The colonial legacy in the Burman view was thus one of disruption and disorder.

One of the main modes of pacification in 1886 was dismantling the royal governmental structure. Inherited offices were abolished and replaced by a combination of British commissioners and British-appointed Burmese officials. These would make tax collections from households more regular and efficient while the former royal mode of exemption due to poor harvest or other problems was abolished. Liberalization thus meant dismantling the traditional moral economy and patron–client relations between officials and civilians.

The Burmese resisted every invasion and organized rebellions after annexation. In 1852 and 1886–90, monks were active leaders of rebellions. They later organized the first Burman nationalist movement in the early 1900s and demonstrated against British rule and colonial policies. They were also active in the widespread Hsaya san rebellions of 1930–31 triggered by the world economic crisis.

Burma's economy was modernized by the colonial rulers. In particular, the British developed the agriculture in the Irrawaddy Delta and in the central dry zone, where new irrigation systems were constructed that expanded the rice area by half a million acres. This increased the output of crops considerably and made the country the 'rice bowl of Asia'. New infrastructure such as railways and the famous Irrawaddy River Flotilla were important for the economy. Forestry, oil production and trade came under British control.

The British gradually allied themselves with Christian missionaries who mainly found converts among the non-Burman ethnic groups (esp. Karen, Kachin and Chin). The colonial rule supported Christian schools, and they favoured Christians in the police, army, in education, as nannies as well as in other jobs. However, the majority of police and army were Indians. The military police was almost entirely made up of Indians whereas the frontier force was composed of Indians and ethnic minorities. About 9% of the police were Karen.[3] In 1946, the colonial army comprised 22,000 men of whom 7,000 were (mostly Christian) Chin, Kachin and Karen; a mere 200 were Burmans.

Another means of breaking up the royal system was territorialization. Burma was gradually scheduled into a Frontier Area, Native States (Kayah) and Ministerial Burma. In 1922, the Frontier Area (i.e the ethnic minority areas) came under direct administration under the British Governor, whereas Ministerial Burma had a Legislative Council. The Burmans resented this divide-and-rule policy and view it today as a cause of the inter-ethnic conflicts since 1948.

The British also imported a large workforce from India to work in the railways, in harbours as clerks, etc. Indian *chettiars* were also the

---

3.   Taylor (1987): 101.

While Yangon can no longer be called an Indian city, many of the colonial buildings from the British period still survive, though not all in a very good condition (photo: Marie Ditlevsen)

hated moneylenders. These migrant workers and *chettiar* capital were important in both the commercial modernization of Burma and its agricultural transformation. But the alien immigration was resented by the Burmans and we may find here the roots to the present anti-Muslim riots.[4] In 1931 there were more than one million people of Indian origin in Burma. Rangoon became an Indian city, half of its population being Indian. Many fled the Japanese invasion in 1942, and about 200,000 Indians left Burma in 1965 due to Ne Win's attack on foreign-owned businesses or his draconian citizenship law of 1982 denying full citizenship to those whose ancestors arrived after 1823.

Only a relatively small, educated Burman elite appeared before 1940. The most important change came via higher education. Rangoon University was founded in 1920 and fostered the student generation of Aung San as well as later rebel generations. Hence colonial rule opened Burma for the modern world but largely denied the majority of Burmans access to modernity, according to J.S. Furnivall, colonial officer, supporter of Aung San and adviser to U Nu.[5] Furnivall argued that colonial

4.   On immigration, see Taylor (1987): 101, 127–128.
5.   See Furnivall (1956); also Furnivall (1957).

rule segregated the ethnic groups and that only a common nationalism could unity the divided 'plural society', as he termed Burma. Thus Burma needed democracy, economic welfare and national unity. 'Yet Burmans cannot lead a healthy life isolated from the outside world', he added.[6]

In the 1930s, students led by Aung San and his 30 more-or-less left-wing comrades, the Thakins ('masters') began to dominate the resistance and staged demonstrations despite the strict sedition law (still used today), while more conservative politicians – such as Ba Maw, premier from 1937 and again during the Japanese occupation, and U Saw, who arranged the assassination of Aung San and seven ministers in 1947 – had their own agenda for obtaining power. Aung San first supported the Japanese invasion but the brutal Japanese rule persuaded Aung San to ally with the British in order to gain independence. 1946–47 were years of chaotic negotiations between Aung San, the British Government and the ethnic nationalities who wanted autonomy or to stay under British protection (see p. 184ff.).[7]

Aung San's nationalist ideology was based on an idea of a unitary state. In a speech at the Shwedagon Pagoda in January 1946, he said: 'A Nation is a collective term applied to people irrespective of their ethnic origin, living in close contact with one another and having common interests and sharing joys and sorrows together for such historic periods as to have acquired a sense of oneness … and desire and will to live in unity.'[8] Although recognizing ethnic, language and religious differences, he argued for a mutual patriotism. This ideology continued during military rule, and its ideas of 'Burmanization' have alienated the ethnic political organizations. It is important to remember, however, that throughout the period of British colonial rule there was no national unity – not even when independence came in 1948. The ideas of a federal union never materialized.

After independence, the small Burmese elite struggled to fill the gap left after the colonial system ended. Ideas of socialism and nationalism were strong and influenced economic decision-making. But the Burmese were not well prepared to run the nationalized British companies or to manage the country. Divisions within the ruling party, the Anti-Fascist Peoples Freedom League, a conglomeration of different political groups,

6. Furnivall (1957), p. 8.
7. See also Maung Maung (1989).
8. Cited in Burma Socialist Programme Party (1963).

and the lack of government control left a power vacuum that the military under General Ne Win (one of Aung San's Thakins) gradually filled.

References

Burma Socialist Programme Party (1963) *The System of Correlation of Man and His Environment*. Rangoon.

Furnivall, John S. (1956 [1948]) *Colonial Policy and Practice. A Comparative Study of Burma and Netherlands India*. New York: New York University Press.

———— (1957) *An Introduction to the Political Economy of Burma*. Rangoon: Peoples Literature Committee & House.

Maung Maung, U (1989) *Burmese Nationalist Movements 1940–1948*. Edinburgh: Kiscadale.

Taylor, Robert H. (1987) *The State in Burma*. London: Hurst & Company.

Myanmar Citizenship Law 1982

Myanmar has a stratified citizenship system based on descent and governed by the 1982 Citizenship Law. This complex law has its origins in the Union Citizenship Act of 1948 and has three categories of citizenship:

1) **Full citizen**. This category applies to those ethnic groups (or *tai yin tha*, 'original people') present in the country before 1823 (at the start of British colonization). Children of citizens (at least one of whom is a full citizen) also hold citizenship. Children of associate or naturalized citizens may also apply for citizenship. By marriage to a foreigner, people lose their full citizenship.

2) **Associate citizenship**. People may apply to become associate citizens if they qualified for citizenship under the 1948 Union Citizenship Act.

3) **Naturalized citizenship**. This category is open to people of a 'good character' (including foreigners) who were living in Burma before 1948 and are of mixed origins and mixed citizenship but who can speak one of the official languages of Myanmar.

All categories are granted by the government, which also decides which ethnic groups qualify for the status of *tai yin tha*.

The number of stateless people in Myanmar, including Rohingya and people of Indian origin not recognized as *tai yin tha*, is unknown but could be much higher than one million.

✍ MG

Ethnic diversity, multiple conflicts

Mikael Gravers

Myanmar/Burma is one of the world's most ethnically diverse countries with 135 'national races' or registered indigenous (or 'original') groups (*tha yin tha*) being officially recognized. But in fact the ethnic picture is far more complex than this. Some ethnic designations are umbrella terms covering a broad array of sub-groups (for instance, the name 'Chin' encompasses about 60 sub-groups/clans, some of whom reject 'Chin' as a term derived from Burmese; they prefer 'Zo'). Moreover, some other groups are not even officially recognized (notably the Rohingya) in the law of citizenship from 1982.

Despite this ethnic diversity, since its independence the country has been largely shaped in the image of its dominant Burman (or Bamar) people, who comprise nearly two thirds of the population. Not only are they often, and imprecisely, called Myanmar national races; Myanmar identity is also closely intertwined with general Burman (Bamar) customs and identity. This conflation of the majority culture with the country as a whole *plus* a keen fear among the ethnic minorities of 'Burmanization' or 'Myanmarfication'[1] have been the wellspring of separatist unrest in the country across the decades. As such, ever since the birth of the modern, independent state in 1948, it has suffered from prolonged conflict between the state/army and armed ethnic organizations.

As is made clear by several authors in this volume, the divide between ethnic Burmans and non-Burmans has its origins long before 1948, mainly in the period of colonial rule. However, the events leading to, and just after, independence deepened this divide; insurrections by

---

1. That is, attempts of cultural assimilation into Buman/Myanmar culture. The new constitution allows minority languages to be used in schools now but the old law prohibiting this seems not to have been changed yet.

the Karenni and Karen date from this period. Later, in the period of political instability leading up to the military coup of 1962, further ethnic insurrections broke out in Shan and Kachin States. Numerous local civil wars escalated in the years of military rule that followed. Some insurgent groups were co-opted by the regime; others were brutally crushed.

Fear has been (and remains) a major factor in this endless cycle of insurrection and repression. The military has long feared the disintegration of the unitary state, whereas the ethnic minorities (or ethnic nationalities, as they prefer to be termed) – fearing for their culture – want more autonomy within a federal constitution. The major challenge for today's fragile democracy in Myanmar/Burma is to bridge this divide, overcome the fear and provide all peoples in the country with full participation and rights within a united state.

One common misconception about the ethnic situation in Myanmar is that it is solely an internal matter. However, the ethnic nationalities largely dominate Myanmar's border areas with Bangladesh, India, China and Thailand and typically their communities straddle these borders.[2] As a result, there are multiple borderland networks of trade, culture, religion and political organizations. The new Myanmar will have to accommodate these networks in a constructive way.

That said, some of this border trade has to be controlled, in particular the drug trade. Burma is the world's third biggest producer of opium and heroin, much of it being produced along the border with China. Although poppy cultivation declined in the Wa region partly as a result of a ban imposed by the United Wa State Army (UWSA) in 2005, cultivation and opium production has been increasing in recent years (for more details, see p. 354ff.). Opium has financed some of the armed ethnic organizations and some profit has been laundered and ended in army pockets.[3] Further, the production of amphetamine tablets (*yaa baa*, 'crazy medicine' in Thai) is another important source of income for the Wa and other armed groups. The drug is smuggled into Thailand and sold in Burma creating many social problems in both countries.

---

2.   The complexity of such cross-border linkages can be seen with the Jinghpaw sub-group of the Kachin. They have kin in Assam and Yunnan who see themselves as part of the wider Jinghpaw family but do not identify themselves as 'Kachin' (see 'Who are the Kachin', p. 263).

3.   On the history of opium in Myanmar, see Bertil Lintner, *Burma in Revolt. Opium and Insurgency since 1948*. Boulder, Westview Press, 1994.

Opium poppy field in the Burmese part of the so-called Golden Triangle (photo courtesy of the United Nations Office on Drugs and Crime)

The widespread illegal logging of precious wood is another problem, and pristine forests are under threat. The border regions have many valuable minerals including rubies and jade (see Map 8, p. 346), which are the country's third biggest export item despite the continued ban on their importation into the United States.

Planned construction of dams in the border regions has further sparked serious concerns among the ethnic groups. The Myitsone Dam in Kachin State is the most high-profile case (see p. 357) but, for instance, in the northern part of Karen State there has been violent opposition to construction of the Hatgyi Dam on the Salween River; erstwhile rival Karen groups have joined forces to stop a Thai-financed project for a 1,200-MW dam that on the Burmese side alone would force the relocation of nine villages (for more details, see p. 198ff.). In the south in KNU-controlled territory, a deep seaport is to be constructed near Tavoy (Dawei) by a Thai–Italian company, the plan being met by local protests over the lack of compensation for land seizures. In line with the widespread land-grabbing being reported from all over Burma, Malaysian and apparently Vietnamese companies have been obtaining land in Karen State via the army.

As such, Myanmar's long-standing armed conflicts have several dimensions – not just ethnic but also political, cultural, religious and economic. The main challenge for the country is to create a fair and truly democratic distribution of influence and resources; justice and peace-building, then, are deeply interlocked. The problem is, however, that all the ceasefires signed between the state/army and armed groups over the decades have not been followed by a political solution; instead, a limited 'armed peace' has existed for many years without an agreement for a way forward. All ceasefires are fragile, as can be seen in the situation in the northern part of the Shan State where recently there has been fighting between the army and Shan State Army North, ending a ceasefire signed by the group back in the 1960s.

Recognizing the fragility of the situation, the ethnic nationalities have long tried to overcome their differences and work together in political front organizations such as the Democratic Alliance of Burma, National Democratic Front and Ethnic Nationalities Council (ENC). Often a mix of political and personal disagreements have caused these organizations to fragment and dissolve. In addition, the army has been able to play them off each other and negotiate separate ceasefires (see 'Peace-building in Myanmar', p. 223ff.). However, in early 2011 the United Nationalities Federal Council (UNFC) bringing together the main ethnic groups was formed to negotiate a political solution with the government. Its goal is a new, federal constitution. A key stumbling block here is the government's push for a nationwide ceasefire; whereas the government wants the ceasefire to come first and political dialogue second, many (but not all) ethnic groups insist on the opposite. In addition, the UNFC seems to be suspicious and resentful of the Euro-Burma Office, a Brussels-based organization with an important background role in the peace process, for its earlier support for the ENC.

Supported by the UNFC, a gathering of representatives from 18 ethnic armed organizations met for the first time inside Myanmar at Laiza in Kachin State in November 2013. Seventeen of them formed a Nationwide Ceasefire Coordination Team, which the UNFC will work with, and agreed to continue negotiations on a nationwide ceasefire as proposed by the government. However, they put forward a number of conditions, summarized here:

- the government must be committed to peace;

- cessation of hostilities (in Kachin State) ;
- recognition of the Panglong Agreement, (i.e. the goal of a federal constitution and a federal army into which are integrated the ethnic armed organizations, who thus get to keep their weapons) ;
- a national political dialogue and building of trust (not only ethnic groups and the government but also other relevant political groups);
- a code of conduct for the army;
- law reform (on land-grabbing, development projects, control of the drug trade and allowing ethnic control of culture).

Moreover, the ethnic nationalities want the Tatmadaw Commander-in-Chief, Min Aung Hlaing, as well as NLD leader Aung San Suu Kyi to participate in reaching any agreement. Without the army chief being involved, they do not see how any agreement can materialize. Whether or not this hardline commander will agree is another matter; the military is against a federation and a federal army – 'one nation and one army' is still their mantra.

Unfortunately, not all armed groups attended the Laiza gathering nor its follow-up meeting at KNU headquarters in January 2014. Significantly perhaps, even though it is a UNFC member, the UWSA attended neither meeting citing 'language barriers' but expressing agreement with much of what has been proposed. The problem now is not only disunity between the ethnic groups but also the fact that the government cannot control the army nor order it to stop fighting in Kachin, Shan or Karen States.

The situation is compounded by the uncertain response of the various ethnic groups to ongoing army incursions into their areas. Fighting between the army and Shan State Army North in northern Shan State has already been mentioned. But next door lie the lands of the UWSA, which has probably the strongest ethnic army in Myanmar. Recently, it bought four helicopters from Thailand and seems determined to protect its interests in the border trade. Despite its earlier ban on poppy cultivation, it is still involved in opium production as well as production of methamphetamine. Moreover, there are many other groups with stakes in the drug business and other illicit trade along the borders.

A further complication are the Border Guard Force (BGF) units of the army, formed from segments of various armed ethnic groups. There are currently 10 BGF battalions in Kachin, Shan and Kayah States and

13 battalions in Karen State. They are paid and armed by the Burmese army and control lucrative trade and resources in the border areas, at the same time taxing the local villagers. There has been fighting between them and their erstwhile ethnic comrades ever since their formation. Sporadic fighting continues to the present day and could thus endanger the peace process.

In March–April 2014, a new census was conducted throughout much of the country though in KIO-controlled territory in Kachin State enumerators were denied access (see p. 269). This was the first census undertaken in Myanmar since 1983 and it was prepared with assistance from the UN Population Fund (UNFPA). Preliminary results are expected to be released at the end of July 2014 and final results in early 2015.

However, long before the count was actually undertaken, the whole process was marked by controversy. It was criticized for being too hastily and badly prepared and for consultations with the ethnic groups coming too late. Although international focus was largely on the denial of Rohingya identity, within the country perhaps more focus was on the concerns of other ethnic nationalities, who complained about the ethnic categories used. For example, the Karen did not want to be registered as Kayin (the Burmese term for Karen); they prefer Karen. They also wanted registration of subgroups. If for example Karen belonging to the Geba were only registered as Geba, they might not be counted as Karen. Moreover, many people are currently registered as Bamar if their father is Bamar; ethnic groups fear this automatic registration will be repeated whatever the person's wishes. Mon, Shan and Karen organizations have conducted their own preliminary census as a check. But they may have a political interest in having all people in their territories registered as Mon, Shan or Karen. The registering of religious denomination is also seen as problematic by many. It was used in colonial times as a divide-and-rule practice and could still be seen as such a means.

In short, the ethnic situation is highly complex and remains volatile. As can be seen, the civil wars between the state/army and ethnic armed organizations involve a struggle not just for political and cultural autonomy but also for the control of local resources and trade. Politicization of ethnicity, internal conflicts and general mistrust has created a complex scenario that is difficult to handle in the ongoing reform and peace process.

Non-Burman ethnic groups

Although Myanmar is largely shaped in the image of its dominant Burman (or Bamar) people, the country's non-Burman ethnic groups are hugely significant and account for about 33–40 % of the total population. In the following, brief overview, the nationalities are ordered by population size (though all figures are rough estimates and may change radically after the 2014 national census). Excluded from this list are the Rohingya (population 800,000 or more), Indians (800,000) and Chinese (400,000); they are treated separately (see especially p. 310 and p. 323ff. for the Rohingya, p. 160ff. for the Indians and Chinese).

Shan (4–5 million), a Tai people originating from Yunnan and inhabiting the Shan Plateau for about 1,000 years; now scattered over much of northern Myanmar with kin found in Manipur, Assam, Yunnan and Thailand. Divided into five sub-groups but many other small ethnic groups are also called Shan, even some speaking Tibeto-Burman and Mon-Khmer languages. Mainly Buddhist.

Karen (3–4 million), a Tibeto-Burman people who perhaps migrated from the Gobi Desert region about 1,500 years ago, arriving before the Burmans. Now living mainly in the Irrawaddy Delta or hilly south-eastern border region, especially Kayin State; some 400,000 live in western Thailand. Divided into 10–12 sub-groups, not all seeing themselves as Karen. Mainly Buddhist but about 25% Christian. For more details, see 'Who are the Karen'.

Mon (2–3 million), part of Mon-Khmer, one of the earliest peoples in Southeast Asia with organized states predating Burman arrival; responsible for the spread of Theravada Buddhism (and building of Shwedagon Pagoda), and a major influence on the dominant Burman culture. Found mostly in Mon State and adjacent areas. Burmese-speaking neighbours of Mon origin are counted as Burman. Buddhist.

Rakhine (2 million), a Tibeto-Burman people closely related to the Burmans; arrived with them from Inner Asia about 1,200 years ago;

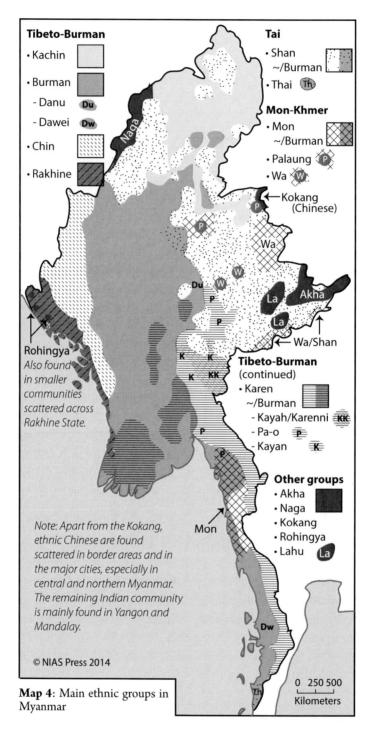

Tibeto-Burman
- Kachin
- Burman
  - Danu Du
  - Dawei Dw
- Chin
- Rakhine

Tai
- Shan ~/Burman
- Thai Th

Mon-Khmer
- Mon ~/Burman
- Palaung P
- Wa W
← Kokang (Chinese)

Wa

Du

La Akha

La

← Wa/Shan

Naga

Rohingya
Also found in smaller communities scattered across Rakhine State.

Tibeto-Burman
(continued)
- Karen ~/Burman
  - Kayah/Karenni KK
  - Pa-o P
  - Kayan K

K   K

KK

K

P

Mon

Other groups
- Akha
- Naga
- Kokang
- Rohingya
- Lahu La

Note: Apart from the Kokang, ethnic Chinese are found scattered in border areas and in the major cities, especially in central and northern Myanmar. The remaining Indian community is mainly found in Yangon and Mandalay.

Dw

Th

© NIAS Press 2014

0 250 500
Kilometers

Map 4: Main ethnic groups in Myanmar

A Pa-o tribal woman near Kalaw, Shan State (photo courtesy of Jialiang Gao)

now found mainly in Rakhine State with kin found in Bangladesh and Tripura State, India. Buddhist.

Kachin (1–1.5 million), a Tibeto-Burman hill people originating from Inner Asia (maybe the Tibetan Plateau); now found mainly in Kachin State and northern Shan State with kin found from Assam to Yunnan. Divided into six sub-groups. Mainly Christian. For more details, see 'Who are the Kachin'.

Chin (1 million), a Tibeto-Burman hill people first inhabiting the Chindwin valley about 1,100 years ago but driven by Shan into the western hills c. 1300. Now found mainly in Chin State but also in Magway Region, Rakhine State, Bangladesh and in Mizoram and Manipur States, India. Divided into six tribal groups; many sub-groups with mutually unintelligible languages. Mainly Christian.

Pa-o (600,000), a Tibeto-Burman hill people closely related to the Karen but asserting a separate identity. The second largest ethnic group in Shan State, they are also found in Mon, Kayin and Kayah States. Mainly Buddhist, some Animist.

Dawei (500,000), a Tibeto-Burman people of mixed origin, regarded as a Burman sub-group but claiming a separate identity; found in Tanintharyi Region. Buddhist.

Two ethnic Wa woman in traditional clothing (photo courtesy of Evangelos Petratos)

Palaung (3–400,000), a Mon-Khmer hill people of Shan State, related to the Wa and strongly influenced by their Shan neighbours. Mainly Buddhist, some Animist.

Lahu (200,000), a Tibeto-Burman hill people closely related to the Akha; found in Shan State but also in Yunnan, Thailand, Laos and Vietnam. Mainly Animist.

Kayah (150,000), a Tibeto-Burman hill people (also called Karenni, Red Karens) regarded as a grouping of Karen sub-groups but asserting a separate identity; mainly found in Kayah State, but also Shan State. Mainly Christian but also many Buddhists.

Wa (1–200,000), a Mon-Khmer hill people of Shan State and Yunnan, related to the Palaung, now quite Sinicized. Prior to the arrival of the Shan, the Wa seem to have inhabited much of the Shan region. Animist.

Akha (100,000), a Tibeto-Burman hill people closely related to the Lahu; found in NE Shan State but also in Yunnan, Thailand and Laos. Mainly Animist.

Kokang (90,000), Han Chinese descendants of Ming loyalists fleeing the Manchu conquest in the 17th century. Buddhist/Confucian.

Danu (80,000), a Tibeto-Burman people usually regarded as a Burman sub-group; found in SW Shan State. Buddhist.

Naga (80,000), a Tibeto-Burman hill people living along the Myanmar–India border, mainly in India, also Sagaing Region and Chin and Kachin States. Divided into 42 tribal groups. Mainly Christian.

Kayan (70,000), a Tibeto-Burman hill people regarded as a sub-group of the Kayah but asserting a separate identity; found in Shan and Kayah State, also Thailand. Divided into several tribal groups of whom the ring-necked Padaung are famous. Mainly Christian, some Animist, others Buddhist.

As can be seen above (and more visually in Map 4 on p. 156), the different nationalities tend not to live in only one area and are often intermixed with others. This is especially so due to the large numbers of internally displaced people after decades of war in the regions with ethnic minorities. Because some of the nationalities are actually composite groups, categories often invented in the colonial era, there is a significant internal diversity – cultural, religious and political. Thus, ethnic identity does not mean identification with the same religious denomination or political interests. Certainly, the ethnic nationalities generally do not like to be identified as 'Myanmars' *or* classified as minorities.

It is important to note that ethnic names differ depending on who is speaking. Names used by ethnic Burmans – and officially – and those used by the groups themselves often differ. For instance, *Shan* is a Burman word. The Shan call themselves *Tai-Yai*, signalling that they are a Tai people related to the Thai and other Tai peoples in Yunnan, Laos and Vietnam. Sometimes the Burman names are seen as derogatory – for example, *Kayin*, the official name for Karen, has a 'hillbilly' flavour and thus is not liked by many Karen who resent its implication that they are less civilized.

While most ethnic nationalities have been studied, at least to some extent, in the past, some groups have never been studied, e.g. the Lutzu or Nusu, a Tibetan-related group in the northern part of Kachin State along the Salween River.[1]

≤ MG/NP

---

1.   A detailed list of references to publications on ethnic groups can be found in Mikael Gravers (ed.), *Exploring Ethnic Diversity in Burma*. Copenhagen: NIAS Press, 2007.

IN FOCUS

Natives and foreigners

Historically Myanmar has been a crossroads in Asia and as such the country has seen many outsiders arrive and settle over the centuries. Moreover, with 135 officially recognized nationalities, Myanmar is a highly pluralistic society. Even so, the growth of nationalism in colonial times was accompanied by a xenophobic reaction against foreign exploitation. This dualistic response has continued to the present day and is one of the motors of anti-Muslim sentiment and violence since 2011.[1] In recent times, the Rohingya have been the people most affected by this rising xenophobia. Their situation is covered in greater detail elsewhere (see p. 310ff. and p. 323ff.). However, two other major ethnic minorities in Myanmar generally not considered to be *tai yin tha* ('original people') are people of Chinese and Indian origin.

The Sino-Burmese[2]

Chinese migration to Myanmar dates back hundreds of years but much of this is from recent times. Chinese traders are first recorded in the Pagan period about 1,000 years ago and by the time of the British conquest they were well established and dominated the kingdom's external trade. In the colonial period, they lost their pre-eminent position to Indians, who were favoured by the British. Even so, there was an influx of Overseas Chinese (mainly from southern China) following new maritime trade networks into Lower Burma at this time. These Chinese were well represented in the colony's commercial and business sector, especially as merchants, traders and shopkeepers, and they established their own chambers of commerce in the larger cities, where Chinatowns were often found. Meanwhile, with the eventual crushing of a Muslim-led rebellion in Yunnan against the Qing in 1873, many Muslim Hui fled

---

1. Rising xenophobia in colonial Burma and after independence is well covered in Gravers (1999. He also argues that the roots of much of modern ethnic violence lie in the violent destruction of the traditional Burman social and political order by the British (see 'The colonial legacy', p. 143, as well as the two chapters starting on p. 173 and p. 293).
2. This section draws heavily on Suryadinata (1997), Ch. 4, and Donald M. Seekins (2006).

Panthay Mosque in Mandalay (photo courtesy of Wagaung)

into northern Burma where they became known as Panthays and soon made a new life working the trade routes between Yunnan and Burma. Here they joined the Kokang, Han Chinese descendants of Ming loyalists, who had fled the Manchu conquest in the 17th century (and the only Chinese group accepted as one of Myanmar's recognized nationalities). More refugees entered Shan State from Yunnan together with defeated Nationalist troops following the communist victory in 1949; many became involved in the development of the Golden Triangle and its lucrative drug trade in the 1950s. In recent decades, they too have been joined by a fluctuating number of illegal migrants from China (just how many is unknown but they are thought to number in the hundreds of thousands).

Over the centuries, many Chinese migrants became assimilated into their local communities; just how many Burmese are thus actually of Chinese origin is unknown but it is thought to be a considerable number. Not only because they adapted to Burmese society more easily but also due to cultural affinities, generally the Chinese were more accepted than other outsiders. Their situation deteriorated in the 1960s, however, after Ne Win implemented a drastic economic policy of 'Burmese socialism' that, among other measures, attempted to limit the power of the

Chinese (and Indians) through the nationalization of private companies. Subsequent food shortages and political xenophobia at home combined with China's ongoing support for communist insurgents in Burma's border regions and its attempts to export the Cultural Revolution were some of the causes of the anti-Chinese riots that erupted in 1967.[3] Although Sino–Burmese diplomatic relations were later repaired, a new citizenship law discriminating against ethnic races of foreign origin was implemented in 1982. Not surprisingly, the number of ethnic Chinese living in Burma declined substantially during the Ne Win period (from 1.6% before the coup to about 0.6% in 1983) though just how many Sino-Burmese chose to fully assimilate rather than emigrate is an open question. The political decision to limit the power of the Chinese is interesting considering the fact that President Ne Win was himself of Sino-Burmese descent.

In the later 1980s and '90s the Chinese started to slowly return to the country, most notably in the service and cotton industries but also very often in opium trafficking and other illegal trade between Myanmar and China. Today the Chinese officially make up around 3% of Myanmar's population though some people believe the figure is much higher depending on how the category 'Sino-Burmese' is determined. Furthermore, the two countries have some common ethnic minority populations (like the Kachin Jinghpaw and Jingpo of Yunnan – see p. 285), which also makes it challenging to distinguish between Chinese and non-Chinese people.[4]

The Burmese Indians

While the Chinese may have adapted more easily to Burmese society, the Indians (or Burmese Indians) are geographically, religiously and culturally closer to the (Bamar) population of Myanmar. Cultural and religious exchanges, trade and population movements between the two countries date back 2,000 years or more. However, the bulk of the Indian influx was during the period of British colonial rule until 1937, when Burma was detached from India and ruled as a separate colony.

Like the Sino-Chinese, until recent times the Burmese Indians were major actors in the Myanmar economy, and in colonial times perhaps

---

3. Clearly, the regime played an active role in these riots with much of the killing carried out by soldiers and rent-a-crowd people. Conversely, many Chinese were rescued, protected and helped by Burmese neighbours. See Steinberg and Fan (2012), ch. 4.
4. See http://www.arakanrivers.net/?page_id=436.

even more so. As recounted elsewhere (p. 145ff.), the British imported a large workforce from India; essentially Rangoon became an Indian city. A key role in the economic transformation of the colony was played by the *chettiars*, a community of moneylenders indigenous to Tamil Nadu. Their provision of capital to Burmese cultivators was behind the dramatic emergence of the Irrawaddy Delta as the rice bowl of Asia in the later nineteenth century but also fuelled indebtedness, land alienation and anti-Indian riots during the Great Depression in the 1930s. The Japanese invasion saw the wholesale flight or destruction of this Indian elite; it was never permitted to return in the years leading to independence.

While the remaining Burmese Indians were treated equally with the Sino-Burmese at the hands of the Ne Win regime in terms of economic privation and restricted citizenship, xenophobia towards Indians was stronger and their suffering was much more severe. Here, an important reason was their political support for democracy. Furthermore, until the 1962 military coup, they were deeply engaged in the country's administrative and economic systems, and thus posed a possible threat to the military government. Another important aspect, which is believed to form part of current discrimination towards the Indians, is their skin colour, which is slightly darker than that of most Burmese. This latter aspect may also play a role in current conflicts between Muslims and Buddhists. As such, since independence the size of the Indian community in Myanmar has declined dramatically from about 5% of the total population in 1948 to about 2% today, in the process leaving more social room for the Sino-Burmese.[5]

References

Gravers, Mikael (1999) *Nationalism as Political Paranoia in Burma: An Essay on the Historical Practice of Power*. Richmond, Surrey: Curzon Press.

Seekins, Donald M. (2006) *Historical Dictionary of Burma (Myanmar)*. Lantham, MD: Scarecrow Press.

Steinberg, David I. and Hongwei Fan (2012) *Modern China–Myanmar Relations: Dilemmas of Mutual Dependence*. Copenhagen: NIAS Press.

Suryadinata, Leo (1997) *Ethnic Chinese as Southeast Asians*. Singapore: Institute of Southeast Asian Studies.

✍ MD/NP

---

5.   Suryadinata, 1997, p. 117.

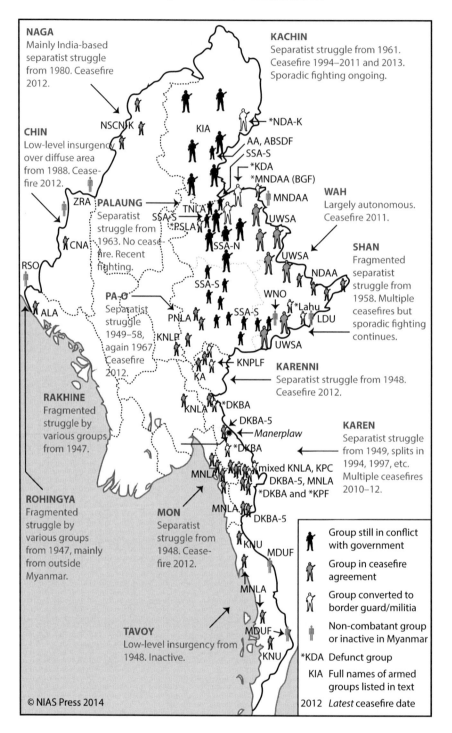

NAGA
Mainly India-based separatist struggle from 1980. Ceasefire 2012.

KACHIN
Separatist struggle from 1961. Ceasefire 1994–2011 and 2013. Sporadic fighting ongoing.

CHIN
Low-level insurgency over diffuse area from 1988. Ceasefire 2012.

NSCN/K

KIA

*NDA-K

AA, ABSDF
SSA-S
*KDA
*MNDAA (BGF)

MNDAA

WAH
Largely autonomous. Ceasefire 2011.

ZRA **PALAUNG**
Separatist struggle from 1963. No ceasefire. Recent fighting.

TNLA
SSA-S
*PSLA
SSA-N

UWSA

UWSA

NDAA

SHAN
Fragmented separatist struggle from 1958. Multiple ceasefires but sporadic fighting continues.

CNA

RSO

ALA

PA-O
Separatist struggle 1949–58, again 1967. Ceasefire 2012.

SSA-S

PNLA

KNLP

SSA-S

WNO

*Lahu

LDU

UWSA

KNPLF

KA

KARENNI
Separatist struggle from 1948. Ceasefire 2012.

RAKHINE
Fragmented struggle by various groups from 1947.

KNLA *DKBA

DKBA-5

*Manerplaw

*DKBA

KAREN
Separatist struggle from 1949, splits in 1994, 1997, etc. Multiple ceasefires 2010–12.

MNLA

mixed KNLA, KPC
DKBA-5, MNLA
*DKBA and *KPF

ROHINGYA
Fragmented struggle by various groups from 1947, mainly from outside Myanmar.

MNLA

MON
Separatist struggle from 1948. Ceasefire 2012.

DKBA-5

KNU MDUF

MNLA

TAVOY
Low-level insurgency from 1948. Inactive.

MDUF

KNU

Group still in conflict with government	
Group in ceasefire agreement	
Group converted to border guard/militia	
Non-combatant group or inactive in Myanmar	
*KDA	Defunct group
KIA	Full names of armed groups listed in text
2012	*Latest* ceasefire date

© NIAS Press 2014

IN FOCUS

Ethnic nationalities – main political organizations and armed groups

It seems very often that a new ethnically based political organization or armed group is formed in Myanmar. This is not surprising given the political volatility and climate of mistrust in the country as well as the rush by some local actors to secure and exploit economic resources as Myanmar opens up to the outside world. Of necessity, then, the following list of political organizations and armed groups affiliated with ethnic nationalities is a provisional one. Entries are ordered in a clockwise direction, starting in Kachin State (see Map 5). Organizations/groups marked by an asterisk (*) are defunct but have historical relevance.[1] Use of '//' identifies the military wing of the respective political organization. Normally, the political organization is highlighted in bold with the military wing in plain text. However, where the military group is the dominant partner (as with the TNLA and UWSA), this is highlighted.

*Burma Communist Party (BCP) // People's Army (PA). Multi-ethnic, Burman leadership with ethnic minority troops. Founded 1939, first led by Aung San. Resisted Japanese occupation. Expelled from AFPFL 1946, rebelled 1948 but fragmented. Supported by China esp. after 1967 anti-Chinese riots when it became powerful, controlling N Shan State, involvement in drug business. Effectively destroyed after ethnic mutiny 1989. Progenitor of many groups, some retaining informal links.

---

1. The term 'defunct' is relative, however. Despite becoming border guard or militia units, some groups like the KPF seem to have retained considerable autonomy whereas others like the NDA-K appear under total Tatmadaw control. For this reason, the KNPLF is not marked as defunct; though converted to a BGF, it seems to have recreated itself as a political and business organization.

Map 5 (*opposite*): Separatist conflicts, ceasefires and armed groups
Size and location of groups indicative only. Not all border guard/militia units shown. Earlier ceasefire agreements omitted. Based on multiple sources, especially Burma News International, 'Deciphering Myanmar's Peace Process: A Reference Guide'. Chiang Mai, 2013; and 'Non-State Armed Groups in Myanmar', The Irrawaddy, Vol. 20(8), Sep. 2013.

*Kuomintang (KMT). Originally c. 2,000 Chinese Nationalist troops fleeing from Yunnan after communist victory in 1949. Entered Shan State 1950, established bases for irregular war against PRC supported by CIA. By 1953 numbering 12,000 incl. Shan auxiliaries and deeply involved in opium trade; heavy fighting with Tatmadaw. Driven into Thailand in 1961 after joint Chinese–Burmese military operation but many spin-off (esp. drug) groups remained, one evolving into SURA.

Kachin Independence Organization (KIO) // ~ Army (KIA). Ethnic Kachin. Lead group pursuing Kachin independence, founded 1961. Strength 7,000–10,000. Member UNFC, NCCT. (For fuller details, see below.)

KIA soldier – see p. 13 for a full-size colour copy
(photo: David Høgsholt)

Kachin Independence Army

One of the larger non-state armed groups in Burma, the Kachin Independence Army (KIA) is the military arm of the Kachin Independence Organization (KIO), a political group composed mainly of ethnic Kachins in the north of the country. Although the KIA is the largest ethno-nationalist armed group in the Kachin region, smaller groups have also been involved in the ongoing Kachin conflicts, most notably groups such as the New Democratic Army-Kachin. However, the KIA and KIO have been the most expansive and best organized grouping both militarily and politically. The KIA has also borne the brunt of recent fighting in the region, although this seems to have strengthened the social basis of its support within many parts of Kachin society, particularly its urban youth. Unlike some other armed groups, the KIA is not seen as being led by petty warlords or opium traffickers driven solely by economic self-interest.

The KIA was founded in early 1961, at which point it declared the start of its armed conflict with the Burmese state. The initial justifications of violent opposition reflected serious political concerns about infringements to the autonomy that the Kachin State had been promised at independence. At first, the KIA was a tiny force but grew rapidly after General Ne Win's military coup in 1962. Some disaffected Kachin troops defected from the Burmese national army to join its ranks, but the KIA also engaged in widespread recruitment bringing new, young soldiers into its ranks (some of it forced).

As a result, the Kachin conflict spread rapidly but with periods of greater and lesser intensity, punctuated by several attempts to negotiate ceasefires. Finally, a ceasefire was settled in 1994 though even this fell far short of a peace agreement. The KIA retained its arms, not least because of the distrust felt towards the Burmese military government and its objectives and the fact that no mutually agreed principles upon which future political developments could be built into the ceasefire at this point. Despite these concerns, the ceasefire held until 2011 when escalating tensions led to an attack by Tatmadaw forces on areas that were considered under KIO control. This was a decisive moment in a progressively deteriorating situation, apparently proving that KIO aspirations for an autonomous Kachin region within a federal national political structure would not be fulfilled. Despite a later statement by President Thein Sein that he had ordered the army to cease its campaign, the conflict continued into 2012 with Chinese-brokered ceasefire talks finally taking place in 2013.

It should be noted that neither at the outset nor subsequently has the KIO/KIA been driven by Christian missionary intent. It has always been more pragmatic than that in its dealings with a wide range of state and non-state actors during the period of conflict, many of which would be hostile to a group making such claims. Nonetheless, the mutual support that the KIO/KIA and the main Kachin churches have been able to offer each other in their respective causes has created an inevitably close convergence of interests and discourse over a period of five decades. (See p. 284ff. for a fuller discussion of linkages between Kachin separatism and Christianity.)

✍ MS

*New Democratic Army-Kachin (NDA-K). Ethnic Kachin, mainly Lachik sub-group. KIA unit, defected to BCP 1988. NDA-K created 1989 after BCP demise, signing ceasefire with regime. Heavily involved in local cross-border timber trade. Ceased to exist 2009 and became a Border Guard Force (BGF).

Arakan Army (AA). Ethnic Rakhine but based in Kachin State. Founded 2008. Has fought beside KIA since 2011. Strength c. 500. Member NCCT.

*Palaung State Liberation Organization (PSLO) // ~ Army (PSLA). Ethnic Palaung. Origins in Palaung National Force, which began uprising in 1963. Ceasefire with regime 1991. Forcibly disarmed, converted into People's Militia Group (PMG) 2005.

Palaung State Liberation Front (PSLF) // **Ta'ang National Liberation Army (TNLA).** Ethnic Palaung. PSLF formed 1992 after PSLO ceasefire. TNLA set up in KNU territory in 2009; redeployed to Palaung homeland in 2011 with KIA help. Currently fighting with KIA and SSA-N against regime in N Shan State. Strength 1,000–1,500. Member UNFC, NCCT.

Shan State Progress Party (SSPP) // Shan State Army-North (SSA-N). Ethnic Shan. Origin in Shan State Army, founded 1964; split in 1970s, northern faction joining BCP. SSA-N created 1989 after BCP demise, signing ceasefire with regime. Most converted into PMG 2010, remainder attacked by Tatmadaw. New ceasefire 2012 but sporadic fighting continues. Strength c. 4,000. Member UNFC.

*Kachin Defense Army (KDA). Ethnic Kachin (NE Shan State). Ex-KIA unit, broke away 1990. Signed ceasefire with regime 1991. Involved in narcotics trafficking. Application to become BGF rejected and forcibly disarmed by regime, converted into PMG units 2010.

Myanmar National Democratic Alliance Army (MNDAA). Ethnic Kokang Chinese. Founded 1989 after BCP demise, signing ceasefire with regime. Major drug supplier (also methamphetamine, *yaa baa*). Rejected order to become BGF, attacked by regime 2009 ('Kokang incident'), converted into BGF. Remnant fled to Yunnan, regrouped with Chinese, Wa and Mongla support. Strength c. 300. Member NCCT, observer UNFC.

United Wa State Party // ~ **Army (UWSA)**. Ethnic Wa. Founded 1989 after BCP demise, signing ceasefire with regime. Strongly supported by China, close ties NDA-K, MNDAA and NDAA. Major drug supplier (incl. *yaa baa*) but has banned poppy cultivation in its territory. Supported regime against MTA 1996, also more recently against SSA-S, a drug-trade rival. Rejected order to become BGF, supported MNDAA during Kokang incident 2009 but not directly attacked. New ceasefire 2011 but building up military resources. Strength c. 30,000 (biggest ethnic army).

National Democratic Alliance Army-Eastern Shan State (NDAA), a.k.a. Mongla group. Ethnic Shan and Akha. Founded 1989 after BCP demise, signing ceasefire with regime. Close ties NDA-K, MNDAA and UWSA. Lucrative casino business with Chinese tourists, also money laundering of drug money. Rejected order to become BGF 2009 but not directly attacked. New ceasefire 2011. Strength c. 3,000.

Lahu Democratic Union (LDU). Ethnic Lahu. Origin in Lahu–Shan rebellion 1958, Lahu National Organization founded 1962, ceasefire 1994. Most Lahu militias converted into BGF 2010. LDU apparently remnant group. Strength <100. Member UNFC, NCCT.

Wa National Organization (WNO) // ~ Army (WNA). Ethnic Wa. Founded 1976, anti-communist roots. Opium producer. Unites with UWSA against Khun Sa, remnant later allied with SSA-S. No ceasefire but today non-combatant. Strength c. 200. Member UNFC, NCCT.

*Shan United Revolutionary Army (SURA). Ethnic Shan. Founded 1971, pro-KMT, involved in narcotics. Joined with Khun Sa to form MTA 1985.

*Mong Tai Army (MTA). Mainly ethnic Shan. Origins in groups led by opium warlord Khun Sa, formed when his Shan United Army joined with SURA 1985. Became dominant Shan group, Golden Triangle's main opium supplier. Weakened by mutiny/SSNA defection 1995, attacked 1996 by UWSA and Tatmadaw, surrendered but remnant spawned SSA-S.

Restoration Council of Shan State (RCSS) // Shan State Army-South (SSA-S). Ethnic Shan. Origin in SURA/MTA. After Khun Sa surrender 1996, remnant regrouped as SURA, merged with other groups to form

SSA-S, continued resisting regime. RCSS established as political wing 2000. New ceasefire 2011 but sporadic fighting continues, also with UWSA. Strength c. 6,000.

*Shan State National Army (SSNA). Ethnic Shan. Formed 1995 by mutineers concerned MTA more interested in drug trade than Shan freedom. Ceasefire 1995. Rejects disarmament and merges with SSA-S 2005.

*Shan State Nationalities People's Liberation Organization (SNPLO). Multi-ethnic, Pa-O dominated. Founded 1967 from several Shan State groups including PNLO. Splits after alliance with BCP 1976. Ceasefire 1994. Forcibly disarmed 2007–08, armed remnant reforming as revived PNLO.

*Pa-O People's Liberation Organization (PPLO). Ethnic Pa-O. Origin in Pa-O National Organization, anti-communist splinter group from SNPLO. Ceasefire 1991, rejectionist group forming PPLO. Combines with PNLO 2009.

Pa-O National Liberation Organization (PNLO) // ~ Army (PNLA). Ethnic Pa-O. Formed 1949, surrendered 1958. Revolt resumed 1966, merges with SNPLO 1967. Revived by remnant group 2007 when SNPLO forcibly disarmed, combines with PPLO 2009. New ceasefire 2012. Strength c. 400. Member UNFC, NCCT.

Kayan New Land Party (KNLP). Mainly ethnic Karen (Kayan and Kayah sub-groups). Founded 1964 opposing Mobye Dam, ceasefire 1994. Pressured to become PMG 2010, refuses but holds ceasefire. Strength c. 500. Observer UNFC.

Karenni National Progressive Party (KNPP) // Karenni Army (KA). Ethnic Karen (mainly Kayah). Origins in struggle from 1946 to preserve nominal independence of Karenni States, anti-communist. Founded 1957, ceasefire 1995 but quickly fails. New ceasefire 2012. Strength c. 600. Member UNFC, NCCT.

Karenni National People's Liberation Front (KNPLF). Ethnic Karen (Kayah). Formed by pro-BCP splinter group of KNPP 1978, ceasefire 1994. Converted to BGF 2009 but continued existence as political party. Observer UNFC.

Karen National Union (KNU) // Karen National Liberation Army (KNLA). Mainly ethnic Karen, Christian-led. Founded seeking Karen independence 1947, fighting 1949. Controls large area from Manerplaw by 1970s, funded by control of black market trade on Thai border. Largely driven into exile after DKBP split and fall of Manerplaw 1994–95. Ceasefire 2012. Strength c. 5,000. Member UNFC, NCCT.

All Burma Students Democratic Front (ABSDF). Multi-ethnic. Formed 1988 after crushing of 8888 Revolt by students fleeing to border regions. Ceasefire 2013 but continues to support KIA. Strength c. 600.

*Democratic Karen Buddhist Army (DKBA). Ethnic Karen (Buddhist). Founded 1994 as Buddhist splinter group from Christian-dominated KNU/KNLA. Supports Tatmadaw capture Manerplaw and drive KNU into exile, wars on KNU also in Thai refuge. Converts to BGF 2010.

Democratic Karen Benevolent Army (DKBA-5). Ethnic Karen (Buddhist). Founded 2010 by DKBA splinter group rejecting conversion to BGF. Ceasefire 2011 but still fighting BGF comrades, cooperation with KNLA. Strength c. 1,500. Member NCCT.

*Karen Peace Force (KPF). Ethnic Karen. Founded 1997 as breakaway KNLA unit seeking peace with regime, ceasefire 1997. Converts to BGF 2010.

KNU/KNLA Peace Council (KPC). Ethnic Karen. Founded 2007 as breakaway KNLA unit seeking peace with regime, ceasefire 2007, new ceasefire 2012. Strength 100–200. Member NCCT.

New Mon State Party (NMSP) // Mon National Liberation Army (MNLA). Ethnic Mon. Origins in Mon uprising from 1948, NMSP formed 1958 after surrender of main rebels. Ceasefire 1995. Rejected order to become BGF 2010 but not attacked. New ceasefire 2012. Strength c. 800. Member UNFC, NCCT.

Myeik-Dawei United Front (MDUF). Ethnic Tavoy (Burman). Origins in BCP insurgency from 1948 in Tenasserim. Founded 1989 after BCP demise. No ceasefire but today non-combatant. Strength 100–200.

Arakan Liberation Party (ALP), a.k.a. Rakhine State Liberation Party // Army (ALA). Ethnic Rakhine. Founded 1967, ALA formed 1974.

Part of fractured Rakhine rebellion. Ceasefire 2012. Strength <100. Member NCCT.

Arakan National Council (ANC). Ethnic Rakhine. Umbrella organization of Rakhine groups including ALP. Member UNFC.

Rohingya Solidarity Organization (RSO). Ethnic Rohingya. Origins in fragmented Rohingya resistance from 1947. Founded early 1980s, based Bangladesh, no presence in Myanmar, links with Taliban and Al-Qaeda. Joins ARNO 1998 but rejects full integration 2001, factional splits. Strength unknown (minuscule).

Arakan Rohingya National Organization (ARNO). Ethnic Rohingya. Formed 1998 to unite fragmented Rohingya resistance. Currently leading Rohingya organization, claimed links with Taliban and Al-Qaeda.

Chin National Front (CNF) // ~ Army (CNA). Ethnic Chin. Founded 1988, limited fighting. Ceasefire 2012. Strength c. 200. Member UNFC, NCCT.

Zomi Reunification Organization (ZRO) // ~ Army. Ethnic Chin (Zomi). Formed 1996 seeking unification of Zomi in Burma and India. Mainly active in India. Strength c. 3,000.

National Socialist Council of Nagaland – Khaplang (NSCN-K). Ethnic Naga. Founded 1980, seeking union of Naga in Burma and NE India. Split 1988, NSCN-K Burma based wing. Ceasefire 2012. Strength 500–600.

In addition to the above organizations/groups, there are many other parties and splinter groups. Most of the organizations have ceasefire arrangements in place with the government or are negotiating these.[2]

The size of the various ethnic armies is difficult to assess. For instance, the KIA is said to have increased in size from 4,000 to 10,000 and even more since the outbreak of recent fighting. However, figures for all of these armies are uncertain; no doubt they are often exaggerated.

✍ MG/NP

---

2. See Tom Kramer, 'Ethnic Conflict in Burma: The Challenge of Unity in a Divided Country'. In I.L. Dittmer (ed.), *Burma Myanmar? The Struggle for National Identity*. Hackensack, NJ: World Scientific, 2010, pp. 51–81, and Zaw Oo and Win Min, *Assessing Burma's Ceasefire Accords*. East–West Center Policy Studies no. 39, 2007. Washington. A major reference source for this section was Myanmar Peace Monitor, *Deciphering Myanmar's Peace Process: A Reference Guide 2014*, Chiang Mai: Burma News International, 2014: http://www.mmpeacemonitor.org/images/pdf/deciphering_myanmar_peace_process_2014.pdf.

Ethno-nationalism and violence in Burma/Myanmar – the long Karen struggle for autonomy

Mikael Gravers

Often heavy fighting in northern Myanmar between army units and especially Kachin separatists has focused international attention on the ethnic situation in the north of the country. However, the world's longest civil war has been played out in the eastern borderlands of Myanmar where, long before 1949 when they rose in revolt, the Karen people have struggled to decide their own destiny. Although a ceasefire was agreed in 2012, the wider political issues have not been resolved nor a mass of outstanding historical issues.

'The most striking aspect of the Burma debate today is its absence of nuance and its singularly ahistorical nature.' – Thant Myint-U: *The Rivers of Lost Footsteps*, p. 41

'I have never known peace, and my father has never known peace.' – P'da Mya, a 30-year-old KNLA soldier, quoted in *The Irrawaddy*, 31 December 2012

The roots of 'ethnic' violence

Unless we trace the historical roots of the so-called ethnic conflicts in Myanmar we shall never comprehend why ethnicity, religion and nationalism became crucial parts of a more than 60-year-long violent conflict between the state/Tatmadaw and the Karen. The roots of this disorder lie in colonial times. The first ahistorical mistake is thus to view ethnicity (and religion) as the generic cause of violent conflict. On the other hand, history cannot explain or determine every action in the pre-

Who Are the Karen?

Making up about 7% of the total population of Myanmar, the Karen are perhaps the country's largest ethnic minority, depending on who is included in this umbrella name. The word *Karen* is used to denote a broad range of people speaking *Karenic* languages, which belong to the Tibeto–Burman group of the Sino–Tibetan language family. These people have similar customs although their actual languages and cultures may vary. The English name Karen derives from *Kayin* in Burmese and Kareang in Mon. The term *Kayin* is viewed as derogatory by many Karen with its connotations of primitive hill people.

The Karen ethnic category comprises 10–12 groups found mainly in the Irrawaddy delta or in the hills bordering the eastern mountainous region. The main groups are the Sgaw (or Pgha G'Nyaw) and Pwo (or Ga Phloung). They are divided linguistically into those in the delta (Western Pwo) and those in the Karen State (Eastern Pwo). The Kayah (also known as Karenni or Red Karens) speak Kayah Li, a central Karrenic language, but prefer not to be termed Karen; instead they define themselves as an independent ethnic and political group. The Pa-o also consider themselves an independent group or nationality; though ethno-linguistically related to the Sgaw and Pwo Karen, they

Karen Baptist wedding in KNU Brigade 5 area, Papun (photo: Vinai Boonlue)

are officially classified as part of the 'Shan National Race'. In Kayah state we find the highest diversity of Karen groups: Kayah (or Karenni in Burmese), Kayan (or Padaung in Burmese), Kekhu, Brè (or Manö), Geba (or Bwe), Zayein (Sawngtun), Pakü (or Sgaw) and Yangtalai. Within these groups, there are subgroups, and variations in the used terms depend on who has done the classification (see Lehman 1967). For example, Kayan seems to be a recent term.

Long before Burmese independence in 1948, the Karen pushed for their own independent state. The insurgency led by the Karen National Union (KNU) that broke out in 1949 has been called the world's longest civil war though a ceasefire agreed in 2012 is largely being observed. (For fuller details, see p. 198ff. later in this volume.)

Because of the mainly Christian leadership of the KNU, outsiders often presume that the Karen are largely Christian like the Chin and Kachin. In fact, the majority of the Karen are Theravada Buddhists, although some, especially in the highlands, also practice Animism. About 25% of Karen, most of these from the Irrawaddy delta region, identify themselves as Christian.

✍ MG

sent even if actions are often interpreted by actors (and observers) with a reference to history. The problem of nuances, then, is also a problem of interpretations.

The first problem is the meaning of 'ethnic conflicts'. Several ethnic groups in Myanmar have been or are still involved in armed struggles against the state/Tatmadaw, among them the Kachin, Palaung, Shan, Wa, Karenni, Pa-o, Karen, Mon and Chin. The term 'ethnic conflict' is often used to categorize these armed struggles. However, ethnicity in itself is not an automatic natural source of violence. We have to look back into the history and politicization of ethnicity in order to explain why the country has suffered from so many conflicts involving ethnic groups since independence in 1948. Though rooted in colonial times, ethnic conflict escalated in the ill-prepared process leading to independence and in the period of failed democratization after independence. Its complexity further involves religious and intra-ethnic divides and conflicts.

Key dates for the Karen

739 B.C.	Approximate date, according to Karen National Union (KNU), of Karen migration into Burma, preceding the Burmans.
pre-1800	Karen subjugated by successive Mon and Burman kingdoms; no Karen state ever formed.
1828	First contact between Animist Sgaw Karen and Baptist missionaries; Christianity spreads especially among the Sgaw but later also among the Delta Pwo.
1852	Christian Karen aid British annexation of Lower Burma, opposed by some Buddhist Karen.
1856–60	Buddhist Karen uprising against the British in the Delta and Salween areas.
1881	Foundation of Karen National Association, forerunner of the modern-day KNU, by Christian Karen seeking greater Karen representation in the colonial government.
1886	British complete their conquest of Burma, abolishing the monarchy; subsequent Burman rebellion quelled with Christian Karen help.
1880s	Increasing British recruitment of Karen and other ethnic minorities in colonial forces.
1942–45	Japanese occupation of Burma; savage attacks on pro-British Karen by Aung San's Burma Independence Army.
1947	Formation of Karen National Union (KNU); Karen refuse to attend Panglong conference on post-independence arrangements called by Aung San.
1948	Burmese independence; growing anarchy across the country; attacks on Karen by nationalist militia led by Ne Win and instigated by U Nu's government.
1949	Outbreak of Karen insurgency of more than 60 years; Karen National Liberation Army (KNLA) overruns northern Burma but narrowly fails to capture Rangoon, and retreats.

1970s	Growing strength of KNU in eastern border areas, with headquarters in Manerplaw.
1984	1984: Major offensive by army using its 4-cuts strategy to deprive the KNU of military, financial and civilian support.
1988	Students fleeing suppression of the 8888 rebellion join forces with KNU and set up pro-democracy bases.
1994–95	Buddhist Karen dissidents split from KNU/KNLA to form the Democratic Karen Buddhist Organization (DKBO); Manerplaw falls to Tatmadaw forces supported by DKBO, with KNLA steadily driven out of Burma; mass flight of Karen refugees into Thailand.
2008	Cyclone Nargis devastates Irrawaddy Delta region, killing many Karen.
2012	KNU agrees ceasefire with new Thein Sein government.

A conflict and armed struggle such as the Karen 'revolution', as the Karen National Union define their struggle, is often termed 'ethnic' and perceived as if the ethnic dimension is the determining factor and an internal substance and quality of ethnicity. In fact, the ethnic dimension often emerges through after-the-fact interpretations. Hence, civil war in Burma is a violent conflict that became 'ethnic' over a long historical process with social memory playing an important role here. For the Karen, suffering, victimhood, fear and mistrust are the major results of their long conflict and these grievances have occupied Karen ethnic identity as dominant elements of their identity together with classification of the Burmans as the 'incompatible other'.[1]

Violence in Burma continued after the end of World War II and winning of independence mainly because the democratic process failed to absorb the divided political and ethnic order left by British rule. Some of the ethnic minorities (or nationalities as they prefer to be called)

---

1. For a fuller exploration of the nature of violence in general and 'ethnic violence' in particular, see Brubaker (2004), 111–115; Kalyvas (2000), 2; Schmidt and Schröder (2001), esp. p. 8; and not least Arendt (1969).

were used by the British as auxiliaries during the initial conquest and pacifications. Further, the frontier zone was administered separately and this segregation created ideas and visions of future independence. A third element of the dynamics of the long conflict is internal struggle and dissension within the Karen and other ethnic groups (none of whom are homogeneous ethnic communities). Missionaries converted some Karen to Christianity and since then conversion has been a source of conflict between Christians (an estimated 20–25% of Karen but only 4–5% of the total population) and the Buddhist majority of Burmans and Karen. Finally, leadership traditions have had a role in a process of continuous fragmentation, as we shall see.

The Karen in the colonial order – divide and rule.

The final British conquest of Burma in 1886 not only abolished the monarchy; it also changed the more or less hereditary administrative system and excluded the frontier area where most of the ethnic minorities lived. The new rulers used Christian Karen, Kachin and Chin in the colonial army and administration while labourers were imported in the thousands from India. In what J.S Furnivall (1956) has termed a 'plural society', there was a division of labour along racial lines – hence, the different peoples mixed economically but never combined culturally or socially. Thus, ethnicity and religion appeared as the main ingredients in a segregated social order. This order – or disorder as seen from a Burman point of view – had come into being with violence. And violence thus became attached to, and more or less justified within, this ethnicized order.[2]

The British colonizers never quite understood the Buddhist cosmological basis of the old royal order in which the king both supported the Sangha (monastic order) and appointed its head. Burmese concepts of power were (and are) based on karma and moral perfection combined in the term *hpoùn* (power based on karma). The king demonstrated his charisma by renovating pagodas and giving donations to the Sangha while his subjects drank holy water when pledging their allegiance. They contributed their labour, services and taxes (or, in the margins of

2. The Burmese historian Michael Aung-Thwin (1985) has defined the colonial order and its 'pacification' as an 'order without meaning'. The British conquest, native resistance, the rise of Burmese nationalism and the impact of this period on modern-day Myanmar are further explored in 'Colonial legacy' (see p. 143).

the royal realm, tribute) in return for royal protection and support for Buddhism.[3] Missionaries often depicted the Karen as repressed by their Burman rulers and burdened with heavy taxes. But this was not necessarily due to ethnic discrimination; it may have been a case of failing to form a protective patron–client relationship with Burmese officials or punishment for having joined the Mon rebellions in the 18th century.[4]

The British abolished the royal patron–client system and its inherited offices and created an administration from governor down to village headman that exercised more direct control over taxes, resources and trade. They employed an army of mainly Indian soldiers (*sepoys*) and found recruits for their Auxiliary Military Police among Christian ethnic minority groups (Karen, Kachin and Chin). Burma was administered under the British Viceroy of India until 1922. The Burmese viewed the massive immigration from India, the Christian conversions and ethnic favouritism as a subversion of their meaningful order and as a foreign disorder. Accordingly, they saw a Christian convert as a person who had adopted an identity as a foreigner (*kala* in Burmese and *khola* in Karen).[5] From this time onwards, then, ethnic and religious identities gradually became more and more politicized.

While Christian Karen aided the second British annexation in 1852, Buddhist Karen opposed them and led by millenarian prophets in 1856–60 in the Delta and Salween areas they rose against the British Raj. They wanted to drive out the 'white foreigners' (*khola*): they believed their time to rule had come and expected the imminent arrival of a Karen King (*min laùng* in Burmese). This guerrilla war proved difficult for the British to quell.[6] The rebels also attacked Christian villages while Christian Karen were involved in suppression of the rebellion. Many Karen were killed,

---

3. The royal realm functioned according to the classic Asian *mandala* principle with a central core, provinces and tributary states in a concentric order where manpower was the crucial resource.

4. See Ito Toshikatsu (2007: 97, 103). Buddhist Pwo were allied with the Mon Kingdom of Pegu (Bago).

5. Christians were called *kala*. See *Baptist Missionary magazine*, vol. 32, 182. 'In the opinion of the Burmese they had become bonâfide strangers having lost their nationality', reported the Catholic Bishop Bigandet (1887: 4). *Kala* is now a derogatory term used for people coming from Bangladesh and India (and now Muslims generally). On the history of conversion to Christianity, see Gravers (2007). The Karen belong to several denominations incl. Baptist, Catholic, Anglican and Seventh-Day Adventist, the Baptist community being the largest.

6. For details and sources on the rebellion and Karen royal imaginary, see Gravers (2001 and 2012a). These rebels were often religious leaders.

or lost their houses and crops, and the rebellion resulted in widespread hunger – the same calamities as have been experienced in recent years.

During the final conquest of Burma in 1886, the Christian Karen were even more active in quelling the subsequent, widespread Burman rebellions that took the British by surprise. The Burmese clearly saw the conquest as more than an occupation; it was a violent attack aimed at the destruction of their religion and indeed of Burman identity. After hesitating to arm the Christian Karen the British saw that they were loyal and distributed arms. Here, they were encouraged by some Baptist missionaries, who called the resistance 'Buddhism in arms against Christianity' and saw the conquest as a final fight against 'despotism' and 'heathen idolatry'. A reward was put on the heads of the rebel leaders who were mainly Buddhist monks. Christian Karen collected some of these and brought one of the main leaders alive to the British.[7] In retaliation, Christian villages and chapels were burned, villagers and Karen teachers killed. But the rebels (dacoits or armed gangs, as the British called them) also burned Burman villages – probably because they, too, had denied them active support. However, the rebellions were gradually suppressed by the Indian army, and in 1890 Upper Burma was claimed to be 'perfectly tranquil'. Even so, resistance was not dead.[8] I suggest that these events became part of a social memory of violence and victimhood for the Karen, and a proof for the Burmans of Karen allegiance to the foreign colonial power. This perception was reinforced when Karen police joined the colonial army against the Hsaya San rebellion in 1930.[9]

Thus, the 'pacification' of Burma turned into a deep disorder where violence escalated and became 'ethnicized'. The Christian Karen saw it as a victory for their God, who was stronger than they first believed.[10] Here, we find an important root of future conflicts with a religious dimension added. However, for the Karen as well as for other people

---

7. Missionary Bunker (1902: 264ff.) describes the capture by two women of 'the great *pongyi*' who had over thousand followers. A woman's skirt was put over the monk's head, an ultimate degradation of his *hpoùn*.

8. See Adas (1982) and Ni Ni Myint (1983) for a fuller account of the final conquest of Burma and subsequent resistance.

9. See Patricia Herbert (1982); Maitri Aung Twinn (2008). 1,600 Christian Chin and Karen from the police participated in the 'pacification'. The leader of the rebellion, Hsaya San – a former monk – mixed Buddhist cosmological notions with nationalism. The British sources emphasized the 'traditional' aspects and dacoity as an anti-colonial disorder.

10. At least in the missionary narrative (see *Baptist Missionary Magazine*, 1866: 331).

in Burma, religion and ritual have traditionally been connected with political allegiance and power as described above. This dimension is often neglected in a modern secularized thinking. Colonialism aimed to erase this allegiance in its 'civilizing' project of modernization but, as we shall see, the religious dimension is still politically important.

Even before the final British conquest, Christian Karen pastors and American missionaries had organized a meeting of 'all Karen Clans' in 1881 and formed the Karen National Association (KNA). It was supposed to be non-religious and aimed at uniting the Karen nation of Buddhists, Animists and Christians and to keep them away from utopian (millenarian) ideas. In reality, the KNA was dominated by Christians and its Christian leaders became the future political elite. Missionaries had long promoted the idea of a Karen Nation and created a national flag 'like other Book nations have' (blue with a Bible and sword) that was presented in New York. The idea was to establish an independent (Christian) Karen nation as a spearhead of civilization and Christianity in the region. For the missionaries, the Karen were one of Israel's lost tribes who had recovered their lost religion. At the same time they were portrayed as 'the Loyal Karen of Burma' fighting Burman rebels and dacoits.[11] From this time, the Karen would argue that they had a legitimate claim to self-determination as a reward for their loyalty. The formation of the KNA in 1881 became a crucial element in the narrative of struggle and suffering. The organization was more than a symbol, however; it was politically active, one of its achievements being to secure for the Karen a special representation of twelve seats in the legislative council after administrative reforms in 1935.[12]

The British Raj was replaced by a new violent order in 1942 with the Japanese invasion and a clash between Burman and Karen nationalism soon took place. The Japanese occupation was supported by the Burma Independent Army (BIA) under Aung San and his 30 comrades or *Thakins* ('Masters'). The British Army in Burma included around 2,800 Karen, and many stayed in Burma after the withdrawal of the

11. See Bunker (1902, 238ff.); Smeaton (1887). Ellen B. Mason (1862: 262–268 especially) describes the evolution of the Karen from a tribal society to a civilized nation; see also McMahon (1876).

12. During the Burma Round Table Conference of 1931–32, the (Christian) KNA representative claimed that the Karen were the aboriginals of Burma; the Buddhist Karen were more cautious. See document MD 4004 vi: 233, in the Oriental and India Office Collections, British Library.

army. The BIA suspected that the Karen were still loyal to the British and had retained their weapons. Clashes between the BIA and Karen escalated in the Irrawaddy Delta, with the BIA killing an estimated 1,800 Karen. Further, 58 Karen villages, and even more Burmese villages, were burnt down after a Japanese officer was killed. However, this conflict was not merely between the BIA and Christian Karen. A Buddhist Pwo Karen, Mahn Shwe Tun Kya ('Tiger') formed a millenarian movement that liberated part of the Delta for some months. Active in the fighting, it also assisted Karen sent in by parachute from India. Shwe Tun Kya was executed by the Japanese in 1944 but is still remembered. Thus, Christian and Buddhist Karen had a shared experience of violence and victimhood that became a crucial part of the social memory.[13]

When the war ended, the British decided to cooperate with Aung San and his Anti-Fascist Peoples Freedom League (AFPFL) after he supported the British in the final battle for Burma. Suddenly, Burma was destined to obtain its freedom together with India as soon as possible. This haste made it difficult for all ethnic groups and organizations to assess their future and reach democratic decisions.

The origins of the federal idea: the Panglong Conference of 1947 – a new order or a flawed one?

The British had divided Burma into Ministerial Burma and Frontier Areas in 1922. The hill areas close to Burma's borders came under the Frontier Areas Administration (FAA), directly under the British governor. The hills were restricted areas for Burmans. After the return of the British in 1945, the new head of the FAA, Noel Stevenson, put forward a plan to merge the whole FAA and its ethnic groups into a federation that would remain under British control until it had achieved a sufficient level of economic and political development to be amalgamated with the rest of Burma. With this aim in mind, Stevenson organized a confer-

---

13. See Kazuto Ikeda (2007) for details and references. The majority of Karen in the Delta were Buddhist Pwo; Christian Karen were only about 8.5% but their intellectuals had a dominant position (ibid.: 67, 73). Estimates of casualties vary. Many Burmese were killed and 17,000 displaced. Perhaps as many as 170 Karen and 180 Burman villages were destroyed (ibid.: 68). Thus there were victims on both sides. In addition, events relating to the British officer Major Seagrim are still remembered. He stayed behind in the eastern hills north of Papun and was helped by Karen who became part of the Force 136 of the Special Operations Executive operating behind enemy lines. The BIA and Japanese threatened reprisals if Seagrim did not surrender, and executed 13 Karen elders. Other Karen elders were tortured and girls were selected as 'comfort women' for the Japanese (see Morrison 1946).

ence in Panglong in the Shan states in 1946.[14] This was a cultural festival but also a platform for political discussions. However, the Burmese nationalists headed by General Aung San protested against Stevenson's plan, believing that he was fragmenting Burma and allowing the ethnic minorities to stay under the British Commonwealth and later to achieve independence. Stevenson was recalled to London. At the main Panglong conference that followed in February 1947, an agreement on the colony's future was signed. Representation was not entirely democratic and some representatives were selected among leaders connected to colonial rule. Many of the minor ethnic groups in the FAA were not represented.

The concepts discussed at Panglong – union vs. federation – were unclear to most non-Burman participants. 'Union' as preferred by the Burman nationalists seemed to have a meaning of unity within a state whereas 'federation' had a connotation of secession of ethnic states. It thus appears that participants were unsure of the exact meaning of the concepts and of the agreement they made. In the constitution subsequently drafted later in 1947, the Shan and the Kayah obtained the right to secede from the Union after ten years because of their traditional autonomy.[15] As for the other minority areas, Kachin State became integrated in the union without right to secession. The Chin opted for aid to develop a special Chin division. The majority of Karen and other groups were not living under the FAA and thus were not parties to the agreement; indeed, their claims were not discussed at Panglong.

There are many stories about promised states and independence. Aung San was said to have promised self-determination but it is more likely that he promised local autonomy. In any case, he was assassinated in July 1947 by a political opponent and his death complicated the process.[16] Likewise,

---

14. This was also hosted by Shan princes (*saw bwas*) who ruled and thus represented Pa-o, Wa, Lahu and other groups. Aung San was not invited but his political opponent and later assassin, U Saw, came and promised fair treatment of the hill peoples, whereas U Nu strongly criticized colonialism.

15. During the colonial period, the traditional Tai princes and lesser rulers of Shan State enjoyed considerable autonomy. As for the Kayah or Karenni States, these were categorized as 'native states' outside of Burma proper though administered by the British governor. Stevenson presented his federal ideas in *Man*, Vol. XLV, 2, 1945. These united the hill peoples in a Supreme Council of the United Hill Peoples and are mentioned in the Panglong agreement.

16. See Silverstein (1987). The federative part of the 1947 Constitution was never implemented. The 2008 Constitution has a similar construction on a chamber of members from the states/regions and a chamber of political parties but not a clear sharing of power between regional assemblies and the national assembly.

the British never gave any direct promises of self-determination to the Karen or other groups. Thus, the whole scenario around the FAA and the Panglong conference, as well as the 'Spirit of Panglong' as it was coined later, seems to have generated a vision of ethnic independence as a British dominion followed by self-determination. As part of the negotiation process, the British organized a Frontier Area Committee of Enquiry so that the wishes of the minorities could be voiced. The exercise was badly prepared and produced ambiguous answers. It also demonstrated the lack of unity among the Karen, especially between the hill Karen from Papun and the urban Karen from Rangoon. Moreover, it seems to have raised expectations of autonomy and federalism among the ethnic minorities.[17]

It is important to understand that this issue is still high on the agenda of the present peace process and cannot be neglected. Aung San Suu Kyi has referred to Panglong and all major ethnic organizations have a federation at the top of their agenda, but no longer is anyone demanding the right to secession as in 1947. The present visions of autonomy, however, are still based on the ethnic nationalism generated in the colonial era. The hasty process of independence and unclear political solutions resulted in several insurrections immediately after independence in 1948 and represented a continuation of the past disorder.[18] Panglong thus represents a vision of future autonomy for the ethnic nationalities whereas it represents a nightmare return to colonial disorder for many in the military. This is one of the reasons why the military is against a federal constitution.

Karen Nationalism since 1946

During World War II, the Karen Central Organization cooperated with the Burman administration in order to protect the Karen from Japanese atrocities. In 1946, the revived KNA sent a delegation to London in the hope of obtaining an independent state, but in vain. The British never replied to the KNA's written memoranda requesting a state under British control. Moreover, the Buddhist-dominated Burma Karen National Association (BKNA) and Karen Youth Organization (Christians and Buddhists linked

---

17. On Panglong conferences, see M/4 2811 and M/4 2854, OIOC, British Library and Universities Historical Research Centre (1999). 'Full autonomy in internal administration for the Frontier Areas is accepted in principle' appears in section V of the Panglong Agreement, the only place where 'autonomy' is mentioned.

18. On the insurrections, see Government of the Union of Burma (1949).

to Aung San's AFPFL) were against sending a delegation to London. They supported the constitution and the elections that provided 24 seats to the Karen constituencies, also arguing that a future Karen State within the Union of Burma was to be decided in the new parliament.[19] However, the Karen National Union (KNU), formed in 1947 and under Christian leadership drawn from the wealthy elite of landowners and business people, boycotted the elections in 1947. The KNU demanded a state that included the present Karen State, Toungoo district, Tenasserim, Insein (north of Rangoon) and Henthawaddy district plus more seats in parliament and that 25% of government ministers should be Karen. Such demands exceeded the more modest aims of the London delegation and split the Karen. After the murder of Christian Karen by Burmese auxiliary forces during Christmas celebrations in 1948, the KNU formed the Karen National Defence Organization (later renamed the Karen National Liberation Army, KNLA) and prepared for the rebellion that began in January 1949.[20]

The arguments for an independent state now appeared in the KNU nationalist discourse, as for example in a memorandum in 1946 distributed in Rangoon and London. In this memorandum, the KNU emphasized the Karen 'as a distinct race' with 'an inborn spirit of nationalism' who were oppressed by the Burmans.[21] From this, a Karen member of the London delegation, Saw Po Chit, drew the conclusion that 'it is a dream that Karen and Burma can ever evolve a common nationality. The Karen are a nation according to any definition of a Nation ... with our own distinctive culture and civilization, sense of value, moral codes, distinctive outlook.'[22] This view continued to dominate the KNU perception that there were incompatibilities between Karen and the Burman majority. It is still related in a KNU publication from 1992: 'It is extremely difficult for the Karen and Burman, two peoples with diametrically opposite views, outlooks, attitudes and mentalities, to yoke together.'[23] This perception is

19. In the event, Karen State only materialized in 1952. On the delegation and its publications in London, see Gravers (1996). On Karen organizations, see FO 643/71 (1946) Public Record Office, London, and Tinker (1967). See also Tinker (1983–84) for a large collection of documents.

20. For details, see Gravers (1999, 2012b) and Thawnghmung (2012). The KNU claim that the British government never told them that their demands were unrealistic and decided to boycott the elections (see Mss. Eur).

21. 'The Case for the Karens', 1946. London, Mss. Eur. E252/22. Sir John Clague Collection.

22. 'Karens and the Karen State'. KNU, 1946. 'Karen's Political Future, 1945–47', M/4/3023 OIOC.

23. KNU (1992).

still alive, with a strong version of this seeming to survive among some in the Karen diaspora in particular.

But many Karen have a more moderate view and in the 1950s many urban Karen supported three political parties during the relatively democratic periods. Political and religious allegiances as well as personal struggles have divided the Karen ever since.[24] Meanwhile, the KNU and their revolution were divided between an eastern and a western command (hills vs Delta) and saw a new split between a right and a left wing. During the 1950s–60s, the KNU was further divided between the socialist Karen National United Party and Kawthoolei Revolutionary Council under Hunter Tha Hmwe.[25] He declared himself a traditional ruler titled 'Lord of Land and Water' and led the Karen until he signed a peace agreement with Ne Win in 1964, resulting in some defections from the KNLA. In 1976, the socialist Mahn Ba Zan was replaced as president by Bo Mya, a right-wing anti-communist and autocratic leader, who died in 2006 after failed negotiations with the military regime. In the years following Bo Mya's accession, the KNU continued their struggle from bases in the hills of Karen State and in the Delta.[26]

The 1962 military coup staged by General Ne Win was explained as an emergency action in order to prevent the fragmentation of the Union and the rumoured secession by Shan and Kayah States during the Toungoo federal seminar. The year before, the Kachin Independence Organization had also begun an armed struggle for an autonomous state. Ne Win soon initiated his 'four cuts policy' in order to eliminate the armed ethnic organizations. Four cuts means cutting the supplies of food, intelligence, finances and recruits – or heads, as in the KNU interpretation. In reality, this four-cuts strategy meant ethnic cleansing. For Ne Win, the ethnic organizations represented remnants of the colonial disorder. He believed in a unitary state and promoted Burman nationalism within his Burma Socialist Programme Party. In order to promote unity he established the Centre for Unity of the National Races in Sagaing.

---

24. See Smith (1999) and Thawnghmung (2008, 2012) for details on internal conflicts in the KNU. Thawnghmung's works provide important insights into the conflict as seen from the silent majority of Karen, who have not been directly involved in the violent conflicts.
25. Hunter Tha Hmwe was a former Force 136 and a regional Karen National Defence Organization commander from the Delta, a charismatic person. When President Saw Ba U Gyi was killed in 1950, Hunter succeeded him.
26. For further details, see Smith (1999).

U Thuzana: detail from a mural at Myaing Gyi Ngu monastery (photo: Mikael Gravers)

Ne Win demanded that the Karen surrender their weapons before negotiations could start. Thus all attempts to solve the conflict stranded since the KNU adhered strictly to the rule laid down in 1947: never to surrender their weapons (this is still a cardinal rule). In 1983–84, the military launched a major offensive against the KNU using its 4-cuts strategy to deprive the KNU of military, financial and civilian support. This resulted in thousands of internally displaced persons and refugees coming into Thailand – at present estimated at 140,000 officially registered and many more living outside camps.[27] The KNU gradually lost control of its base areas and adopted guerrilla tactics.

The divide between Buddhist and Christian Karen in 1994

The rise of U Thuzana and eventual splintering of the KNU in 1994 foreshadowed the worst infighting between Karen in living memory. Ostensibly, the cause was religious. Many Buddhist Karen had become KNLA front-line soldiers, with Buddhist and Animist Karen from the hills an important source of recruits and taxes for the KNU in the border region. However, Buddhist Karen complained that they bore the brunt of the fighting in the KNLA while its leaders lived a safe, rich life,

---

27. On Karen refugees, see TBBC (2011) and South (2011). On Christian influence among refugees, see Horstmann (2011).

Monastery in Myaing Gyi Ngu: U Thuzana's HQ (photo: Mikael Gravers)

sending their children off to be schooled in the USA or UK. They also complained that Buddhism was discriminated against by the KNU.

When the Sgaw Karen monk and former KNLA runner, U Thuzana, began to mobilize the Buddhist Karen in search of peace, the KNU leadership became highly suspicious. It believed he was acting for the Tatmadaw and betraying the KNU. How otherwise could the monk finance the construction of a huge monastery in Myaing Gyi Nu on the Salween River and feed thousands of internally displaced persons? U Thuzana proclaimed a prophecy that, after 50 white pagodas had been constructed, peace would come. He then mobilized the Animist Karen in the hills (a KNU backwater) and began constructing a white pagoda above the KNU headquarters in Manerplaw. After fighting between supporters and opponents of the pagoda broke out near the building site, the Democratic Karen Buddhist Organization (and Army) were formed with the monk as patron. The rebellious Buddhist soldiers drank holy water when pledging their allegiance to the monk, perhaps emulating the old royal ritual. In the beginning they used yellow headbands with protective Buddhist inscriptions on them to distinguish themselves from their former comrades.

The formation of the DKBA (recently estimated at 4–6,000 soldiers, twice the size of the KNLA forces), and its prompt ceasefire with the regime were hard blows for the KNU, which soon lost its base areas in

Burma. During the 1990s, DKBA soldiers in alliance with the Tatmadaw attacked Christian villages and refugee camps in Thailand, where they engaged in looting, kidnapping and murder. In 2006, two Karen (probably paid by Burman officers) assassinated the Karen leader, Padoh Mahn Sha, and a fierce campaign against the KNLA in 2009 generated a new flow of refugees. Meantime, U Thuzana managed to collect huge donations from influential Thai business people wishing to invest in both religious merit and the border trade. Donations have largely been used to establish schools and clinics, to build roads and bridges, and to construct pagodas. It is not clear if some of the money has been used to supply the DKBA. However, the monk provides vegetarian food to his followers.[28]

After significant pressure from the regime, much of the DKBA became part of the Border Guard Force (BGF) before the elections in 2010 and hence, instead of being an autonomous ally of the regime, it was integrated into the Tatmadaw. However, significant numbers of DKBA troops (especially from its fifth brigade and apparently encouraged by U Thuzana) rejected this change and broke away to form the Democratic Karen Benevolent Army (DKBA-5). Some of the former DKBA, now BGF units, are thus no longer loyal to U Thuzana and their officers act like warlords. In these changed circumstances, the DKBA-5, under U Thuzana's influence, has forged an alliance with the KNU. They have held meetings and even celebrated martyrs days in commemoration of Saw Ba U Gyi, the KNU president killed in 1950. A DKBA-5 officer whom I interviewed regretted that Karen had been fighting Karen since 1994 and said that there should be unity.[29] The BGF units rely on support from the Burmese army and want to maintain their share in the border region's twilight economy, taxation and forced labour. The subalterns always follow their leaders, a DKBA-5 major told me. They form patron–client networks and their loyalty is rewarded with weapons, pay and protection. Thus, in this conflict, a combination of religion, economy, politics and personal loyalties – as much as ethnicity – are the sinews of the networks of trust. The problem with the internal divisions within the Karen, especially in Karen State, is that sometimes they have generated violent conflicts within the larger conflict.

---

28. See Gravers (forthcoming).
29. During an interview in January 2012, KNU leader Saw David Tackabaw assured me that the KNU and DKBA-5 collaborated and that there was no conflict between Buddhist Pwo and Christian Sgaw.

Amidst this main divide between Christians and Buddhists, more splinter groups broke away from the KNU after 1994. One of these was the Karen Peace Council, formed by an officer and former member of the KNU's Central Committee, who felt excluded and disgruntled. In addition, many of those who deserted the KNU obtained a ceasefire and lucrative economic deals with the Tatmadaw, including personal payments and gifts of cars. Examples are Tay Lay and Nehr Day, sons of KNU president Bo Mya who lost influence after their father's death, and Pado Aung San, former Minister of Forests in the KNU, who defected with a unit in 1997 and is now in business south of Hpa-an. KNU leader David Thackabaw explained that these deserters all made off with large amounts of money from the KNU, indicating that the harm done to the KNU was not only political but also financial. Recently, Mahn Robert Ba Zan, the late KNU president Mahn Ba Zan's son and a Christian, returned from the USA and formed a political organization within the DKBA-5 called the Klo Htoo Baw Karen Organization (KKO). U Thuzana is one of the KKO's patrons. This group still recognizes the KNU and Saw Ba U Gyi's principles. Thus, the scenario for peace process and a future political settlement is complicated by such interpersonal fragmentation, which I believe is also a sign of 'conflict fatigue' and a dwindling of support and resources. The Burmese army has exploited these divisions and obtained more control of the frontier zone in the Karen state.

Furthermore, the KNU is split internally between a sceptical faction, who largely mistrusts the intentions of the government and most Burmans, and a more collaborative faction. The older KNU leadership emphasizes how they have been chided and tricked in previous negotiations and demand a solution which includes all ethnic groups and a federal constitution. Many in the younger generations of Karen are tired of the conflict and hope for a political solution. This may be found among three Karen parties that participated in the elections in 2010. The most important is the Phloung-Sgaw Democratic Party, with a broad support in the Karen State. It obtained nine seats in the national parliament and four in the Karen State assembly. Its patron is a Buddhist monk, Ashin Pinnya Thami (Taungalay) in Hpa-an, who is organizing education and development.[30] The Karen Democratic and Development Party, linked to the DKBA-5,

---

30. The monk is a controversial figure, critical of all other Karen organizations and leaders, and he is said to have had close relations with Senior-General Than Shwe.

Improved relations between the KNU and government/military. A visit to Naypyidaw in June 2014 by the top leadership of the KNU drew much attention, not least when KNU Chairman Mutu Say Poe emerged from a KNU–Tatmadaw meeting holding hands with the commander in chief (photo: Senior General Min Aung Hlaing/Facebook)

is also based in Karen State. In contrast, the Kayin People's Party is found mainly in Yangon and the Delta and is a party of former government officials. It has support among those urban Karen in the centre of the country who desire an accommodation with the state and the new government.

After inauguration of a quasi-civilian government, the KNU split again. This time it was after a group lead by the KNLA commander in chief, General Mutu Say Poe, inaugurated a liaison office in Hpa-an, the capital of Karen State. He and three other leaders were demoted for disloyalty to the KNU political leadership but reinstated after long talks in the lead-up to the KNU congress in November 2012. The congress resulted in a victory for the peace camp. The new chairman is General Mutu Say Poe while Naw Zipporah Sein is vice-chairman, Kwe Htoo Win is the general secretary, General Johnny is military chief of the KNLA and Saw Roger Khin, who was ousted in 2012, is now defence minister.[31] In all, this was a major victory for the peace camp but divisions remain and there is a concern that Mutu, who met President Thein Sein in January 2014, will accept the government's emphasis on development and foreign investments before a lasting peace is established (for

---

31. Naw Zipporah and the vice-chief General Saw Baw Kyaw He, commander of the strong 5th Brigade, represent the conservative faction. See *The Irrawaddy*, 31 December 2012 and 7 January 2013. See also *Karen News* (karennews.org), 2012–13.

fuller details, see p. 262ff.). The division inside KNU is also a divide between those with personal business interests and those who oppose big development projects.

In 2011, a Karen Affairs Committee was formed with more than 200 representatives from all Karen areas in order to advise the KNU in the negotiations, for example on the national census. This is led by U Kyaw Swa. Another important step to reconcile the internal disagreements among the Karen was taken in March 2013 when 400 delegates met in Hpa-an to discuss the peace process. Leaders who formerly refused even to meet seem to have joined this event. This meeting was followed by the formation of a 37-member Karen Unity and Peace Committee (or Consultations) (KUPC). The leader is a Buddhist monk, and the aim is to strengthen political unity and cooperation among the various organizations, including religious and military. Christian leaders such as Catholic Bishop Raymond saw Po Ray are also involved. This could be an important step towards internal reconciliation by including the opinions of civil organizations.[32]

CR

Four main themes can be deducted from this history:

1) Political and religious leadership is still deeply connected among the Karen. Charismatic leadership and personal loyalty are important. This has generated many internal conflicts and factionalism, even violent struggles. Ethnic unity is considered crucial for a political resolution and agreement with the government. Those who differ from the KNU leadership and act on their own are thus often branded as 'traitors' incompatible with the cause. Besides these internal dissentions, there is a deep mistrust towards the government and all Burmans. This mistrust and related fears have to be taken into consideration. To overcome them is an important dimension of the whole peace process.

2) The longer the conflict and the more violence used, the more emphasis there is on ethnic incompatibilities. The result is that the conflicting parties have more difficulties in creating mutual trust and in reaching a sustainable peace.

---

32. *Karen News*, 4 April 2013.

3) A meta-narrative of political deprivation, suffering and victimhood has come to dominate the political discourse among the Karen. For many, it has also become a dominant element of their Karen identity.[33]

4) The KNU, DKBA and BGF as well as minor groups depend on a war economy. Essentially, by force of arms they practice a predatory form of capitalism to obtain more arms, raising funds from illegal logging, drugs,[34] trade, taxation and use of forced labour. Thus, greed has perhaps become as important as ethnic grievances.[35]

5) All informants interviewed in 2012–14 agree that mistrust is the main obstacle to a nation-wide ceasefire and political resolution of the long conflict.

Resolution of the conflict?

After a meeting of 18 ethnic armed groups in Laiza, Kachin State, in October 2013 there is a hope for a more lasting nationwide ceasefire but to date this has not been reached. At issue is if a national political dialogue and settlement should precede any ceasefire. The United Nationalities Federal Council (UNFC), the main organization representing the armed ethnic groups, has outlined 11 points for agreement, among these the recognition of the Panglong Agreement, the formation of a federal army (vehemently opposed by the Tatmadaw), the building of mutual trust, basic rights for ethnic nationalities, peace and a political dialogue.

However, negotiations between the state and the armed groups are not enough. It is urgent that the peace process also includes civilian community organizations – in particular the religious movements and denominations that are the fundament of Karen civil society. A ceasefire is urgent but it must encompass a plan for negotiation of a future political settlement and offer a clear prospect of local autonomy in Karen State and in major Karen constituencies elsewhere. A federation is a future project that has to be carefully prepared and agreed upon by all

---

33. See Violet Cho (2009), Zoyah Phan (2010) and Falla (1991). Karen identity construction in history is discussed in Harridan (2002).

34. Local commanders of some groups are known to be involved in the drug trade and the KKO leadership, which opposes drug trafficking, was severely embarrassed when the DKBA-5 leader was indicted for trafficking by Thai authorities in 2012. The KNU has an active drug-eradication programme.

35. For a more detailed discussion of violence, victimhood and the problems in reconciling this long conflict, see Gravers (2012).

those involved. A third, neutral party should be involved in the ongoing negotiations.[36] Security for civilians, IDPs and returning refugees must be provided and land rights and livelihoods secured. Land grabbing in Karen State, as elsewhere, is a major problem that could destabilize the whole peace process. Thus, economic security and a secure livelihood for civilians as well as for combatants are crucial.

The internal conflict within the KNU and the conflicts between Karen groups, parties and leaders must be addressed. Convening an all-Burma Karen reconciliation conference might be the initial step needed to create confidence and help the different actors reach an agreement on what unites them in a democratic future; it might even help them agree that diversity in religion and politics is a part of a democratic polity. Some Karen politicians hope that all Karen parties can be merged with the KNU if it is legalized as a political party. This is seen as a necessity in order to strengthen ethnic interests vis-à-vis a potential NLD landslide victory in 2015. But this could also mean more communal politics and less focus on the overall democratic process. Establishing some kind of provisional justice by acknowledging such crimes as rape and land grabbing is crucial for creating confidence. Finally, the sufferings and victimization of all sides must be listened to and given official recognition. Two generations Karen have never experienced peace but perhaps the next generation will have a chance.

References

Adas, Michael (1982) 'Bandits, Monks and Pretender Kings: Patterns of Peasant Resistance and Politics in Colonial Burma 1826–1941'. In R.P. Weller and S.E. Guggenheim (eds): *Power and Protest in the Countryside: Studies of Rural Unrest in Asia, Europe, and Latin America.* Durham, NC: Duke University Press.

Arendt, Hannah (1970). *On Violence.* Boston, MA: Houghton Mifflin Harcourt.

Aung-Thwin, Maitri (2008) 'Structuring Revolt: Communities Interpretation in the Historiography of the Saya San Rebellion'. *Journal of Southeast Asian Studies,* vol. 39(2): 297–317.

Aung-Thwin, Michael (1985) 'The "Pacification" of Burma: Order without Meaning'. *Journal of Southeast Asian Studies,* Vol. 16(2): 245–61.

Bigandet, Poul A. (1887). *An Outline of the History of the Catholic Burmese*

---

36. On the peace negotiations, see 'Peace-building in Myanmar', p. 223ff.

Mission from the Year 1720 to 1887. Rangoon, Hanthawaddy Press (Reprinted by Bibliotheca Orientalis 1996, Bangkok.).

Brubaker, Rogers (2004) *Ethnicity without Groups*. Cambridge, MA: Harvard University Press.

Bunker, Alonzo (1902) *Soo Thah. A Tale of the Making of the Karen Nation*. New York: Flemming H. Revell Company.

Cho, Naw Violet (2009) 'News Media and Burmese Diaspora Identities in New Zealand'. B.A. (Hons) dissertation, School of Communication Studies, Auckland University of Technology.

Falla, Jonathan (1991) *True Love and Bartholomew. Rebels on the Burmese Border*. Cambridge: Cambridge University Press.

Furnivall, John S. (1956) *Colonial Policy and Practice. A Comparative Study of Burma and Netherlands India*. NY: New York University Press. (First edition in 1948).

Government of the Union of Burma (1949). *Burma and the Insurrections*. Rangoon: Government of the Union of Burma Publications.

Gravers, Mikael (1996) 'The Making of a Karen Nation'. In Stein Tønnesson and Hans Antlöv (eds): *Asian Forms of the Nation*. Richmond, Surrey: Curzon Press, pp. 237–269.

——— (2001) 'Cosmology, Prophets, and Rebellion among the Buddhist Karen in Burma'. *Moussons* no. 4: 3–31.

——— (2012a) "When will the Karen King Arrive? Karen Royal Imaginary in Thailand and Burma." *Journal of Southeast Asian Studies*, vol. 43(2): 340–363.

——— (2012 b). 'Disorder as order: The ethno-nationalist struggle of the Karen in Burma. A discussion of the dynamics of an ethnicized civil war and its historical roots'. (Paper presented at the workshop, 'Can Political Reforms bring Peace to Myanmar?' Organized by PRIO and Myanmar Egress in Yangon, 12–14 October 2012.)

——— (forthcoming) 'Religious Imaginary as an Alternative Social and Moral Order – Karen Buddhism Across the Thai–Burma Border'. In Alexander Horstmann (ed.): *Building Noah's Ark: Refugees, Migrants and Religious Communities*. New York, Palgrave-Macmillan.

——— (ed.) (2007) *Exploring Ethnic Diversity in Burma*. Copenhagen, NIAS Press.

Harridan, Jessica (2002) '"Making a Name for Themselves": Karen Identity and the Politicization of Ethnicity in Burma'. *Journal of the Burma Society*, vol. 7: 84–144.

Herbert, Patricia (1982) 'The Hsaya San Rebellion (1930–1932) Reappraised'. *Working Papers*, Centre of Southeast Asian Studies, Monash University, Melbourne.

Horstmann, Alexander (2011) 'Sacred Networks and Struggles among the Karen Baptists Across the Thailand-Burma Border'. *Moussons*, no. 17: 85–104.

Ikeda, Kazuto (2007) 'The Myaungmya Incident during the Japanese Occupation of Burma: Karens and Shwe Tun Kya'. In Kei Nemoto (ed.): *Reconsidering the Japanese Military Occupation in Burma (1941–45)*. Research Institute for Languages and Cultures of Asia and Africa, Tokyo University of Foreign Studies.

Kalyvas, Stathis (2000) 'The Logic of Violence in Civil War: Theory and Preliminary Results'. Centro de Estudios Avanzados en Ciencias Sociales. Working Paper.

Karen National Union (1992) *The Karens and their Struggle for Freedom*. Kawthoolei.

Mason, Ellen B. (1862) *Civilizing Mountain Men: Sketches of Mission Work Among the Karen*. London: James Nisbet & Co.

McMahon, A.R. (1876) *The Karens of the Golden Chersonese*. London: Harrison.

Morrison, Ian (1946) *Grandfather Longlegs. The Life and Gallant Death of Major H.P. Seagrim*. London: Faber and Faber Ltd.

Ni Ni Myint (1983) *Burma's Struggle Against British Imperialism (1885–1895)*. Rangoon: The University Press.

Phan, Zoya (2010 [2009]). *Little Daughter. A Memoir of Survival in Burma and the West*. London: Pocket Books.

Schmidt, Bettina E. and Ingo W. Schröder (2001) 'Introduction'. *Anthropology of Violence and Conflict*. London: Routledge, pp. 1–24.

Silverstein (1987) 'Ethnic Protest in Burma: Its Causes and Solution'. In: R. Ghose (ed.): *Protest Movements in South and South-East Asia. Traditional and Modern Idioms of Expression*. Centre of Asian Studies, University of Hong Kong, pp. 81–94.

Smeaton, Donald M. (1887) *The Loyal Karens of Burma*. London: Kegan Paul, Trench and Co.

Smith, Martin (1999 [1991]) *Burma. Insurgency and the Politics of Ethnicity* (second revised edition). London: Zed Books.

South, Ashley (2011) *Burma's Longest War. Anatomy of the Karen Conflict*. Transnational Institute and Burma Centre Netherlands, Amsterdam (www.burmacentrum.nl).

TBBC (2011) 'Displacement and Poverty in South East Burma/Myanmar'. Thailand Burma Border Consortium, Bangkok (www.tbbc.org).

Thawnghmung, Ardeth Maung (2008) *The Karen Revolution in Burma: Diverse Voices, Uncertain Ends*. Policy Studies 45. Washington, D.C.: East–West Center and Singapore: ISEAS.

———— 2012. The 'Other' Karen in Myanmar. Ethnic Minorities and the Struggle without Arms. Lanham, MD: Lexington Books.

Thoshikatsu, Ito (2007) 'Karen and the Kon-baung Polity in Myanmar'. *Acta Asiatica*, 92: 89–108.

Tinker, Hugh (1967) *The Union of Burma. A Study of the First Years of Independence*. Fourth Edition. Oxford: Oxford University Press.

———— (1983–84) *Burma: The Struggle for Independence 1944–48*. 2 Vols. London: Her Majesty's Stationery Office.

Universities Historical Research Centre (Yangon) (1999) *The 1947 Constitution and the Nationalities*. Volume 1. UHRC and Inwa Publishing House, Yangon. (Compiled by U Kyaw Win, U Mya Han, U Thein Hlaing and U Tun Aung Chain.)

Documents from colonial Burma

Baptist Missionary Magazine, Vol. 16, 1886.

FO 643/71 (1946) 'Notes on Various Karen Associations'. Public Record Office, Kew, London.

M/4/3023 'Karen's Political Future 1945–1947'. The Oriental and India Office Collections (OIOC), British Library, London.

M/4/2854. (1947). *Frontier Areas Committee of Enquiry*. OIOC, British Library, London.

Mss. Eur. E252/22. *Sir John Clague Collection*, OIOC, British Libray, London.

Mss. Eur. F. 169/20e. Rance Papers. OIOC, British Library, London.

M/4/2811 Panglong Conferences Burma 1946–47. OIOC, British Library, London.

MD/4004 vi. Oriental and India Office Collections, British Library, London.

The Karen in Myanmar's southeast – great hopes and many unresolved issues

Tim Schroeder and Alan Saw U

Introduction

The reform process in Myanmar, which over the past 2–3 years has led to many political and economic changes, has been positively welcomed by foreign governments, the international community and private sector. Government reforms in the economic sector, especially the introduction of an investor-friendly foreign investment law, have created great interest of the international business community. Consequently, Myanmar is now experiencing an influx of international aid and foreign investment.

Next to the introduction of political and economic reforms, the government has also taken first steps to resolve longstanding ethnic conflicts in the country, through signing ceasefire agreements with various ethnic armed groups (EAGs). A major achievement was the signing of a ceasefire agreement between the government and the Karen National Union (KNU) in January 2012, which has, for the time being, suspended the world's longest running civil war. As a result of the ceasefire agreement, the conditions for Karen populations living in the conflict-affected areas of southeast Myanmar have improved tremendously. They remain vulnerable, however, during their struggle to recover from the conflict.

While the government has heavily restricted project implementations by international aid agencies in the past, recent government reforms and ceasefire talks have opened up a new chapter for humanitarian and development aid in the region. As the situation continues to improve, more and more international donors and aid agencies are lining up to establish themselves in the region. Donors have pledged to provide sufficient funding for project implementations in the fields of humanitarian and development aid. Their engagement, however, has not been without controversy as many step prematurely into unknown territory. This rush is joined by local and international companies, which are waiting to tap into one of the country's most resource rich regions.

International aid and foreign investment can contribute to post-conflict reconstruction and development. However, it can also help escalate further ethnic conflict and fuel local grievances if aid interventions and business investments are not done in a responsible approach (do-no-harm) and transparent way to ensure optimum benefit to local populations. In order to effectively support the peace building process in Myanmar, international donors, aid agencies and international companies need to carefully analyse and understand the conflict situation, its dynamics and stakeholders.

Humanitarian and development dynamics

Karen-populated areas have seen decades of armed conflict between Burma/Myanmar-led governments and the KNU, with severe consequences on their daily lives. Poverty and displacement as well as human-rights abuses have been widespread across the region and almost become normality. The Border Consortium and its local partners estimate that there are still 89,000 internally displaced people (IDPs) within Karen State in addition to 130,000 mostly Karen refugees in nine camps on the Thai–Burmese border as of 2012.[1]

Humanitarian and development assistance in conflict-affected areas of southeast Myanmar has been limited for local and international agencies for many years. Only a handful of UN and INGO agencies have been able to operate in government-controlled areas, and here with heavy restrictions and under close government supervision. Humanitarian assistance to conflict-affected communities, such as IDP and host communities, has mainly been carried out by cross-border agencies from Thailand as well as local/faith-based agencies from inside Myanmar.

Local agencies operating from inside Myanmar consist mainly of Christian and Buddhist networks. These agencies work on a very low-

---

1.   The Border Consortium (2012).

profile level in order to avoid government repression and to maintain access to vulnerable populations in areas of ongoing armed conflict or ceasefire zones. Project implementations focus on humanitarian aid, such as medical care in the form of mobile health teams, supply of food rations, and small-scale development projects in the fields of water and sanitation (e.g. well renovation, gravity-flow system, provision of household latrine materials), education (e.g. teacher training, provision of teachers' stipends, school gear for primary students) and capacity building in the fields of agriculture and community mobilization. Next to working on a very low-profile level, organizations have been able to utilize their valuable networks and contacts in order to gain a certain degree of protection against government and EAG restraints. Christian faith-based organizations, for instance, might operate under the protection of influential local monks or receive permission by important local politicians to reach conflict-affected populations.

The recent ceasefire negotiations between the Myanmar government and various Karen armed groups have so far provided the greatest opportunity for peace in southeast Myanmar. This has also been acknowledged by the international donor community, which has pledged to support the peace process on the ground by funding of humanitarian and development projects. In the international community, however, only a few people are familiar with the protracted conflicts between successive Bamar-dominated central governments and the country's other ethnic groups.[2] The international donor community therefore needs to better understand the 'emerging political complexes' and conflict dynamics on the ground.

As the international community pays more attention to the southeast of Myanmar and pledges more funds to the region, the interest of international organizations to enter this area has significantly increased. Where funding and coordination among humanitarian actors has been limited to the southeast of Myanmar in the past, various workshops, information sessions and coordination meetings have been held in recent months by different organizations and donors in Yangon, with dozens of INGOs attending. The term 'gold rush' to the southeast has become a frequently used term, when referring to the rush of international organizations to enter these formerly closed regions and secure fund-

2. Saw U (2007): 219.

ing for their operations. The absence of representatives of local NGOs from southeast Myanmar, as well as other states and regions, from coordination meetings is a striking phenomenon and shows the neglect of involving local civil-society organizations and communities in project planning and implementations from the start. While there is some fruitful cooperation between INGOs and local Karen organizations, Karen civil society actors as well as Karen politicians have criticized the lack of information sharing and cooperation by international organizations over the past year. A civil society leader described current coordination among donors as 'a loose cannon', without proper strategic planning and consultation.[3] Civil-society organizations have served their communities for decades under extremely difficult circumstances and should be included in finding best solutions for conflict-affected communities and contribute to post-conflict reconstruction in the southeast of Myanmar.

As INGOs are not able to reach all conflict-affected communities, especially IDPs in remote ceasefire zones, they should partner with Karen organizations from both sides of the border. A convergence process between organizations from inside Burma/Myanmar and organizations from the Thai–Myanmar border should also be supported in order to avoid conflict between these groups. INGOs from within Myanmar will gradually expand their operations into territories served by Karen organizations, many of whom are aligned with the KNU and are deeply rooted in their communities. Cooperation and coordination between these groups are therefore absolutely essential. In fact, INGOs can encourage the emergence of community-based organizations (CBOs) and local NGOs in Karen and other ethnic states. Donors and INGOs should promote increased coordination among local NGOs and CBOs and between civil-society groups and international agencies. More strategic planning and organizational development services to local NGOs and CBOs should be provided, not only in Yangon but also in ethnic states.[4]

A great challenge that UN and INGO agencies will face is the recruitment of suitable field staff for their project implementations. The limited amount of experienced Karen personnel, such as doctors, engineers, project managers, etc., will make recruitment of individuals from

---

3.   Personal interview, 24 February 2013.
4.   South (2008): 46.

other ethnic groups necessary. While there is a decent amount of highly experienced NGO workers within Myanmar, there is only a limited number with experience in Karen State and the southeast of Myanmar in general. Conflict-affected Karen populations regard the Myanmar government as largely illegitimate and have experienced the Myanmar army as a predatory and violent force. Consequently, they show deep mistrust and fear towards non-Karen-speaking outsiders and especially ethnic Bamar people, as they identify them with the government and army. These communities have been victims of brutal counter-insurgency warfare and various forms of human-rights abuses in the past. Often, Karen villagers avoid receiving treatment at government health facilities and refrain from receiving immunization for their children from government mobile health clinics during health campaigns. Karen EAGs have also accused ethnic Bamar people of being government informants or spies. INGOs should therefore be very careful in their project implementations and fully inform EAGs about their project activities as well as project staff. Consequently, trust and peace-building must be an essential part of project activities and must be made a priority in any implementation.

While more and more INGOs are accessing the southeast and UN organizations are expanding their operations, the government has made it clear that it will closely monitor all agencies' activities. They will have to report frequently about their activities and be fully transparent about their ground implementations. INGOs that have contacted the KNU for project implementations in mixed control areas have also been informed that they need to report monthly to the relevant Karen Departments (e.g. the Karen Department of Health and Welfare, KDHW) about their project implementations.[5]

The current situation is a unique opportunity for the international community to cooperate with local Karen organizations on project planning and implementation. Local NGOs, including faith-based organizations, possess a unique understanding of the situation on the ground in Karen State, including conflict dynamics, populations and political stakeholders. However, local civil society leaders feel excluded from the current humanitarian aid and development dynamics and are not always informed about recent funding opportunities and implemen-

---

5. Personal Interview with an INGO employee, 30 January 2013.

tations. One-sided aid interventions by international organizations in partnership with the government could do more harm than good in the long run. Therefore, the international community needs to realize that, in order to foster peace-building in ethnic states, all assistance needs to proceed in a participatory manner and that international actors must not dictate solutions imposed from outside the country or by Bamars on ethnic minorities.[6]

Involving civil society and local populations in the peace process

Peace-making efforts in the conflict between successive governments and the KNU have not been limited to recent efforts but show a long history. Most significantly, in the past it has been religious leaders who have been at the forefront in trying to mediate between the government and KNU. In the years from 1948 to the present, there has been series of attempts to resolve the issues of conflict between the two parties.

The first attempt in building peace was made in 1948 by Archbishop Francis Ah Mya, the very first national bishop, a Karen of the Anglican Church in Burma, at the request of the government when armed clashes broke out between the KNU and government troops. The attempt was shortly followed by the appeal of the KNU sent by Saw Ba U Gyi and Thra Saw Tha Din, which resulted in a commission headed by Sir U Ba U for negotiation. A third attempt occurred in 1949 following an outbreak of fighting at Insein Township in Yangon and was designed to end the fighting. A fourth attempt was made in January 1960 in Rangoon following the elections when General Ne Win took over from Prime Minister U Nu in a caretaker government.

The fifth attempt at serious negotiations occurred following the coup d'etat by General Ne Win and lasted from October until the second week of November 1963 in Rangoon/Yangon. Saw Hunter Tha Hmwe, a respected Christian, formed the Karen Revolutionary Council (KRC), a splinter group of the KNU, in order to engage in peace talks with the government. A peace treaty was signed on 12 March 1964 between the KRC and the Burmese military government. The KRC included well-known Christian Karen leaders such as Saw Ba Tun, P'doh Wareegyaw, General Ohn Pe, Brigadeer Lin Htin and Saw Truman.

---

6. Callahan (2007): xv.

The sticking point in all those attempts is clearly that the Burmese government and the KNU had diametrically opposed views with regard to autonomy. Autonomy from the government's viewpoint would have allowed for only local self-government with ultimate control over the approval of personnel to head the Karen state as well as control over the finances too be allotted thereto. To the KNU this provided no bases for self-determination and without control over its own territory, no freedom was possible.[7]

After a long period of silence, an attempt was again made in 1991 by the late Reverend Andrew Mya Han, the former General Secretary of the Myanmar Council of Churches and later Archbishop of the Anglican Church. His visit to the KNU headquarters resulted in the formation of a five-member mediator group, comprising leading Karen Christian figures. They served as go-betweens during the four rounds of talks between the regime and KNU from 1995 to 1997. Unfortunately, the talks broke down after the fourth round.

The formation of the Karen State Peace Committee (KPC) in 1999 had been a positive sign in bringing religious leaders together. This consisted of four Karen Buddhist monks and five Christian clerics, and was headed by a Karen Buddhist monk, the Venerable U Pyinya Thami, and Bishop Saw Daniel Hoi Kyin of the Hpa-an Diocese of the Anglican Church, who had been working on establishing peace between the KNU and Burma/Myanmar government. Its objective had been 'to work for peace-building through the leadership of the Karen religious leaders and to work with other existing Karen civil-society organizations for the emergence of peaceful Karen communities'.[8] Religious leaders are highly respected by their local Karen communities and able to influence and mobilize them. They have often protected local communities from armed conflict and exploitation and have created havens of peace and refuge.[9]

The unfailing efforts of this five-member mediator group between 1997 and 2003 resulted in a visit by General Saw Bo Mya of the KNU to Yangon in 2004, where a gentlemen's ceasefire agreement was reached. The agreement however was short-lived due to the untimely death of

7.   See Klein (1995) for fuller details.
8.   Saw U (2007), p. 228.
9.   A more comprehensive account of the above-described emerging political complexes can be found in South (2011).

General Saw Bo Mya and the purge and jailing of General Khin Nyunt, the chief architect of various ceasefire accords and then Premier Minister. The ensuing period of silence and stalemate in the ceasefire process for a couple of years was a true nightmare for Karen people who had been looking forward to at least a partial normalization of the national situation that would have been achieved by a ceasefire between the KNU and the military regime.

It was a moment of great joy for the Karen communities when the government and the KNU officially signed a ceasefire agreement on 12 March 2012. The first meeting between the KNU delegation and the Union-Level Peace Delegation was held on 6 April 2012 in Yangon. At the meeting, an agreement to be implemented by both sides was adopted for the realization of a ceasefire in practice involving trust building and a guarantee for security of the people.

After the ceasefire talks between the KNU and the government's Union Level Peace Team, on several occasions the KNU has met with community representatives, civil-society organizations and religious leaders in order to consult on the current ceasefire processes. The meetings were not only held with both the religious leaders and key figures of the Karen and ethnic-based official political parties but also with the Ministers of Karen Ethnic Affairs of Yangon, Ayeyarwaddy, Bago and Tanintharyi Regions and Mon State. Moreover, there has been a series of meetings and consultations between the Karen Armed Groups and Karen political parties for mutual sharing and edification. These meetings and forums have resulted in the formation of a nationwide 37-member Karen Unity and Peace Committee (KUPC) at the very first Pan-Karen Assembly held on 29–30 March 2013 in Hpa-an, the capital of Karen State. The KUPC comprises elders from various Karen communities, leaders of civil-society organizations, religious institutions, political parties, ministers of Karen Ethnic Affairs, members of parliament and key leaders of the KNU.[10]

The KUPC is now in the process of convening Karen community consultations in various regions in Myanmar with a view to collect opinions and suggestions from the local communities regarding issues on peace process and its consolidation. All the feedback and findings will be compiled and shared with both the government and the KNU. It

10. See Weekly Eleven News of 25 November 2013 for more details.

remains to be seen if the KUPC will be able to speak on behalf of their communities and encourage peaceful ways in dealing with conflict.

Today, all Karen EAGs have signed individual ceasefire agreements with the Union-level government. These groups include the Karen National Union, Democratic Karen Buddhist Army and KNU/KNLA Peace Council. Most battalions of the DKBA and all of the troops of the Karen Peace Force were incorporated into the Tatmadaw command structure in August 2010 and became known as Border Guard Forces (BGFs). Ceasefire groups control significant amounts of territory along the Thailand–Burma Border, with thousands of people under their control. However, several areas are still being contested between different non-state armed groups as well as the government, represented by the Burmese Army. Till today, Karen-populated areas remain highly militarized, with much of the political power still in the hands of the military and EAGs. Karen political parties joined the group of political actors in 2010 after the nationwide elections. Since then, they have been able to use the space created by recent political reforms to give voice to their communities and advocate on their behalf. Until the beginning of 2013 however, they were not involved in the peace process as mediators but only granted occasional observer status at ceasefire talks.

The KUPC is convinced that the ceasefire talks between the Burma/Myanmar government and KNU in 2012 represented the best opportunity to resolve the longstanding conflict. The talks established some degree of trust among the stakeholders and conditions for conflict-affected communities have improved.[11] However, huge challenges and obstacles remain on the way to establish a sustainable peace process. Ceasefire talks have only been conducted between the EAG and representatives of the Myanmar Peace Making Working Committee, mainly Minister Aung Min and representatives of the Myanmar Peace Centre (MPC), on individual basis. The MPC is a government-organized non-governmental organization (GONGO) and its main function is to handle logistical matters related to the peace process.[12] While most observers believe that Aung Min and his team are serious about the peace process, questions remain about their ability to deliver, specifically whether the Myanmar

---

11. See Weekly Eleven News of 25 November 2013 for more details.
12. See Jolliffe (2013).

Army is willing to follow the peace process.[13] For example, various clashes were reported between government-led BGFs and KNU and/or DKBA troops during 2012–13. In addition, government troops have been accused of resupplying and fortifying their camps and outposts during ceasefire negotiations. Until today, the Myanmar Army has not withdrawn any of its troops from Karen EAG territories even though this is needed to build trust and confidence in the ceasefire process and bring relief to local populations.

It has to be noted that the KNU is still regarded as an illegal organization and the unlawful association law originally used by the Myanmar/Burma government to ban the KNU is still in force. It is no wonder that the Karen people in local communities are afraid to associate themselves with the KNU for they could be arrested any time according to that law. This includes officially registered Karen political parties. The result is that instead of serving as centres for discussion and resolution of the political and military conflicts during the early stage of the ceasefire processes, the KNU/KNLA liaison offices have merely become havens frequented by business people and personnel of the special police branch, the government's intelligence unit. Re-defining the roles and re-enforcing the actions of the liaison offices of the KNU/KNLA and other EAG as avenues for political negotiation fronts is crucial.[14]

Despite the efforts of the KUPC and Karen civil-society organizations, outside observers have noticed that there is a lack of grassroots participation in the ceasefire processes, also of involvement by women. The challenge is thus how to empower, encourage and enable local populations who have been the victims of armed conflict to engage in the current ceasefire and subsequent peace processes. It has also not been decided who will effectively monitor the ceasefires at the grassroots level.

The greatest hope of the Karen people in Burma/ Myanmar is that there can emerge an official consolidation of the ceasefire agreement followed up by a process of negotiated settlement of underlying political differences.

---

13. South (2012): 14.
14. Indeed, Saw Greh Moo (2014) warns of a developing economic war.

Economic dynamics

Most parts of the southeast of Myanmar have experienced armed conflict in the recent past as well as conflict-related instability. This instability has profound implications for the economic development of the region. Due to decades of armed conflict, economic development is often non-existent in areas controlled by EAGs and limited in government areas. While areas under DKBA control show some signs of economic development due to a previous ceasefire, including paved roads and brick buildings, the physical infrastructure in KNU-related areas is limited or non-existent. After decades of armed conflict and underdevelopment, there is a great need for economic development, education/vocational training and job creation. Much of the rural Karen population are subsistence farmers with day-to-day survival their prime concern. The militarization of Karen-populated areas has limited private investments by local villagers and reduced them to a minimum. Conflict-related instability has therefore great consequences on both the private and public sector.

Local populations have suffered the most from armed conflicts in the past. Not only have they been victims of atrocities and war crimes; conflict has also kept them in deep poverty. Militarization of the region and its characteristics (such as displacement, forced labour, illegal taxation, loss of livelihoods and restriction of movement) have limited people's ability to engage in livelihood activities and make investments for the future. In order to cope with this situation, thousands of Karen people have crossed the border into Thailand to seek better job opportunities to support their families back home. The situation since the ceasefire of 2012 has however tremendously improved for local populations on the ground. People are now free to travel and engage in livelihood activities.

Recent political and economic changes have attracted many foreign businesses, governments and international financial institutions into Myanmar. Most of the country's natural resources are located in its borderlands, home to many ethnic groups, who have suffered from decades of armed conflicts. These regions have caught the attention of foreign investors and are considered to be Asia's last frontier. While many large-scale projects are already in the process of being implemented, others are currently in the planning stage. Various conferences on investment possibilities have been conducted in Yangon, with foreign investors rushing into the former capital. Topics of conferences have included investment possibilities in the sectors of oil and gas, mining, rubber plantations, commercial farming, etc. However, little information is given to investors about the complex situation of many of the borderlands, and how they are currently recovering from armed conflicts and their overall socio-political situation remains fragile. Areas under Karen EAG control are some of the borderlands that potentially will attract large amounts of foreign investment. The Greater Mekong Sub-region initiative of the Asian Development Bank, mainly the Asia Highway from Myawaddy to Hpa-an as well as the East–West Economic Corridor will change southeast Myanmar dramatically. In addition, special economic zones are planned in Hpa-an, Myawaddy and the Three Pagoda Pass area, with hydro-power dams planned on the Salween River as well.

Ethnic conflicts in Myanmar cannot be labelled as 'new wars' that are only based on control of natural resources (greed) rather than competing political ideologies (grievances). However, the government and EAGs have increasingly battled over natural resources since the 1990s.[15] While many motives of conflict actors for reaching ceasefires might not be limited to humanitarian assistance for conflict affected populations, war fatigue, establishment of a political dialogue, etc., but also include aspirations of profiting from business opportunities, especially in the exploitation of natural resources.[16] Lasting ceasefires might have several dramatic consequences for the economy and local populations, if large-scale development projects and trade are not done in a transparent and participatory way by the government and EAG. Lessons should be drawn from previous ceasefires in Northern Burma/Myanmar during the 1990s. While the ceasefires had positive impacts for populations in terms of safety and security, the truces provided space for large-scale unsustainable investment and natural resources extractions, causing environmental damage and loss of local livelihoods.[17]

Local DKBA (now BGF) commanders and their families have been the ones who have most profited from the ceasefire arrangements made in 1994 in Karen State. Large amounts of profits were generated through mostly illegal resource extraction, such as mining and logging, agricul-

---

15. Smith (2007): 3.
16. South (2012): 26.
17. Kramer and Woods (2012): 78.

ture plantations and the illegal trade across the Thailand–Myanmar border. Hpa-an has seen an increase of large housing constructions and the establishment of companies and businesses by these groups and their related families. Rural communities in DKBA- and BGF-controlled areas, however, remain for the most part in deep poverty.

One of the larger-scale development projects in Karen State is the Hpa-an Industrial Zone on the way to Hlaingbwe. This is still under construction with only a few companies having set up factories and starting operation. Local villagers have reported of forced relocation and land-grabbing in relation to the establishment of the industrial zone. Hpa-an residents fear that wages of labour-intensive production (e.g. garment manufacture) will not attract local Karen populations, who will rather continue to seek better-paid employment in Thailand, but will attract migrants from the Dry Zone and other parts of Burma/Myanmar. Crucial issues that will be faced by investors to successfully operate the special industrial zone are the lack of a one-stop service, an effective zone management, including power and water supply, water treatment and road infrastructure.[18] Due to its strategic location on the East–West Economic Corridor, the Hpa-an Industrial Zone might have a better future than the neighbouring Mawlamyine Industrial Zone, which has lost much of its importance in recent years.

Another large-scale development project is the planned Hatgyi Dam, which is supposed to be the first of several dams to be built on the Salween River. An agreement between Burma/Myanmar's Ministry of Electric Power, the Electricity Generating Authority of Thailand (EGAT), and China's Sinohydro was signed in 2006. With a construction cost of around $1 billion USD, the dam would have an installed capacity of 1,200 MW. Most generated electricity would go to Thailand, however. The construction preparations have led to increased militarization and armed-conflict in the area. In March 2011, for instance, six villages with a population of around 1,000 were displaced due to renewed fighting between the conflict parties along the Salween River.[19] The KNU and Karen civil-society organizations have frequently called for suspension of the dam project, which would have a severe impact on local communities and the environment. In addition, the site of the

18.   Zaw and Kudo (2011).
19.   Assessment report, 16 March 2011.

dam is strategically important for the KNU. Dozens of Karen villages will need to be relocated from the dam's floodplain, while the dam will also have an impact on the riverine eco-system and people's livelihoods. Construction of the dam was suspended in 2007 due to violent conflict between the KNU and Myanmar military around the dam site. While the current ceasefire process has allowed EGAT to resume the construction preparations for the Hatgyi Dam, the situation around the dam remains tense and heavily militarized. A conflict between an alliance of the KNU/KNLA 5th Brigade and the DKBA against government troops could have a severe impact on the local population and the overall ceasefire process.

Large-scale development projects such as the Hatgyi Dam construction, which were planned under the former military regime, need to be re-evaluated and handled in a transparent way in order to avoid further conflict. All activities should be suspended until a common decision is made by all involved stakeholders including local communities. It has been Karen civil-society organizations and other conscientious lobbying civil-society groups that have voiced their concerns on topics such as large-scale economic projects (hydro-power dams, cement factories, etc.), land-grabbing, mining and logging in post-conflict regions over the past year, and have urged both the government and the KNU to currently suspend such projects and focus on the current peace process and involve local organizations in the decision making process. It is evident that the major grievances of the local people in KNU-related areas are increased militarization and violence around large-scale development projects, lack of ownership and management over natural resources, land confiscations as well as negative environmental and social effects of development projects on local communities.

Such voices of grievance, however, are often ignored by the government and businesses have already moved into conflict-sensitive areas. Despite the ongoing ceasefire talks and preparation process for refugee repatriation, the government has also started to confiscate land in order to lease it to local and foreign investors.[20] It is also quite remarkable that local and national governments have already granted local businesses and their foreign partners business concessions and access to conflict-

---

20. 'Burma based Karen Organizations concerned over massive land grab', *Karen News*, 26 November 2012.

affected areas while local NGOs and INGOs have been denied access to displaced populations in the same areas. Companies, however, are not able to enter conflict areas without the permission of both the government and EAGs.

As many areas are contested by different Karen EAGs and the government, such business endeavours are likely to fuel conflict. Frequent clashes between the Tatmadaw-aligned BGF and units from the KNLA 5th Brigade and DKBA units in Southern Hpa-pun Township can mostly be traced back to a struggle for control of territory and business interests in the mining sector.[21]

The government believes that, if economic conditions have improved for the Karen communities, they will no longer wage wars of resistance against the Union. From the very beginning, the motives of the government to conclude ceasefires have been all about business and profit-making projects. It is grounded more in economic and business interests than on any grand strategy to find a solution to political problems. Hence, local and foreign companies have been part of the 'emerging political complex' as well, and have been able to extract high profits during times of conflict.[22]

Concluding remarks

Ceasefire talks between the Burma/Myanmar government and Karen EAGs, mainly the KNU, have been a positive first step in establishing more trust between the negotiation parties. Fighting has decreased significantly between the conflict parties in recent months and the security and safety of conflict-affected communities have improved. However, many populations in Karen State remain vulnerable to conflict-related human-rights abuses. Another concern is the role of the Tatmadaw and its willingness to follow the current peace process. So far, the Myanmar military has not accepted the KNU-proposed 'code of conduct' and has not withdrawn any troops from EAG-controlled territories.

---

21. On 11 February 2013, a truck from a construction company that was erecting buildings at a BGF outpost at Kadaing Di, Southern Hpa-pun Township, hit an anti-tank mine at Way Shan village while collecting river sand at the Yuzalin River. Construction workers had been warned by local villagers not to use the road. The incident left four workers dead and one severely injured.

22. See especially Saw Greh Moo (2014). The concept of an 'emerging political complex' is employed by Callahan (2007).

The political and economic reforms, as well as current ceasefire talks have opened up a new chapter for humanitarian aid and development in KNU-related areas. The international community has responded positively by pledging funds for humanitarian aid and the recovery of conflict-affected communities. As international donors, INGOs and businesses move into the region, they need to be aware of the 'emerging political complex' on the ground, a situation that has been a reality for decades.

To effectively contribute to the peace process and development in Karen-populated areas, it is crucial that these newcomers work closely together with Karen civil society actors, such as CBOs and local NGOs, as well as populations at the grassroots level. All strategic planning and consultations should be done in a participatory way and lead to the strengthening and empowerment of local communities and networks. Currently, local communities that have suffered for decades are often not consulted or included in decision-making processes and are excluded from ongoing ceasefire talks. It is these civil society actors, however, who have assisted their communities under extremely difficult circumstances for decades.

The southeast of Myanmar is entering into a new phase of investment and economic development, as the country opens up to the international community. Foreign investment in the form of regional infrastructure projects as well as natural resource extractions is being planned or already under implementation. While KNU-related areas are in desperate need of economic development, it is necessary to ensure that foreign and local investments in conflict-affected areas will not create new grievances among local communities and bring about new conflicts. In fact, current economic development and investment plans should not be implemented apart from the ceasefire process but be included in the agenda of ongoing peace talks. Any failure to do so will have negative consequences on conflict resolution and – ultimately – on local populations.

The conflicts in KNU-related areas have had severe consequences for local populations over the last six decades and will take many more years to be resolved. Ceasefire agreements are a first step but, to end the conflict, much more needs to be done. The peace process needs to continue with an inclusive political dialogue at the national level, one that addresses main ethnic grievances and aspirations.

Only if it is possible to establish a new political culture that is free of deep mistrust and open to negotiation, dialogue and compromise will the country be able to develop socially, politically and economically. This is especially true for the relationship between ethnic minorities and ethnic Bamar but also for the relationship of ethnic minorities with each other.

References

Callahan, Mary B. (2007) *Political Authority in Burma's Ethnic Minority States: Devolution, Occupation, and Coexistence.* Washington, DC: East–West Center Washington.

Gravers, Mikael (ed.) (2007) *Exploring Ethnic Diversity in Burma.* Copenhagen: NIAS Press.

Jolliffe, Kim (2013) 'People's War: People's Peace: How Can International Peacebuilders Facilitate Reconciliation of the KNU Conflict and Address Local Security Concerns?' MA Dissertation, King's College War Studies Department.

Klein, Harold E. (1995) 'The Karen People of Burma: Their Search for Freedom and Justice'. Unpublished.

Kramer, Tom and Kevin Woods (2012) *Financing Dispossession: China's Opium Substitution Programme in Northern Burma.* Amsterdam: Transnational Institute.

Saw Greh Moo (2014) 'Caught in a Two-Front War in Post-Ceasefire Karen State'. Salween Institute for Public Policy: http://www.salweeninstitute.org/home---two-front-war.html.

Saw U, Alan. (2007) 'Reflections on Confidence-building and Cooperation among Ethnic Groups in Myanmar: A Karen Case Study'. In N. Ganesan and Kyaw Yin Hlaing (eds), *Myanmar: State, Society and Ethnicity.* Singapore: Institute for Southeast Asian Studies, 2007.

Smith, Martin (2007) *State of Strife: The Dynamics of Ethnic Conflict in Burma.* Washington, DC: East–West Center Washington.

South, Ashley (2008) *Civil Society in Burma: The Development of Democracy amidst Conflict.* Washington, DC: East–West Center Washington.

—— (2012) *Prospects for Peace in Myanmar: Opportunities and Threats.* Oslo: Peace Research Institute Oslo.

The Border Consortium (2012) 'Changing Realities, Poverty and Displacement in Southeast Burma/Myanmar'. Bangkok: TBC.

Zaw, Myinmo and Toshihior Kudo (2011) 'A Study on Economic Corridors and Industrial Zones, Ports, Metropolitan and Alternative Roads in Myanmar'. In Masami Ishida (ed.), Intra- and Inter-City Connectivity in the Mekong Region. Bangkok: Bangkok Research Center, IDE-JETRO, BRCR Report No. 6, 2011.

Ready to defend the people – new KNLA recruits (photo courtesy of KNU/Facebook)

'If they come again ...'

In November 2013 in the Tanintharyi Region, a column of Myanmar Army troops set out on a patrol to the surrounding jungle areas. Its objective was to enter a formerly closed and so-called black area under the control of the Karen National Union (KNU). Previously heavily contested and mostly inaccessible, the area had seen an increase in stability since the KNU–government ceasefire in 2012. This stability and the increase of trust and confidence in the peace process that followed encouraged a Karen IDP community to rebuild its former village in the area. With the assistance of an NGO consortium and funding from international donors, the IDP community was able to do this in an impressive way. The decision to return home, however, had not been an easy one. Only half of the population had so far returned; the rest of the community waited in hiding site to see how the peace process matured.

As the Army column entered KNU-controlled areas, it became evident that the soldiers would pass through the village along the way. Realizing the impact of the presence of a Myanmar Army column in the area, local KNU administrators pleaded with the commanding officers not to enter the area or the village as this would create fear among the villagers. Their plea was ignored and the Army column continued its patrol. Realizing the tense situation, the KNU administrator warned both the villagers and the local Karen National Defence Organization (KNDO) before the arrival of the Tatmadaw column. KNDO soldiers decided not to engage the intruders, as probably this would have led to increased fighting in the area with devastating consequences for local population, but to avoid confrontation.

The news of the imminent arrival of Tatmadaw troops in the village led many Karen villagers to flee their homes. From a safe distance in the surrounding hills, they watched the patrol as it passed by. Even though the overall situation was contained, it left villagers in doubt about the overall peace process and the intentions of the Myanmar Army. The incident surely did not increase the trust and confidence of local people in the peace process and many expressed: "If they come again, we will go back to our old hiding places."

Such military operations have not been the only incidents that have put pressure on the local population in the past two years since the ceasefire. The opening up of former conflict-affected areas and a sense of stability have also attracted private businesses to explore the area, leading to increased logging and mining activities. Land grabbing is rampant in the Tanintharyi Region and the local people fear that their land will soon be taken away from them. In most cases, economic endeavours are never discussed with the local population but decided by local KNU and national elites.

The example of this one village in the Tanintharyi Region shows the complex situation and immense challenges faced in the current peace process in Burma/Myanmar. Even after two years of a ceasefire process, it has not been possible to establish a code of conduct or ceasefire monitoring mechanism – yet regulated and unregulated business activities in conflict-affected areas are gathering pace.

Coming home!

Lian H. Sakhong

Among the many exiles who have returned home in recent years is Lian Sakhong, who recounts his homecoming to Chin State in 2012.

I was in the Kinokuniya Bookstore in Singapore when my wife called me from Uppsala. Being inside a bookstore, I kept my voice low, but at the other end of the line my wife sounded happy and loud, almost hilarious: 'Lian, your name is removed.' I was at first confused and asked: 'Removed from what?' She said: 'From the blacklist!'

I didn't know how to react: should I be happy or angry? In a way I was happy because I could now go back to my native country, and angry because such a thing should never have happened in the first place. What drove me away from my homeland? We were just students demanding freedom of movement and expression within our campus. But what we got was the bullet not the ballot, and from March to September 1988 our campus became almost like a battlefield. Hundreds of thousands of students and ordinary people died, and thousands more fled to the border areas controlled by ethnic armed groups. I was one of them. Luckily for me, I managed to get a valid passport (but not Burmese, of course), and able to go further to Singapore.

What a coincidence! In September 1991, I was granted asylum by the Swedish Embassy in Singapore with the help of the UNHCR; and now, in September 2012 also in Singapore, I received news that my name was removed from the blacklist. In 1991, I was young and full of dreams: to continue my study, work for my country, and one day go back to my country and serve the people! During all these years, I never stopped campaigning for democracy and freedom in my country, not even when I was studying at Uppsala University. As soon as I finished my studies, I came back to the Thai–Burmese border and worked fulltime for my country. The very reason that I was in Singapore now was to renew my visa – simply by leaving and returning to Thailand – in order to stay longer on the border.

Now the time to go home had come! But to go back where? To the campus? There was no campus anymore. The Rangoon University campus became like a jungle when the country was ruled by the jungle law. To go home? But where was my home? That made me more and more angry. Who will compensate for the loss of those youthful and happy years in the campus! Who will bring back our lost friends? Who will build memory stones for those who lost their lives in the jungle, and on the streets of our (then) capital Rangoon, which literally means the 'City of Peace'. When the demonstrators, mostly students, were killed on the streets of the City of Peace, so many bodies could not be collected, not even by relatives and loved ones!

Though angry, I was determined that, no matter what, I would go back, at least to see my old campus. Luckily, the Peace Research Institute in Oslo and Myanmar Egress in Rangoon invited me to present a paper at their jointly organized seminar. Just before I left, I gave a training course on 'principles of democracy and federalism' in the KNU-controlled border areas. Being in the jungle, I was unaware that the news of my plan to return home was broadcast by the BBC, VOA and Radio Free Asia. Actually, it was I who had given an interview but I was unable to listen my own interview from the jungle camp. When I arrived back in Bangkok from the KNU camp via Sanglaburi, my friends told me that my plan to return home had been rather widely publicized but I was unable to imagine what I would encounter in my native land.

I went home, finally! At Rangoon Airport, quite unexpectedly, my big brother came to see me all the way – almost to the aircraft – and guided me through the VIP diplomatic channel. My bother looked so happy but I was not quite sure of myself. Just a few years back, he wrote a letter to me and complained that because his two younger brothers (me and our younger brother) were in the camp of anti-government ethnic armed groups, he had missed getting a promotion several times. Now, after a few words of greeting, he told me happily that finally he had got a promotion a few days after Aung San Suu Kyi was released from house arrest. And he also told me that there were many people waiting for me at the arrival hall. I expected, of course, that there must be some friends and relatives who would welcome me home after all these years in exile!

Homecoming in Haka (photo: Lian Sakhong)

But it was more than I expected! I was simply shocked to see all these peoples, old and young, carrying banners bearing my name. I did not expect such a crowd! Around three hundred – maybe more – were lining up in the arrival hall of this rather small airport. And still more to my surprise, they handed me bunches of flowers and even put strings of flowers round my neck, making me feel like an Indian politician! Why had all these people come to see me and offer me flowers? What did they expect from me? What can I do for them? I am not a hero, not even a politician: just an activist!

In retrospect, I realized that my encounter with the public at Rangoon Airport was merely a portent. Many more such events happened during my short return to my native land. In Kalemyo, due to the delaying of my flight, we arrived after dark. Since it was the day of the Chin traditional harvest festival, I was brought directly to the podium erected at the corner of the football stadium where several thousand people had gathered to greet me by clapping hands and making beautiful noises, a reception that literally thrilled me. I thought I was just lucky because the audience actually may have been waiting for a concert to begin. As I was handed the microphone, I did not know what to say, so I opened my Bible and read the verses from Exodus: *Let my people go!* And I related the story of the Israelites from the book of Exodus, comparing this with our current situation, telling them that the waiting had been so long.

219

The next stop was Haka, my native town. It was a bright, sunny day but on the far horizon a thick black cloud was forming. The elderly family friend who accompanied me from Kalemyo, and who knows about my family background rather well, told me that my ancestors worshipped the rain god; so whenever they entered the town after some kind of victory – whether a successful hunt or victorious war game – the rain accompanied them. I told him that we are now Christians and do not believe in old traditional religious beliefs anymore. Nonetheless, he insisted, the rain is a blessing. I demurred: not for today.

Just before we entered to the town, several forerunners came to see us at the gate. They brought me the traditional Chin blanket, but it was black. That was another shock to me; the most I would have expected was a red one, not black! A red blanket looks more beautiful but it is for warriors and dancers. The black one is for respected elders, especially for the chiefs, priests and counsellors. They dressed me well, and we entered the town.

Hundreds of people (around 1,500, the local newspaper reported the next day) were gathered in front of the State Parliament Building, known in olden days as Chin Usi Zung, wearing their most beautiful traditional dress, carrying banners with my name, offering bunch after bunch of flowers and their greetings. And finally, in front of the newly built Union Guest House, people gathered together and sang traditional Chin warrior songs and fired the gunshot several times. Once again, I was asked to deliver a speech. Instead of giving a long speech, I recited the names of our friends who had lost their lives in this struggle, especially those who were from this town and surrounding areas. I told the audience that they also wanted to come home but could not do so in person anymore. And I asked the audience to remember them and what they had sacrificed their lives for.

After a short impromptu welcome-home ceremony at the Union Guest House, we drove home. A few minutes after we arrived, the rain poured down heavily. This time I was no longer worried: maybe this really was a blessing from God. But whether it was a blessing or not, the reality that we faced was that the roof of my sister's house (this is the house where I was raised) was leaking heavily. And the living room looked so small compared to what it used to be. So, I went out and checked, and saw that the side of the house was reduced by almost a half. And there stood three other houses in our compound! There were no more apple and pear trees, nor the cherry

Returning to the land with wife Run Pen (photo: Lian Sakhong)

tree that used to stand at the right corner of the house. My sister looked so sad when I stood on the balcony and faced the reality, and she told me that life had been very difficult during the military regime, and the only means for the family to survive was to sell the land. They divided the family compound into four: the garden into two and where the house stood also was divided into two. They sold three parts of the compound and reduced the house to half its original size. It was not that grand but a very comfortable house when I left Haka in December 1990.

The reality struck me more the next day. I used to think that my hometown, Haka, was located in the most beautiful place on this planet, surrounded by a thick forest that covered mighty Mt. Rungtlang, where wild orchids and other kinds of flowers bloomed. But where have all the forests gone? Rungtlang is almost a barren hill now; no more blooming trees, let alone orchids. Maybe a few cherry trees are still there but nothing like before.

Within the vicinity of the town, at least seven lakes – though they were not that big – once added to the beauty of Haka. Now only one lake barely survived. Not only the trees and forest but also the water was gone. Water scarcity has become a huge problem in the summertime, something that was unknown in my youth. It seems to me that after all these years of struggle for freedom, what we gained, if anything, is incomparable to what we lost. Rebuilding – from planting trees to nurturing people's character – will be a huge job that will take generations to accomplish. How are we going to get back our forests, our trees, our flowers and even our water?

After a few days in Haka, my wife joined me from Uppsala and we went to Thlantlang, her native town. It rained. Despite of the rain, hundreds of

Thanksgiving dinner at Carson Hall in Kaka, 2012 (photo: Lian Sakhong)

people bearing their umbrellas had lined up to see us. They were beating the drums and playing trumpets and singing traditional warrior songs. And I still asked to myself: why have they come to see us? What did I do for them? Almost nothing! What could I offer them? Nothing!

One evening, when family members and friends hosted a dinner for us at the Carson Hall in Haka, one elderly gentleman, who could not even pronounce my name properly, delivered rather a long speech. It was rather a grand dinner attended by some five hundred people and combined with a thanksgiving worship service. So many friends went up to the podium and delivered their speeches. That elderly gentleman said that it was a celebration for freedom, and that freedom is bigger than any individual human being. So, his speech made me realise that the reason why they all came to see me and welcome me in huge crowds was not only about me but also the celebration of their own freedom.

I happened to be the person who had been fighting for freedom for so many years. And when I returned to my homeland, my homecoming coincided with the time for a celebration of freedom. So, no matter rain or shine, let the people come out and celebrate their freedom together. It was not about me, not about any single person, but freedom that matters for all.

Peace-building in Myanmar

Charles Petrie and Ashley South

The peace process currently underway in Myanmar represents the best oppor-
tunity in half a century to resolve ethnic and state–society conflicts. Critical to
the success of this peace process will be the role that is played by various actors
in the country's civil society. In an earlier chapter, the nature of civil society
in Myanmar was examined. In this chapter on peace-building in Myanmar,[1]
among other issues the actual engagement of these various actors in the peace
process is explored in greater detail.[2]

Conflict and peace in Myanmar

For more than half a century, rural areas of Myanmar populated by
ethnic nationalities have been affected by conflicts between ethnic insurgents and a militarized state, widely perceived to have been captured
by elements of the ethnic Burman majority. For decades, communist
and dozens of ethnic insurgents controlled large parts of the country.
Since the 1970s, however, armed opposition groups have lost control of
their once extensive 'liberated zones', precipitating further humanitarian and political crises in the borderlands. For generations, communities
have been disrupted, traumatized and displaced. In 2011 there were an
estimated 500,000 Internally Displaced People (IDPs) in the southeast
alone, plus some 150,000 predominantly Karen refugees living in a series

---

1. *Peace-making* aims to reduce and control levels of violence, without necessarily addressing
   root causes. *Peace-building* involves a commitment to transformative action, going beyond
   conflict management to address underlying (structural) issues and inequalities.
2. This chapter was first drafted in early 2013. In the year since then, much effort has gone
   into securing peace throughout Myanmar but to date with few concrete results. As such,
   the text of this chapter has been updated where appropriate but the bulk of the chapter has
   been left unchanged; its deft analysis of the overall peace situation has not been affected by
   the short passage of time. This chapter is followed by an update of the peace process as it
   stands in March 2014 and a timely reminder of the critical issues involved. (MG)

of camps along the Thailand–Burma border. Following lengthy ceasefire negotiations in 2011–12, the number of displaced people in southeast Myanmar was considerably reduced but it increased dramatically in Kachin and Rakhine States as a result of war and communal violence.[3]

A previous round of ceasefires in the 1990s brought considerable respite to conflict-affected civilian populations. These truces (about 25 agreements in total) provided the space for civil society networks to (re-)emerge within and between ethnic-nationality communities. However, the then military government proved unwilling to accept ethnic-nationality representatives' political demands. Therefore, despite some positive developments, the ceasefires of the 1990s did little to dispel distrust between ethnic nationalists and the government.

The election of a military-backed, semi-civilian government in November 2010 represented a clear break with the past. Although opposition groups (including most non-state armed groups, NSAGs) continue to object strongly to elements of the 2008 constitution, this has nevertheless seen the introduction of limited decentralization to seven States, predominantly populated by ethnic nationalities.

Despite such positive developments, in June 2011 the Myanmar army launched a major offensive against the KIO (Kachn Independence Organization), the main Kachin armed ethnic group in northern Myanmar, breaking a 17-year ceasefire. As a result of this resumption of armed conflict, at least 80,000 people were displaced along the Chinese border, with tens of thousands of more IDPs in the conflict zones and government-controlled areas.[4] This resurgence of armed conflict included some of the most significant battles of Myanmar's civil war, now soon in its 60th year. The reasons behind the resumption of armed conflict in Kachin areas are complex and contested, and largely beyond the scope of this chapter, including sometimes opaque political-economic and geo-strategic factors. At the time of writing (March 2014) – after several false starts – a Chinese-brokered ceasefire seemed to be holding between government forces and the KIO.

Meanwhile, in late 2011 and through 2012, preliminary ceasefires were agreed and/or re- confirmed between the government and 10 of the 11 most significant NSAGs, representing the Wa and Mongla, Chin,

---

3. For fuller details, see Thailand Burma Border Consortium (2012) and The Border Consortium (2012).
4. Human Rights Watch (2012).

Chin Liberation Army soldier (photo courtesy of Daniel Sakhong)

Shan, Pa-O, Karen, Karenni, Arakan/Rakhine and Mon. By mid-2012, the only major group still at war was the KIO though sporadic fighting involving different NSAGs is still reported elsewhere, especially in Shan and Kachin States.

Many communities have experienced some of the benefits of the peace process. In areas where ceasefires have been effective, it is far easier to travel than previously. In the past, villagers had to fear rough handling (or worse) on the part of Tatmadaw personnel and/or insurgent forces. In contrast, 2012 travel restrictions greatly eased in many areas, so that villagers can move more freely, spending more time in their fields and getting products more easily to market. While these benefits may not seem significant to political elites, they mean a great deal to local communities. Nevertheless, the human-rights situation in remote, conflict-affected areas needs to improve further, in order to reach acceptable international standards. In the meantime, many problems remain on the ground. In particular, people living in remote, conflict-affected areas are concerned about business activities expanding in ceasefire zones. Often, commercial activity in previously inaccessible areas is focused on natural resource extraction, with little benefit to the local community and often involving very serious impacts on the natural environment.[5] The

---

5. Karen Human Rights Group (2013). The effect of more freedom of movement is explored in greater detail in the next chapter (p. 250).

relationship between business interests and the peace process is hugely important, but under-examined. The political economy of both armed conflict and peace in Myanmar involves significant economic interests, on the part of both government and NSAG actors. If such concerns are not addressed, the grievances of local communities (and the advocacy groups seeking to represent them) are likely to increase, in relation to the peace-business nexus. Already, some NSAG leaders have been accused of profiting personally from the peace process. Such concerns could lead to outbursts of local violence, with highly negative consequences for both communities and the peace process more broadly.

The peace process currently underway in Myanmar represents the best opportunity in half a century to resolve ethnic conflicts in this troubled country. However, the political, social and economic issues at the heart of the conflict will not be easily resolved. In order to address deep-rooted, structural problems, both the government and NSAGs must act with courage and imagination. Otherwise, the present window of opportunity may close, as the peace process loses momentum. Failure of the peace process would have significant negative impacts on President U Thein Sein's reform agenda.

The most significant challenges facing the peace process are: 1) to initiate substantial political dialogue between the government and NSAGs (*broaden* the peace process); 2) to include participation of civil society and affected communities (*deepen* the peace process); and 3) to demonstrate the Myanmar Army and NSAG's willingness to support the peace agenda. Additional issues include the need to ensure free and fair elections scheduled for 2015, and to establish effective governance and rule of law – which is particularly lacking in conflict-affected areas on the periphery of state control, where civilian populations are often subject to multiple state and non-state authorities. As noted, a related issue is the need for regulation of the private sector, particularly in relation to natural resource and other extractive industries, which are making significant inroads in remote and previously armed conflict-affected areas. This should be a key topic for capacity building among newly decentralized State and Regional governments, where ethnic-nationality political parties have some voice. Also essential to sustainable transition in Myanmar will be economic reform, at the macro-level and more locally in the conflict-affected countryside.

A particularly significant, but largely unremarked, challenge lies in conceptualizing and working constructively on the relationship between government structures and those of NSAGs. Many armed opposition groups have long-established, if chronically under-resourced, para-government structures, for example in the fields of education, health and local administration. Peace talks have yet to address, let alone resolve, how these non-state local governance structures will relate to formal state structures. This is a particularly pressing question in areas of recent armed conflict, where communities are subject to multiple authorities (government, Myanmar Army and one or more NSAGs, plus local militias and other informal power-holders). For many displaced and other communities in the conflict zones, NSAG structures and personnel are perceived as more legitimate and effective than those of the state. As noted below, civil-society actors in conflict-affected areas often enjoy very close relations with (and personnel overlap with those of) NSAG service provision actors. It is essential that such individuals and networks enjoy a sense of ownership in the peace process, if momentum is to be maintained. Deepening of the peace process should therefore include participation of affected communities and other stakeholders, such as civil society and political actors, with special attention to the roles of women and young people. (However, this additional and unpredictable dynamic between NSAGs and these other actors may in the short term threaten the momentum rather than help to maintain it.)

The government's ability to deliver reforms is hampered by deep-rooted conservative-authoritarian institutional cultures, and limited technical capacities. This is also the case with Myanmar's diverse NSAGs. Furthermore, the government (composed mostly of ex-military personnel) exercises only limited control over the Myanmar Army.[6] One consequence of the Kachin conflict has been to activate and empower 'hard-line' elements within the Myanmar Army who actively oppose civilian control over the military. Perhaps the greatest challenges facing the government are therefore to ensure that the Myanmar Army implements its policy and to build new civilian institutions. For many actors and observers, such reforms will require significant changes to the 2008 constitution.

---

6. Perhaps the best way of addressing this issue is through the development of codes of conduct and other monitoring mechanisms, details of which lie beyond the scope of this volume but should include significant local participation (see below).

The President having promised so much, Myanmar may experience a 'revolution of rising expectations': prospects of change have been talked up, and people may become frustrated if the government and its partners are unable to deliver. The reform process in Myanmar may be likened to taking the lid off a pressure cooker. In a society where tensions have been building for more than half a century, ethnic and other grievances can easily spill over, with disturbing consequences. One example is the recent violence and ethnic hatred in parts of Rakhine State and central Myanmar described elsewhere in this volume. These events remind us that there exist not only conflicts between the Myanmar government/ Army and various armed ethnic groups but also intra-communal conflict, with the potential to be extremely violent, between some ethnic communities. Outbursts of horrific violence in Rhakine constitute a complex phenomenon, beyond the scope of this chapter, involving deepseated mistrust of the 'other' and the politics of citizenship, immigration and representation – issues that have been exacerbated and mobilized by local and national-level political entrepreneurs. Among other things, these events indicate that there are spoilers on the sidelines, waiting to utilize tensions to provoke violence in order to undermine the reforms.[7]

The peace process in Burma/Myanmar is indigenous, driven in the first instance by government initiative. In the context of limited international involvement, the process has been quite ad hoc in nature. Furthermore it is highly complex, with some 20 parallel sets of discussions underway between the government and various NSAGs. In 2013, more coordinated efforts to reach a nationwide peace agreement came to the fore but intractable issues at the local level still have a major influence.

Given the essentially indigenous nature of the peace process in Myanmar, the role of the international community context is necessarily limited. On the one hand, international stakeholders should continue to remind the government, and NSAGs, of their commitments and responsibilities under international human-rights and humanitarian laws, of the need to resolve outstanding armed conflicts, and of the necessity for an inclusive political dialogue, and ultimately a substantial political settlement acceptable to key stakeholders. Beyond that, the international community can support peace-building initiatives which build trust and confidence in

---

7. Arguably, among these spoilers are certain nationalist groups determined on exploiting local tensions between different ethnic and religious communities.

the peace process, and at the same time test the sincerity of the Myanmar government and Army, and NSAGs, to deliver the peace which citizens long for. One way of doing so is to engage constructively with various parties to the process including civil society actors, encouraging their participation in and principled support for the peace process.

Key stakeholders and relationships with peace-building

As noted in our earlier chapter, civil society in Myanmar has undergone a gradual re-emergence since the 1990s. Until 2011, many of the more dynamic sectors of Myanmar civil society were situated among ethnic groups. The re-emergence of civil society within and sometimes between often highly conflict-affected communities was partly a result of the previous round of ceasefires in the 1990s. Assessments of the earlier ceasefires should address both the failures (in terms of inability to achieve a political settlement) and the successes of this period, which included a dramatic decline in human-rights abuses in ceasefire areas and the re-emergence of civil society in conflict-affected areas.

Since the new government took power in Myanmar in 2011, the space for civil and political society has again expanded dramatically. Previous surveys of the sector (e.g. South 2008b) are therefore largely redundant. The following section provides an overview of key civil-society and related stakeholders in relation to peace-building in Myanmar. This is not a comprehensive overview of the civil-society sector, and even within the parameters of exploring the peace process provides only a limited sketch. Moreover, this material risks being overtaken by events. For instance, when this chapter was finalized in March 2014, a national ceasefire had still not been agreed while concerns were growing that implementation of the 2014 census would lead to widespread violence across the country. The issue of constitutional changes affecting the 2015 elections could also provoke civil disobedience in the cities and beyond.

To aid clarity and brevity, Myanmar peace-building civil society is mapped according to the following sectors: urban/Burman areas; established ethnic actors operating from government- controlled areas; the borderlands, including areas of on-going armed conflict; and refugee and diaspora communities. It should be noted that reality is more complex and messy than intellectual schema, with many actors and networks operating between and beyond these categories.[8] Furthermore, this mapping focuses mostly on indigenous actors, and does not include the significant new presence of 'international civil society actors', including 'think tanks' and others that have sought involvement in the peace process over the past two years.

Urban/Burman areas

As noted, the 'saffron revolution' of 2007 and the response to the following year's Cyclone Nargis, demonstrated the capacity of Myanmar civil society and its potential as a socio-political catalyst. In relation to the peace process, until very recently the repressive political environment in Myanmar has limited citizen engagement in urban areas, with the exception of some ethnic-minority communities (see below).

While urban and peri-urban dwellers include significant minority communities (including populations of Chinese and Indian origin), for analytical purposes it is possible to identify a Burman majority-orientated civil society. Before the socio-political opening of the past two years, the roles and scope of civil-society action in government-controlled areas were severely restricted. Nevertheless, Christian (mostly ethnic-minority) civil-society groups have enjoyed considerable space and been able to maintain strong international connections while remaining mostly disconnected from Burman-majority civil society. Recent positive developments include meetings (in January 2013) between Myanmar civil-society actors and the President and later, his main peace envoy, U Aung Min.

Over the past decade, urban civil society in Myanmar has grown, and also become more politicized. In part, this politicization is due to the decision by some Burman elites to engage in civil-society-based activism, with the intention of promoting democracy in their country.[9] Those aiming to 'build democracy from below' have established a number of predominantly Burman-staffed national NGOs, many of which can claim significant achievements in the fields of service delivery (e.g. education and community development). Several of these organizations

---

8. Due to the rapidly changing situation in Myanmar, there is little published material upon which to base this mapping. The following section is based on the authors' first-hand experience, when working to support the peace process in Myanmar through the Myanmar Peace Support Initiative (see below).

9. See South (2008b).

grew substantially in response to Cyclone Nargis and some are now well established. A number of these new NGOs have quite self-consciously emulated the model of Christian/ethnic minority civil-society organization. The trend towards a more politically-engaged civil society was magnified by the decision of the National League for Democracy (NLD) to engage in social work, as a way to engage with communities and mobilize support while outflanking the government, in a context where explicitly political ('big-P political') work was subject to outright suppression by the authorities. The NLD's engagement in the civil-society sector has potentially threatened the activities of longer-established actors with less explicitly political agendas.

Since mid-2011, there has been a huge increase in civil-society activism in government- controlled, and particularly urban, areas. While not exclusively identified with the majority community, activism is nevertheless focused particularly around Burman intellectual classes. A newly energized civil-society sector has engaged in public discourse and protests regarding rule-of-law and natural-resource issues – one notable achievement being pressure mobilized on the government to suspend the giant (Chinese-implemented) Myitsone Dam on the headwaters of the Irrawaddy River (this was indeed suspended by Presidential decree on 30 September 2011). More recently, civil- and political-society actors have protested against widespread land seizures and other rights violations across the country. These land protests have reached beyond urban civil society with many localized disputes in the rural countryside organized by aggrieved local farmer communities, an example being the protests against the Letpadaung copper mine in late 2013.

Some mainstream civil-society and political leaders have adopted strong and high-profile positions in relation to the peace process, including in particular members of the '88 generation'.[10] For example, on his release from jail in early 2012, veteran 'student leader' Min Ko Naing drew attention to the Kachin conflict, and since then he and colleagues have undertaken study tours to conflict-affected parts of the country, including the main KIO-HQ town of Laiza. Members of the '88 generation' have also visited the Philippines to better understand the peace process in Mindanao and how lessons might be applied to Myanmar.

---

10. Political activists, prominent in the 1988 democracy uprising, who spent much of the next quarter century in jail or under close surveillance by the authorities.

Urban-based peace activists have initiated a number of public events (demonstrations in Yangon, Mandalay, Meiktilla and elsewhere as well as t-shirt campaigns, art events, public seminars, etc.) and undertaken high-profile visits to Kachin IDP camps. In the process, new understandings and alliances have developed between Burman elites and (in particular) ethnic Kachin communities. However, such activities have been accompanied by significant continued state suppression, including the arrest of a number of 'peace walk' activists (who face up to six years in jail). Although such activities have thus far produced limited results on the ground, they are nevertheless of political-cultural importance. For the first time in two decades,[11] middle-class activists and elites from the urban-Burman community (who enjoy considerable domestic political following) have expressed compassion for and solidarity with struggling ethnic nationalities. For the peace process in Myanmar to be sustained and deepened, it is essential that members of the ethnic Burman community gain better understandings of the grievances, aspirations and realities of their minority brethren.[12] In the past, under half a century of military rule, urban (particularly Burman) citizens had little exposure to the realities of armed conflict and its impacts in the ethnic-minority-populated countryside, beyond highly distorted government propaganda (plus the counter-narrative provided by news on the BBC, VOA, etc.).

These events have been covered widely in the Myanmar print and online and social media, which experienced a significant improvement in freedom of expression during 2012. The easing, and finally abolition, of censorship of the print media are some of the most visible and tangible results of the democratic reforms (though difficulties remain there – see p. 39ff.). While the (Burman-dominated) media has a limited understanding of ethnic minority affairs and conflict dynamics, the coverage

---

11. Following suppression of the '1988 democracy uprising' and the government's failure to recognize the results of the 1990 general election, a wave of predominantly urban-based student and other democracy activists fled to the border areas, where many made common cause with the country's ethnic insurgents. This was the first time in a generation (since the mid-1960s and the 1974 'U Thant' protests) that elites from the Burman majority had been exposed to the realities of life for minority communities in conflict-affected areas (Smith 1999). Over the past year or so, many exiles from 1988–90 have returned to Myanmar, including prominent student activists, some of whom have contributed towards the peace process by joining the quasi-governmental Myanmar Peace Centre.

12. There is also the prospect that urban/Burman elites may seek to mobilize alliances with regard to ethnic issues for their own political purposes.

of peace activism and the peace process has increased dramatically. Moreover, the Kachin conflict has regularly been front-page news in domestic media, often highlighting the grievances of ethnic communities and the KIO. Such reporting (often facilitated by peace activists) has included interviews with local communities and ethnic leaders as well as war reporting from near the front lines. In recent times, the government has also stepped up its engagement with the media, seemingly to counter the dominance of peace activists and the KIO of the conflict narrative. However, biased media coverage of the Rakhine conflict highlights the lack of understanding of conflict-sensitive journalism in Myanmar and demonstrates how the media as part of civil society can act as a powerful factor in inciting violence or enforcing stereotyped perceptions of ethnicity, discrimination and historic narratives.

With a few exceptions, the peace process in Myanmar is heavily dominated by men. Nevertheless, women activists play more prominent roles in civil society, particularly among ethnic nationality communities (see below).

Many of those who have emerged as peace activists over the past two years are members of a younger generation who have gained valuable experience in national and international NGOs in Myanmar. Peace activism among the Myanmar majority is therefore a welcome development – so long as this remains focused on peace-building rather than on the mobilization of ethnic issues for essentially political ends. As well as the political elites mentioned above (who by some definitions would not be included in civil society), other urban-based civil and political society networks have (re-)emerged over the past few years. These include activities extending into rural areas and ethnic nationality communities – illustrating the arbitrary nature of 'inside'/'outside' majority/minority distinctions in the rapidly changing context of Myanmar politics. Initiatives such as Paung Ku and others have developed contacts between Burman and ethnic-nationality communities, and between urban areas and the conflict-affected countryside. In doing so, they have engaged constructively with civil-society actors in the borderlands (see below).

In addition to 'traditional' organizations (see below), other CBOs operating in securely government-controlled areas include farmer-interest and village-development groups, community-savings groups, early-childhood centre committees and local Parent–Teacher Associations. Some are staffed by retired state officials.[13]

Ethnic actors in government-controlled areas

As noted, civil-society actors in government-controlled areas of Myanmar have long been subject to state suppression and penetration, and thus have had to work with great caution.[14] Ardeth Thawnghmung (2011) describes and analyses how ethnic-nationality communities in government-controlled areas have adopted a variety of (public and private) positions in relation to state–society and armed conflicts. Often, a surprising amount of space has been available to ethnic communities, providing they have been careful to situate themselves under the 'protective umbrella' of well-connected patrons, and have situated their discourse and activities within an overall pro-Union narrative.

Over the past few years, ethnic-nationality civil-society actors in Myanmar have enjoyed more space for action. The dynamics of this fast-changing situation vary, according to the context of particular conflict and peace processes. Among several communities (e.g. Shan, Karen), there have been long-standing, low-profile contacts between ethnic civil-society actors in government-controlled areas and those in the conflict-affected borderlands and in neighbouring Thailand. Often, these networks have been mediated by religious leaders (monks, pastors, priests). Since 2012, these contacts have been practised more openly, with a number of meetings convened in both Thailand and Myanmar. However, the 1908 Unlawful Associations Act (Section 17/1) still exercises a major restraint on relations between civilian populations and NSAGs, with the former fearing that contact with the latter could expose them to retaliation on the part of the state.

For the Shan, growing NSAG–community contact have involved major gatherings in Yangon (November 2012) and Taunggyi (January 2013), bringing together civil-society and political actors from inside, and activist groups and representatives of armed groups from the borderlands. For the Karen, a number of community leaders have travelled to Thailand, to discuss the peace process with the KNU and border-based civil-society groups, and represent the concerns and aspirations

---

13. Lorch (2006).
14. South (2008b).

of communities living in or accessible to government-controlled areas. In its engagement with the peace process, the KNU has undertaken a number of community consultations in the borderlands (and online), as well as high-profile missions to government-controlled areas. For example, KNU leaders met Yangon- and Karen State-based civil society leaders, immediately following the historic 4 April 2012 talks in Yangon, which consolidated the KNU–government ceasefire. Other consultations have been organized more independently, including a large event held during the 2012 rainy season in KNU/KNLA 2 Brigade territory (Taungoo District), which was brokered by trusted local civil-society intermediaries. Like other ethnic groups in Myanmar, the Karen community is highly diverse in terms of language-culture and religion (fuller details in 'Who are the Karen'). This diversity is reflected in the broad range of Karen civil-society actors, and in tensions between Yangon-based elites (mainly Christian and Sgaw dialect-speaking) and political and civil society networks in Karen State (and also, to a lesser degree, in the Irrawaddy Delta). The challenge for peace-building in Karen and other communities in Myanmar extends beyond relations between minority groups and the central (historically militarized and assimilationist) state, to include the need for trust and confidence-building between sub-groups of the ethnic community. Furthermore, civil society in Karen and other ethnic communities extends beyond Western-oriented (and often internationally-funded) CBOs and national NGOs, to include faith-based and other more traditional types of association. While the latter may 'fall beneath the radar' of Western observers (and particularly donors, with their understandable requirements for 'programmability'), this indigenous civil society constitutes the heart of the communities in question, being a great reservoir of 'human capital' and strategic capacity for change.

In contrast to the larger and more diverse Karen community, Mon populations in southeast Myanmar are numerically smaller and generally more homogenous culturally.[15] In many areas, the two ethnic

15. Demographic data in Myanmar are notoriously unreliable. The *CIA Factbook* estimates the ethnic breakdown to be Burman 68%, Shan 9%, Karen 7%, Rakhine 4%, Chinese 3%, Indian 2%, Mon 2% and other 5%. At time of writing, preparations were underway to conduct a new national census in April 2014 (i.e. prior to the 2015 elections). While this may give better data, there is also a risk of reinforcing unhelpful essentializations of ethnicity in Myanmar. As Sadan and Robinne observe (2007), ethnicity is a fluid category, subject to re-imaginations. While the fixing of ethnic identity may be convenient for administrative

communities live side-by-side, providing opportunities for cultural interchange as well as potential for inter-communal tensions. A ceasefire was agreed between the government and NMSP in 1995. Although political relations broke down in 2010, and tensions remained very high for some time, fighting did not break out again between government forces and the NMSP (unlike in the case of Kachin). In this context, Mon civil-society actors have long enjoyed close relations and much overlap between those working 'inside' Myanmar, those operating out of the NMSP-controlled ceasefire zones and in neighbouring Thailand which overlap with NMSP service-providing NSAG–GONGOs. Mon women have been prominent in the peace process, particularly in relation to community development and education activities.[16]

Until two years ago, similar observations could be made regarding Kachin civil society. In the decade and a half following the 1994 KIO ceasefire, Kachin civil society flourished in many sectors. Among the best-known NGOs to emerge were the Shalom (*Nyein*, peace) and Metta foundations, both of which originated in the Kachin community but grew to encompass nationwide networks with a special connection to ethnic-nationality communities and well- connected to international civil-society actors. Inevitably, with the breakdown of the KIO ceasefire in June 2011, security concerns have curtailed the work of Shalom and Metta in some localities. Furthermore, in some (but not all) Kachin circles, the breakdown of the earlier ceasefire has somewhat undermined Shalom's credibility, due to its founder's close association with the 1994 agreement.[17] The roles of these two Kachin foundations have been particularly important due to the committed engagement of Kachin women involved. In the context of the resumption of armed conflict in Kachin areas, a number of CBOs and national NGOs have supported IDP and other vulnerable communities. These include pioneering Kachin groups operating in KIO-controlled areas along the Chinese border. Like their Karen counterparts on the Thailand border (see below), Kachin CBOs

and political elites, this does not necessarily reflect lived realities; see also Sadan (2013). A key challenge in the census will be to decide who is considered a citizen, in which state or region.

16. Mon education is discussed by Ashley South in the next chapter (from p. 250).

17. Shalom has been closely involved with a number of initiatives in relation to the current peace process, including supporting community-based monitoring networks in some areas.

are characterized by a variety of relationships with the KIO, ranging from 'GONGO' status as the armed group's relief wings through being much more independent community-based groups to being more activist-orientated groups. In the Kachin IDP camps, local organizations (often channelling international funding but also in receipt of money from the KIO and the Kachin diaspora) have been the only agencies assisting highly vulnerable communities. In government-controlled areas, the Kachin Baptist Convention and the Catholic Church (KMSS/Karuna), as well as Metta and Shalom, have been active in helping such communities. A number of Kachin civil society actors and individuals in Myanmar have also engaged in peace advocacy, including the Kachin Peace Network. Kachin civil society is marked by relatively high levels of participation on the part of women.

There is a widespread perception among Kachin civil- and political-society actors that it is inappropriate for the broader national peace process to move forward too quickly while the KIO armed conflict is unresolved. Indeed, some consider that efforts by the government and international community to promote the national peace process at this time is counter-productive as it undermines the Kachin cause. More broadly, civil-society actors in Myanmar tend to feel excluded from the peace process. Perhaps inevitably, thus far this has consisted of ceasefire negotiations between armed actors: the government (and, more problematically, the Myanmar Army) and NSAGs. As noted, in order for the peace process to be representative of the community/communities, it will be necessary to deepen participation to include civil society and political actors. This will be particularly important, as and when the peace processes is 'broadened' to include substantive political discussions. If political talks are to contemplate structural changes within a more decentralized state and address citizens' key grievances and aspirations, they must include discussion of issues concerning all in the country – including the Burman majority.[18] Given the lack of opinion surveys in Myanmar over the past half-century, observers may be surprised by some of the issues and concerns identified as priorities by various communities.

---

18. For an overview of political, social and economic issues for possible inclusion in the peace process, see p. 250 ff, also South (2012).

Discussion of mainstream civil society in Myanmar tends to focus on cosmopolitan elements, following a broadly democratic-progressive agenda. However, this narrow framing reproduces some widespread and unhelpful assumptions regarding civil society in Myanmar, and beyond. While the sector can certainly be a vehicle for progressive political change, recent grassroots violence in Rakhine State shows that Myanmar civil society is not necessarily cosmopolitan in nature but can include dark elements working towards decidedly non-liberal aims. The combination of populism, contested identities and interests with long suppressed political and communal passions can be a volatile mix.

Returning from issues of intra-communal violence, to discuss armed conflict in the borderlands, those most directly affected by the peace process include communities in areas of on-going or recent armed conflict. Efforts to support the peace process, such as the Myanmar Peace Support Initiative (MPSI),[19] have worked with communities in areas where access was previously heavily restricted, to undertake assessments of participatory needs, in order to implement locally-owned projects helping households/villages recover from decades of insurgency, and brutal counterinsurgency campaigns. In the process, spaces have been created, allowing for substantive discussions between representatives of the Myanmar Army and government, NSAGs, the international community and displaced ethnic-minority villagers. These unprecedented engagements have been profound and moving experiences for those involved (including the authors of this paper).

It is essential that such efforts are extended and replicated, in order to bring the victims of armed conflict in Burma/Myanmar into dialogue with both the government and the NSAGs (i.e. to win recognition of

---

19. The Myanmar Peace Support Initiative aims to build trust and confidence in (and test) the peace process by supporting peace agreements between the government and NSAGs. The MPSI was initiated in January 2012 when Myanmar asked the Norwegian government to help support the peace process. Since then, a number of other governments and donors have become involved. The MPSI has sought to move quickly in response to political imperatives in a fast-changing context. It is committed to substantial consultations with conflict-affected communities, civil society, and government and non-government political and military actors, and to consulting and sharing information with a broad range of stakeholders. The MPSI is committed to working in a manner that does not expose vulnerable populations or other partners to increased danger (including due to any breakdown in the peace process). It is supporting local partners and NSAGs to implement projects in Rakhine, Chin, Shan, Karen and Mon States, and in Bago and Tanintharyi Regions. For regularly updated information on the MPSI (in English, Burmese and minority languages), see http://www.emb-norway.or.th/News_and_events/MPSI/.

civilians as autonomous actors). In such efforts to test the emerging peace, the roles of women and youth will be particularly important. Other ways in which the MPSI has sought to deepen participation in the peace process include supporting consultations between NSAGs and the communities that they seek to represent, and also working with civil society and NSAGs to support community-based monitoring of the peace process.[20]

The borderlands; areas of ongoing armed conflict

Most literature on armed conflict and its humanitarian impacts in Myanmar distinguishes between areas of ongoing conflict (and assistance provided mostly cross-border from Thailand and other neighbouring countries) and ceasefire and government-controlled areas (e.g. South 2008b). As the peace process gains ground (with the important caveat of recent heavy fighting in Kachin areas and elsewhere in Shan State), this distinction is beginning to break down. Vulnerable, armed-conflict-affected communities in remote areas are increasingly accessible from inside the country, making the case for cross-border assistance more problematic (see below).

In areas where ceasefires have taken hold, conditions on the ground have improved for civilians. However, conflict-affected communities and other non-armed actors have so far been largely excluded from meaningful participation in ceasefire negotiations (which constitute the initial door-opening stage of a longer peace process). Initiatives such as the MPSI are endeavouring to build trust and confidence in (and test) the peace process by facilitating engagement on the ground between conflict-affected communities, NSAGs and Myanmar government/Army. As noted above, Myanmar civil-society actors are also engaged in processes of trust and confidence-building, developing networks between previously isolated (and sometimes mutually fearful) communities.

Myanmar civil-society networks include those based in the insurgent-influenced and opposition-oriented borderlands, as well as actors work-

20. Other elements of Myanmar society with a claim to be key stakeholders include ethnic political parties, representatives of which were elected to provincial and national-level parliaments in 2010. These parties have a credible claim to represent their communities – but have so far been largely excluded from the peace process. Increasingly, above ground, civilian ethnic politicians are demanding a voice in the peace process, and particularly in emerging political discussions. To a degree, such actors are rivals to the NSAGs for the support of ethnic communities.

ing out of government-controlled areas. Over the past two decades, a veritable 'aid industry' has grown up along the Thai border, under the broad patronage and protection provided by the refugee camps (home to some 150,000 ethnic-minority refugees, mostly Karen and Karenni).[21] Under Western/donor tutelage, a number of civil-society groups have flourished, staffed by dedicated Myanmar personnel as well as long-term foreign actors.

During the many years of armed conflict and state suppression in Myanmar, border and exile- based civil-society networks were among the few viable mechanisms for supporting anti- government and pro-democracy activities in ethnic-nationality-populated areas. During this period, enterprising and committed local actors learned to orient their rhetoric and activities along lines favoured by Western donors and solidarity networks, and were able to communicate the plight of their communities to international audiences. From the late 1990s, increasing amounts of cross-border assistance were provided to highly vulnerable IDP and other conflict-affected civilians, particularly in southeast Myanmar (in areas broadly adjacent to the refugee camps in Thailand). Some cross-border organizations have the characteristics of CBOs, or at least local NGOs, cooperating with (but fundamentally being quite independent from) NSAGs; others constitute the relief wings of armed groups. Donors have encouraged the latter to distance themselves from their 'mother organizations' and focus on the impartiality and supposed neutrality of their work. While most cross-border NSAG–GONGOs can be said to be impartial, inasmuch as assistance is provided regardless of beneficiaries' ethnic/religious identity, most are far from neutral, being actively engaged in anti-government and solidarity struggles. Indeed, some border-based organizations resent their patrons' insistence on camouflaging the political nature of relief work in the borderlands.

A number of cross-border groups have undertaken important work in the fields of community development and the provision of essential health and education services. As the peace process in Myanmar moves forwards, these activities should be integrated constructively with existing state governance and service-delivery mechanisms rather than displaced by the latter.

---

21. Thailand Burma Border Consortium (2012).

Other cross-border groups and networks focus mostly on advocacy work. Their activities include documenting and denouncing the systematic human-rights abuses which occur (primarily, but not exclusively, on the part of Myanmar Army) in conflict areas, as well as more general anti-government messaging. The changes in Myanmar over the last three years have caught many of these actors by surprise, challenging long-held assumptions. Rather than a radical decapitation of the military regime – in the context of some kind of popular uprising, with the expectation that exiled political elites would be parachuted into positions of power – there has instead been a pacted, incremental and still very fragile and uncertain transition. Many border-based groups have responded to the changes in Myanmar with strategic vision. As noted, there are growing contacts between civil-society and political actors 'inside' the country, and those in the borderlands and overseas. Large numbers of exile activists have returned home, either permanently or on scoping visits, including some 'intellectuals' who have been drawn into the President's 'advisory group' working in support of the peace process. However, for some border- and exile-based activist groups, the changes in Myanmar are perceived as threatening. Over the past two decades exile-based activist groups and networks have become used to controlling the political agenda, framing ethnic conflict in Myanmar for international consumption, and in the process channelling donor funds to their own conflict-affected client populations. Local opposition groups face a dilemma: whether and how to reinvent themselves and work for change around the new peace scenario, or to become increasingly marginalized in the borderlands and overseas, frustrated and angry as the political narrative shifts 'inside' Myanmar.[22] In many respects of course, concerns regarding the trajectory of the peace process are both credible and legitimate. The peace process in Myanmar is fragile and unfinished, and many stakeholders remain understandably sceptical regarding the true intentions of the government (and in particular of the Myanmar Army).

---

22. Meanwhile, civil-society actors in Kachin State enjoy no such luxuries. Local communities and CBOs have been struggling to respond to a humanitarian crisis, with the Myanmar Army and KIO engaged in intensive armed conflict. The recent negotiation of a tentative ceasefire in Kachin State may prove a very positive development, moving the peace process in Myanmar onto a constructive new phase.

Such issues raise key questions. Who speaks on behalf of civil society? Whom does civil society represent? In the past, exile-based organizations could represent themselves as spokespeople for conflict-affected ethnic communities in Myanmar, despite having access to the conflict zones only. However, as and if the peace process (and broader reform agenda) gathers momentum, communities will increasingly be able to speak for themselves, and should be supported to have direct access to political dialogue and to donors and diplomats seeking to support the reform and peace processes in their country.

The peace process is also raising interesting questions along another dimension of state–(NSAG)–society relations. As noted, ethnic civil-society Myanmar is highly diverse, including in the borderlands. In the past, there was generally little distinction between the (sometimes implicit) political positions of opposition-orientated civil-society groups and the NSAGs with whom they cooperated closely. However, as the peace process gains momentum, some (e.g. Shan and Karen) civil-society actors have grown critical of the NSAGs they have long worked alongside, accusing the latter of lacking transparency and failing effectively to engage with local communities (or at least in the ceasefire negotiations failing to take account of the positions of well-established border-based activist groups).

Refugee and diaspora communities

Over the past several decades, millions of (predominantly, but not exclusively) ethnic-nationality civilians have been internally displaced in Myanmar. In 2012, up to half a million IDPs still remained in southeastern Myanmar but the numbers are falling.[23] Their plight and prospects are covered above, in relation to situations of ongoing armed conflict in recent ceasefires.

Among those with the greatest stake in the peace process in Myanmar are refugee communities in Thailand and elsewhere. Many of these people have legitimate concerns regarding agendas for possible repatriation (on the part of the Thai and Myanmar governments, UNHCR and perhaps NGOs), which have not been widely discussed with beneficiary communities. As the peace process gathers momentum, it can be expected that large numbers of refugees (and IDPs) will return 'spontaneously' to Myanmar, rather than wait for assistance through officially

---

23. Thailand Burma Border Consortium (2012).

sanctioned and organized packages. Such patterns of migration have the potential to provoke conflicts over land and resources, as well as to increase the danger of accidents in the context of widespread landmine contamination in conflict-affected areas.

Besides the refugee communities in Thailand, there are some two– three million migrant workers and their dependents in the kingdom. Many of these have fled for similar reasons as those who enter the refugee camps but, instead of seeking asylum in the border areas, have sought to enter the 'grey' and 'black' economies. Some may return to Myanmar once political conditions allow but most will presumably re-quire significant social and economic changes before deciding to return home. Their situation is explored in greater detail later (see p. 364ff.).

Refugee and migrant communities have been largely excluded from discussion of the peace process, except for some limited opportunities to communicate their concerns and aspirations to the KNU and other NSAGs. As noted, many activist and exile groups in Thailand and be-yond have sought to play constructive roles in the peace process while others feel more threatened by the changes in Myanmar, and have posi-tioned themselves as 'spoilers'. Such dilemmas are particularly acute for refugees in third countries and other members of the diaspora. To the extent that the reality of change in Myanmar is recognized, this raises issues regarding whether refugee and exile communities may be willing to return home.

Opportunities – potential entry points, mechanisms and issues

As recently as ten years ago, observers – and donors – were asking whether civil society existed in Myanmar. Since then, commentary has shifted towards mapping this dynamic sector, and discussion of which actors to engage with, and how. Although such deliberations have sometimes proceeded according to a rather simplistic understanding of civil society, they nevertheless represent a positive development.

During the previous round of ceasefires in Myanmar in the 1990s, international donors failed to adequately support the peace process, resulting in lost opportunities to move from peace- making towards an environment of genuine peace-building.[24] It is essential that these mis-takes are not repeated. The reforms underway over the past three years,

24. South (2008b).

and particularly the peace process since late 2011, remain fragile, incomplete – and still problematic. In particular, the relationship between the government and Myanmar Army remains fraught with tension, with serious implications for the long-term prospects for peace. Nevertheless, this represents the best opportunity in many decades to address issues that have long structured state–society and armed conflicts in Myanmar. In order to succeed, the peace process must be broadened (to include political talks), and deepened (to include participation on the part of civil society and other key stakeholders).

As well as their underlying strategic-political and emerging peace-building roles, civil-society actors have for some years been involved in service delivery in Myanmar. In the context of a militarized and predatory state, civil-society actors have provided services that in other countries are more commonly provided (at least in part) as part of government health and welfare programmes. In Myanmar, in areas of on-going armed conflict, such activities have included assistance to highly vulnerable communities. From the 1990s until very recently, many conflict-affected communities, particularly in the southeast, were accessible only – or mostly – to local agencies working across-border from Thailand. Such cross-border aid has saved many lives, and also served to build the capacity of local actors; it has largely been complementary to relief and community-development assistance provided by actors working 'inside' the country. In areas where the security situation still precludes access to vulnerable communities from 'inside' Myanmar (such as much of Kachin State), cross-border assistance remains viable, and indeed often the only way to access highly vulnerable groups. However, in areas where the peace process is taking hold, such as most of southeast Myanmar, access is increasingly possible from inside the country. Cross-border assistance can be limited to situations where vulnerable communities can *only* be accessed from the neighbouring country. Rather than being the default approach to providing assistance, continued cross-border assistance needs to be justified on the case-by-case basis. That said, groups previously characterized primarily by cross-border modes of operation will often continue to have important roles to play if they can re-imagine their work in relation to supporting – and testing – the peace and broader reform processes.

In this context, it is important to address emerging relationships between government structures and those of (or associated with) NSAGs. As noted, many armed opposition groups have long-established, if chronically under-resourced, para-governmental structures, for example in the fields of education, health and local administration. Peace talks have yet to resolve how these non-state local governance structures will relate to formal state structures. This is the case also for border-based civil society actors, some of which have access to vulnerable communities, and whose should be supported to enhance their capacity, rather than being marginalized in the peace process. Such an approach can help to build trust and confidence in the peace process.

Opportunities for support of civil society engagement in the peace process include to:

- Support the engagement of mainstream mainly Burman civil (and political) society with the peace process – including activities to expose the majority community to the realities, grievances and aspirations of ethnic-nationality groups, and people in conflict-affected areas.

- Encourage the government (including, but not limited, to the Myanmar Peace Centre) to continue engagement with Myanmar civil society – and to extend this to groups working in conflict-affected areas, including border-based actors.

- Build the capacity of Myanmar media (including ethnic-nationality media), in relation to the peace process and political reforms more generally.

- Engage sensitively with 'traditional' civil society, building capacity and providing resources where appropriate, while avoiding tendency to re-configure local groups in line with donors' expectations/demands.

- Provide financial and capacity-building resources in line with the needs of civil society actors, rather than top-down, donor-driven priorities. This should include donor support that facilitates the evolution of civil society actors' priorities.

- Support voices of women and youth in the peace process, including through awareness-raising and information-sharing activities.

- Support constructive engagement of Myanmar (particularly ethnic-nationality) political parties with the civil-society sector, and the peace process more broadly.

- Support the agreement (between government and NSAGs, in the first instance) of Codes of Conduct and monitoring mechanisms; support community and civil society participation in ceasefire and peace-process monitoring.[25]

- Provide political and timely financial support to peace mechanisms: support consultations between NSAGs and conflict-affected communities (including civil society and political actors); support local peace-monitoring networks (capacity-building, financial support and encouragement to government and NSAGs).

Civil society participation in political consultations, as part of the peace process, could be facilitated by establishing sectoral 'working groups' to address key issues, eliciting significant input from a broad range of stakeholders.[26] Issues likely to elicit substantial engagement from civil society actors include:

- Land rights issues and land-use conflicts (including compensation for and/or restitution of property confiscated from or abandoned by forced migrants);

- Environmental regulation and natural resource management (including revenue sharing between the central and State/local governments);

- Language policy and education (including the status of minority languages in government administration, the justice system and schools, and the situation of non- state ethnic education regimes);

- IDP and refugee resettlement, including the complex issue of secondary settlement (where displaced or other communities have resettled on land previously occupied by people who themselves have been displaced), and roles of local, national and international agencies; and

- Economic development, job creation and vocational training.

---

25. Continue facilitating exposure of state and non-state actors to other country contexts in which monitoring mechanisms have been used successfully, particularly those that have included participation by civil society and affected communities (e.g. the southern Philippines).

26. For details of such an approach, see South (2012).

Caveats, assumptions, risks

As noted, intra-communal violence in Rakhine State, and elsewhere, and the on-going conflict in Kachin State threaten to undermine the peace process and potentially derail still fragile nationwide reforms. Clashes in southwest Myanmar are a salient reminder that grassroots activism and popular mobilization can be undertaken in a spirit far removed from the normative progressive–cosmopolitan framework within which most discussions of civil society are framed.

This issue touches upon another concern: to a significant degree, civil-society actors working on the peace process are identified with particular ethnic communities. There is a need to continue building bridges between ethnic nationality and Burman majority communities, developing Myanmar's long-suppressed civic traditions, rather than encouraging a further 'ghettoization' of civil society. The risk otherwise is that an expanded civil society may take the form of separate networks of ethnically and religiously based associations, reflecting existing lines of ethnic and political conflict, rather than bridging such divides.

Peace is an issue that affects all sectors of society, and everyone in Myanmar is a stakeholder. The exclusion of conflict-affected communities, and more broadly of civil-society actors and networks, is both unjust and liable to cause resentments that could undermine the peace process itself. In this context, the question of who speaks for communities will become increasingly urgent. Those working to support the peace process in Myanmar have a responsibility to ensure that they engage respectfully and constructively – and above all, safely – with communities which have suffered so much, for so many years.

On the relationship between conflict-affected communities and peace-building support, it is essential that outside interventions respect local agency and operate in a manner that does not expose vulnerable (and often traumatized) individuals and communities to further risk. Well-intentioned international agencies visiting previously inaccessible areas should be cautious about the impact of their brief visits on longer-term security and political dynamics in remote areas. When engaging with civil-society actors and conflict-affected communities, those supporting the peace process in Myanmar should ensure clarity regarding the distinctions between information sharing (engaging with a wide range of stakeholders, to ensure that they are informed) and consultations (which imply some kind of veto on the part of interlocutors).

Another risk is that the influx of peace-building 'think tanks' and other support networks currently entering Myanmar can severely stretch the limited capacities and time of local actors. Therefore, those seeking to support the peace process in Myanmar should consider carefully what added value they bring, and not over-tax local resources.

A further concern of many communities in relation to the peace process is widespread environmental damage, especially in the context of increased business activities in previously inaccessible, conflict-affected areas – a problem which is on the increase.[27] Those supporting the peace process should work to address these concerns, in partnership with affected communities, civil society actors, government and NSAGs. Issues of environmental protection and business regulation should be placed on the agenda for forthcoming political talks.

If civil-society and political parties are not included, there is a risk that Myanmar may experience a backlash in relation to the peace process. If they do not feel a sense of ownership and participation, civil-society and political actors – especially ethnic political parties and urban-based civil society – may begin to mobilize to demand their inclusion as stakeholders. This could lead to protests on the part of groups who should be partners in the peace process.

As Myanmar approaches the 2015 elections, these concerns are likely to become more pressing, as national politics enters a zero-sum mode. Given the demands of the country's chairmanship of ASEAN from January 2014, followed by the elections, there remains a small window of opportunity. Despite the many problems, there are great possibilities for social and political progress in Myanmar, including in the peace process. However, more needs to be done to engage the broad spectrum of actors in the peace process, or these opportunities may be missed.

Authors' Note

As with the earlier description of civil society (see p. 87), this chapter is based on (and updates) material from the background paper 'Mapping of Myanmar Peacebuilding Civil Society', which was prepared by the authors for a meeting of the Civil Society Dialogue Network focused on the evolv-

---

27. Karen Human Rights Group (2013).

ing peace processes in Myanmar and held in Brussels on 7 March 2013 (more details at http://www.eplo.org/civil-society-dialogue-network. html). Part of this extracted material is drawn from South (2012b).

References

The Border Consortium (2012) 'Changing Realities, poverty and displacement in South East Burma/Myanmar', Bangkok.

Human Rights Watch (2012) 'Untold Miseries: Wartime Abuses and Forced Displacement in Burma's Kachin State' http://www.hrw.org/sites/default/files/reports/burma0312ForUpload_1.pdf.

Karen Human Rights Group (2013) *Losing Ground: Land conflicts and collective action in eastern Myanmar*, KHRG 2013-01, March.

Lorch, Jasmine (2006) 'Civil Society under Authoritarian Rule: The Case of Myanmar'. *SÜDOSTASIEN/aktuell* (*Journal of Current Southeast Asian Affairs*), 2006: 2.

Maung-Thawnghmung, Ardeth (2011) 'Beyond Armed Resistance: Ethno-national politics in Burma (Myanmar)'. Washington, DC: East–West Center, *Policy Studies*, no. 62.

Sadan, Mandy (2013) *Being & Becoming Kachin: Histories Beyond the State in the Borderworlds of Burma*. Oxford: Oxford University Press.

Sadan, Mandy and Francois Robinne (eds) (2007) *Social Dynamics in the Highlands of South East Asia: Reconsidering 'Political Systems of Highland Burma' by E. R. Leach*. Leiden: Brill.

Smith, Martin (1999) *Burma: Insurgency and the politics of ethnicity*. London: Zed Books, 2nd ed.

South, Ashley (2008a) *Ethnic Politics in Burma: States of Conflict*. London: Routledge.

— (2008b).'Civil Society in Burma: The Development of Democracy Amidst Conflict'. Washington, DC: East–West Center, *Policy Studies*, No. 51.

— (2012) 'Prospects for Peace in Myanmar: Opportunities and Threats'. Oslo: Peace Research Institute Oslo, PRIO working paper, December.

Thailand Burma Border Consortium (2012) 'Program Report 2012: January to June'. Bangkok.

Update on the peace process

Ashley South[1]

The lives of civilians affected by decades of armed conflict in Myanmar are undergoing profound transformations for the better, thanks to the ceasefires agreed since late 2011 between the government and more than a dozen ethnic armed groups. However, the emerging peace process is unlikely to be sustainable unless negotiations soon begin regarding the underlying political, social and economic causes of conflict.

Part of the problem is that different actors, from the military to donors to conflict-affected communities, have different understandings of what 'peace' is, and act accordingly. Because key stakeholders often fail to define what they mean by peace, dominant positions and actors tend to prevail.

For most ethnic stakeholders, the primary need is for structural changes to the state and real autonomy for ethnic communities (usually expressed as an aspiration for constitutional federalism). However, historically in Myanmar, the Army has opposed such changes as threatening to national unity and sovereignty. The government has sought to escape this thorny issue by focusing primarily on the perceived development needs of ethnic communities.

Unfortunately, international support to the peace process has largely supported the government's view of what peace-building means, proceeding in accordance with donors' assumptions and agendas rather than an understanding of political concerns and local needs and realities. There is a risk of missing opportunities for long-term peace if donors continue to support activities that mostly suit aid agency agendas and are understood by many ethnic stakeholders as playing into the government's hands.

---

1. This article is based on 'Inside the peace process', an op-ed by Ashley South that appeared in *The Myanmar Times* on 6 January 2014. It builds on the situation in Myanmar as at the end of February 2014.

Conflict-affected communities: hopes and fears

The Myanmar Peace Support Initiative (MPSI)[2] has recently completed the first phase of a 'listening project' with conflict-affected communities in remote parts of Myanmar. The aim is to listen to Karen, Mon and Karenni (Kayah) communities – particularly women – to better understand their experiences before and after the ceasefires. Initial findings indicate that many people have benefited greatly from preliminary ceasefires between the government and the Karen National Union, New Mon State Party and Karenni National Progressive Party. For example, before the KNU ceasefire, villagers often had to flee from fighting and to avoid forced conscription and portering. Today people report greatly decreased levels of fear. Many of those who spoke with the MPSI said that for the first time in decades they did not have to worry about fleeing into the jungle to avoid being subjected to serious human-rights abuses. In some cases, displaced people are beginning to return to previous settlements and attempting to rebuild their lives. Many villagers mentioned that before the ceasefire they were unable to travel or visit their farms – or could only do so by paying bribes. Even then, villagers were severely restricted in terms of the amount of food or other supplies that they could carry while travelling, as they risked being accused of supporting the KNU. Villagers told terrible stories of abuse at the hands of the Tatmadaw, including beatings and killings – even the beheading of suspected insurgents.

After the ceasefire, however, villagers have been able to travel much more freely and to tend their rice fields. Levels of taxation, paid to either the Tatmadaw or ethnic armed groups, have decreased significantly over the past two years in both Karen and Mon areas. In many communities, livelihoods have improved as a result of villagers' better access to their farms and a reduction in predatory taxation. Villagers greatly appreciate these changes although they worry whether the ceasefire and emerging peace process can be maintained. "Since the ceasefire, I can go to my rice fields and weed regularly, so I got more rice for my family", one villager said. "Now I can also travel freely and, unlike before, sleep out in the rice

---

2. The MPSI was launched in March 2012 following a request from the Government of Myanmar to the Government of Norway to lead international support to the peace process. The MPSI facilitates projects implemented by conflict-affected communities, civil society actors and ethnic armed groups, which aim to build trust and confidence in – and test – the ceasefires, disseminates lessons learned from these experiences and seeks to strengthen local and international coordination of assistance to the peace process.

fields in a hut without having to fear for my life. Now the Tatmadaw still move around but we don't have to fear meeting them." Another man told the MPSI that "our villagers are like ducklings that have been in a cage for so long, and now they are released. They are so pleased to leave their cage! Our villagers are free to travel day and night, and are more busy and productive than before."

Despite such positive views, there is widespread anxiety that the government and ethnic armed groups may fail to reach a political settlement and the peace process may yet break down. One man told us: "If the ceasefire breaks down, it's not worth living for me."

Supporting the peace process: missed opportunities?

The agreement of ceasefires is a historically important achievement of peace-making. In order to sustain the peace process and move towards a genuine peace-building phase, it will be necessary to start a multi-stakeholder political dialogue and consolidate the existing ceasefire agreements. The government and most ethnic armed groups have agreed to continue negotiations towards a nationwide ceasefire to address these issues. However, many ethnic stakeholders remain sceptical about whether the government is willing or able to deliver. The govern-

Intense discussions at national ceasefire negotiations in May 2014 (photo: Lian Sakhong)

ment can maintain the present truces more or less indefinitely without reaching a political settlement; for ethnic communities, the status quo is a losing game. Political dialogue is essential.

As of February 2014, there are still important differences between the Nationwide Ceasefire Agreement drafted by the ethnic armed groups' Nationwide Ceasefire Coordinating Team (NCCT) and provisions acceptable to the government (and particularly the Myanmar Army). Nevertheless, a positive outcome from recent negotiations is the emergence of greater clarity regarding positions on both sides. Since November 2013, when representatives of ethnic armed groups met at a historic conference in the KIO headquarters at Laiza, a fairly cohesive approach to the peace process has emerged on the part of the groups in the NCCT. Likewise, on the government side, since late 2013 the military has been more engaged in the peace process. This is extremely important, given previous concerns that the Myanmar Army was not sufficiently involved in negotiations.

The peace process in Myanmar is unique in many ways, not least because of the limited role of the international community: negotiations are undertaken between the government and ethnic armed groups with no significant external mediation and only limited international facilitation. Outsiders, however, can help communities to recover from conflict while supporting initiatives that build trust and confidence in the peace process and test the sincerity of the government, Tatmadaw and ethnic armed groups. A number of international donors have pledged financial support to the peace process. Already some funds have been distributed, including to MPSI-supported projects in a number of conflict-affected areas that are implemented by local communities, civil society actors and ethnic armed groups. Several key donors are keen to expand their assistance on the understanding that supporting the peace process can help to consolidate the wider government-led reform process. Of course, there are very substantial needs among conflict-affected communities.

Unfortunately, international support to the peace process has been mostly characterized by a lack of direction and by strategic drift. Donors seem largely content to provide funding channelled through traditional – and generally government-controlled – structures. This is an easier approach than seeking out appropriate local partners on the ground.

This situation is not unique to Myanmar. Around the world, aid donors tend to frame the concerns of vulnerable communities as technical problems to be fixed by professional aid regimes rather than sites of contestation requiring political solutions. The exceptions are in contexts where a state's legitimacy is very clearly and persistently challenged, such as Myanmar before 2011, or when regional or global powers' interests are directly involved.

As a result, it is not uncommon for peace-support initiatives to fail to engage with the real issues affecting communities and other stakeholders; instead they fall in behind government-led development and rehabilitation projects. However, the problem in Myanmar is not primarily one of a failing or weak state that needs to be strengthened or fixed but rather an urgent need to re-imagine and negotiate state–society relations – and in particular mend relationships between the Burman majority and ethnic-nationality communities.

The commitments made by international donors under the Busan New Deal in 2011 are meant to guide the international community toward addressing the causes of conflict.[3] Donor support to the Myanmar peace process demonstrates the difficulties of implementing this approach. For example, most Asian governments' support to the peace process is channelled almost exclusively through Myanmar state structures, demonstrating very limited consultation with conflict-affected communities or ethnic armed groups. This approach to peace-building frames armed conflicts as problems to be resolved through foreign aid, rather than expressions of deep-rooted social and political grievances.

Aid agencies working in conflict-affected areas need to better understand local political cultures and perceptions, and the dynamics of peace and conflict. Illustrating how peace means different things to different people, ethnic communities are concerned that the government has an 'economic development first' agenda and wants to use aid as an alternative to political dialogue. They also worry that aid activities constitute efforts by the government to intensify its presence in and control over ethnic communities. This is deeply problematic for many ethnic stakeholders, who still regard the government as largely illegitimate and whose experience of the Tatmadaw is as a violent and predatory force. As the leader of a major ethnic armed group recently told me, "We are

---

3.   The New Deal addresses the many issues relating to fragile states (development, security, engagement, etc.). It is an agreement aiming at strengthening partnerships and ownership in peace-building and state-building between donor organizations and the fragile states where they operate.

worried that the government and donors are pushing ahead with their own plans, without consulting us – and that the aid agenda is getting ahead of the political agenda."

Meanwhile, a number of needs articulated by key stakeholders in the peace process are going unmet. For example, there is a need to provide funding and training to more than thirty liaison offices established by ethnic armed groups under an agreement with the government. The liaison offices play important roles in sustaining the peace process but, apart from some start-up funding, donors have mostly failed to support this key component of the peace process.

Another example of unmet needs is the failure properly to support education activities in conflict-affected ethnic minority areas. Despite requests to donors dating back more than a year, ethnic-nationality schools in Mon areas, for example, are still unable to pay their teachers. This is leading to a local perception that international donors are happy to support the government – in this case through the state education system – but are unwilling to engage constructively with ethnic na-tionality systems of service provision. The Mon National Schools are administered by the NMSP, and provide an ethnic-language introduc-tion to schooling for minority children – most of whom do not speak Burmese – allowing them the best possible start in education. At the same time, the Mon National Schools teach the Myanmar language and mostly follow the government curriculum, ensuring that graduates can sit state matriculation exams and enter the higher education system. The Mon National Schools represent the best of both worlds: a locally owned and delivered education regime which is closely linked to the state system, producing students who are proud of their ethnic cultures, but also equipped to be citizens of the Union. Despite widespread recognition that the Mon National Schools represent a model of best practice – which is in line with the government's reformed education policies – donors have so far provided only limited amounts of funding to the Mon school system.

International donors and diplomats need to better demonstrate their understanding of the complexities in Myanmar and play a more strategic role in supporting the peace process. Failure to brighten the glimmers of hope experienced by conflict-affected communities would constitute a terrible lost opportunity to support lasting peace in Myanmar.

Casualties of war

In what has been described by the United Nations as one of the world's most intractable refugee situations, people have been fleeing Burma/Myanmar for more than half of a century. The root causes of the country's refugee problem lie in the ethnic and political conflicts since independence in 1948 from the British. Tragically, the Burmese nation has since then never known a single day of peace.

Most of those affected by conflict are minorities living mostly in the rugged hills and mountains bordering Bangladesh, China, India, Laos and Thailand. The core of these conflicts is that the government does not recognize ethnic political aspirations. The absence of durable and sustainable solutions mean that forced labour by the military, forced relocation of villages, enforced disappearances, rape and other forms of sexual violence, torture, arbitrary detentions, and discrimination against ethnic minorities are all cited as concerns by the United Nations and international rights and humanitarian groups.

The refugees and internally displaced people are vulnerable to human traffickers and people smugglers. Where there are no refugee camps, they receive little support and are routinely subject to detention, discrimination, harassment and exploitative working conditions.

None of the main asylum countries in Asia is a signatory to the 1951 Convention Relating to the Status of Refugees or its 1967 Protocol, leaving refugees from Burma/Myanmar with little protection or recognition of their rights. The affected Asian countries lack national refugee legislation, with the result that legitimate asylum seekers and refugees are instead treated as migrants in breach of immigration laws.

Along the Thai border

The intractable nature of the emergency is illustrated by nine refugee camps in Thailand along the 1,800-kilometre-long border with Burma/Myanmar, where some 150,000 Burmese refugees live. The camps are run by the refugees themselves, with support from NGOs. The origin of these camps dates back to 1984, when the then military government's bid to seize more control of areas in the east sent the first large influx of 10,000 mainly Karen refugees into Thailand. Since 2004, the International Organization for Migration (IOM) has helped to resettle more than 80,000 Burmese refugees from Thailand, who primarily belong to the Karen and Karenni ethnic groups. They were mostly resettled in the US, as well as in Australia, Canada and New Zealand. However, this is an option only for the estimated 60% of refugees with official registration papers.

As of 2014, the Thai-Burmese border is home to approximately 130,000 refugees, many of whom over decades of ethnic conflict have lost their lands, families and livelihoods. Countless children born in makeshift camps have neither set foot in the country of their parents' birth nor do they speak their parents' native tongue.

Thailand does not have a refugee law or functioning asylum procedures. Different ethnicities are treated arbitrarily. Karen people are allowed to register as refugees or migrant workers, Shan can only be migrant workers, while the Rohingya are not allowed to register officially as either.

The landmines problem

While the existing data available on landmine victims indicate that Burma/Myanmar faces one of the most severe landmine problems in the world today, little is known about the actual extent of the problem, its impact on affected populations, communities' needs to sort out the mine problem and how different actors can become more involved in mine action.

The government in Naypyidaw has until recently prohibited almost all forms of mine action with the exception of a limited amount of prosthetic assistance to people with amputated limbs through general health programs. Some Mine Risk Education (MRE) is conducted in areas that are partly or fully under the control of non-state armed groups (NSAGs) as is victim assistance and some survey work, however, without government authorization. A substantial part of the MRE activity is carried out by DanChurchAid (Folkekirkens Nødhjælp), a humanitarian NGO based in Copenhagen.

Since starting operations in 2006, humanitarian groups like Geneva Call and DanChurchAid Mine Action, like other local and international

A young landmine victim gets a new start in life. The Danish NGO, DanChurchAid, works with local physiotherapists, teaching them how to make prosthetics and artificial legs for victims of landmines and unexploded ordinance (photo: Jonas Leegaard, courtesy Dan-ChurchAid)

actors wishing to undertake mine action, have been struggling to identify how best to do this in the limited humanitarian space available in Burma/Myanmar.

The problem with anti-personnel mines originates from decades of armed conflict, which is still ongoing in some parts or the country. Anti-personnel mines are still being used today by the armed forces of the government (the Tatmadaw), by various NSAGs, as well as by businessmen and villagers. Ten out of the country's 14 states and regions are contaminated by mines.

The eastern states and regions bordering Thailand are heavily mined. Some areas bordering Bangladesh and China are also mined, and accidents have occurred there. An estimated five million people live in townships with mine-contaminated areas; they are in urgent need of

Mine Risk Education (MRE) to reduce risky behaviour, and victim assistance for those already injured.

Until recently, the government's refusal to grant permission for mine-action activities and the ongoing conflict have left little space for humanitarian demining. However, some de-mining has been undertaken by the Tatmadaw and by NSAGs, although it is unclear whether these activities should be regarded as of military or humanitarian nature.

Inside the country

According to a 2013 estimate by the Norway-based Internal Displacement Monitoring Centre, there are currently 458,000 internally displaced people (IDPs) inside Myanmar, while UNHCR estimates there are an additional 215,000 refugees living in camps along the Thai border in areas where UNHCR is operating. UNHCR's main focus in the southeast will be to be prepared for the potential return of refugees from Thailand; however at the end of 2013, conditions were not yet conducive for such a return.[1]

The opening up of the once-isolated Myanmar after the 2010 elections led to installation of a hybrid military–civilian government, and more international aid has poured into the country and NGOs from the West have rushed to set up headquarters there.

Although Thai authorities bar residents from leaving the camps, many do find work locally, leaving themselves vulnerable to arrest and exploitation. They usually receive less than the minimum wage, and unscrupulous employers often refuse to pay them at all. Young women are especially vulnerable to sexual abuse by employers and authority figures such as policemen and government officials.

Critics warn that housing, land and property rights of Burma/Myanmar's displaced ethnic people have been largely ignored during the on-going peace process involving the central government and various armed ethnic rebel groups.

Despite the fact there is a general understanding by all parties involved in the peace process about the importance of land and property rights, all too little progress has thus far been made to address these issues in any detail; nor have practical plans commenced to resolve on-going displacement of either refugees or IDPs. Despite the fact that the land and housing rights of the hundreds of thousands of displaced people

1. Nor do they necessarily wish to return (see p. 364).

Kachin IDP camp, February 2012 (photo courtesy Burma Campaign UK)

is a glaring problem, the government has yet to formulate any concrete policies or positions on these questions during the negotiations process.

Although the central government has officially owned all the land in the country for decades, large numbers of rural people – both from the Burman majority and the country's ethnic minorities – have lived and farmed land using centuries-old forms of customary land-ownership, which determined inheritance and succession issues, as well as land-sharing.

Rape as a weapon

According to the Thailand-based Women's League of Burma (WLB), the military in Myanmar is still using rape as a weapon of war, with more than 100 women and girls raped by the army since a 2010 election brought about a nominally civilian government that has pursued rapprochement with the West. The WLB said in a report that 47 of the cases documented were gang rapes and 28 of the women were either killed or had died of their injuries. Several victims were as young as eight. Furthermore, in the period of 2009–12, the Kachin Women's Association Thailand had documented 59 cases of sexual violence by Myanmar government soldiers. The Shan Women's Action Network reported another 30 cases involving 35 women and girls.

The widespread and systematic nature of rape indicates a structural pattern: it is still used as an instrument of war and oppression. The WLB report said that more than 38 different army battalions were implicated in the cases it had documented: the incidents took place in at least 35 different townships and it was suspected that the reported cases were only the 'tip of the iceberg' as many cases went unreported.

The 2012 US State Department Human Rights Report on Burma referred to rapes by both government forces and ethnic minority insurgent groups in Shan and Kachin states. It said that when government soldiers committed rape in ethnic minority areas, the army rarely took action to punish those responsible. The January 2013 Human Rights Watch report on Myanmar said that sexual violence by the military remained a serious problem.

Child soldiers

Children in Myanmar have been widely used in armed conflicts by both state armed forces and non-state armed groups. Despite a minimum age of 18 for military recruitment, over the years many hundreds of under-age boys have been recruited, often forcibly, into the national army (Tatmadaw) and deployed to areas where state forces have been fighting armed opposition groups. Border guard forces, composed of former members of armed opposition groups and formally under the command of the Myanmar military, also have under-age boys in their ranks. In June 2012, after protracted negotiations with the UN, the Myanmar government signed up to an action plan under which it has committed to release all soldiers under 18 from Tatmadaw and border guard forces.

Child recruitment and use by armed opposition groups is also reported. These include the Democratic Karen Buddhist Army (DKBA), Kachin Independence Army (KIA), Karen National Union/Karen National Liberation Army (KNU/KNLA), Karenni National Progressive Party/ Karenni Army (KNPP/KA), Shan State Army South (SSA-S) and United Wa State Army (UWSA). The KNU/KNLA and KNPP/KA have sought to conclude action plans on child soldiers with the UN, but the UN has been prevented from doing so by the Government of Myanmar.[2]

✍ FY

2.   Sources: UNHCR, Geneva Call, DanChurchAid, Burmanetnews.

The struggle for peace in northern Myanmar

Wai Moe

At the time this volume went to press in July 2014, a nationwide ceasefire had yet to be reached between the Myanmar state/the army (Tatmadaw) and various armed ethnic groups. One of the major stumbling blocks to an agreement was sporadic fighting in Kachin and northern Shan State between government forces and the Kachin Independence Army (plus its allies). The following account, prefaced by a brief historical background, illustrates how complex and difficult the peace process is proving to be.

Background to the conflict and recent peace talks

Armed rebellion against the Burmese state by Kachin separatists broke out in 1961, shortly after the formation of the Kachin Independence Organization (KIO) and its military wing, the Kachin Independence Army (KIA).[1] A ceasefire was agreed upon in 1994 that for many years was the only written agreement the regime had with any armed group. This left the KIO/KIA both armed and controlling a swathe of territory in Kachin State that was virtually independent. For the next 17 years, there was relative peace in the north and the KIO earned large revenues from exploitation of the rich natural resources in its domain. In particular, logging became an important revenue source and trade with Chinese businesses and officials expanded. Although logging was later banned by the KIO, and China and Burma agreed to stop illegal logging, environmental degradation, illegal trade and trafficking seem to have continued.

However, the military and its business partners benefitted most from the ceasefire. Not only do they now seem in control of major parts

---

1. For a fuller description of the KIA, the links between the Kachin resistance and the church, etc., see p. 166.

Who are the Kachin?

As noted earlier in this volume (see p. 159), ethnic names differ depending on who is speaking. They can be also used to combine a number of separate groups under a common identity. So it is for the Kachin, whose name is a modern umbrella term for six sub-groups. These are the Jinghpaw, Lawngwaw, Lachik, Zaiwa, Lisu and Nung-Rawang, all of whom traditionally resided in the northernmost parts of the country, having strong links with the Salween River and Yunnan to the east, Tibet to the north, and Assam and Arunachal Pradesh in India to the west. The traditional heartland of the Kachin region for many of these people, but especially for the Jinghpaw, is known in English as The Triangle. This is the land that sits just above the confluence of the great Irrawaddy River.

The Kachin people are not confined to Burma. For instance, in pre-colonial times the Jinghpaw controlled many of the major mountain passes in the region between Assam and Yunnan (fuller details in 'Religion, identity and separatism', later in this volume). In India, the Jinghpaw developed a local identity known as Singpho and associated with Theravada Buddhism. They do not readily identify themselves as Kachin – this is a term that has very specific Burma context – but they maintain affinities with Jinghpaw groups and others across the region. In China, Jingpo is an umbrella category, much as is the term Kachin in Burma, and in Yunnan it includes groups such as the Bolo, who are not considered Kachin in Burma (indeed they are not even known in Burma as a separate ethnic group). However, in Burma, the Lisu have been included in the Kachin ethnic category, while in China they are not considered part of the Jingpo. There is not, therefore, a neat correlation between the terms Singpho, Kachin and Jingpo as used by groups and national political systems in India, Burma and China respectively.

The key point here is that while the political category Kachin has traction only in Burma (and to a limited extent in Thailand), it is also recognized by those within the Kachin nexus that they have affinities, sometimes very close and substantive, with a range of communities across national boundaries. These linkages have also proved very important in the development and sustainability of long-term conflict in the post-independence Burmese state. They have helped to secure ethno-nationalist military, religious and political elites with geographical, political and social conduits through which they have been able to access external actors, such as other armed groups or sympathetic representatives of neighbouring national or regional governments, as part of their conflict with the Burmese government.

But what do Kachin people mean when they refer to themselves as such? In reality, most are referring to a very specific *ideological* construct of kinship. Again, this is something with which any visitor to Kachin State or engaging with Kachin people in any setting will become aware very quickly. In normal social interaction, there is no need for Kachin people to use a term such as 'Kachin' with each other to define their kinship bonds; they would instead use the complex system of kinship categories that defines one's place as a sister, brother, cousin, mother, grandfather and so on, to define their relationships. It is, then, in the context of inter-cultural rather than intra-cultural communication that the term Kachin is used, as a kind of shorthand, a useful tool of communication and classification. It is to this broader ideological concept of kinship to which Kachin people refer when they say 'I am Kachin'. Decades of recent conflict have undoubtedly brought changes to the understandings of this kinship system in practice, but at an ideological level it remains the key referent in what makes someone 'Kachin' and for integrating a diverse range of communities within this identity over time and space.

✍ MS

of the lucrative jade mining industry in the state but also the army used the ceasefire to extend its control over trade and land in a process that Kevin Wood has termed 'ceasefire capitalism'. After areas had been cleared of forest, the land was confiscated and turned into large-scale rubber plantations guarded by the army. Local peasants were forced out and army officers in cooperation with Chinese companies took over the land. In some cases local Kachin were also involved. In this process of 'silent conquest', the army seems to have expanded its area of control and thus in part provoked the recent fighting.[2] In addition, from 2009 tensions began to rise because of the KIA's refusal to join the govern-

2. See Wood (2011). China also began an opium substitution programme but poppy cultivation actually increased by 26% in 2013.

Kachin IDPs attend a small Christmas Day service in a home at Jeyang refugee camp outside of Laiza, December 2012 (photo: David Høgsholt)

ment's Border Guard Force scheme and due to the construction of the giant Myitsone Dam, whose reservoir would flood wide areas of Kachin land and pristine forest.

Fighting broke out in June 2011 – less than three months after the new, nominally civilian government took power – when the army moved in troops to protect three dams under construction near the Chinese border. There was an agreement on this move but the KIA suspected that the army was bringing more troops in than had been agreed upon. The resulting conflict has caused many casualties, including civilians, and an estimated 100,000 Kachin people have been displaced, many fleeing over the border into Yunnan. At least 66 churches and 55 schools have been destroyed, crops have been burned, and many new bridges wrecked, the Human Aid Relief Trust reported in 2013.[3]

Following several rounds of inconclusive peace talks, the army launched an offensive during Christmas 2012 against the border town of Laiza where the KIO has its headquarters. According MPC officials whom I interviewed, the Tatmadaw's purpose in its December offensive against KIA posts was to 'give a lesson'. Artillery fire landed on the

---

3.   Human Aid Relief Trust, London 2013, www.hart-uk.org.

Chinese side of the border, provoking local protests. Beijing then finally intervened in the situation. On 19 January 2013, it sent a high-level delegation to meet with President Thein Sein, who ordered the army to stop the fighting. Within days the Chinese hosted new peace talks in Ruili, Yunnan, between Aung Min, the president's negotiator with the ethnic armed groups, and General Gun Maw of the KIA. Aung Min also brought observers to the talks: General Saw Mutu Say Poe, head of the Karen National Union, Sai Lu from the Shan State Army (South) and Harn Yawnghwe, head of the EU Burma Office. The talks, however, did not stop the fighting despite a positive atmosphere and permission being given for the UN special envoy to Burma, Vijay Nambiar, to visit Kachin refugees near Myitkyina. The army followed its own agenda and did not react to the intervention. However, the army is reported to have suffered heavy casualties due to the KIA's well-organized guerrilla warfare. Throughout June 2011 to December 2012, hundreds of Tatmadaw officers and many other ranks were hit by KIA snipers and roadside mines. In March 2014, Jane's Defence Weekly reported that 5,000 government troops had been killed and two helicopters crashed during military operations against the KIA in 2012. At the same time, KIA officials told local Burmese media that at least 1,000 Kachin troops had died as well.

≤ MG

Further talks between the government and the KIO

The government and the KIO met again in early April 2013 in Ruili but the result was as inconclusive as previous talks. The next round of peace talks was in late May in Myitkyina, the capital of Kachin State. It was the first time the Kachin leaders had travelled to the government-controlled area since the civil war broke out again on 11 June 2011. Thousands crowded the streets of Myitkyina to give a hero's welcome to the Kachin delegation led by Gun Maw. However, the result of the meeting had no real meaning for genuine peace. According to Min Zaw Oo, a director of the Myanmar Peace Centre (MPC), the semi-government organization headed by Minister U Aung Min, the government could not use the term of 'ceasefire agreement' with the KIO since the Kachin leaders did not agree to the term. They argued they had already signed a 'ceasefire agreement' in 1994 but this had been broken down overnight in June

2011. Therefore, Kachin leaders did not wish to use the term again before a genuine peace agreement takes place.

However, the result of the meeting in Myitkyina was that both sides agreed to form a 'Peace Technical Team' to resolve immediate tensions and conflicts as well as to work out matters in detail before the meetings of the high-level peace committees. The government's team was made up of MPC members who were former exiles and mid-level business-men while the KIO's team was filled with second-line officers used to dealing with alliances.

More recent tensions in Kachin State occurred in September 2013 following a skirmish between Tatmadaw and KIA forces in Machanpaw Township (in Putao District) in the far north of Myanmar. During the skirmish, some government soldiers including an officer were killed. Shortly afterwards, the Tatmadaw accused Kachin troops of beheading their officer after catching him in hiding. KIO spokesman La Nan rejected the accusation in an interview with media. Machanpaw is a transit point to nearby high mountains in Myanmar. At the time of the conflict, five American climbers were trapped in these mountains by the fighting, heightening international attention on the Kachin situation, but Burmese authorities and Tay Za, a businessman, arranged their return by helicopter.[4]

On 4 November 2013, new talks were held in Myitkyina between the Union-level Peace Making Committee and ethnic groups. Observers were UN Special Envoy Vijay Nambiar and Wang Ying Fang representing China. Only Skynet TV and MRTV plus the KIO information committee were allowed to report from this closed-door meeting. Here, Nai Hong Sar, the general secretary of the United Nationalities Federal Council (UNFC), outlined the conditions for a nationwide ceasefire agreed by ethnic groups at their Laiza meeting, including 'genuine federalism' and formation of a (federal) Union Army.[5] He also laid out their roadmap for peace:

---

4. The climbers (who included one Burmese) were the first ever to reach the summit of Myanmar's second highest mountain. The mountaineering expedition was indeed financed by Burmese billionaire Tay Za's Htoo Foundation and the nearby fighting took place on land to which Tay Za was in the process of acquiring the licence in order to pursue a large-scale gold-mining project for his company. (*Kachin News*, 23 September 2013).

5. The Myitkyina meeting immediately followed a UNFC-supported gathering of 18 armed ethnic groups in Laiza at which conditions for a nationwide ceasefire were laid down (for fuller details of these conditions, see p. 152).

1. Agreement on a framework for national political dialogue.

2. Signing of a nationwide ceasefire agreement.

3. Holding a national-level political dialogue.

4. Signing a union accord from a national convention held in the spirit of the 1947 Panglong conference.

5. Ratification and implementation of the union accord.

Ethnic groups in Myitkyina also called for abolition of Article 17/1 of the Illegal Organizations Act.[6]

However, Lt-Gen. Thet Naing Win, Minister of Border Affairs and chief of the Tatmadaw's Bureau of Special Operations-4, repeated the six policies on the peace process articulated by the Tatmadaw commander-in-chief, Senior-General Min Aung Hlaing. These included ethnic groups' respect for the 2008 constitution and the Three Main National Causes.[7]

Meanwhile, sources in Naypyidaw said that while ethnic groups were holding their earlier meeting in Laiza, the National Defence and Security Council, the highest body in Myanmar's power structure, held its own meeting to prepare a new draft for the nationwide ceasefire agreement. The government negotiation group headed by Minister U Aung Min brought the new draft to the peace talks in Myitkyina but failed to persuade ethnic leaders to sign the agreement. All that both sides could agree, then, was to announce another round of peace talks in Karen State in December.

After the failed meeting in Myitkyina, Major-General Sumlut Gun Maw, deputy chief of staff of the Kachin Independence Army said: 'In the peace process, we are still at [the stage of] a precondition agreement, not yet nodding on the nationwide ceasefire.' He reiterated: 'The government's negotiators and ethnic armed groups have been still in discussions on a precondition agreement.'

'Regarding federalism, everybody including the president is talking [about this] except the military', Gun Maw said. 'The president sent a

6. Until recently, this law was used to imprison people belonging to, or attending the meetings of, banned organizations. The army may wish to keep this law in force until a final settlement is signed.

7. That is, to preserve the nation, national solidarity and national sovereignty. Military representatives at the conference were said to be utterly opposed to the idea of a federal army or reorganization of the Tatmadaw to incorporate ethnic armed groups and instead insisted that all ethnic groups should disarm.

letter to us saying autonomy and self determination have to be provided to ethnic minorities.'

'We have been talking with government negotiators such as U Aung Min for more than two years. But the precondition agreements during two years of talks were not included in their latest draft of a ceasefire agreement. The federal union could be possible. But we all have to try and work hard', Gun Maw said.

Even though Naypyidaw's ceasefire/peace talks have lasted for more than a year since the heavy military offensive against Laiza in December 2012 and January 2013, armed conflict between Tatmadaw and KIA troops continued at different levels of intensity throughout 2013 and in early 2014 in both Kachin State and northern Shan State. Most clashes between ground forces are over deployment territories and control of natural resources and trade. At the time of writing, the latest of such clashes was on 25 March in Momeik Township, northern Shan State. An online news outlet, Kachinland News, which is close to the KIO's information department, reported that Tatmadaw 'infantry units are commanded by their superiors to launch ground operations to combat illegal logging while expanding their foothold in southern Kachin State. The source said that Burmese army's frontline battalion commanders are warned against contact with KIA troops despite ongoing peace talks between ethnic armed groups and [the] Burmese government.'[8]

Another fresh source of tension between Naypyidaw and Laiza has been in the implementation of the first national census in more than three decades, launched on 30 March 2014. In early March, the KIO announced that territory under its control would not participate in the census process. During an interview with Burmese media, KIO spokesman U Lanan explained that the KIO had decided against the census because Kachin representatives had not been invited to discussions with national census officials and in any case armed conflicts were occurring in KIO territory. The KIO's rejection of the census process came after negotiations between the central government and KIO in how different ethnicities in Kachin State were to be recorded in the census. A KIO official at the War Office in Laiza said that Kachin felt Naypyidaw was

---

8. 'Battles Resume in Northern Shan State', Kachinland News, 25 March 2014, http://kachinlandnews.com/?p=24290.

using the census to generate disunity between Kachin and non-Kachin people in Kachin State.

The China factor

The international community and neighbouring countries also play a significant role in the conflict in northern Myanmar. The main actor here is Myanmar's powerful neighbour, China, which is especially important because many of its state enterprises are engaged in Myanmar while Chinese nationals and other people linked to China are assuming key roles in the country's economy. But there are also longstanding links between China and the Kachin themselves. For centuries, the Jinghpaw, the main Kachin sub-group, have lived in both northern Myanmar and China's Yunnan province (see p. 263). Kachin can be found running restaurants, hotels, jade companies and other businesses in Yunnan and elsewhere in China. And traditional Kachin 'Manaw' statues are noticeable in Yunnan.

Military links have also been important. When the KIO launched its armed insurgency in 1961, China's People's Liberation Army (PLA) provided it with arms either directly or via the Burma Communist Party. Throughout more than five decades of their separatist struggle, KIO leaders have maintained relationships with China while Kachin armed groups have maintained key outposts on the border to China.

As part of their geopolitical balancing act, Kachin leaderships never forget to deal with New Delhi, too. As such, the KIO is the only ethnic armed group in Myanmar that has liaison offices in both China and India. 'We Kachin have to play a geopolitical game too', explained Tuja, an official with the KIO's Strategic and International Studies Department. 'We have to deal not only with Beijing or Kunming but also with New Delhi since [the] KIO's territory is strategically wide from the Sino–Burmese border in the east to the Indo–Burmese in the west.'

However, Laiza's external relationship with the Chinese seems more important because the Sino–Burmese border is crucial for them. But the relationship is not without problems. According to KIO officials interviewed in Myanmar, China and Thailand, Kachin feel the Communist Chinese may have distrusted the KIO for decades because the Kachin leadership is Christian and seen as being close to the West. For instance, the KIO maintain relations with American missionaries. Despite possible distrust, China, and particularly Yunnan, enjoyed the benefits of access to Burmese natural resources, border trading and other business activities in KIO territories during the 17 years of ceasefire between the central government and KIO.

China's involvement in the current conflict predates the collapse of the ceasefire in 2011. In December 2008, Beijing was reminded of the intractability of Myanmar's ethnic issues when it received a letter from Kachin and Wa leaders asking for help. This was sent shortly after ethnic groups came under pressure from the military regime for their armed groups (including the KIA) to join the new Border Guard Force established under the 2008 constitution. The letter's authors stated their preference for an autonomous arrangement such as Hong Kong has within the PRC and they asked China's leadership to convince Naypyidaw of its merits. According to the letter, the ethnic leaders said:

> We solemnly ask the Chinese government to relay our request to the Myanmar government: first, we support the constitutional reform. When the new government forms in 2010, the leadership based on national public elections should promise to leaders of the autonomous states that we will be part of high leadership of the new government and build upon the method of management of China's autonomous region.[9]

Since the outbreak of armed conflict in northern Burma/Myanmar, China has attempted to ease tensions between the central government and the Kachin. It hosted 'peace talks' on the conflict in Kachin state in 2012 and 2013 and sent observers to talks in Myanmar in response to a Kachin request for a mediator in the negotiations. However, according interviews with staffers from the MPC, China is being careful in its involvement as Burmese officials have shown that they are not very comfortable even with the Chinese playing a third-party role.

This kind of concern is expressed by Chinese officials, too. In an email interview with a Chinese official from Yunnan province's International Culture Exchange Centre made on the basis of complete anonymity, the respondent pointed out that, although China is involved in Myanmar's ethnic issues including those involving the Kachin, Beijing maintains its 'non-interference policy in the internal affairs of other countries in [the] first place.' Secondly, the official said, 'that [involvement] is to solve the

---

9. Quoted in *The Irrawaddy*, 'China's Autonomous Regions Eyed as Model for Burmese Ethnic Areas?', 13 July 2009: http://www2.irrawaddy.org/article.php?art_id=16316.

problem, or reach peace through a dialogue and talks, and on this aspect, in Feb[ruary] 2013, China played the role of mediator of the talks between [the] KIA and Myanmar government.' He added thirdly that 'it's my view that China doesn't want to see its interests hurt by [either] side'.

The exact nature of China's policy towards the Kachin resistance movement is unclear, however. For instance, it appears that Chinese objections have influenced their close allies in Myanmar, the Wa and the Mongla armed groups,[10] not to participate in the Burmese ethnic alliance group, the United Nationalities Federal Council (UNFC). In contrast, the KIO has been playing an active role in this organization. On the other hand, the Kachin leadership has maintained its relationship with the United States and European countries. It has also expanded its relationship with Tokyo, who wants to counterbalance Beijing's influence in the Southeast Asian mainland. In the past three years, the Japanese have also been involved in peace and ethnic issues by providing funding. According to the Myanmar Peace Monitor, the Nippon Foundation, a sister organization of the right-wing Sasakawa Peace Foundation, has put more than US\$ 28.86 million into Myanmar projects since 2012 when it started to involve itself with the UNFC and in the peace process generally.[11]

The Kachin and their alliances

Since it was founded in 1961, at various times the KIO has forged alliances with other ethnic armed groups. It was a key member of the Democratic Alliance of Burma (DAB), an alliance formed in 1988 between ethnic armed groups and pro-democracy groups following the crushing of the 8888 Revolution. However, the role of Kachin within the alliance was set back after the KIO signed a ceasefire agreement with the Burmese military regime in 1994. At the time, other members of the DAB – including another key member, the Karen National Union (KNU) – condemned the KIO's move; its unilateral ceasefire agreement with the central government betrayed a core principle of the alliance,

---

10. The United Wa State Army and National Democratic Alliance Army-Eastern Shan State, respectively (MG).

11. The extensive Japanese involvement in the peace process is made clear by the Myanmar Peace Monitor (2014) (MG).

that 'any ceasefire and peace talks' should not be undertaken individually but together within the umbrella group.

After signing the ceasefire, the KIO's relationship with other ethnic groups became informal rather than part of a formal alliance. The KIO leadership even attempted to demonstrate to the central government that they wanted to avoid any issues with which the generals were not comfortable. For example, like the KNU in eastern Myanmar, the KIO had previously hosted student activists in the north who fled the big cities shortly after the brutal suppression of the pro-democracy uprising in September 1988 and helped them form the All Burma Student Democratic Front (ABSDF-North). The KIO's hosting of the ABSDF dramatically changed after the 1994 ceasefire agreement. According to separate interviews with former ABSDF members and KIO officials, under pressure from the generals the KIO leadership abandoned the ABSDF and forced its former student activists either to join up with the KIA or leave its territory. Even so, during the 17-year ceasefire, the KIA was reported to have significant relationships with certain ethnic armed groups including the Wa, Shan, Chin and Rakhine. The Kachin also trained small ethnic armed groups such as the Chin National Front and Arakan Army, hosting them in KIO territory for decades and providing them with arms and ammunition. Moreover, Gurkhas and Shan were among other ethnic minorities in northern Myanmar integrated into the KIA, with a Gurkha battalion formed within the Kachin forces.

It was towards the end of the ceasefire period, in 2008–09, that the KIO began to strengthen its alliances. The impetus was an aggressive push by the central government for all ethnic armed groups who had signed ceasefire agreements with the regime to be absorbed into the previously mentioned Border Guard Force established under the 2008 constitution. The ceasefire groups saw this 'One Nation, One Army' policy as a 'disarmament policy' without guarantees. After the regime began actively pushing its BGF strategy in late 2008, the affected groups expected war at any time and started to work out formal or informal alliances with each other. The KIO/KIA's strategic relationships in the BGF crisis were particularly with ceasefire groups in the northeast of the country who also disagreed the regime's plan – the Shan State Army-North, the United Wa State Army (UWSA), the ethnic Chinese Kokang armed group known as the Myanmar National Democratic Alliance

Army (MNDAA) and the Mongla armed group (National Democratic Alliance Army, NDAA). At the time, the cooperation between these allies included logistical and armed support but this was insufficient to hinder Tatmadaw troops which overran the Kokang armed group at its headquarters in Laokai in 2009.

After the Kokang incident, the KIO strengthened its efforts to forge alliances with other armed groups, even renewing contacts with ethnic umbrella groups like the DAB. In 2009–11, KIO envoys travelled to the territories of other ethnic groups along the length of Myanmar's eastern border with China and Thailand. Finally, for the first time in 17 years, the Kachins rejoined the ethnic alliance, now called the Committee for the Emergence of Federal Union (CEFU). Headquartered in the northern Thai city of Chiang Mai, home to many Kachins and Kachin leaders, this significant alliance was formed in November 2009 by ethnic armed groups. In February 2011 the alliance became the United Nationalities Federal Council (UNFC), also based in Chiang Mai.

KIO involvement in the formation of the CEFU and UNFC was motivated by the need to strengthen its financial and political will. As such, from the beginning the Kachin worked to convince the key ethnic armed groups to join the alliance and thereafter the KIO has played a key role in all offices of the CEFU and later UNFC. All members of the CEFU were ethnic armed groups – the KIO, KNU, New Mon State Party (NMSP), Karenni National Progressive Party (KNPP), Chin National Front (CNF) and Shan State Army (SSA), both North and South. Moreover, the UNFC has an informal alliance with the UWSA and Mongla group.[12] Other ethnic but non-armed civic groups have subsequently joined the UNFC.

As with the DAB, the ceasefire/peace policy of the new alliance is that all talks with the central government should be held jointly rather than individually and that there should be more focus on political dialogue to find a genuine political solution. However, although the UNFC represents the united voice of ethnic groups, in 2012 this unity (and the KIO's whole alliance strategy) was suddenly undermined by the leadership of the KNU unilaterally entering into negotiations with the central government. Initially this action actually split the Karen leadership but

---

12. As noted above, in line with Chinese wishes, the UWSA and NDAA-ESS are UNFC observers only. At this stage, also the SSA-South is only an observer.

those leaders who wished to negotiate with Naypyidaw outside the alliance consensus eventually gained control of the organization.

Perhaps because of the above setback, the KIO continues to pursue individual alliances with different ethnic armed groups. Significant here is the KIO's alliance with the Ta'ang National Liberation Army (TNLA), which is based in northern and eastern Shan State. It is alleged that not only did the Kachin facilitate redeployment of the embryonic TNLA from KNU territory to its Palaung homeland in 2011 but they have also trained and armed the Ta'ang. Today, the KIA and TNLA are the two main ethnic armed groups still fighting the Tatmadaw.

Divide and rule?

An obstacle to real peace in Burma/Myanmar is the government and army's divide-and-rule tactic of providing improved opportunities to ethnic armed groups that have a better relationship with Naypyidaw. Since 2011, President U Thein Sein and the commander-in-chief of the Tatmadaw have met repeatedly with two groups in particular, the KNU and Shan State Army (South). The Karen and Shan rebels are Naypyidaw's biggest success stories since President Thein Sein took office in March 2011. However, the Kachin rebels, who had a 17-year ceasefire agreement with the Burmese regime, have not received this kind of favours after the ceasefire broke down in June 2011.

In January 2014, the KNU's chairman, General Mutu Say Poe, was received in Naypyidaw by both President Thein Sein and the Tatamadaw commander-in-chief, Senior-General Min Aung Hlaing. The meeting was significant for Naypyidaw as it approached this key ethnic armed group ahead of another conference of ethnic armed groups held at a jungle base in Karen rebel territory.

'We discussed the nationwide ceasefire agreement, and plans regarding another conference of ethnic armed groups [to be held] in February, as well as the upcoming meeting in Hpa-an [between ethnic armed groups and] the government's Peace Making Committee', the general secretary of the KNU, Saw Kwe Htoo Win, was quoted by the Democratic Voice of Burma. 'We spoke with the commander-in-chief about the ethnic groups' endeavours. He also stressed that peace is necessary for the country's development, and that he will continue his efforts with no reversal.' The state media also reported on the meeting, quoting Min Aung Hlaing: '75 per cent of the peace process has been completed between the government and KNU and coordination would be the final stage of the process.'

After meeting with Thein Sein and Min Aung Hlaing in Naypyidaw, the KNU's policy on the ceasefire became different from the common ground agreed in Laiza. While ethnic leaders had agreed that there should be genuine political dialogue before the nationwide ceasefire, Karen leaders said at the follow-up meeting of ethnic armed groups in Chiang Mai that they now wanted the signing of a ceasefire agreement before political dialogue. The Karen leadership even reportedly threatened others in the UNFC that they would leave the umbrella group if others disagreed.

This new stance seems to directly challenge the KIO who repeatedly have said that meaningful political dialogue would be a gateway to better guarantees for ethnic minorities. KIO leaders such as Gun Maw said that Kachin had had a 17-year experience with a ceasefire agreement with the central governments and a ceasefire agreement alone could not be a guarantee for them. On the other hand, the Karen leadership is used to responding to the KIO that they betrayed the ethnic alliance in 1994 by signing their own ceasefire agreement with the Burmese regime.

Ethnic groups and the government's peace negotiation group led by Minister Aung Min had previously agreed that another meeting on the ceasefire should take place in Karen State's capital, Hpa-an, on 20 January but this was postponed. 'Before peace facilitators of the Myanmar Peace Centre travelled to Chiang Mai, U Aung Min told them not to come back to Yangon without something in their hands', said Khin Maung Shwe, co-ordinator with Burma News International, which is monitoring the peace process. 'U Thein Sein and U Aung Min want for the nation-wide ceasefire agreements before the Union Day on February 12.' However, MPC facilitators failed to convince ethnic leaders to signing ceasefire agreements before the Union Day and the Hpa-an meeting was postponed to 20 February.[13]

In mid-March 2014, President Thein Sein was accompanied by Tatmadaw commander in chief Min Aung Hlaing on a trip to Kachin State that was described by the Ministry of Information as a 'snap visit' without advance notice. On the trip, the president and commander-in-

---

13. After multiple postponements of the Hpa-an meeting, peace talks were finally held in Yangon in May 2014. At time of writing, follow-up negotiations are still in progress. (MG)

chief, clad in Kachin dress, met with local leaders in Myitkyina. They also visited Myitkyina University, meeting students there. However, a meeting with KIO leaders was not on the agenda. As with other VIP trips in Myanmar/Burma, officials arranged a public welcome by local people for the country's two most powerful figures from central government and the military. But, in comparison with crowds who turned out in past months to welcome KIO delegations led by General Gun Maw, the state visitors had less of a welcome.

The military is still the most important key

Even though the Burmese military regime's rule was 'officially' concluded at the end of March 2011 with the transition to the government led by U Thein Sein, a retired general, the Tatmadaw is still powerful particularly on ethnic issues. Armed conflicts were escalating in northern Burma within months of U Thein Sein being sworn in as president and led to the breaking of the 17-year ceasefire agreement between the central government in Napyidaw and the Kachin armed group.

The spark to the breakdown was around Tapaing Dam in Kachin State near the Sino–Burmese border when government troops attacked KIA troops. To restore the ceasefire, Thein Sein's government and KIO negotiators have been meeting since June 2012. Initial talks were unable to halt the fighting, which escalated near KIO headquarters in late December 2012 with the Burmese military even using air raids on KIA outposts. It was President Thein Sein personally who reportedly ordered the ceasefire in Kachin State.

Therefore the question is what influence Thein Sein really has on the Tatmadaw even though its commander-in-chief, Senior-General Min Aung Hlaing, has publicly said that he backs the administration. What is Min Aung Hlaing's policy on ethnic issues?

'Our efforts for peace in the country do not mean we are afraid. We are not afraid', said Min Aung Hlaing during a speech to senior military officers at the command centre of the War Office in Naypyidaw on 29 November 2013, according to a confidential official document leaked by military sources. 'Peace is for stability and development for the country to compete shoulder to shoulder with other countries.' However, Min Aung Hlaing added, 'I would like to say clearly that democracy and peace do not mean decentralization.'

In his speech on the 69th anniversary of Armed Forces Day on 27 March 2014, Min Aung Hlaing said that the 2008 constitution was 'supported by 92.48 per cent of 26.7 million voters' in the 2008 referendum in May.[14] He also said the 2008 constitution was not written for 'one person, one organization, one ethnic group or the Tatmadaw'. Min Aung Hlaing assured his audience yet again that the Tatmadaw is the 'main [institution] responsible for safeguarding the constitution'.

Postscript

As of June 2014 no nationwide ceasefire agreement has been signed and there is still sporadic fighting in Kachin State while more Kachin people have been displaced despite a preliminary agreement signed to ease tensions. It is not a genuine ceasefire but IDPs were promised a fast and safe return. Even so, within the KIO there exists a deep mistrust of the army and government. The Tatmadaw is also attacking the Ta'ang National Liberation Army, a Palaung ethnic armed group active in nearby northern Shan State, causing 5,000 people to be internally displaced. However, the army argues that it only acts in self-defence and the TNLA does seem to be on the offensive. Overall, however, what can be seen is a strategic struggle for control of these resource-rich border regions, an area over which the state has never had control. The KIO has refused to participate in the ongoing national census and the army is now going into some Kachin villages to complete it. This may escalate the conflict further. Kachin, like most ethnic groups resent the Burman ethnic categories and terms being used in the census.

✍ MG

References

Myanmar Peace Monitor (2014), *Deciphering Myanmar's Peace Process: A Reference Guide 2014*, Chiang Mai: Burma News International: http://www.mmpeacemonitor.org/images/pdf/deciphering_myanmar_peace_process_2014.pdf.

Wood, Kevin (2011) 'Ceasefire capitalism: Military-private partnerships, resource concession and military-state building in Burma-China borderlands'. *Journal of Peasant Studies*, Vol. 38,4: 747–770.

---

14. Critics described the referendum as the 'Nargis referendum' as the Burmese military regime held it shortly after Cyclone Nargis hit Myanmar killing at least 134,000 people.

The religious dimension

Mikael Gravers and Marie Ditlevsen

From the large number of pagodas, churches, mosques, temples, etc. decorating the country, it is easy to see that religion plays a very important role in the culture and everyday-life of Myanmar. Visitors to the country will also quickly find that religion does not simply belong to the physical landscape; in many ways, but especially in the form of Buddhist monks and nuns on their alms rounds, it is an integral part of the human landscape.[1]

Novice nuns making house visits to collect alms in Yangon (photo: Marie Ditlevsen)

The vast majority of the population is Buddhist (about 89%), while the rest are Christian, Muslim, Hindu or Animist. Not only does the

---

1. Monks and nuns offer an opportunity for lay people to make donation or alms in order to obtain religious merit. Monks and nuns do not actually beg and normally wander in silence on their alms rounds.

The world's largest reclining Buddha lies south of Mawlamyine (photo: Mikael Gravers)

Buddhist Sangha play a key role in civil society, providing schooling, health services, etc. for many Burmese (see p. 66), but also Buddhism itself has a dominant role in *official* descriptions of national culture and identity (also in the national constitution – see below). Mainly concentrated in the central parts of the country, Buddhism is practised in particular by the Bamar (Burmans). However, significant ethnic minorities are also Buddhist, notably the Mon, Rakhine, Shan and a majority of Karen (see Map 6, p. 282).

About 4% of the population are Christian. The result of Western missionary work during the colonial period, especially among the ethnic minorities, Christianity is mainly practised by the Kachin, Chin, Kayah and a minority of Karen, as well as by some other groups. The main Christian denominations are the Baptists and Catholics, with smaller numbers of Anglicans and Seventh-Day Adventists among others.

Islam has a far longer history in Myanmar than Christianity, dating back to Muslim traders who arrived along the Arakan coast and Ayeyarwady River delta more than a thousand years ago. Its followers, mainly Sunni, account for about another 4% of the population. Although the Rohingya are the Muslims in Myanmar attracting the greatest international attention today (especially in the news media) (see pp. 310 and 323ff.), significant numbers of Muslims are found outside Rakhine State. These include people sometimes called Pathi, who are scattered across the Bamar heartland. Of Persian/Indian origin, some Pathi reached high positions in successive Burmese royal courts. The Panthay, who originated from Hui Muslim communities in Yunnan, mainly live in northern parts of Myanmar (fuller details p. 161), Muslims have had a significant influence as small-scale traders, a role in which some have been targeted – as was recently emphasized in Meikhtila, north of Yangon. The unrest between the city's Muslim and Buddhist communities was sparked by a dispute at a gold shop between a Buddhist customer and the Muslim shopkeeper.[2]

Mosque in old Rangoon (photo: Mikael Gravers)

Officially, very few Burmese (about 1% of the population) are Animists/spirit worshippers. However, Animist beliefs are widespread and can be discerned in the practice of other religions, e.g. in the Burmese Nat cult of guardian spirits. Every monastery and house can have a Nat and these spirits are consulted before commencement of construction work or repairs, even if they are not formally part of Buddhism as such. Very often, small dwellings raised for the spirits can be seen in front of people's homes. Non-Buddhist spirit worship and animal sacrifice are still practised among some ethnic groups.

---

2. See http://www.irrawaddy.org/political-parties/state-of-emergency-in-meikhtila-to-be-lifted.html.

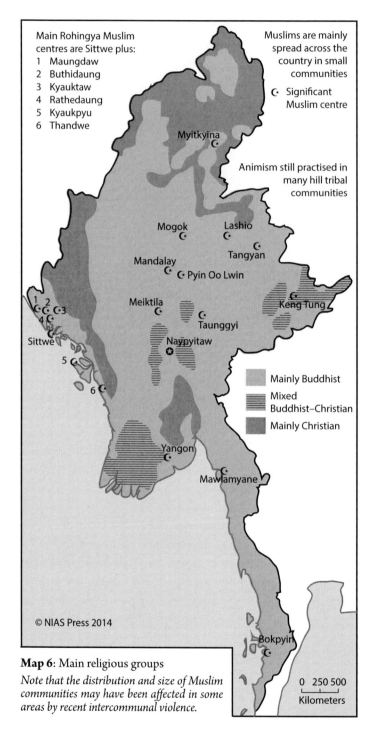

Main Rohingya Muslim centres are Sittwe plus:
1 Maungdaw
2 Buthidaung
3 Kyauktaw
4 Rathedaung
5 Kyaukpyu
6 Thandwe

Muslims are mainly spread across the country in small communities

☪ Significant Muslim centre

Animism still practised in many hill tribal communities

Myitkyina ☪

Mogok ☪   Lashio ☪

Tangyan ☪

Mandalay ☪   ☪ Pyin Oo Lwin

Meiktila ☪   Keng Tung ☪

☪ Taunggyi

Naypyitaw ✪

Sittwe

5 ☪

6 ☪

Mainly Buddhist

Mixed Buddhist–Christian

Mainly Christian

Yangon ☪

Mawlamyane ☪

© NIAS Press 2014

Bokpyin ☪

Map 6: Main religious groups

Note that the distribution and size of Muslim communities may have been affected in some areas by recent intercommunal violence.

0   250 500
Kilometers

Astrologers shop, Kaba Aye Pagoda, Yangon. Regardless of religious background, spiritualism in many different guises is an integral part of the country's culture (photo: Mikael Gravers)

The 2008 constitution includes provisions that ostensibly provide religious freedom for all religions, with article 34 giving every citizen 'the right to freely profess and practise religion subject to public order, morality or health and to the other provisions of this Constitution'. However, while article 362 'recognizes Christianity, Islam, Hinduism and Animism as the religions existing in the Union at the day of the coming into operation of this Constitution', article 361 states: 'The Union recognizes [the] special position of Buddhism as the faith professed by the great majority of the citizens of the Union.' Interestingly, article 364 warns that 'the abuse of religion for political purposes is forbidden' – a warning that has become highly relevant in relation to recent events in Burma relating to political Buddhism and the plight of the Rohingya (for more details, see pp. 293ff. and 323ff. respectively).

Religion, identity and separatism – the case of the Kachin

Mandy Sadan

Religion is commonly cited as a major cause of the deep social and cultural barriers between ethnic groups such as the Kachin and their Burmese neighbours; the Burman heartland is Buddhist whereas ethnic minorities on the periphery tend to be Christian. This is a gross simplification as the Mon, Rakhine, Shan and a majority of Karen (as well as many other minority groups) are Buddhist. Even so, the stereotype persists and has been often used to explain many of the country's separatist conflicts. The links between ethnic identity, religion and separatism become even more tenuous, however, when an actual case is thoroughly examined – as, for instance, the Kachin.

It is often stated that more than 90 per cent of the Kachin people inside Burma today are Christian (and some claims go as high as 99 per cent). The main denominations are the Baptist and Roman Catholic congregations, the result of especially American and French missionary work from the 1870s, but there are many smaller groups, including the Assembly of God and various house church and evangelical movements. Initially, the missionaries made slow progress in obtaining and retaining Christian converts. However, the dominant perception today is that in the years leading up to the independence of Burma in 1948, there was an exponential increase in the numbers of Christian congregations; it is generally accepted that 'most' Kachin were Christian.

Some claim that one of the primary causes of the longstanding conflict between the Burmese government and the Kachin has been this religious division, reflecting the hostility that emerged between an assertively Burmanizing centre that wanted to extend Buddhism as the state religion and an ethno-nationalist inspired Kachin Christian society that sought to oppose it. Also important was that the Kachin were seen as essentially loyal to the colonial order and actively participated in the British policy of recruiting colonial troops among the ethnic minorities. This latent loyalty to the colonial military order is then used to explain the apparent reluctance of Kachin elites to join wholeheartedly with the new Union in the years between war and independence, and critically why they should feel no sense of disloyalty by rebelling against the Union government.

However, the above claim about religion is a simplification of the many serious political and economic fissures that have become only further embedded during decades of violence, of which religious affiliation is but one. Moreover, in terms of their supposed loyalty to the British and the extent that they were Christian in 1948, an entirely different picture of the Kachin emerges from a careful examination of the historical record.

The stereotype of the Kachin historically has traditionally been that before the arrival of British colonizers they were isolated, disconnected from the wider world other than as payers of tribute or bringers of chaos, resistant to the normative political values of state-based polities and non-participants in the conduct of trade. Burmese nationalists have thus seen the Kachin as susceptible to brainwashing by the British, hence their supposed loyalty to colonialism and easy conversion to Christianity. In reality, the Jinghpaw (a major sub-group of the Kachin) was fully established as an important cultural and political grouping in the region long before the establishment of colonial rule. By the end of the eighteenth century, Jinghpaw elites controlled many of the major passes across the northern Patkai Hills between Burma and the Ahom kingdom of Assam, as well as some of the most significant trade and diplomatic routes between northern Burma and Yunnan. Although some elites were symbolically sometimes tributary to the Burmese and Qing courts, this was not always the case and Jinghpaw elites could even in those cases assert considerable influence over the flows of goods, people and international diplomacy that required passage through these passes.

This interaction with the wider region changed dramatically in the colonial period with the British delineating the Kachin Hills as an Excluded Area, a restricted zone over which they exerted indirect control through a system of deliberate separation. Hence, for the Kachin, isolation, disconnection and dissociation were consequences of new forces of globalization and imperialism, not the inherent reality of daily experience prior to this time. Another result was that, with independence in 1948, the new constitution established Kachin State as a relatively autonomous part of the Union, having its own State Government and some control over its internal budget and other arrangements. That a degree of autonomy was appropriate in this case arose from the historical reality that neither the pre-colonial Burmese state nor its colonial successor had fully incorporated this region into either of their respective political systems.

It is true that Kachin men were recruited to serve in to the colonial forces, some even serving abroad in World War I. However, this practice involved far more than simple loyalty to the British and, in any case, by the end of the colonial period there were signs of significant discontent among communities in the region with the practice. In the years immediately prior to the Japanese invasion in World War II, it was becoming harder to enlist young Kachin men into the army, and those who had demobilised were helping develop a more strident (even anti-colonial) political nationalism. Furthermore, those who fought with the Allies in the war were mainly new volunteers who joined to protect their own homes and communities from an enemy that was confronting them on their doorstep.

Only at this stage, with independence in 1948, did religion start to gain real political significance. The idea that most Kachin people were Christian by that time has been promoted largely without proper historical analysis, taking the accounts of missionaries at face value. In fact, at that stage it is clear that the majority were *not* Christian, although in key urban areas those who had made public proclamations of their Christian faith were increasing. More significant than numbers alone, however, were the important niche places that Christian elites and some former elite soldiers who were also converts occupied in the new, urban based Kachin society that was starting to emerge in the period of late colonialism.

It was in this environment that Kachin ethno-nationalism as a modern political entity had its roots. It built upon the dislocations and disruptions to traditional economic and social systems that colonial rule and wider changes in the geopolitics of the region had brought upon a

Group of Kachin Rangers in 1944 (photo courtesy of Sam Spector)

society that increasingly referred to itself as 'Kachin'. Indeed, it was at this time that the term Kachin itself began to be politicized and used to reflect modern political concepts of territorialism and rights (see 'Who are the Kachin' on p. 263 for a fuller analysis). Yet as far as the prevalence of Christian faith as a modern symbol of Kachin identity was concerned, this was boosted considerably by the experience of conflict in the post-independence state and it was only during this time that it can reasonably be said that 'most' Kachin became Christian.

However, it is also true to say that today, the identification of oneself as being both Kachin and being Christian in Burma has become important in the discourse of ethno-nationalism. The churches, too, have played an important role in providing relief and support to communities badly affected by conflict. They have also established local higher-education institutions that have become very important in developing ethno-nationalist oriented, educated, confident young men and women at a time when state-funded university education was erratic and frequently inaccessible. These young people have become important in the emergence of a politically literate, status-bearing youthful ethno-nationalist demographic, which has in turn been important for sustaining general levels of support for the conflict across more than one generation.

Moreover, the churches have been important in developing Christian ethno-nationalism as a bulwark for armed resistance to what has been interpreted locally as a self-aggrandizing state determined to impose Buddhism on the region. However, as noted in the account of the Kachin Independence Army (see p. 166), the Kachin ethno-nationalist movement has never been inherently Christian and has tended to act pragmatically. Nonetheless, the mutual support that the KIA/KIO and the main Kachin churches have been able to offer each other in their respective causes has created an inevitably close convergence of interests and discourse over a period of five decades. However, it would be a mistake to see these developments as already inevitable at the point of independence in 1948. In this respect, the failings of the independent state to address issues of economic and political concern have been as significant as the experience of colonialism in seeing the establishment of Christianity as a major ideological support of the Kachin ethno-nationalist movement.

Christianity is important in the lives of many in Myanmar – Kachin mother bearing her 10-year-old daughter, paralysed by Tatmadaw mortar fire (photo: David Høgsholt)

IN FOCUS

Aung San Suu Kyi: Translating Buddhist concepts into democracy

'Of the four Buddhist virtues conductive to the happiness of laymen, *saddha*, <u>confidence in moral, spiritual, and intellectual values</u>, is the first.' – Aung San Suu Kyi, *Freedom from Fear*, p. 178 (my emphasis)[1]

Daw Aung San Suu Kyi believes that the Burmese, who are not used to Western discourses of democracy, turn to Buddhism in their quest for democracy and moral leadership. She considers Buddhism to be liberal, including within that concept free subjects who can realize truth by their own free will and helping others (p. 174). Thus, Buddhism can be used to criticize a despotic and immoral rule. Buddhist concepts of the moral leader are then translated into universal notions of modern democratic leadership. A traditional Buddhist cosmological imaginary is merged with a globalized imaginary of universal democratic freedoms and rights in a modern hybrid form – both with a focus on the moral subject.

'The Lady' argues that political leaders must follow the ten moral perfections of a righteous king (*dasa-rājadhamma*), some of which are similar to the perfection of a Buddha (see p. 295). She translates the last duty as forbearance or non-obstruction (non-opposition) against the will of the people. She writes that the leader who stops moral and social chaos is a Mahāsammata in Buddhism, 'a ruler by unanimous consent of the people' with reference to a mythological king (p. 169). The *dhammarāja* concept was earlier used by Aung San Suu Kyi in order to criticize the junta for not following these perfections and not following the will of the people by moving towards a more democratic society. Moreover, it is the duty of a ruler to prevent moral decline and material decay. According to Aung San Suu Kyi's interpretation, the junta could be held responsible for 'failure to recover that which has been

---

1.   Aung San Suu Kyi refers to the four streams of merit (*punna-dhara*) produced by giving alms to monks following the Buddha's teaching. Subsequent page references in this text (with the exception of the last one) are to *Freedom from Fear*.

Buddhism is one aspect of Aung San Suu Kyi's public persona; she is also her father's daughter – detail of a painting in a gallery in Bagan (photo: Flemming Ytzen)

lost, omission to repair that which has been damaged, disregard for the need of a reasonable economy, and the elevation to leadership of men without morality or learning' (p. 169). The junta followed the wrong path (*agati*) with unwholesome roots (*akusala*) in suffering, which creates greed (*lobha*), hate (*dosa*), delusion (*moha*), and cowardice (*bhaya*) and was therefore the opposite of the path of freedom. This was a clear sign of lack of a moral leadership. Moreover, the military rulers of that time showed clear signs of ignorance (of the moral concepts) and ignorance (*avijja*) is the fundamental root of all vices and violence. Dhamma, the Buddhist law of existence based on righteousness, virtue and non-violence, is as universal as the 1948 Universal Declaration of Human Rights, Daw Suu Kyi argues (p.177). She quotes the Human Rights declaration, 'if a man is not to be compelled to have recourse, as a last resort, to rebellion against tyranny and oppression, human rights should be protected by law' – a clear reference to the situation in Burma.

In Buddhist cosmology, a world conqueror (*cakkavatti*), acting on behalf of King Indra, will cleanse the world of its vices before the next Buddha arrives. Indra will use water to wash away anger, fire to burn away lust and wind to erase ignorance. This part of the cosmological imaginary is easily read into specific events, such as Cyclone Nargis or an earthquake.

Prophecies (*tabaung*) are prevalent in Burma and easily spread as rumours in a country where all information, until recently, was strictly censured and reduced to what the generals had to say.[2]

Aung San Suu Kyi may not be compared to a coming ruler in the classic Buddhist sense. But she emphasizes that Burma needs a 'spiritual revolution', a 'spiritual movement' and 'new spiritual values' – in other words, a new moral order based on notions of *mettā* (loving kindness).[3] She practises meditation to improve her knowledge of Buddhism and stresses the importance of mindfulness. Meditation is very popular in Burma, especially among women.[4] One female informant, who took part in the Saffron Revolution and now teaches *vipassanā* meditation via the Internet, told me that by improving the moral self one can contribute to countering the increasing immorality in Burma. This comes in the form of the four vices – greed, hate, delusion and ignorance – as evidenced in the corruption, extravagant spending, economic and social decline, drugs, prostitution and violence found in society. The mindfulness (*sati*) achieved from meditation also neutralizes fear.

Fear is something often addressed by Aung San Suu Kyi, for instance in her book *Freedom from Fear*. Fear corrupts people: 'It is not power that corrupts but fear. Fear of losing power corrupts those who wield it and fear of the scourge of power corrupts those who are subject to it' (p. 80). Fear contributes to the isolation of the person, and isolation is one of the mechanisms used by totalitarian regimes. In a strictly censured society, it becomes impossible to separate facts from fiction, and rumours from reality[5] and dissimulation becomes a dominant condition of inter-subjective actions. Trust networks are difficult to maintain, except perhaps when they are strictly underground. In Buddhism, one should respect a teacher but one should also question his teachings. Likewise, one should not fear a tyrannical ruler nor submit to the paranoia of a

---

2. See Tosa (2005) on the use of supernatural imaginary as rumours. Before the demonstrations and Aung San Suu Kyi's speech in 1988, a *tabaung* (prophecy) had predicted auspicious events: 8x2 + 8x2: 8 August 1988.

3. See Aung San Suu Kyi (1997): 51. On her use of Buddhism as political rhetoric, see McCarthy (2004).

4. See Jordt (2007); Houtman 1999 provides a detailed analysis of the political role of meditation. He counterposes *vipassana* (insight meditation) and *samatha* (concentration meditation) as democratic versus autocratic. However, *vipassana* is also supported by the generals, according to Jordt, who criticizes this dichotomy.

5. See Fink (2001): 227–231.

ruler. Here, mindfulness (*sati*), equanimity (*upekkhā*), altruistic joy (*muditā*) and *mettā* (loving kindness) are important notions. Buddhism defines the moral and knowing subject to be the best, or only, bulwark against tyrannical rule. Knowledge, as we shall see below (p. 308), is an important notion used by the young monks. The question is, of course, if morally enchanted subjects constitute a sufficient kind of empowerment against an increasingly totalitarian rule.

In this way, the discourse on power in Burma takes its point of departure from the qualities of the person and his moral capital and then analyses the actual power and its implementation in tactics, organizations, and in the structuring of society at all levels by connecting specific acts to the morality of the person. It is very much a struggle between persons and their symbolic power. Daw Suu Kyi is seen as an enchanted leader with her father's perfections and a potential *bodhisatta*. When asked if she could become a female *bodhisatta*, she replied: 'Oh for goodness sake, I am nowhere near that state' – but not denying the possibility.[6] The question is, now that Aung San Suu Kyi has entered the world of *realpolitik*, if she can uphold these high moral standards in the eyes of her supporters.

✍ MG

References

Aung San Suu Kyi (1991) *Freedom from Fear: And Other Writings*. London: Penguin Books.

—— (1997) *The Voice of Hope. Conversations with Alan Clement*. London: Penguin Books.

Fink, Christina (2001) *Living Silence. Burma under Military Rule*. Bangkok, White Lotus.

Houtman, Gustaaf (1999) *Mental Culture in Burmese Crisis Politics. Aung San and the national League for Democracy*. Tokyo, Institute for the Study of Languages and Cultures of Asia and Africa, Tokyo University.

Jordt, Ingrid (2007) *Burma's Mass Lay Meditation Movement. Buddhism and the Cultural Construction of Power*. Athen: Ohio University Press.

McCarthy, Stephen (2004) 'The Buddhist Political Rhetoric of Aung San Suu Kyi'. *Comtemporary Buddhism*, Vol. 5, No.2: 67–81.

Tosa, Keiko (2005) 'The Chicken and the Scorpion.' In Monique Skidmore (ed.) 2005: *Burma at the Turn of the 21st Century*. Honolulu: University of Hawai'i Press, pp. 154–174.

6. Aung San Suu Kyi (1997: 9).

Politically engaged Buddhism – spiritual politics or nationalist medium?

Mikael Gravers

Introduction

Buddhism is a fundamental part of Burmese society and is involved in all parts of the social fabric. An estimated 89% of the population is Buddhist and, as mentioned above (p. 279), the constitution of 2008 emphasizes that Buddhism has a 'special position' in Burma. Although this and previous constitutions state that 'the abuse of religion for political purposes is forbidden', Buddhism has been a part of the country's politics since pre-colonial times. This chapter provides a brief insight into the complex relationship between the monks and the political arena and its changing conjunctures.[1]

In Burma/Myanmar today, there is an uneasy relationship between the worldly or mundane sphere (*lokya*) defined by Buddhism and the supra mundane or sacred sphere (*lokkutara*). These two spheres are interdependent: monks and monasteries need material support from the lay community while the latter needs spiritual support from the monks in order to accumulate religious merit and enhance karma. Thus, Buddhism and its monks have to engage with the political and economic conjunctures, whereas the laypeople often look to the monks for support and protection against an unjust rule. However, the support must be moral and spiritual more than (directly) politically active. Since 1948, monks have not had the right to vote and the law does not allow them to be politi-

---

1. On Buddhism in Burmese history, see Schober (2005) and (2011), Sarkiyanz (1965) and Spiro (1982).

cally active. Nonetheless, what the so-called Saffron Revolution of 2007 demonstrated was that monks could turn Buddhist ethics into political spiritualism, using it as a moral resistance to unjust rule.

Monks who participated in the Saffron Revolution are still in exile and are not welcome in the monastic order (*Sangha*) or in the monasteries. Recently, one of its leaders, U Gambira, was jailed and although released on bail he is accused of breaking into his monastery and insulting the Maha Nayaka Sangha Council, the supreme authority of the Sangha. He was forced to disrobe when released from jail in 2011 after serving four years of a 63-year sentence. Since his release, no monastery will accommodate him after he criticized the elder monks for accepting his illegal disrobing in 2007. The elder monks in the Sangha Council are appointed by the former military junta and utterly against monks' participation in politics. Many abbots supported the criticisms made by the young monks in 2007 but warned against demonstrating. Many laypeople also supported the monks but there was also substantial opposition to monks becoming involved in politics.

Despite the suppression of the Saffron Revolution, some monks remain politically active. In December 2012, for instance, monks joined a demonstration in Letpadaung, Sagaing Region, against the confiscation of land for a copper mine to be run by a Chinese company. Riot police attacked the demonstrators and 70 monks were severely injured and burned by grenades. Thousands of monks then demonstrated demanding an apology from the government, which after some hesitation complied. This incident demonstrated that the military is still wary of the monks and considers their engagement in civil affairs as being political and thus illegal.

However, there is another side of Buddhism's political engagement: nationalism. 'To be Burmese is to be Buddhist' is often quoted in reference to Buddhism as a main ingredient in Burmese national identity. Recently, this aspect was recalled when monks demonstrated against Muslims in Rakhine State. The demonstrators viewed the local Rohingya as non-Burmese or 'Bengali illegal immigrants' (see Ardeth Thawnghmung, p. 323ff.). This was not the first time that monks have demonstrated against Muslims. Indeed, Buddhism and nationalist politics were deeply intertwined in the colonial era, an interrelationship that has continued since independence. The military regime often used Buddhism in its nationalist rhetoric.

An estimated 400,000 monks and 40,000 nuns are a sign of the important role that Buddhism plays in Burma today – a civil force of the same
size as the army. Besides their spiritual functions, the monasteries also run
schools and many children frequent the schools, especially those from
poor families who cannot pay the extra money often demanded by the
poorly-paid teachers at state-run schools. Some monasteries also run clinics treating eye diseases, HIV/AIDS and other ailments. The monastic
order thus fills important roles in a state where civil-society organizations
have been limited and strictly controlled. An example here is the famous
Sitagu Hsayadaw ('venerable abbot') from Sagain, Ashin Nyanissara,
who established the Sitagu Association, an important foundation that has
development projects, a hospital and an International Buddhist Academy
with a branch in the USA. In 1988 he stood up and criticized the military
by referring to the ten rules for a *Dhammaraja*. He was active in helping
the victims of Nargis and had contacts with Aung San Suu Kyi. Today,
his development projects provide water pumps to the dry zone where the
rainfall has been reduced due to climate changes.[2]

In short, the Buddhist Sangha is an important institution in Burma, its
social and political engagement having roots far back in history. Moreover,
Buddhism and its cosmology provide important definitions of power and
righteous rule that are still important. But, in order to understand how
Buddhism functions as a modern political medium, we need to consider
its role under the old monarchy and during the colonial era.

Royal power, Buddhism and resistance to colonialism

According to Buddhist cosmology a ruler follows two sets of ideals: as
cakkavatti (Pali, *setkyamin* in Burmese), a world conqueror who will use
force, and as *dhammaraja*, a righteous ruler who follows the ten moral
rules: liberality, morality, self-sacrifice, integrity, kindness, restraint and
austerity, non-anger, non-violence, tolerance and forbearance or non-
obstruction (non-opposition). A righteous ruler has a solid moral virtue
(*parami*) and he must be like Maha Thamada, the 'first elected (by
the people) monarch' according the Buddhist legend.[3] Besides secular

---

2. On the Sitagu monk, see *The Irrawaddy*, 'Serving the People', vol. 16, no. 3, March 2008:
   http://www2.irrawaddy.org/article.php?art_id=10644; see also http://www.sitagu.org/
   burma/.
3. Aung San Suu Kyi referred to Maha-Sammata (Maaha-Thamada) in her article 'In Quest
   for Democracy' as a moral ruler 'by unanimous consent of the people' (1991): 169.

power, all rulers possess karmic power (*kan-hpoùn* in Burmese). *Hpoùn* is power based on religious merit accumulated in previous existences as well as in the present.[4] It is sometimes translated as 'glory', with *hpoùn-gyi* ('great glory') being the designation for a monk. Thus power has a moral aspect and is tied to a person. A rule based only on violence is unjust and not based on the wisdom called for in the Dhammapada.[5] An unjust ruler thus may be challenged by a rebel leader, a *mìn laùng* (imminent ruler, prince or pretender). Sometimes former monks became rebels. The Sangha depended on royal support and power – but also had to ensure that this was righteous rule according to Buddhist ethics. If the socio-economic order declined due to royal neglect, this disorder could endanger Buddhism. And if the Buddhist Sangha became corrupted by profane activities, this endangered the mundane world as well, requiring that a ruler purify the religion. The Buddha admonished rulers to listen to wise monks and during this period the *sangharaja* (primate) heading the Sangha was generally a powerful figure. Thus a monk's spiritual power is seen as being above that of all laypeople including rulers. Yet the Buddha also told laypeople to criticize monks who made their own distorted version of *dhamma*. This sermon (the Kalama Sutta) was referred to by the rebellious, young monks in 2007.

These concepts of power were crucial for traditional royal power and have been adapted to modern politics although often only implicitly. In order to manifest the karmic power a ruler had to support and (if necessary) reform the Sangha. A material sign of righteous power was the construction of pagodas or renovation of a famous one. At the end of the work, the king would hoist the royal umbrella (*hti daw*) decorated with precious stones, on top of the pagoda as the sign of his *hpoùn*. When the British colonized Burma their perception of rule collided with these indigenous, Buddhist-based concepts and perceptions.

After the final annexation of Burma and humiliating exile of King Thibaw in 1886, monks became particularly active as rebels against the British. They also attacked local Christians who had recently been converted by

---

4. See Kawanami (2009) on *hpoùn*.
5. Verses 256 and 257 of the Dhammapada state: 'A man is not just if he carries a matter with violence; no, he who distinguishes right and wrong, who is learned and leads others, not by violence but justly and righteously, and who is guarded by the law and intelligent, he is called just.'

Close-up of the hti daw *above Uppatasanti Pagoda, Naypyidaw (photo courtesy of the Government of Thailand)*

the Western missionaries now entering the country.[6] However, when colonial documents mention rebel monks it is not always said that they had 'left the robe'. Most likely they did indeed disrobe in order not to break the ethics and *vinaya* rules (227 rules of conduct); otherwise they would have become *parajikka*s ('defeated') and been excommunicated. Disrobing is crucial because a monk who acts violently acts against Buddhism. After Britain's annexation, several pretenders with titles such as *Buddha-raja, Setkya Mintha* ('ruler of the universe') and *Mìn Laùng* appeared. Some of the rebels were former monks often posing as princes or their descendants and using royal symbols such as white umbrellas. Among these rebels was the famous U Oktama (or Ottama) who had 5,000 followers and kept the British out of the Minbu area. He disrobed before he raised the golden (royal) umbrella and led the rebellion. Regarded by his followers as a *dhammaraja*, he was caught and hanged by the British in 1889. Another rebel was the Mayanchaung Hpoùngyi, a Shan monk, who issued royal orders and flew the royal flag with a peacock. He was captured by Christian Karen who collected a reward of 5,000 rupees 'on his head' and he too was hanged. These monks and several others saw themselves as fighting against heretical foreigners (*kala*) whom they believed would destroy Buddhism as well as Burmese culture.[7] Though no longer formally monks, they acted in defence of Buddhism in danger. The British neither supported Buddhism

6.   On the confrontation of Buddhism and Christianity, see Gravers (2010).
7.   See Ni Ni Myint (1983): 42, 62–71 for more details of these rebel monks.

nor, after the death of the incumbent *sangharaja*, intended to appoint a new head of the Sangha. With the British behaving like a *cakkavatti* rather than a *dhammaraja* and more concerned about monasteries becoming hatching places for anti-colonial resistance, the Sangha lost not only its political protection and main support but also its traditional leading role.

In the 20th century the *min laùng*-inspired struggles against colonial rule gradually took root but were transformed into a modern nationalist movement. College students formed the Young Men's Buddhist Association (WMBA) in 1906, imitating the Christian WMCA but inspired by monks in Sri Lanka. Although it promoted nation, language and Buddhism, the WMBA was not part of the Sangha. It was more like a political and cultural club, a critical riposte to the segregated British clubs,[8] but it opened the anti-colonial field for activist monks. One of its most famous members was U Ottama (1897–1939), who is often mentioned as an inspiration for the young monks of 2007.[9] As perhaps the first modern engaged monk, he initiated the organization of local nationalist movements (*wunthanu athins*: 'protectors of national interests' associations). Inspired by Gandhi's non-violence strategy, he spoke against colonial rule, favouring a boycott of British goods, and against Europeans wearing shoes in Buddhist temples. U Ottama travelled and had contacts in many parts of Asia and learned from anti-colonial struggles in Ceylon and India: he was a modern monk who even planned to supply weapons to the resistance.[10] He met King Thibaw and the Prince of Mingun both living in exile. U Ottama represents the encounter between the modern global and Burmese tradition. He was arrested several times but managed to mobilize part of the Sangha in the struggle. Monks became members of the local association of Sangha Sameggi Aphwe (United Sangha Organization) under the general Council of Sangha Sameggi (GCSS). It became a religious counterpart to the (estimated 10,000) lay *wunthanus* all over Burma. The *wunthanu* organizations were set up under the central leadership of the General Council of Burmese Association (GCBA) in 1920. Monks and lay nationalists were separately organized, since the monks are under the monastic rules, but

---

8. U Maung Maung (1980): 4.
9. AAPP (2004): 11. Recently, the 100th anniversary of U Ottama's birth was celebrated. He is seen as an idol by the democratic opposition. The All Burma Monk's Alliance (from 2007) says they can learn from him and that he was 'well-versed in world affairs, brave and courageous'. He is thus an idol of modern, engaged monks (*The Irrawaddy*, 28 December 2009).
10. Mendelson (1975): 205.

this did not prevent the monks from becoming more and more active in politics. Ex-monks became *dhammakatikas* (*dhamma* lecturers) who travelled and agitated while also preaching *dhamma*. Reading the complex history of these organizations one cannot miss the parallels to today's struggle: charismatic leaders (monks and students) in agreement about the main aim yet involved in factionalism and personal power struggles.

The main rift during the 1920s and 1930s was between those favouring engagement in elections to the legislative council and those who were for a boycott and even contemplated violent resistance. Mainly the young monks supported the boycott.[11] This disagreement created several splits of the organizations. Moreover, when monks engaged in secular struggles they came close to money and other material things and were thus in danger of moral pollution (*kilesa*). This period saw many examples of monks who were tempted by entertainment in the secular domain. U Ottama was not only incarcerated but forcibly disrobed, beaten and forcibly fed during a hunger strike, giving hints of the recent treatments of monks. He was widely considered a *bodhisatta*, a coming Buddha. Another cultural-hero monk, U Wissara (Pakokku Dhammakatika), was disrobed and jailed. He died as a martyr after a hunger strike. At least 120 monks were jailed in the late 1920s. The Sangha increased its involvement in politics while the global economic crisis escalated and landed the vast majority of peasants in debt. The elder monks found that the young monks and the *wunthanu* organizations were generating violence and transgressing the *vinaya* rules. The conflicting views led to a split in the GCBA. The engagement of monks provided clear indications of a schism for the Sangha when monks get involved in politics and risk compromising their adherence to Buddhist ethics and *vinaya* rules. It was a clear illustration of the conflict between the mundane activities in the *lokyia* and the rules in the sacred *lokkutara* domain, a dilemma that is still relevant today.

Meanwhile in the late 1920s, the price of rice plunged dramatically while taxes and usury rates went the opposite way and moneylenders including Indian *chettiars* took the land from indebted Burmese peasants. The nationalist organizations began organizing volunteer corps or 'armies' (*tat*) sporting the red royal battle banner with a green peacock.[12]

---

11. See further: Maung Maung (1980).
12. The fighting peacock is the emblem of the National League for Democracy as well as a former royal symbol.

These developments in the 1930s provide the second lesson from this period: when the lay society suffers and *lokiya* is in crisis, Buddhism and its spiritual domain (*lokuttara*) is in danger. The ensuing rebellion was inevitable and one of its leaders was a prominent *wunthanu* leader and ex-monk, Hsaya San, who had been collecting data on the seriousness of the rural debt: more than 80% of all peasants had debts and half of all land in the Irrawaddy delta was owned by landlords. He was part of the boycott faction of the GCBA and it seems logical that he went against the cooperative faction and began to prepare an uprising. The rebels were poorly armed and prepared. They had received traditional tattoos and amulets against the British bullets but seemed to be loosely organized through the local *wunthanu* associations. There are clear relations to a *min laùng* rebellion.[13] It is likely that the peasants conceived Hsaya San as a person with *hpoùn* and similar to a traditional rebel. He called his movement Galon (Garuda) Wunthanu Athin, signifying the mythological Garuda bird and its fight against the evil Naga dragon (i.e. colonial power). He titled himself Thamada, 'President' (cf. Maha Thamada, the first 'elected' monarch, see above). But the peasants could well have seen him as a *setkyamin* (*cakkavatti*) who would cleanse their land of the greed and immoral conduct of their foreign rulers. There were also references to the ten rules for a *dhammaraja*.[14] Monks played a significant role in the prelude to the rebellion. Some agitated in support of the rebellion, others intervened trying to stop the fighting, once more a confirmation of the dilemma facing engaged monks. In the event, the rebellion ended in disaster with about 2,000 killed, 580 of these executed (Hsaya San among them), and 890 deported.

The confrontation between the secular and the spiritual worlds meant that the students and young Thakin ('masters', a riposte to the British) in the nationalist Dobama Asiayone ('We Burmans' Association) during the 1930s emphasized that their political struggle was secular, even though the movement had a traditionalist and royalist faction. The socialist faction used a neologism *lawka neikban* (*lokiya* nirvana: 'this-world nirvana') for a future egalitarian society but they did not want the monks as patrons. Meanwhile, there was a resurgence in lay Buddhism and meditation as

---

13. On the nationalist Buddhist organizations, see Maung Maung (1980). British sources emphasize the traditional and religious symbols of Hsaya San. Recent discussions have questioned this representation; see Aung Twin (2006).

14. Herbert (1992): 9.

well as a focus on personal *parami* ('moral perfection'). There was also a movement against vices such a smoking, drinking and gambling.[15] The scholarly monks, not the political, were sought by laypeople for studying meditation. U Ottama was called home in order to revive the struggle but was not treated with respect by young monks and the Thakins. He died alone and poor in 1939. However, the young monks were active again and seven were killed by Kachin Riflemen during large anti-Muslim demonstrations in Mandalay.[16] The peacock flag was carried in front of the funeral procession. The young monk's movement (Rahan or Yahan Pyo Aphwe) was a forerunner of today's young monks – some were conservative and anti-Marxist and in opposition to the left-wing students such as U Nu, Thein Pe and Aung San among others. These monks agitated for a boycott of Western clothing, particularly women's transparent blouses. The left-oriented monks disrobed in order to join the Thakin movement. The political involvement of monks thus demonstrated the continuous difficulties in adhering to the *vinaya* rules as when young monks participated in lootings and carried weapons during anti-Muslim riots[17] – acts sadly repeated in recent years.

To summarize these historical illustrations, four trends appeared during the anti-colonial struggles: 1) Buddhism became a vehicle of active social, political and moral criticism with increased focus on the subjective moral habitus of leaders; 2) there was an ongoing contradiction between the secular and spiritual domains and their opposing values – very much like the present situation; 3) Buddhism was transformed into a crucial, modern medium for the nationalist struggle against colonial rule; and 4) the Buddhist engagement was inhibited by factionalism and splits as in the present struggle.

As we shall see, after independence from the British in 1948, Buddhism also played a significant role, again with nationalist connotations.

Buddhism, nationalism and military rule

When General Aung San entered Burma in 1942 as head of his Burma Independence Army he was seen as a *setkyamin*, a *cakkavatti* clearing out

---

15. Maung Maung (1989): 112–115. On Dobama, see Daw Khin Yi (1988).
16. Daw Khin Yi (1988): 96, 128.
17. See Mendelson (1975): 212.

the British.[18] Aung San had attended a monastic school as a boy but as a student leader during the 1930s he was against monks' participation in politics. His view on the role of Buddhism is stated in his inaugural speech to the AFPFL convention in 1946. He referred to 'the majestic Shwe Dagon pagoda', 'a symbol of consecrated land' with 'memories of great men' and a 'monument of our nation's labour of love'.[19] The famous pagoda in this speech is part of the historical memory and a national symbol. Interestingly, he espoused a highly modern, secularist view on religion, condemning charlatans using astrology and magic in politics, and emphasized that religion is not a matter of politics but one of individual conscience whereas politics is 'a social science'. Significantly, he referred to one of Burma's cultural heroes, King Anawratha, who purified Buddhism and expelled the Ari priest who lived an immoral life and focused on a Naga cult. King Anawratha also acted as a *cakkavatti* and plundered Pegu for its famous Buddhist relics. In his speech, Aung San admonished the Sangha: 'Reverend Sanghas! Purify Buddhism and broadcast it ... go among the people and preach the doctrine of unity and love ... spread the Dhamma anywhere, freedom from fear, ignorance, superstition, etc. etc.'[20] His secular view was thus coloured by the use of the royal imagery and imbued with Buddhist ethics offering a kind of national morality.

While Aung San was clearly for a strict separation of the secular and religious domains, his successor U Nu, Prime Minister from 1948 to 1962, acted like a *dhammaraja* and made Buddhism serve the otherwise secular state. Although his aim was an egalitarian welfare state that he called Pyidawtha ('Royal Golden Land'), U Nu spent large sums of public money on pagoda construction and religious ceremonies. For instance, he constructed the Kaba Aye Pagoda, endowing it with enshrined relics collected in Sri Lanka as well as the Lion Throne returned from Britain, plus a cave large enough to house ceremonies with 5,000 monks and 10,000 laypeople. All of this was in the style of a monarch, said his critics in the AFPFL, who believed that U Nu's main concern was the accumulation of merit. This is not necessarily why he saw and promoted Buddhism as the national religion, however. To this end, a

---

18. Prager (2003): 18–19.
19. Silverstein (1993): 93–94.
20. Ibid.: 97; also cited by his daughter Aung San Suu Kyi (1991).

Buddhist mission was formed to convert non-Buddhist minority peoples and integrate them into the Burmese nation, a project supported by the army. Perhaps for the same reason, U Nu also transformed the royal cult of the 37 guardian spirits (*nat*) into official national ceremonies in order to ward off threats (such as insurgency) that endangered the nation. Buddhism was also promoted internationally, with U Nu organizing the Sixth Buddhist Council (Synod) in 1954–56. The purpose of the Synod was not only to celebrate the 2,500th year of the Buddhist era but also to review and purify Buddhist texts and to rescue a faith and morality that had gone into decline from colonial times.

At the same time, by living an ascetic life as a vegetarian, celibate and practitioner of *vipassana* meditation, U Nu demonstrated that a leader must have special moral qualities and spiritual power. During political crises he would renounce the world as a monk or withdraw from the secular world and meditate. His style of rule evoked many contradictory notions when he posed quite explicitly as a potential saint (*arahant*) and a *bodhisatta* and ruled in the style of a Maha Thamada. Despite his identity as a socially engaged democratic leader, he transformed Buddhism into a modern political force and concluded that it was democratic and incompatible with Marxism (communism) and its materialist (*lokiya*) orientation.[21] His actions polarized the Sangha, at the same time provoking the military and their secular worldview. Some of these contradictions had unexpected consequences, as for example when some monks demonstrated against Muslim ritual slaughter. In Rangoon the demonstrations turned violent, monks destroying a mosque and killing two Muslims. U Nu acknowledged the significant contradiction between the subjective moral qualities founded in Buddhist ethics and modern real politics. Nonetheless, he emphasized that the country depended on morally good leaders and equated his personal *parami* and *hpoùn* with the destiny of the nation. However, even though such an 'enchanted leader' might govern according to absolute moral values, his rule was still vulnerable to criticism and rebellion of a *mìn laùng*.[22]

---

21. In 1959, General Ne Win launched an anti-communist campaign and distributed a pamphlet titled 'Dhammantaraya', (Buddhism in danger) and mobilized monks and laypeople in mass meetings. See Smith (1965: 133).

22. On U Nu and Buddhism in 1948–1962, see Smith (1965), Sarkisyanz (1965), Buttwell (1963) and Mendelson (1975).

Such a *mìn laùng* came in the shape of General Ne Win, head of the army, who toppled U Nu's civilian government in 1962. Ne Win was not new to power; he had been 'called' by U Nu to act as caretaker prime minister between 1958 and 1960 and deal with problems and conflicts that had accumulated after parliament had approved a constitutional amendment making Buddhist the state religion of Burma and expectations had been raised among the Shan and other ethnic groups of greater independence. The issue of state religion alienated Burma's Christian and Muslim minorities and angered the secularist politicians, who accused U Nu of violating §21 of the constitution regarding political abuse of religion.

Ne Win reacted against U Nu's religion-inspired policies by banning ceremonies for the guardian spirits (*nat*) and giving away the shrines to anthropologists! Not only did he separate the mundane and the spiritual worlds; he also began a strict state control of the Sangha and monks. He conferred honorary titles to senior monks and seems to have gained the tacit support of the most conservative sect, the Shwegyin. Formed during King Mindon's reign (1853–78), this is the second largest of the nine official sects and has often been hailed for its purity and strict adherence to the *vinaya* rules by the military. It keeps a clear distance from the mundane world and its activities – including attempts to enlist it for political purposes – almost in the style of the forest monks.

Ne Win's ideas of purification seemed to resonate with his perception of socialism. He attempted to create a secular socialist ideology or philosophy for the Burma Socialist Programme Party, published in *The System of Correlation of Man and His Environment* (1963). It included concepts from the Buddhist cosmology such as *nama* (mind) and *rupa* (matter). Though often called a hodgepodge of Buddhism and Marxism, arguably its eclectic use of Pali concepts was an attempt to combine the material and the spiritual (ideological) domains in a discourse signifying not just a scientific and modern but also a traditional foundation of the Burmese way to socialism. His socialism was a strict communitarian moral order subsuming all subjective acts under the party and the state. Thus, it formed a modern nationalist and socialist rule and cosmology based on Burmese tradition. General Ne Win introduced a new Sangha Act in 1980, which demanded registration and identification cards for individual monks. The new Sangha Maha Nayaka Committee of 84 senior monks came under strict state control. Monks who protested against the law were accused of rape and other preposterous acts, then disrobed. The committee began a purification of temples and evicted laypeople living inside monasteries.

Even though Ne Win was more in the style of a secular ruler, a *cakkavatti* who wanted to subsume Buddhism under a modern unitary state, he did collect 50 mio kyats from the public and began constructing the Maha Wizaya Pagoda close to the famous Shwedagon, enshrined Buddhist relics there and hoisted the *hti* in 1986. This was only two years before his *hpòn* finally faded and he was forced to step down during the events of 1988. At that time a prophecy said that 'when the pagoda umbrella was hoisted, the sun [Ne Win would] set'.[23]

The generals of 1988 and Buddhism

After the violent repression of the democratic movement in 1988–91, the generals now ruling the country were often seen hoisting the pagoda umbrella, making donations and renovating pagodas. Not least, a new umbrella was raised on the Shwedagon, made of 0.2 tons of gold and half a ton of gemstones. The generals are said to have spent an estimated 440 million kyats from public donations on the renovation of pagodas (making such donations of course was difficult to refuse for the lay population). In the new capital, Naypyidaw, Than Shwe had constructed a replica of Shwedagon called the Uppatasanti (or Peace) Pagoda (see p. 297). Its inauguration took place after the Saffron Revolution and those monks attending were kept at a distance from their rulers. The regime also bestowed new religious titles as well as money and valuable presents on those leading monks who were loyal.

Besides controlling the Sangha via the State Sangha Mahā Nāyaka Council – the Supreme Sangha Council – the generals attempted to restrict monks' participation in secular affairs. Since the time of independence, monks have never been allowed to vote and they are not supposed to participate in political activities. After monks demonstrated in 1988 and 1990, the regime issued an order in July 1990 prohibiting monks from participating in non-religious activities, especially political ac-

---

23. See Sarkyiyanz (1965) for a discussion of Buddhism and socialism; for the Sangha reforms, see Tin Maung Maung Than (1993); and for Ne Win's pagoda building, see Maung Aung Myoe (2006).

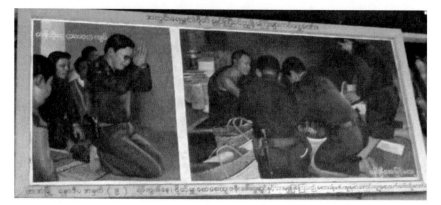

General Khin Nyunt, then head of military intelligence, pays respect to U Thuzana: mural at Myaing Gyi Ngu monastery (photo: Mikael Gravers)

tivities. This was backed up by the new constitution, which has a clause warning against abuse of religion. The regime also prohibited NLD members from making public donations to monks and from entering monkhood.

The generals thus recognized the Sangha as a political force that they needed to control. On the other hand, they had to demonstrate that they were the legitimate protectors of Buddhism, which for them symbolized the unity of the nation, its identity. The regime used the Buddhist *mangala sutta* (on good fortune) to instruct people on national moral values while one of Than Shwe's slogans was 'uplifting the morality of the entire nation'. The aim was the creation of a *mangala* (Bur. *mingala*) nation – a prosperous nation. This was also used as a reason for attacking and beating demonstrating monks in September 2007 (see Saffron Revolution below). They were defined as 'bogus monks' put in place by destructive elements that wanted to destroy peace and stability. In its Orwellian language the *New Light of Myanmar*, a government mouthpiece, said that 'destructive elements inciting instigation to grab state power through short cut foreign radio stations aiming exaggerated means ... and planting bogus monks.'[24] It was further claimed the monks not only broke the *vinaya* rules but had had a political agenda.

At the same time, young monks discussed whether the generals' donations and religious observations had the right intentions (*cetana*) and concluded that they used Buddhism more as a kind of preventive magic

---

24. *New Light of Myanmar*, 18 September 2007, cited in NCGUB (2008): 44.

(*yadana*) in order to ward off misfortune; the generals were *a-dhamma* (anti-*dhamma*) by killing monks. However, other monks said that they could not assess their intentions and that the generals seemed to possess karmic power – otherwise they would not be in power.

The Saffron Revolution of 2007

After the brutal attacks on demonstrators including monks between 1988 and 2003, young monks in Mandalay and other towns began to organize classes in English and computer studies as a cover for political discussions. They communicated on the Internet and by cell phone, planning new actions. In August 2007, students and monks demonstrated against the rise in fuel prices and the decline of Burma's economy. On 5 September in Pakokku, a town with a Buddhist university, soldiers beat up young monks and tied them to a lamppost. The next day, in protest, some monks briefly took 10–20 government officials hostage and set fire to their vehicles. Three days later, a group of monks formed the illegal All Burma Monks' Alliance (ABMA) and demanded an apology from the military before 17 September. If this were not received, monks would boycott all donations from military personnel (indeed, some monks were already throwing military donations into the street).[25] This act, called *pattam nikaujjana*, is normally used against individuals who have insulted the Sangha or a monk. Here it would be used as a collective act of excommunicating the military. This is a strong act for a Buddhist to make because a denial of access to merit-making means that the condemned person's karmic status is in jeopardy.

No apology was made. Suddenly, thousands of monks were walking along streets in all major towns chanting the *metta sutta* on loving kindness to all creatures in the world, one of the most important sermons of Buddha. Laypeople lined the streets replying, 'our cause, our cause'. Using the slogan 'For peace on Earth and in Burma', the young monks also demanded a dialogue between the regime and opposition. One group of monks managed to walk to Daw Aung San Suu Kyi's house and chant the *metta sutta* outside. She briefly looked out from her compound and said *sadhu sadhu* ('well done'), words comparable to 'amen'. At the beginning of the protests, the monks tried to keep laypeople and students with NLD logos and banners away from the demonstrations

---

25. Human Rights Watch (2009): 64, also NCGUB (2008): 41.

in order not to politicize their actions directly. The monks carried the Dhamma banner, whose eight colours symbolized loving kindness, karma, virtue, the purity of *dhamma* and the wisdom of the Buddha's teaching, as well as pictures of the Buddha. Many monks also showed the alms bowl upside down, symbolizing the boycott.

The young monks argued that it is their duty to react when Buddhism is endangered by economic mismanagement leading to a significant decline in donations, when society is pervaded by immorality – corruption, theft, drug trade, prostitution and other vices – and when the rule is violent and unjust. The generals had committed many sins such as killing monks and laypeople and disrobing monks by force. The young monks found that the SPDC junta acted against *dhamma* (*a-dhamma*), this being an attack on the Buddha, *dhamma* and Sangha. The rulers lacked knowledge and were not acting according to the *desa-dhammaraja* (as outlined above). Thus spiritual politics and what the monks termed 'study-power' (*hpoùn acariya*) were necessary means to counter the decline. 'Study power' is the dissemination of Buddhist ethics (loving kindness, compassion, non-violence) as well as secular knowledge about the world, human rights and democracy. The young monks defined de-

Not all monks supported the Saffron Revolution (photo still taken from the award-winning documentary by Anders Østergaard, 'Burma VJ', reproduced by permission of the director)

mocracy as 'people's power'. As an example, they referred to the Buddha who would teach kings as well as laypeople. For them, a ruler without *parami* (moral perfection) cannot rule in a righteous way.

However, the young monks also defied the Sangha elders who were either supporters of the regime or, even if not, were still reluctant to let the young monks take to the street. They feared retaliation by the regime would damage Buddhism. Some laypeople were also against the demonstrations saying that they provoked the army and entangled Buddhism in politics. Even among the organizers, there were disagreements. Some did not like the term Saffron Revolution, probably coined by the media, since it entailed violence, and they objected to letting NLD students join the demonstrations in the last days of September. They blamed these students for provoking the violent response when it came. However, there was general agreement on the economic and moral decline of Burma and that the blame lay with the regime. However, the military maintained that national disintegration and lack of national morality and cooperation were to blame for the decline. Thus, once again, nationalism reappeared in a dangerous collision with violence.[26]

The military regime responded to the demonstrations with force. Monasteries were raided, monks beaten up and disrobed in public then sent to jail and labour camps. An estimated 1,400 monks were arrested and 250 jailed. It is uncertain how many monks were killed (a UN estimate says 30). Many monks went underground or fled to Thailand where many are still in exile. Monks were further restricted in their popular *dhamma* talks, where they used their exposition of Buddhist ethics as an indirect criticism of the regime. Also their travelling was restricted, and new identity cards were issued. The military intelligence system, which had been unable to monitor preparations for the protests, expanded its surveillance of the monks.

The leaders of the All Burma Monks' Alliance, which organized the demonstrations, are now out of jail. U Gambira, the main leader, has not been allowed to return to the Sangha. He has health problems after being tortured in jail and is now married. Ashin Issariya (King Zero) is still in Mae Sot and organizing teaching in Best Friends Libraries.[27] He has

---

26. For more details and references, see Gravers (2012).
27. See Kuijper and Kovida (2012) for an interview with King Zero. Ashin Kovida is a co-founder of Best Friend Library and now lives in Switzerland.

been back in Burma and is currently engaged in reviving the libraries. He is critical of the anti-Muslim movement, which he believes is a result of military indoctrination and lack of education, and condemns its leader, U Wirathu (see below), for being politically naïve and lacking modern education and knowledge.

Monks and xenophobic nationalism: anti-Muslim riots in 2013 and their roots

The recent clashes between Buddhists and Muslims in Rakhine State and central Burma are alarming examples of the volatile situation in Burma. Ethnic and religious violence is not easy to overcome without just and properly functioning laws and an ingrained democratic rule. That said, this conflict has its roots in colonial Burma, during which period the British imported workers from India, many of them Muslims (see pp. 143 and 160). As a result, from colonial times but especially since independence, there have often been clashes between Buddhists (including monks) and Muslims. Especially in Rakhine State there has been violence since 2012 between the Buddhist-majority Rakhine and the Muslim-minority Rohingya, the latter numbering between 800,000 and 1.3 million people (approximately one fifth of Rakhine's population).

Even though the Rakhine–Rohingya conflict is in part due to anti-*kala* xenophobia ignited during the British period, it is likely that at least some of the Rohingya are not recent arrivals; they descend from Muslim traders and fishermen who were present in the old independent kingdom of Arakan before its conquest by Burma in 1785. Even so, the current Myanmar government argues that most are Bengalis and recent illegal immigrants and more widely, especially among the Rakhine, the ethnonym Rohingya is disputed (see Ardeth Thawnhmung, p. 323). The term may have been introduced in the 1950s but its origin is uncertain. British traveller Francis Buchanan-Hamilton refers to the term *Rooinga* in 1799.[28] He wrote that Muslims who had settled in the old Arakan kingdom, some working for the royal court in Mrauk-U, used this term. The meaning is not clear but could be a reference to the state, i.e. Rakhine.[29] With the government and broad sections of the populace not accept-

---

28. See Buchanan-Hamilton (1799).
29. A Rohigya refugee in Denmark explained that the term refers to Rohang – 'a town or area in Rakhine'. The term could be an ancient version of 'Rakhine'. However, this does not clarify its origin.

ing this history, the ethnonym 'Rohingya' is not officially recognized as one of the '135 Myanmar races'.[30] Thus, according to the Myanmar Citizenship Law of 1982 (see p. 148), the Rohingya are not citizens. In order to obtain full citizenship, a group has to be registered as *tai yin tha luo myo*, that is have an indigenous ethnic ethnonym. Nor were Rohingya allowed to register as such in the recent census, instead being categorized as 'Bengalis'. At the moment, Rohingyas are living in a state of exception, being excluded (for instance) from public education. Moreover, two international aid organizations working on their behalf were recently accused of insulting Buddhism and expelled from the state.

At present the government rejects calls from the UN to give these people citizenships, saying that 'Bengalis' born in Burma/Myanmar before 1982 can apply for 'naturalized citizenship' if they can prove that their ancestors had lived in Burma before 1948. But it is uncertain if this will be granted. Bangladesh does not recognize the Rohingya as natives of its country and considers the about 270,000 Rohingya living in Bangladesh to be from Myanmar. Most of this group are probably refugees from 1991 when the army launched an offensive against a rebel Mujahedin organization. The refugees and internally displaced were supported by the UN and this helped create a deep resentment among poor Rakhine who felt that they deserved help, too. The Rakhine see themselves as repressed by Burman rule while the army considers the province to be the most volatile region in the country.

There seems to be a general resentment against Muslims among a majority of ethnic Burmans. This problem needs further research, and the following below is a cautious attempt to find some answers. In conversations that this author had with Burmans during a recent visit, the same cultural and economic explanations are repeated. Muslims only trade among themselves. Some big business people are said to have obtained favours during the military period by helping the regime to avoid sanctions. There are stories of Muslims bribing the military to enter Burma illegally. When Muslims settle in a town or village, they are accused of taking over the place, buying the land and controlling

---

30. A smaller Muslim group, the Kaman, descendants of Muslims in the old Arakan royal guards, *is* among the five officially registered ethnic groups in Rakhine State. There had been no animosity between Kaman and Rakhine until October 2013 when a village near Tandwe was burned and four killed – probably by outsiders. Houses flying the Buddhist flag were spared, indicating some organization behind the attack.

trade. Such complains must be scrutinized before drawing conclusions. Importantly, in cases of interfaith marriage, Islam demands conversion of the Buddhist spouse. This enforced conversion is resented by most Burmans. Buddhists consider their religion to be inclusive whereas Islam is seen as exclusive with Muslims viewing other religions as opponents. The custom of polygamy was also raised in these conversations and the view put forward that Muslims have too many children; they do not care enough for them and let them beg in the streets, according to some informants. In all, there is an image of a social disorder at work, an image that has to be taken seriously even though other social and political problems are the main reason behind the grievances.[31]

Thus these statements are difficult to assess but they are treated as facts in the narratives of ethnic categorization even though many Buddhists seem to have good personal relations with individual Muslims. However, among Buddhist Karen there is even a ban on establishing new Muslim settlements and in some parts of Karen State Muslims are not allowed to settle. 'They conquer the whole place and dominate trade', Karen informants told me. True or not, we have to consider such views and grievances since negative ethnic categorization may enforce and legitimize organized violence even though they may not be based on personal experience.[32]

When, in an interview with the BBC in October 2013, Aung San Suu Kyi said that the violence came from both sides and was based on mutual fear, she described the general mood in Burma. She also denied that there is an ongoing ethnic cleansing of Muslims (i.e. the 140,000 internally displaced in Rakhine State). Maung Zarni, founder of the Free Burma Coalition (opposition in exile) criticized her statement. Nevertheless, the 1988 students support her and reject the term 'ethnic cleansing' as used by Human Rights Watch. There is a feeling that Muslims have lived in a segregated community since colonial times and this has generated misunderstanding, mistrust and now fear. Some communities in Yangon and Moulmein appear to be well off while smaller communities

---

31. Jean Berlie (2008) provides a general description of Muslims in Burma and the problems of assimilation. The Muslim community is a mix of a Sunni majority and better-off Shia minority. Major communities including mosques and Islamic schools are found in Yangon, Mawlamyaine and Mandalay (with more than 70 mosques in still found Yangon). Muslim traders and bankers form close networks that also have international linkages.

32. One Burman informant said that she hated Muslims. But it turned out she did not know any and had never had direct encounters with Muslims. In short, the national resentment also has a scapegoat function.

in other towns seem relatively poor. Popular resentment focuses on the larger Muslim businesses, such as transportation companies, which thrived during military rule according to some informants. This claim and the interpretation of Muslims' cultural and economic expansion are given an 'ethnic' and 'national' explanation by many Burmans, including monks, as described below, thus generating resentment and even hatred.

But the most important catalyst for sectarian violence is the widespread discourse on Buddhism being in danger – that is, being under threat from globalization, and first of all from Islam. Many believe Muslims have contacts with radical Islamic groups and potential terrorists outside Burma. This globally derived imaginary of fear is, in my view, crucial for understanding the resentment. It is translated into a nationalist, xenophobic imaginary of race, culture and nation being in danger. This has a wide resonance among people in Burma who often use the derogatory term *kala* for Muslims (i.e. 'black foreigners from India'). However, this imaginary dislike is found not just in Myanmar but in Europe as well. Religion and nation in danger evoke our fear of losing identity, and is easily translated into a localized political agenda.

The global imaginary of an endangered Buddhism is further fuelled by reference to its historical dimension. Muslims came to Burma as cheap labour and traders during the colonial period – and thus as ethnic aliens in the view of many Burmese. In 1938, right-wing politicians and monks raised anti-Indian and anti-Muslim feelings in Burma. The monks said that Buddhist women married to Muslims were suffering. Rumours were spread that the Sule and Shwedagon Pagodas were in danger of being destroyed. In response, monks with sticks attacked Muslims and committed arson and looting. They were young monks from All Burma Council of Young Monks whose aims were to protect Buddhism, race and language. This was basically an anti-colonial struggle. However, the monks proclaimed Muslims to be the 'enemy number one'. Riots spread all over Burma, and 186 persons were killed, most of them Muslims. In response, the Buddhist Women's Special Marriage and Succession Act was enacted in 1939 to discourage interfaith marriages.[33] In 1961, when Buddhism briefly became state religion, there were new anti-Muslim demonstrations and the destruction of two mosques by young monks.[34]

---

33. See Berlie (2008): 23 for further details.
34. Smith (1965): 109–114.

Further anti-Muslims riots followed the 1988 uprising, in 1997 and 2003. The recent riots thus have deep historical and nationalist roots.

The anti-Rohingya riots in 2012 continued in 2013 and left 192 people dead and about 140,000 displaced. It is estimated that 80,000 have left for Malaysia and other countries. Some 9,000 Rohingya arrived in southern Thailand, finding refuge with local Muslims, but at least 2,000 perished at sea in small boats.[35] Ardeth Mung Thawnghmung (see p. 323) is one of the first academics to investigate the background of this serious conflict, although it is very difficult to work on this controversial subject. Any support for the rights of Muslims or reference to human rights and human security concepts is met with strong rejection and references to national security needs due to the threat of possible radical Muslim intervention.

In March 2013, the religious violence spread to central Burma. Meiktila, a town with about 100,000 inhabitants, has a community of 30,000 Muslims. A quarrel at a gold merchant's shop flared into violence with at least 43 people killed, 8,000 displaced and several mosques and many houses burned. From Meiktila, the violence escalated, spreading across a broad swathe of the central plains as well as to other parts of Burma including Mon and Shan States (see Map 7, p. 316).

As it turned out, the riots seem to have been instigated and perhaps organized by a radical nationalist Buddhist organization with the code-name 969 (a numerological reference to Buddha, *dhamma* and Sangha) of militant monks and thugs who are active all over Burma. Their stated aim is to protect 'race and religion'. They claim that Muslims force Buddhist women into marriage, while Muslim women are not allowed to marry Buddhist men let alone convert to their husband's religion. They also argue that Muslims will not buy from Buddhists and thus should to be boycotted. The organization has distributed anti-Muslim propaganda all over Burma claiming that Muslims control Burma's economy even though they constitute only 4% of the population. Mosques are 'enemy bases', *The Irrawaddy* reported the 969 leader claiming in September 2013.

The leader of 969 is a 46-year-old monk, Ashin Wirathu (see also p. 56). He was jailed for 25 years in 2003 after organizing anti-Muslim

---

35. Thomas Fuller with Wai Moe, *New York Times*, 23 June 2013. In 1979 and 1991 the army conducted campaigns against Muslim separatist organizations. In 1979, 200,000 Rohingya fled to Bangladesh, followed by another 260,000 in 1991. Here they are not recognized as a local ethnic group.

riots causing more than 10 deaths in Kyaukse and Mandalay; he was released under an amnesty in 2012.[36] He is the abbot of the Mesoeyein Monastery in Mandalay and seems to have gained followers from all over Burma for his fast-growing movement. He emphasizes Myanmar nationalism and the protection of race, culture and Buddhism. In a recent interview, Ashin Wirathu said: "Don't take nationalism lightly." He also criticized Aung San Suu Kyi for indirectly supporting the Muslims. In so doing, she does not take nationalism seriously enough, in the monk's view. U Wirathu also fears that a change in the constitution could open the way for a Muslim presidential candidate in the future.[37] U Wirathu and his followers use a highly derogatory and demonizing language. For example, he said: 'You can be full of loving kindness, but you cannot sleep next to a mad dog'. Likewise, monks in a demonstration carried a banner saying, 'Islam is similar to animalism' (i.e. Muslims have uncontrollable birth rates).[38] The words of monks have an enormous impact upon laypeople due to their spiritual and symbolic power and status. Such strong language also resonates with the Buddhist cosmological imaginary of a decline in Buddhism predicted by the Buddha – the coming of a *Kala Yuga*, a 'Dark Age', when knowledge of *dhamma* and morality erode.

Even learned and highly respected monks ask Muslims to 'behave nicely as guests'; in other words, Muslims are aliens. However, many monks tried to help the Muslims and most monks are against religious violence. Moreover, the police and military never confronted the rioters directly, leaving the suspicion that higher powers were behind the violence or at least sought to exploit it. The police response was that they had not been ordered to intervene. Interfaith organizations and the students from 1988 have tried to mediate in different conflict situations, but in vain, the only result often being threats against those who

---

36. The origin of 969 goes back to 1997 in Moulmein where an anti-Muslim booklet, titled *969*, was published. There was an incident in Karen state in 2003 near Hlaingbwe where 200 Karen monks and DKBA soldiers attacked a Muslim village and mosque, burning them down (*The Irrawaddy*, 30 April 2003) – an incident little noticed at that time. Ashin Wirathu appeared on the cover of the 1 July 2013 edition of *Time* magazine under the heading 'the face of Buddhist terror'. U Thein Sein and many Burmese reacted against what they saw in the article as an overly generalized and offensive picture of Buddhism as being violent.

37. *The Irrawaddy*, 2 April 2013.

38. *The Irrawaddy*, 2 December 2013.

tried. Aung San Suu Kyi has said that only the rule of law will protect the Muslims. What worries outside observers is that there is no discourse on human rights, basic protection of life nor freedom of faith in the current

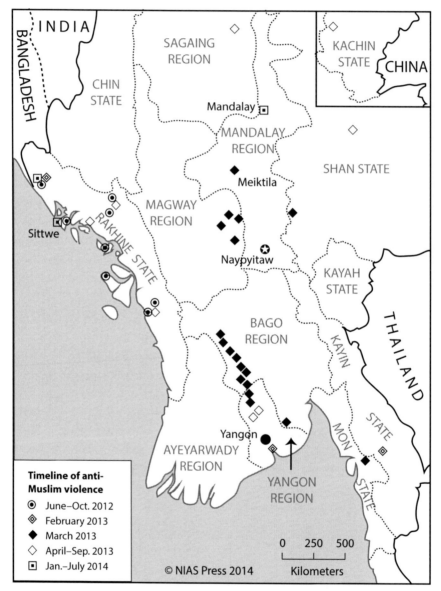

Map 7: Anti-Muslim violence 2012–14

Based on a map in Physicians for Human Rights, 'Patterns of Anti-Muslim Violence in Burma: A Call for Accountability and Prevention', August 2013.

situation. This is a crucial issue that must be investigated by researchers in due course. Otherwise, this conflict could impede democratic reforms and provoke the army into calling a state of emergency according to the new constitution. This could mean that halting the reforms is part of the hidden agenda of this campaign. Indeed, there is a suspicion that persons related to the ruling Union Solidarity Development Party are behind these monks or use them. If this is the case, they probably aim to stall the reforms and revision of the constitution before the election in 2015, thus preventing Aung San Suu Kyi from running for president.

However, in September 2013 the Maha Nayaka Sangha Council banned the 969 organization as illegal and criticized its proposal of a law banning Buddhist women from marrying Muslim men without permission from their parents and local authorities. The draft law further required such Muslim grooms to convert to Buddhism. The Sangha Council did not prohibit the monks from promoting the nationalist ideology, however. U Wirathu responded by saying that the council was 'undemocratic' and operating 'under the gun', i.e. under military command.

In January 2014, the nationalist monks convened a new meeting at Tu Mo Shi Monastery in Mandalay. Some sources said 33,000 monks participated; another estimate was 10,000. Ashin Wirathu participated but, interestingly, so too did some well-known monks including one of the most influential ones in the country, the Sitagu Hsayadaw (Ashin Nyanissara). The meeting aimed at collecting signatures for a law restricting interfaith marriages. This is the same idea as promoted by the 969 movement. President U Thein Sein supports the proposed legislation whereas Christian leaders oppose this restrictive law.

The meeting also urged people to oppose local and international business people who support proposals to recognize non-indigenous ethnic groups (i.e. Rohingya) as citizens. This would be a violence of sovereignty, the monks said.[39] The nationalist monks have allied with the National Democratic Front, the party that split from the NLD in 2010, in order to promote the draft law in parliament. The strong turnout in Mandalay could signify that the monks will intervene in the 2015 elections and perhaps 'advise' the electorate not to vote for parties who are against their nationalist and anti-Muslim agenda. The meeting resulted in the formation of a new movement, the Sasana Wuntha Parla, or Mabatha (Association to

---

39. *Myanmar Freedom Daily*, 16 January 2014.

Protect Buddhist Race and Religion; the word 'race', though, seems not to be in the Pali title). During an interfaith meeting in Yangon later in January organized by Columbia University, the Sitagu Hsayadaw urged all sides to avoid violence. Ashin Wirathu, who also attended the meeting, talked about a dialogue and that he would advise his followers in Rakhine State to follow the rule of law. The role of the Sitagu Hsayadaw is obviously to take the violence out of the movement in order to protect the position and image of Buddhism. Certainly, Mabatha poses a serious challenge to the NLD and Daw Suu Kyi before the elections in 2015.

According to *The Irrawaddy* (5 May 2014), Mabatha has now collected four million signatures for the law and involved the Ministry of Religious Affairs and the Attorney-General's Office in their effort to promote the law.[40] More than hundred NGOs have protested against these restrictions on individual and religious freedom. This resulted in U Wirathu calling the NGOs 'traitors'. It can thus be seen that this nationalist movement is creating new frictions and political confrontations in Burma. The government seems to follow the nationalist turn of the monks and it seems as if the movement also has support from about half of the 400,000 monks including some who were active in the Saffron Revolution. It is perhaps a clear sign of the risks that democratization faces in an uncertain period of transition.

There is an interesting global dimension to the movement. The nationalist Burmese monks of the 1930s had close connections to India and Ceylon (Sri Lanka). The present movement has drawn inspiration from the Sri Lankan Buddhist movement Bodu Bala Sena ('Buddhist Power Force') formed in Colombo 2013. This movement holds the same views against marriage, forced conversion, halal slaughter and wearing of burkas. These monks refer to a long anti-Muslim and anti-Christian tradition that originated as part of the anti-colonial struggle around 1909–15 led by the famous monk Anagarika Dharmapala.[41] Sri

---

40. Actually this is not one but four connected laws: the first on interfaith marriage, which is only allowed if the parents of the woman as well as officials give permission, while the other three laws will ban polygamy, enact population control (of Muslims?) and restrict religious conversions. About 30% of Muslim men are married to Buddhist women. On paper at least, their children all become Muslims, according to Berlie (2008): 23.

41. Interestingly, the multi-coloured Dhamma flag used in Burma during the Saffron Revolution and now by the 969 movement has its origins in Sri Lanka in the early 1900s. It was invented by Colonel Olcott and Madame Blavatsky, who were not only supporters of Dharmapala and his Buddhist revival but also the founders of the Theosophical Society.

Lanka is a Buddhist country, they argue. They consider Buddhism to be in danger and thus in need of a revival. Recently, some of these monks have been directly involved in violent actions against Christians and Muslims. Young Burmese monks visit Sri Lanka to study Buddhism and have imitated the idea of Dhamma Sunday schools aimed at strengthening Buddhism. There are more than 100 *dhamma* schools in Burma.

In lieu of thorough research on this issue, it is safe to say that the conflict is a result of the long repressive rule and renewed historical anti-Muslim feelings combined with widespread poverty and neglect of education. This is also the argument of Aung San Suu Kyi and some monks. A strong nationalist sentiment with origins in colonial society and deeply rooted in the identity politics of post-colonial society is understandable. However, its current xenophobic form is perhaps a result of nationalist paranoia promoted in military propaganda for decades under totalitarian rule. Nationalism is thus deeply ingrained not only in the Burman ethnic majority but among ethnic nationalities as well. Such primordial sentiments are easy to use in generating resentment and fear in times of transition and uncertainty. What is termed foreign is a danger to race, language, Buddhism and nation in the Burman nationalistic perspective. And what is seen as Burmanization is a danger to ethnic identities, cultures and languages. Thus, it is important to take these sentiments seriously, including the anti-Muslim resentment, as they challenge not only unity but also the democratization of Myanmar. However, it is not *Buddhism* that has turned violent – it is a social and inter-ethnic conflict in which religious difference and violence appear as solutions to social and political conflicts for people who have been deprived of democratic experience. A modern, secular and democratic interfaith dialogue as well as trust and toleration of other religious and ethnic identities are badly needed in Burma. Neither the constitution's ban on 'abuse of religions for political purposes' nor other laws will solve this divide.

Concluding remarks

Buddhism and monks will no doubt continue to play a significant role in the democratization of Burma. In a somehow simplified version, it has two 'lines': one is the political spirituality of the NLD and young monks aimed at establishing a new moral and democratic order. It is critical of corruption, violence and repression. The other is the conservative,

Dhamma flag flying over the Shwedagon Pagoda (photo: Mikael Gravers)

nationalist 'line' of 'Burmanization' or 'Myanmarification', which emphasizes Burman cultural hegemony, Buddhism as the national religion, and the order established by the state as above the Sangha. This line still has the upper hand and seems to be growing into a sectarian direction. There has also been criticism of monks soliciting donations in a time of crises and poverty in exchange for merit and rebirth or as a means of accumulating wealth and power. For instance, the commentator Min Zin describes monks with the loudspeakers soliciting alms: 'Donations have become big business ... I often heard the loudspeaker broadcasts pushing the message that it is the lack of generosity, and not poverty as such, that is the reason for the destitution. "If you say you can't make donations because you lack wealth, you can never expect to become wealthy," I heard at one point.' He also reports growing talk of 'crony monks'.[42] Beyond these money issues, many in Burma including monks are against the involvement of monks in politics. However, Buddhism and monks still play a significant role in local communities, providing spiritual advice, aid and development, and this social engagement can eventually not avoid also engaging in politics.

---

42. Min Zin, 'Worrying about Burma', contribution to Foreign Policy's Transitions blog, 1 February 2013: http://transitions.foreignpolicy.com/posts/2013/02/01/worrying_about_burma; Min Zin, 'The People vs. The Monks', *International New York Times*, 7 June 2014.

References

AAPP (Assistance Association for Political Prisoners [Burma]) (2004) *Burma: A Land Where Buddhist Monks are Disrobed and Detained in Dungeons.* Mae Sot, Thailand: www.aappb.net.

Aung San Suu Kyi (1991) *Freedom from Fear: And Other Writings.* London: Penguin Books.

Aung-Thwin, Maitri (2008) 'Structuring Revolt: Communities Interpretation in the Historiography of the Saya San Rebellion'. *Journal of Southeast Asian Studies*, vol. 39(2): 297–317.

Berlie, Jean A (2008) *The Burmanization of Myanmar's Muslims.* Bangkok: White Lotus.

Buchanan-Hamilton, Francis (1799) 'A Comparative Vocabulary of Some of the Languages Spoken in the Burma Empire. *Asiatic Researches* (The Asiatic Society), 5: 219–240.

Burma Socialist Programme Party (1963) *The System of Correlation of Man and his Environment.* Rangoon.

Buttwell, Richard (1963) *U Nu of Burma.* Stanford: Stanford University Press.

Fuller, Thomas and Wai Moe (2013) 'Extremism Rises Among Myanmar Buddhists'. *New York Times*, 23 June.

Gravers, M. (1999) *Nationalism as Political Paranoia in Burma. An Essay on the Historical Practice of Power.* Richmond, Curzon. Second revised edition.

——— (ed.) (2007) *Exploring Ethnic Diversity in Burma.* Copenhagen: NIAS Press, introduction.

——— (ed.) (2010) *Exploring Ethnic Diversity in Burma.* Copenhagen: NIAS Press, second revised edition.

——— (2012) 'Monks, Morality and Military. The Struggle for Moral Power in Burma – and Buddhism's Uneasy Relation with Lay Power'. *Contemporary Buddhism*, vol. 13(1): 1–33.

Human Rights Watch (2009) *The Resistance of the Monks: Buddhism and Activism in Burma.* New York.

Jordt, Ingrid (2007). *Burma's Mass Lay Meditation Movement: Buddhism and the Cultural Construction of Power.* Athens, OH: Ohio University Press.

Kawanami, Hiroko (2009) "Charisma, Power(s), and the Arahant Ideal in Burmese-Myanmar Buddhism." *Asian Ethnology*, vol. 68(2): 177–183.

Khin Yi, Daw (1988) *The Dobama Movement in Burma (1930–38).* Ithaca, NY: Southeast Asian Program, Cornell University.

Kuijper, Elke and Ashin Kovida (2012) *Burma Voices: People of Burma in Their Own Words.* Mae Sot, Thailand: 54 Project Printing.

Maung Aung Myoe (2006) 'The Road to Naypyitaw: Making Sense of the Myanmar Government's Decision to Move Its Capital'. Singapore: Asia Research Institute, Working Papers Series No. 79.

Maung Maung, U (1980) *From Sangha to Laity: Nationalist Movements of Burma 1920–1940*. New Delhi: Manohar.

——— (1989) *Burmese Nationalist Movements 1940–1948*. Edinburgh: Kiscadale.

Mendelson, Michael (1975) *Sangha and the State in Burma: A Study of Monastic Sectarianism and Leadership*. Ithaca, Cornell University Press.

NCGUB (2008) 'Bullets in the Alms Bowl: An Analysis of the Brutal SPDC Suppression of the September 2007 Saffron Revolution'. [Thailand]: National Coalition Government of the Union of Burma: www.ncgub.net.

Ni Ni Myint (1983) *Burma's Struggle Against British Imperialism (1885–1895)*. Rangoon: The University Press.

Prager, Susanne (2003) 'Coming of the "Future King": Burmese Min Laung. Expectations before and during the Second World War'. *Journal of Burma Studies*, vol. 8: 1–32.

Sarkisyanz, Emanuel (1965) *Buddhist Backgrounds of the Burmese Revolution*. The Hague: Martinus Nijhoff.

Schober, J. (2005) 'Buddhist Visions of Moral Authority and Modernity in Burma'. In M. Skidmore (ed.): *Burma at the Turn of the 21st Century*. Honolulu: University of Hawai'i Press, pp. 113–132.

——— (2011) *Modern Buddhist Conjunctures in Myanmar: Cultural Narratives, Colonial Legacies, and Civil Society*. Honolulu: University of Hawai'i Press.

Silverstein, Josef (1993) *The Political Legacy of Aung San*. Ithaca, NY: Southeast Asian Program, Cornell University, revised edition.

Smith, Donald E. (1965) *Religion and Politics in Burma*. Princeton: Princeton University Press.

Spiro, Melford E. (1982 [1970]) *Buddhism and Society: A Great Tradition and Its Vicissitudes*. Berkeley: University of California Press, second edition.

Tin Maung Maung Than (1993) 'Sangha Reforms and Renewal of Sasana in Myanmar: Historical Trends and Contemporary Practice'. In Trevor Ling (ed.): *Buddhist Trends in Southeast Asia*. Singapore: ISEAS, pp. 6–63.

Newspapers and magazines

New Light of Myanmar: www.myanmar.com/newspaper/hlna/index

The Irrawaddy: www.irrawaddy.com

Mizzima News: www.mizzima.com/inside-burma/

Myanmar Freedom Daily: http://www.mmfreedom-daily.com

Contending approaches to communal violence in Rakhine State

Ardeth Maung Thawnghmung

Introduction

Recent communal violence in northern Rakhine State, triggered by the alleged rape and murder of a Buddhist Rakhine girl and the subsequent lynching of eight Muslim pilgrims and two other Muslims, is a manifestation of ongoing and deep-seated problems that have been fuelling tensions in the area for many years.

Foreign media, Western and Islamic governments, and human rights organizations have framed the problem mainly in terms of the violation of human rights by successive Burmese governments that have denied citizenship to the descendants of Bangali immigrants, practised various forms of discrimination, and placed restrictions on their movements. In addition, outbreaks of communal violence are attributed solely to manipulation and provocation on the part of the government or local media. Outside efforts have therefore been limited to putting collective pressure, often unsuccessfully, on the Myanmar government to repatriate displaced Rohingyas and to provide humanitarian assistance. The government, on the other hand, has framed the issue in terms of 'illegal' immigration and the security threat posed by militant Islamic resistance groups, and advocated for stricter monitoring and law enforcement as the main solution to the problem.

The Myanmar government has no doubt been responsible for the violation of human rights, for fuelling the conflicts, and for failing to implement the rule of law in the region. However, any approach that fails to take account of the character and dynamics of communal relationships, and focuses solely on the policies and actions of government, is incomplete at best and counterproductive at worst.

This chapter assesses the rationales behind these two seemingly ir-reconcilable approaches and argues that both sides have thus far dealt with the symptoms rather than the deep-seated roots of the problem, and have aimed at containing rather than addressing it. The nature and complexity of the issues involved also demonstrate that many intercon-nected layers of the problem need to be addressed, and tackled from a variety of perspectives. The first step is to understand the complicated relationships among actors who are involved in the conflict and assess their competing and complementary interests. In addition, both short-term and long-term comprehensive strategies will have to be developed to deal with underlying issues such as citizenship, national security (for Myanmar as well as Bangladesh), entrenched racism and Burma's long-term relationships with both Islamic and Western countries.

This chapter first traces the historical roots of the animosity between Buddhist and Muslim communities in northern Rakhine State. It then identifies a number of core issues that have divided the two communi-ties, and examines the relationships among the multiple actors involved in the conflicts. The final section offers some concluding and cautionary remarks.[1]

History

'Rohingya' is a controversial term that refers to a minority religious group of around 725,000 people concentrated in northern Rakhine State. They practice Sunni Islam and are the descendants of Bangali immigrants from the Chittagong area across the border in Bangladesh.[2] Rohingyas consti-tute about 90% of the residents of Maungtaw and Buthidaung and about 40% of the population of Sittwe township. The 'Rohingyas' represent a truly displaced group, being accepted as original settlers in Burma neither by the Myanmar government nor by the local Rakhine population – nor are they considered Bangladeshi by the Bangladesh government.[3] The Burmese government and Rakhine Buddhists do not acknowledge the

1. This project is based on the author's observations and conversations with members of Rakhine political parties, businessmen, civil-society organizations, Burmese and other minority residents, NGO staff and researchers working in Rakhine State since 2011. It is supplemented by secondary resources such as the report by the government-appointed commission on communal violence, Burmese-language newspapers, magazines and web-sites, and scholarly articles and books.
2. Lewa (2009).
3. See New Mandala (2011).

term 'Rohingyas' but officially describe them as 'Bengali' Muslims in Myanmar. In this chapter I shall use the term Rohingya to differentiate them from Buddhists of Bangladeshi descent (Maramangyi), Kamar nationals in Rakhine State who are Muslims, and the descendants of Indian migrant populations, many of whom are Hindus.

Early evidence of Bengali Muslim settlement in Arakan dates to the time of King Narameikhla (r. 1404–06 and 1430–34). When he regained the Arakanese throne and founded the Mrauk U kingdom, this was with military assistance from the Sultanate of Bengal. There were signs of Islamic cultural influence under his and his successors' rules, which included the Arakanese kings' adoption of Islamic titles, the employment of Muslims in the royal administration, and the adoption of the Bengali coinage.[4] While this evidence is not disputed by Burmese and Rakhine nationalists, it is used by the Rohingyas as evidence of their occupation of the land prior to British rule and as confirmation of their claim as 'original settlers' in Myanmar.

The numbers of Bengali immigrants – along with animosity between the local Rakhine Buddhists and Rohingya Muslims – increased following the British occupation of western Burma in the early 19th century. The British encouraged the migration of Bengalis from neighbouring regions to farm the fertile valleys of Arakan and to take up work of other kinds. British census figures show that the numbers of Muslims in Arakan increased from 58,255 in 1891 to 178,647 in 1911. The Japanese invasion of Burma during World War II expelled the British and left a political vacuum that resulted in mass killings by both sides. The accounts of the roots of this communal violence vary depending on the source of the information. According to Mosher Yegar, Arakanese villagers instigated the conflict, while Arakanese accounts put the blame on Muslim villagers who murdered a Rakhine village headman and his two younger brothers, thus sparking a wider conflict.[5]

Rakhine historian Aye Chan lays the blame for the violence at the door of the British colonial administration, which in 1942 formed and armed the Chittagonians of the Mayus Frontier into a volunteer force charged with waging guerrilla operations against the Japanese, and with collecting information and acting as interpreters for the British.[6] The Rakhine com-

---

4.   Berlie (2008) and Chan (2005).
5.   Yegar (2002).
6.   Chan (2005).

munity responded by forming the Arakan National Congress (ANC) and, later, the Arakan branch of the Anti-Fascist Organization (AFO) which first sided with the Japanese and the anti-British Burma Independence Army. According to Aye Chan, Rohingya volunteers destroyed Buddhist monasteries and pagodas, torched houses in Arakanese villages and massacred thousands of Arakanese civilians. This communal violence, in which thousands of people from both sides were killed, also led to the displacement of many villagers who fled to the Bangladesh border areas.

The government of U Nu, which came to power after Burma gained independence in 1948, practised a more accommodating policy toward the Rohingyas. Muslim civilians in Buthidaung and Maungdaw townships were issued with national registration cards, and allowed to vote and elect four Muslims representatives to the state parliament. When U Nu promised statehood for the Arakanese and Mon peoples, Muslim leaders announced a rival proposal to establish a Rohingya state.

General Ne Win, who led a caretaker government in 1958–60 and took power following a military coup in 1962, adopted a stringent policy toward the Rohingyas and foreigners in general. Not only did Ne Win nationalize the retail trade in Burma, thereby dispossessing some 100,000 Indians and 12,000 Pakistanis and driving them back to their homelands; he also initiated a series of military campaigns aimed at cracking down on 'illegal' immigrants from Bangladesh. The citizenship law of 1982 (which was enforced from 1987 – see p. 148) stripped Rohingyas of their Burmese citizenship and categorized them as 'Bangladeshi'. The first military campaign against the Rohingyas, code-named the Dragon King (*Naga Min*), was carried out in 1978 and drove more than 200,000 Rohingyas over the border into Bangladesh. The second campaign, which took place in 1991 and expelled more than 250,000 Rohingyas, ignited strong international reaction. Talks between the UN and the Burmese government resulted in an assurance by the government to repatriate the expelled communities and assist the inflow of international aid to the areas affected. In 1995, the intensive campaign mounted by the UNHCR to pressure the Burmese government to document the Rohingyas resulted in the introduction of a Temporary Registration Card (TRC). However, the card fails to mention the bearer's place of birth and therefore provides no official evidence of birth in Burma as the basis of a claim to Burmese citizenship.[7] There were

---

7.   Blitz (2010): 30.

still an estimated 20,000 Rohingyas living in refugee camps along the Bangladesh–Burma border in 2011.

The communal violence between Rakhine Buddhists and Rohingyas that broke out in June 2012, following the alleged rape and murder of a Buddhist Rakhine girl and the subsequent lynching of eight Muslim pilgrims and two Muslim bus passengers, resulted in the deaths of hundreds of residents (estimates range between 78 and 650), the destruction of buildings and the displacement of tens of thousands of people. Unfortunately, however, this first incident set the stage for a chain of violent events across the country triggered by spontaneous reaction as well as systematic and violent attacks coordinated by religious leaders using established networks for mobilization. The attacks mainly targeted Muslim houses and mosques and spread to Karen State, to Meiktila, Othekone, Tatkone and Yamenthin in central Burma and Okkan town in Yangon Region, killing 42 civilians, and displacing thousands of people by April 2013 (see Map 7, p. 316). They were followed by an anti-Islamic movement launched by ultra-nationalist Buddhist monks and laymen whose aim is to revive or introduce laws that restrict religious conversion and interfaith marriage, and control birth rates and immigration. A report by the official Rakhine Inquiry Commission offers in-depth assessment of the roots of violence, current socio-economic situations and popular opinions and provides lengthy recommendations (from improving the economy and welfare of the residents to the rule of law to tackling the issue of citizenship) to improve the situation.[8] The President's public assurance to protect 'minority rights' can be interpreted as the first step in the right direction to resolve these long-term grievances despite a few outstanding issues that were not mentioned in the report and challenges associated with the implementation processes.

Rakhine communal violence in historical perspective

The ongoing communal hostility in northern Rakhine is influenced by a variety of factors including cultural and religious differences, historical relations, policies pursued by colonial and postcolonial governments, and concerns about national security.

---

8. Rakhine Inquiry Commission, Final Report of Inquiry Commission on Sectarian Violence in Rakhine State, 8 July 2013.

Indigenous versus immigrant populations

One major issue in the ongoing tension and violence has been the disagreement over whether 'Rohingyas' are the original inhabitants of the land. With the exception of the U Nu government in the post-independence period, which pursued a relatively conciliatory approach toward foreign immigrants and promised a degree of autonomy in the areas occupied by Rohingyas, successive military governments in Myanmar and the Rakhine Buddhist population have denied their claim to be the first settlers of the region.

Some scholars and Rohingya commentators have argued that the Rohingyas were indeed the original settlers of the land. Historian Aye Chan, however, contends that the Rohingyas were 'the direct descendants of immigrants from the Chittagong District of East Bengal (present-day Bangladesh) who had migrated into Arakan after the province was ceded to British India under the terms of the Treaty of Yandabo, an event that concluded the First Anglo–Burmese War (1824–1826).' This view disqualifies them, along with the descendants of Chinese and Indian immigrants, for Burmese citizenship under the 1982 law, which reserves citizenship for members of the 135 national races settled in Burma before 1823, at the beginning of the British colonization of Arakan.[9]

The overwhelming majority of Rakhine Buddhists adamantly deny the very existence of 'Rohingyas' and react strongly to use of the term. They argue that there was no historical record of the name under either Burmese or British rule, and that it was 'invented' in the early 1950s by a few Bengali Muslim intellectuals from north-western Rakhine State. A now-defunct blog by a Burman nationalist,[10] for instance, challenges the statements made by Bengali historians who argue that: (1) Rakhine and Bangali share common Negroid ancestors, some of whom migrated to northern Rakhine, met with Arab traders in the 8th century, and became Muslims, while others went south toward central Rakhine and adopted Buddhism; (2) Rohingyas constitute half the population of Rakhine; and (3) Rakhine was ruled by Muslim Rohingyas from 1430 to 1784,

---

9. Many descendants of immigrants cannot meet Burma's stringent requirements for other forms of citizenship. These include associate citizenship, granted to those whose application for citizenship under the 1948 Act was pending on the date the Act came into force, and naturalized citizenship, granted to those who could provide 'conclusive evidence' of entry and residence before Burma's independence on 4 January 1948, who were fluent in one of the national languages and whose children were born in Burma. Fuller details in Blitz (2010).

10. 'Paduak Myay' blog, with the cited posts published in April 2011.

when it was taken over by the Burmese monarchy. Another Burmese nationalist who responded to the blog suggests that the reason for the predominance of Rohingyas in two of Rakhine's townships was the killing of Rakhine citizens by the Muslim population during the Japanese occupation: 'During the 1942 riot, our ancestors recounted that 20,000 Rakhine people perished, although there was no evidence to back this. Only 68 out of 129 Rakhine villages in Maungtaw were reclaimed by Rakhine who fled the areas to the south during the war. Rohingyas became [the] majority.'

The refusal of Rakhine and Burman Buddhists to accept the Rohingyas as the original settlers of the land reflects their concerns about culture, language and religious differences as well as the separatist aspirations of some of the political and armed organizations run by Rohingyas. In the above-mentioned blog, a Burmese nationalist noted that, 'if we accept the Rohingyas as the original settlers in Burma, we will be obligated to give them a self-autonomous region since the current constitution (2008) gives such status to nationalities who constitute the majority in two adjacent townships.'

Consequently, both sides have devoted considerable effort to unearthing historical evidence favourable to their own position. On 7 April 2012, the National Democratic Party for Development, a Rohingya political party, submitted a thick document to the National Parliament. It was titled 'In Respect of the Fact that the Muslim Inhabitants of Rakhine State are Natives by Race and Citizens of the Republic of the Union of Myanmar Under Law or By Natural Birth'. A month later, the Rakhine Nationalities Development Party countered by publishing an equally hefty document showing how the Rohingyas have 'fabricated history' to claim the status of original inhabitants of the land.[11] Resistance from Rakhine radicals has since resulted in the government's last-minute decision to prevent Rohingyas from identifying themselves as 'Rohingya' in the nationwide census recently undertaken in April 2014.[12]

Eligibility for Citizenship

Another bone of contention that has polarized the two sides is the question of whether Rohingyas should be granted citizenship. The 1948 citizenship law (which ostensibly granted citizenship to members of

11. See NDPD (2012) and RNDP (2012).
12. International Crisis Group (2014).

ethnic minorities who had been settled in the country for more than two generations) allowed Rohingyas in Rakhine State to hold national registration cards and recognized them as an independent ethnic community, one of the then 144 groups defined as eligible for Burmese citizenship.[13] This right was rescinded by the 1982 citizenship law, which was promulgated 20 years after the military took over the country in 1962. The 1982 law established three criteria for citizenship – full, associate and naturalized – and granted full citizenship rights only to the 135 national races settled in Burma before 1823. The Rohingyas were not included in this group and therefore were no longer eligible for full citizenship and the political and economic rights that accompanied it.

As a further obstacle, many immigrants and their descendants cannot meet Burma's stringent requirements for other forms of citizenship. Associate citizenship is granted to the offspring of mixed marriages between ethnic Burmans and members of immigrant communities and the spouses of ethnic Burmans. It also applies to anyone who had lived in Burma for five consecutive years, or for eight out of ten years preceding 1942 or before independence in 1948. Those having associate citizenship had the right to earn a living but could not take up any government office. To obtain associate citizenship, however, the application must be pending on the date the 1948 Act came into force. The third category of naturalized citizenship is generally offered to members of immigrant communities who could furnish 'conclusive evidence' of entry and residence before Burma's independence on 4 January 1948, who are fluent in one of the national languages and whose children were born in Burma.[14] Naturalized citizens are prohibited from holding any important political office and from serving in the armed forces. The majority of the Rohingyas have been unable to obtain either associate or naturalized citizenship, either because they or their predecessors failed to apply for citizenship by the 1948 deadline or because eligible individuals failed to keep proper documentation or were not given it, or their rights taken away.[15] Over time, it has become increasingly difficult to distinguish between those who are eligible for citizenship and those who are illegal immigrants.

---

13. NDPD (2012).
14. Yegar (2002): 62.
15. Blitz (2010): 11.

In 1989, colour-coded citizens' 'scrutiny cards' were introduced: pink cards were issued to full citizens, blue to associate citizens and green to naturalized citizens. The Rohingyas were not issued with any cards. In 1993, the Department of Immigration began seizing illicit citizenship cards held by Rohingyas and replacing them with a white Temporary Registration Card (TRC). Neither the TRC nor the household registration certificate (which is required to be possessed by every family in Burma) includes the bearer's place of birth and thus cannot be used to claim citizenship. More white cards were issued in response to UNHCR's intensive advocacy efforts to document the Rohingyas. However, Rohingyas face increasing restrictions: they are prohibited from travelling outside Rakhine State, are restricted to having no more than two children and are required to obtain marriage authorization from local officials.[16]

Today, views within the state on whether members of the Rohingya community should be granted citizenship are mixed. While popular opinion in Rakhine has been against granting citizenship, some moderate voices support the granting of citizenship to Rohingyas on a 'case-by-case basis'. In return for this concession, however, they argue that the Rohingyas should give up their claim to be "original inhabitants" of the land and to the territories in which they currently reside. Efforts by the Burmese government to carry out a survey to verify the legal status of Rohingyas that would allow a significant number of them to become naturalized citizens have been stalled due to political instability in the region and strong resistance from Rakhine extremists.[17]

Actors in the Conflict

Current analyses of communal riots in Rakhine State generally portray the issue as a result of the tension between two opposing parties with diametrically opposing interests. Rakhine Buddhists are lumped together in the same category as their Burman counterparts and the government dominated by Bamar Buddhists due to their shared hostility to the Rohingyas. Generally speaking, Burman and Rakhine Buddhists share an anti-Muslim and anti-Indian prejudice, a widespread attitude that can be traced back to the colonial period. The growing numbers of Indian immigrants who came to dominate various aspects and levels of the economy during the British colonial period ignited a strong reaction

16. Ibid.
17. International Crisis Group (2014).

of fear in the Burmese population, combined with a sense of superiority. The Burmese speak of South Asian peoples in derogatory terms such as "Kala" and, given these deep-seated racist attitudes, it is hardly surprising that even some pro-democracy dissidents from Burma's ethnic Burman majority and a number of monks' organizations that have been at the forefront of Burma's struggle for democracy have reacted strongly against the Rohingya community.

Rakhine Buddhist communities are particularly concerned about the growing numbers of Rohingyas whose cultural and religious practices differ from their own, and feel that they have been bypassed by the international assistance, which is most often directed to the Rohingyas. While acknowledging that some of their ancestors may have settled in the state in pre-British times, Rakhine nationalists still regard Rohingyas as illegal immigrants and have strongly supported government policies aimed at cracking down on Rohingya settlers. Rakhine Buddhists have also resisted domestic and international efforts and pressure to promote inter-religious peace and dialogue in the region.

There is also an important economic dimension that is at stake. The Rohingyas in Myanmar have historically dominated the lower economic rungs in the Rakhine region and have been mostly employed as unskilled labourers – such as domestic and construction workers – earning meagre wages working for Rakhine employers. Rohingya fishermen are known to be more risk-prone than their Rakhine co-workers and accept relatively lower wages, demonstrating that very little has changed since the colonial period.[18] Aye Chan reports that many of their ancestors (most of whom were coolies) came from the Chittagong district to Burma for better economic and employment prospects, given the relatively better wages offered in the host country. Chan also notes that the colonial administrators of India regarded the Bengalis as amendable and 'frugal folk' who paid their taxes, while characterizing the indigenous Arakanese as defiant, rebellious, and addicted to gambling and opium-smoking. Land disputes between the Rakhine and Bangali immigrants became common under colonial rule, evident in an increase in lawsuits and litigation over land ownership. Eighty-five per cent of litigation over land heard in the courts was initiated by Chittagonians, Chan reports. The loss of land and economic opportunities by Rakhine residents

18. Material from the author's interviews in 2011–12.

during the colonial period served in their eyes as a warning against any conciliatory policies directed towards immigrant populations.[19]

These sentiments, however, do not accurately reflect the ongoing interdependent economic relationships between the two communities. A significant number of Rakhine businesses employ Rohingya workers and some Rakhine businessmen complain of their inability to find Rakhine workers who are willing to work in the low-paid jobs currently performed by Rohingyas. Informal conversations with Rakhine business-owners during field research in Rakhine State by the author carried out in 2011 also reveal that many of them have obtained loans from Bangladeshi traders and financiers who serve as a major source of capital and in some areas form the backbone of the local economy.

In addition, while Rakhine Buddhists display strong negative attitudes toward Rohingyas, this by no means implies that they have friendly relationships with their Burman counterparts or the Burmese government. Their animosity toward the Burmans dates back to 1785 when the Burmese conquered the Arakan kingdom and persecuted the Arakanese population. Rakhine Buddhists have joined armed resistance movements against the Burmese government and formed political parties with the aim of gaining greater autonomy for Rakhine State. They also claim that they are carrying a disproportionate share of the nation's burden by helping block the spread of Islam into the rest of Burma as the result of the official restrictions against the movements of Rohingyas outside Rakhine areas. Indeed, some Rakhine nationalists favour the lifting of restrictions on the movements of Rohingyas to give them free access to the rest of Burma.[20]

Burman politicians have historically courted the Rohingyas to counterbalance the popularity of the Rakhine political parties in Rakhine State. In order to undermine the popularity of the Arakan National United Organization Party and its demands for greater autonomy for Rakhine State, the post-independence U Nu government attempted to mobilize support among the Rohingyas by promising them radio air-time following the 1956 elections, autonomous status for the Mayu district (where the majority of Rohingyas live), and the right to vote and to elect their own representatives.[21] U Nu also added a constitu-

---

19. Chan (2005), especially p. 399.
20. Author's interviews in 2011–12.
21. Bigelow (1960). In 1960, for instance, the Arakan United Organization Party won 8 seats, compared to U Nu's Clean AFPFL's 3 seats, and the stable AFPFL's 1 seat (Bigelow 1960: 73).

ency in Buthidaung township – a district dominated by Rohingyas – to increase his party's chances in the state, offered an amnesty to Rohingya armed resistance fighters, offered citizenship rights, and allowed Bengali groups into Burma in return for their votes.[22]

Four to six Muslim members were elected to the upper and lower parliaments from Maungtaw and Buthidaung townships during the 1951, 1956 and 1960 elections.[23] Despite being denied citizenship, Muslim constituents in Rakhine State were allowed to vote for their representatives in the national elections and in popular referenda under the socialist government (1972–88), in the 1990 and 2010 elections, and in the referendum on the constitution in 2008.[24] They voted either for Rohingya parties (1990 and 2010 elections) or for Rohingya community leaders representing the pro-government party (2010 elections). The pro-government Union Solidarity and Development Party (USDP), which won a landslide victory in 2010, allegedly enlisted the support of a well-known Rohingya leader in order to generate votes among the Rohingya community.[25] This was seen as an attempt to undermine support for the Rakhine Nationalities Development Party (RNDP), which won the fourth largest total of parliamentary seats (35 seats or 3% of total seats) in the 2010 elections. In fact, in 2010 the RNDP won the largest number and percentage of seats in the state legislature of any party (the USDP won 29.8% of the seats in the Rakhine State legislature and the 25% of seats reserved for the military.)[26]

Thus, while Burman politicians and military leaders may share anti-Muslim sentiments with their Rakhine counterparts, they do not hesitate to exploit the Rohingyas as a source of political support against rival Rakhine political parties.

There have also been other minorities who are caught in the conflict. Kamar – Muslims but recognized as one of Burma's '135' races, for instance – have allegedly offered support to Rohingyas to register as Kamar and eventually obtain citizenship. A political party representing Kamar has come under fierce pressure by Rakhine nationalists to divulge their population figure to match with their claimed population numbers. The Chin – another minority group from among Myanmar's recognized 135

---

22. Myint Thein (2009): 21.
23. Ibid.: 23.
24. NDPD (2012): 17.
25. Author's interview 2011.
26. Transnational Institute (2010).

races and claiming to have an estimated population of 100,000 in Rakhine State – felt pressured and threatened by Rakhine hardliners to use violence against Rohingyas, even though they express sympathy toward the Rohingyas and would like to remain neutral in the conflict.

National security and Islamist militancy

National security concerns have played a major role in the hostile policies adopted toward the Rohingyas by successive military governments in Burma. The Burmese army – as well as Burman and Rakhine Buddhist nationalists – are particularly concerned about the separatist aspirations expressed by some Rohingya organizations and the threat posed by militant extremists in the region.

The notion of an autonomous Muslim state in Rakhine goes back to the end of colonial period, when in 1946 a Muslim delegation visited Karachi to discuss with the leaders of the Muslim League the possibility of incorporating Buthidaung, Maungdaw and Ratheedaung townships into Pakistan (or Eastern Pakistan, which later became Bangladesh). However, the British ignored their proposal. In 1947, Rohingya activists founded the Mujahid Party to push their demands for an autonomous Muslim state in Arakan in the area between the west bank of the Kaladan River and the east bank of the Naaf River; for acceptance of the Muslims in Arakan as one of the official nationalities of Burma, and of Urdu as their national language; and for the resettlement of Muslim wartime refugees from the Kyuaktaw and Myohaung townships. When these demands in turn were ignored, a further round of communal violence was ignited. A proposal for the creation of a separate or autonomous Muslim state by Muslims from the Mayu Frontier region was again turned down in 1962 by the revolutionary government, which was seeking public submissions prior to the drafting of a new constitution. Although the Ne Win government later waged a series of military operations against the Muslim insurgency, the Burmese mujahideen (Islamic militants) are reported to have been active in remote areas of Arakan.

More recently, there have been increasing concerns about the close association between Burmese mujahideen and Bangladeshi mujahideen and their growing international networks, which provide religious and military training outside of Burma. Rohingya refugee camps in the Cox's Bazar District of Chittagong have also reportedly served as fertile ground for recruitment by Islamic militants (including Bangladesh's most extreme Islamic organization, Harkat-ul-jihad-i-Islami, which was set up in 1992 with financial support from Osama bin Laden), and have become a hideout area for militants from Jemaah Islamiah, a militant group with connections to Al-Qaeda (Lintner 2002).[27]

Rohingya armed organizations active in the Burma–Bangladesh border area include the RSO (Rohingya Solidarity Organization), ARIF (Arakan Rohingya Islamic Front), RPF (Rohingya Patriotic Front), RLO (Rohingya Liberation Organization), and IMA (Itihadul Mozahadin of Arakan). The Rohingya Solidarity Organization and the Arakan Rohingya Islamic Front are fighting for autonomy or independence for the Rohingyas. According to Lintner, the RSO has allegedly been supported by one of Bangladesh's right-wing political parties and has established ties with the Islamic terrorist organization Jamiat-ul-Mujahideen Bangladesh (JMB). Last but not least, the repression of Muslim populations in Asian nations in general and Burma in particular could create a backlash in majority Islamic countries, thereby increasing the severity of existing conflicts.

Conclusion

The establishment of the rule of law (defined in terms of enhanced state capacity in law enforcement and non-discriminatory arbitration in judicial and legal disputes) and the promotion of economic development are urgently needed in the conflict-ridden and poverty-stricken Rakhine State. In addition, deeper and interrelated issues such as eligibility for citizenship, the persistence of anti-Muslim and anti-Indian prejudice, and the spread of radical militant Islam will have to be addressed. These issues are technical as well as political.

Proper documentation of residents will be a step in the right direction since it will lay the groundwork for establishing criteria and eligibility for citizenship, and protection and rights for guest workers and refugees. It is also important that a neutral party, which is trusted by both sides, is tasked with the responsibility to carry out the process. However, efforts to collect demographic data or to foster better interfaith dialogue and peaceful coexistence have been met with resistance in Rakhine State.

Thus far, the voices expressing either strong anti-Rohingya or pro-Rohingya sentiments are the loudest; those who strike a conciliatory or indecisive note, including Daw Aung San Suu Kyi, have been condemned

---

27. See Rahman (2010) and Lintner (2002), also Abuza (2003).

by both sides.[28] One nationalist blogger complained: 'I heard Daw Su saying that whoever is born in Burma should be considered [a] Burmese citizen ... I hope this is not what she meant.' At the same time, Aung San Suu Kyi was criticized by international human rights organizations sympathetic to the Rohingyas for remaining silent over the issue. There seems to be no 'middle way' approach to the situation. It is difficult to judge what proportion of Burmese either harbour feelings against the Rohingyas, are sitting on the fence or are sympathetic to them. The situation is far from clear-cut. Some Burmese nationalists, while rejecting the Rohingyas' claims to Burmese nationality, have expressed a desire to protect their rights: 'We are not against them because of differences in culture, ethnicity or religion; we respect their human rights, they should freely worship and speak; they should fight against oppression, but we cannot accept them as original settlers of Burma; we cannot accept illegal immigrants.'[29]

Burma shares the concern of illegal immigration, anti-Islam sentiments and fear of radical Islam movements with other countries in the region. Given the persistence of comparable conflicts in other parts of the world, one should not expect a quick-fix solution to Burma's age-old problems. The study also shows the tendency of the existing literature to overlook differences between groups with seemingly shared positions and emphasizes the need to develop a new research agenda that looks at conflicts where three or more parties are involved.

References

Abuza, Zachary (2003) *Militant Islam in Southeast Asia: Crucible of Terror.* Boulder, CO: Lynne Rienner Publishers.

Berlie, Jean (2008) *The Burmanization of Myanmar's Muslims.* Bangkok: White Lotus Press.

Bigelow, Lee. (1960) 'The 1960 Elections in Burma'. *Far Eastern Survey*, May.

Blitz, Brad (2010) 'Refugees in Burma, Malaysia, and Thailand: Rescue for the Rohingya'. *The World Today*, vol. 66(5), May.

---

28. Aung San Suu Kyi refers to the situation as a rule-of-law or illegal-immigration problem – issues that will be discussed in parliament while the human rights of all should be protected.
29. Defunct 'Paduak Myay' blog, April 2011.

Chan, Aye (2005) 'The Development of a Muslim Enclave in Arakan (Rakhine) State of Burma (Myanmar)'. *SOAS Bulletin of Burma Research*, vol. 3(2), Autumn.

International Crisis Group (2014) 'Counting the Costs: Myanmar's Problematic Census'. Yangon, 15 May.

Lewa, Chris (2009) 'North Arakan: An Open Prison for the Rohingya in Burma'. *Forced Migration Review*, Issue 32, April, pp. 11–13.

Lintner, Bertil (2002) 'Bangladesh: Breeding ground for Muslim terror'. Available at: http://www.scribd.com/doc/12964470/Rohingya-Terrorism-Link-by-Bertil-Lintner.

NDPD (2012) 'In Respect of the Fact that the Muslim Inhabitants of Rakhine State are Natives by Race and Citizens of the Republic of the Union of Myanmar Under Law or By Natural Birth'. Yangon: National Democratic Party for Development.

New Mandala (2011) 'BBC under fire on Rohingyas', 3 November: http://asiapacific.anu.edu.au/newmandala/2011/11/03/bbc-under-fire-on-rohingyas/.

Rahman, Utpala (2010) 'The Rohingya Refugee: A Security Dilemma for Bangladesh'. *Journal of Immigrant & Refugee Studies*, vol. 8(2), April–June, pp. 233–239.

Rakhine Inquiry Commission, Final Report of Inquiry Commission on Sectarian Violence in Rakhine State, 8 July 2013.

RNDP (2012) 'A Critical Assessment of the History Fabrication of Bangali Who Assume the Name of Rohingya to Claim Identity as a National Group'. Sittwe: Rakhine Nationalities Development Party (RNDP), May 2012 (in Burmese).

Thein, Myint. (2009) 'Rakhine Day Tha Thoe Muslim Myar Win Yauk Lar Chin Hint Naing Ngan Yae Loke Shar Pone Ah Sint Sint' [The Inflow of Muslim populations into Rakhine region and their various stages of political activities]. Naypyidaw: Ministry of Culture.

Transnational Institute (2010) 'A Changing Ethnic Landscape: Analysis of Burma's 2010 Polls'. Amsterdam: Burma Centrum Netherlands, Burma Policy Briefing, no. 4, December.

Yegar, Moshe (2002) *Between Integration and Secession: The Muslim Communities of the Southern Philippines, Southern Thailand, and Western Burma/Myanmar*. Lanham, MD: Lexington Books.

PART THREE

Economy, development and environment

Traders selling fruit and vegetables at a local market in the Ayeyarwady Delta (photo: Marie Ditlevsen)

The economy of Myanmar is changing and developing at an incredible pace, and it brings opportunities as well as challenges to the state administration, local people, and the environment. In the following section of this volume, these changes and developments will be presented, discussed and analysed in order to give the reader a deeper understanding of the situation.

In so doing, this section will start with a general overview of the economic fundamentals and resources on which the Burmese economy is dependent. These will be then elaborated and analysed in relation to the current political situation in the country, the main focus being on economic and political reforms (or lack thereof) and lifting of sanctions. Based on this analysis, it will be discussed how economic development might have a positive influence on social conditions and help reduce poverty and what impact it has had on the environment. At this point, a showcase development project that is also a controversial environmental issue, the Myitsone Dam project in the Kachin State, will be explored. The section ends by focusing on these issues viewed from the perspective of international donors and NGOs who, together with national and local NGOs, are expected to play an important role in the development of Myanmar.

Economic fundamentals, ongoing challenges

Marie Ditlevsen

Rapid change is affecting not just Myanmar's political situation but also its economy. The following chapters focus on aspects of these changes but first, in this chapter, the most important economic fundamentals of Myanmar will be presented and discussed, particularly in relation to the role of the military/ cronies and foreign investors.

Myanmar is currently experiencing internal and external changes that may pave the way for economic improvements. The floating of the kyat, new financial laws, the lifting of sanctions, and foreign support and investment are all factors that could contribute to economic development. While the country will continue to exploit and benefit from existing natural resources, new sources of income are arising first of all from tourism and foreign investment. And these new resources carry opportunities as well as challenges with them.

The new quasi-civilian government, supported by civil-society organizations and the people in general, is gradually gaining power to influence the economic situation. However, the military and the so-called 'cronies' are expected to keep playing an important role in economic development. As described elsewhere in the book (see p. 362ff.) the cronies have the economic foundation, and possibly also business experience, required to implement development projects in collaboration with foreign investors, and thus to boost the country's economic development. The question is, however, to what extent the Burmese people in general will benefit from this.

Agriculture

A century ago, Burma was the wealthiest country in Southeast Asia and the world's largest exporter of rice. War and a succession of failed or downright ruinous economic policies turned the country into one of the world's most impoverished ones. Since 2011, the Thein Sein government has been preparing comprehensive reforms in the area of agriculture, particularly with the objectives to increase productivity through improvements in rural infrastructure, access to affordable inputs, and expanded credit availability (via microfinance).

However, the implementation of the reforms has thus far been of limited nature. The agricultural sector is continuously bedevilled by export restrictions and production controls, and farmers are still struggling with poor infrastructure, lack of access to fertilizers, silted-up irrigation systems, etc. (for more details, see p. 369 ff). Furthermore, certain areas of the agricultural sector are monopolized by large, crony-owned businesses, with the result that the income of individual farmers is negatively affected. Many farmers thus work hard but achieve little.

Lack of tenure is one of the most serious challenges faced by the Burmese farmers. In spite of the political reforms, which are gradually granting people more freedom in general, land rights have not changed. Land in Myanmar is still ultimately owned and controlled by the state. Hence, individual farmers and farmer organizations depend upon usage rights, as they are unable to obtain ownership rights to the land.[1] This lack of tenure also applies to the lake and delta areas: here fishermen have to rent the water areas in which they wish to fish.

In the wake of the influx of foreign investment, tenure issues have shown themselves to be particularly problematic. Due to the fact that the farmers have no secure title to their farmland, the state and foreign companies have practically the right to confiscate/grab their land for the purpose of large infrastructural dam or large-scale agricultural projects.[2] Such forced land confiscation, which in most cases is uncompensated, is a source of conflict, and protests and fear of 'land grabs' have been escalating.[3] A number of people participating in these (usually non-violent) protests have been punished, some even jailed.

The issue of land rights could also have a negative impact on large-scale development projects, based on foreign investment, that may be

---

1. See http://usaidlandtenure.net/burma.
2. Ibid.
3. Nang Lao Liang Won, 'Luk ikke øjnene for vold i Burma', *Jyllands-Posten*, 3 December 2013.

Flower-growing as an alternative, or in addition, to rice farming in the Delta (photo: Marie Ditlevsen)

needed for the economic development of the country. If the rights and values of the rural population (around 70% of the total population) are not respected, there is a risk that local resistance to these projects will increase, thus hampering the country's overall economic development.

A positive aspect of this conflict, however, is that the growing freedom of speech has resulted in the farmers actually expressing their dissatisfaction about the land situation. In August 2013, farmers presented a list of 17 demands to legislators to amend the country's land laws and to provide greater protection against forced evictions.[4] The primary objectives were to amend the 2012 Land Law, to end the arrest of farmers protesting against land grabbing, and to require outright compensation for the loss of land. Hence, although farmers are being punished for holding non-violent demonstrations, they are now able to apply for amendments to the law. Whether this will result in political changes or not is difficult to predict.

Another challenge faced by the farmers is the continued lack of access to credit. In order to establish private, small-scale businesses, it

---

4.   See   http://www.atimes.com/atimes/Southeast_Asia/SEA-01-210813.html#.UhUfziRXkIg. twitter.

is crucial for farmers to have initial capital as well as the possibility of investing in their business. Generally speaking, the access to credit has improved slightly since the beginning of the political reforms. This is the case for example in certain rural areas, partly as a result of international NGOs establishing or strengthening existing microfinance mechanisms in villages, and partly because the state is now granting farmers larger amounts of money than before. The establishment of microfinance mechanisms enables villagers to save as well as borrow money in their own village – in most cases at lower interest rates.[5]

In spite of this slight improvement, however, people's access to credit is still limited. According to the International Finance Corporation, in 2013 only 16% of households used formal financial services.[6] Hence, the majority still relies on informal lenders, such as fellow villagers and family members, to fulfil cash-flow needs. A possible explanation may be that although the new Law on Microfinance is undoubtedly a positive approach towards economic development, it is still based on rules and regulations restricting people from fully benefitting from the microfinance mechanisms. (For more details, see p. 369ff.)

The combination of continued lack of tenure and difficulties in getting access to credit presents a serious challenge to farmers. Even so, despite the number of barriers and challenges mentioned above, agriculture remains the most important sector in the economy, employing 61% of the population and utilizing about 60% of the land area.[7] Rice is still the main crop, accounting for 97% of total food grain production by weight. However, other crops have been introduced recently or their production is on the increase, for example rubber, beans, soybeans and palm oil.[8]

Forestry

Myanmar has been one of the world's main sources of teak wood, which is popular worldwide because of its natural durability and its termite

---

5. These issues are explored in Marie Ditlevsen, 'Strengthening Civil Society in Myanmar – the influence of political reforms'. M.A. thesis, International Development Studies and Communication, Roskilde University, 2013.

6. See http://www.cgap.org/sites/default/files/Microfinance%20in%20Myanmar%20Sector%20Assessment.pdf.

7. Ibid.

8. See http://faostat.fao.org/DesktopDefault.aspx?PageID=339&lang=en&country=28 and http://faostat.fao.org/desktopdefault.aspx?pageid=342&lang=en&country=28.

Despite increased legal protection of forests, illegal logging is still common – timber trucks lined up near Laiza, Kachin State, to cross the border into China (photo: David Høgsholt)

repellence. Teak grows throughout Southeast Asia, with almost half of the natural forests found in Myanmar.

One of the reasons for Myanmar's success in teak-wood export is that Myanmar has not enforced a logging or export ban on teak wood – the only country in Southeast Asia not to do so. As a result of this, all naturally harvested teak wood in the international market is Burmese – a factor contributing to the wood being sold at a high price.[9] Hence, the export of teak wood plays an important role in the Burmese economy. But there has been a severe degradation of forest cover in Myanmar as a result of this (see Map 8 on p. 346).

In late 2012, the government passed a timber export bill to be enforced in 2014. The main reasons for passing the bill were to preserve the remaining teak forests and develop a sustainable timber production and export industry.[10] Hence, the environmental issues related to the teak-wood industry are being taken into consideration, a crucial factor that will be discussed later (see p. 387). Initially, the timber export bill may have a hampering impact on the industry but in the longer term

---

9. See http://www.eastbysoutheast.com/burmese-teak-turning-a-new-leaf.
10. Ibid.

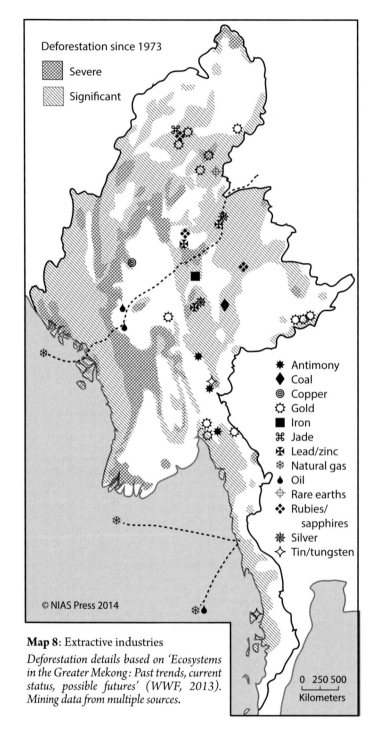

Map 8: Extractive industries

Deforestation details based on 'Ecosystems in the Greater Mekong: Past trends, current status, possible futures' (WWF, 2013). Mining data from multiple sources.

it will be beneficial for the environment as well as for sustainable economic development.

Mining

Other natural resources of significant economic importance are the various gemstones (jade, rubies etc.) and various minerals like gold, tin and copper extracted from mines (see Map 8). This resource, if extracted, processed and traded in a sustainable and respectful manner, could be beneficial to the economy. Unfortunately, about half of all gemstones are traded on the black market so the state earns less revenue from this trade than it could. Moreover, the mining business often causes conflicts and protests, in many cases because the extraction process requires the confiscation of large areas of rural land.

An important example is the Wanbao Mining Corporation project, implemented in October 2004, in which Aung San Suu Kyi sought to address the issues of land rights and shared interests. The project is a joint venture between a subsidiary of China's state-owned arms maker, Norinco, and the military-run Myanmar Economic Holdings Ltd. The objective was to build a vast new pit for the mining of copper, a project that called for the acquisition of the lands of 26 villages at the base of Letpadaung mountain. This caused considerable controversy leading to a public inquiry supported by Aung San Suu Kyi.[11]

To the relief of Wanbao, the inquiry ruled that the company could continue to expand and Suu Kyi, anxious not to alienate China, urged the farmers to cooperate with the project. Her inquiry ordered the company to pay market prices for farmers' land, and compensation for three years worth of crops. Furthermore, the company was requested to conduct an environmental impact study, but the enforcement of the result of the studies was not being emphasized. Hence, in order to create a basis for the mining project to continue, Suu Kyi called for both parties involved to make compromises – compromises that for the farmers and local residents may appear more like sacrifices.

Apart from the acquisition of land and environmental degradation, the mining industry involves issues related to work environment. On the one hand the mining projects provide work for local residents but on the

11. See http://www.globalpost.com/dispatch/news/regions/asia-pacific/myanmar/130425/myanmar-burma-mine-quarry-china-copper-dirt.

other hand the extraction of gemstones, copper, etc. is physically challenging and harmful to the health of the workers. The mining industry is often controlled by the military, and the work involved sometimes includes slave-like conditions and use of child labour.[12]

Energy sector

The energy sector is one of Myanmar's major sources of foreign income. The country has large reserves of oil and gas, and foreign companies are flocking to get a share of the wealth (see Map 9). In June 2013, a total of 145 joint ventures between local and international energy companies had been registered with the Ministry of Energy.[13] Generally speaking, the state has the sole right to explore and extract oil and gas, but the strong interest in foreign investment has made the government welcome the participation of foreign companies. According to Myanmar's most recent foreign-investment law, foreign companies are generally required to form joint ventures with local companies in order to invest in the oil and gas sectors.[14]

The resources of oil and gas are primarily exported to neighbouring countries, most importantly to Thailand and China. Hence, the Burmese people are not directly benefitting from it. Not utilizing the oil and gas resources (or the revenues from the oil and gas exports) in developing the country's own energy supply and infrastructure is an obstacle to the overall development of the country. According to the Asian Development Bank, 'Myanmar's energy sector is critical to reducing poverty and enhancing the medium- and long-term development prospects of the country'. However, despite the increasing focus and investment in the oil and gas sector, only about 50% of the Burmese population has access to electricity.[15]

Oil and gas are transported and exported through a growing web of pipelines, which in most cases cross the borders into neighbouring countries; the China-backed Shwe Gas Project in Rakhine State in western Myanmar is a good example. The project contract was finalized

---

12. See http://latitude.blogs.nytimes.com/2012/10/17/clashing-over-jade-ethnic-kachin-continue-to-oppose-the-myanmar-government/?_r=0.
13. See http://elevenmyanmar.com/business/2526-over-140-joint-ventures-in-myanmar-s-growing-oil-and-gas-sector.
14. Ibid.
15. World Bank: http://wdi.worldbank.org/table/3.7.

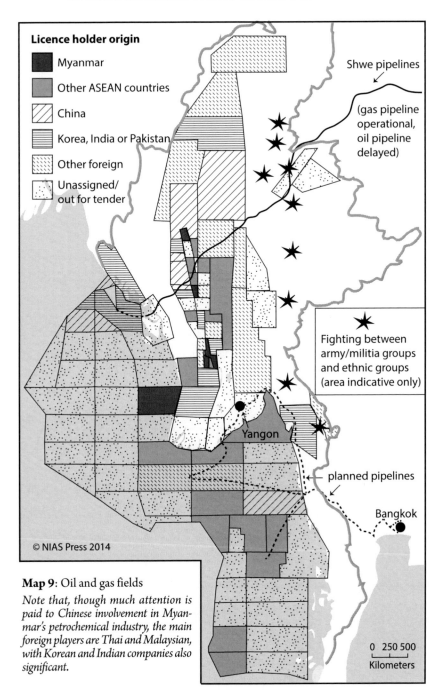

Licence holder origin

- Myanmar
- Other ASEAN countries
- China
- Korea, India or Pakistan
- Other foreign
- Unassigned/ out for tender

Shwe pipelines

(gas pipeline operational, oil pipeline delayed)

Fighting between army/militia groups and ethnic groups (area indicative only)

Yangon

planned pipelines

Bangkok

© NIAS Press 2014

0   250 500
Kilometers

Map 9: Oil and gas fields

Note that, though much attention is paid to Chinese involvement in Myanmar's petrochemical industry, the main foreign players are Thai and Malaysian, with Korean and Indian companies also significant.

between China National Petroleum Company (CNPC) and Myanmar's Ministry of Energy in December 2009, with a total investment of US$ 2.54 billion. The involvement of the local people in the project turned out to be reprehensible, as they experienced inadequate compensation, a continued poor transport infrastructure and insufficient salaries for local workers. These circumstances resulted in protests from hundreds of residents in April 2013.[16] Apart from the residents not benefitting from the project, the construction of the pipeline furthermore resulted in the pollution of rivers from which local fishermen earn their living.

In spite of the protests, however, the Shwe gas pipeline was completed in May 2013 and is now operational. The oil pipeline was expected to be finished before the end of 2013 but, in addition to the local protests, it has been held up by rare public protests in China forcing the relocation of the associated oil refinery in Kunming. Labelled as China's 'fourth largest energy transportation route' after the Central Asia pipelines, sea transportation and the Sino–Russian pipelines, the project is seen by China to be of national strategic importance by diversifying China's energy transportation system (see Map 3, p. 97). In addition, although the pipelines have a Chinese identity, the project is a multinational endeavour. The gas pipeline involves six stakeholders from four countries (China, Myanmar, India and South Korea) and is aimed at delivering gas from a Daewoo-led consortium operating in the Shwe field to China.

In a country geographically divided by numerous ethnic minority territories, some dominated by ethnic or religious conflicts and unrest, the establishment of far-reaching pipelines may prove problematic. In most cases local villagers affected by the pipelines are not consulted before the implementation of the projects,[17] and if they do not approve of the government, or the foreign investment upon which the pipeline project is based, resistance may arise.

In addition to oil and gas, Myanmar has the potential to generate huge amounts of electricity via a large number of hydroelectric dams. Again, there has been much local opposition to the construction of these dams (for more details, see p. 357).

Without doubt, these large-scale energy development projects have the potential to generate large revenues to be used in upgrading the

---

16. See http://www.shwe.org/hundreds-protest-pipeline-in-burmas-rakhine-state.
17. See http://www.burmapartnership.org/2013/07/shwe-gas-pipeline-a-sign-of-things-to-come.

national energy supply and the infrastructure, and ultimately to improve the living conditions of the citizens in the country. The challenge, however, is to develop the projects in a way that respects and is beneficial for the people of Myanmar, and not just for the military/cronies, Chinese resource companies and multinational businesses.

Manufacturing

In Myanmar's manufacturing industry, garment and textile products have been amongst some of the most important export products. Countries like China, Thailand and Bangladesh are considered the leading actors in the Asian garment/textile industry but Myanmar has also contributed significantly to this particular export market. From the mid-1990s until 2004, 85 per cent of Myanmar's export products were garments or textiles. During this period, the United States was the country's largest export market, receiving an estimated 25% of its garment/textile export products. This situation ended abruptly after the imposing of increasingly strict sanctions from the late 1990s, and actual banning of imports from Myanmar in 2003. With the U.S. being Myanmar's largest export market, these comprehensive U.S. sanctions had a devastating impact on the sector and resulted in a severe decrease in the value of exports from Myanmar.[18]

Today, after the lifting of sanctions and reopening of trade, Myanmar's manufacturing industry is slowly regaining its strength in the Asian garment/textile export market. As is the case with other sectors in the Myanmar economy, this development is partly being realized through joint ventures between foreign investors and local manufacturers/factories. A number of leading Thai clothing manufacturers are also moving part of their production to Myanmar. Whether or not it will encourage the huge numbers of Burmese factory workers in Thailand to return home is another matter, however (see p. 364).

Apart from the traditional garment/textile industry, the inflow of foreign investors is also resulting in international brands like Coca Cola and Carlsberg being introduced and manufactured in Myanmar. Coca Cola believes that now is the right time to invest in the country, and

---

18. See http://www.forbes.com/sites/connorconnect/2012/10/18/can-manufacturing-succeed-in-myanmar.

that the establishment of a joint venture will create jobs for the Burmese people and hence result in a positive economic development.[19]

There are certain factors that contribute to Myanmar manufacturing being particularly lucrative, at least for the time being. One of the most important factors is the young, low-cost labour force. As the poorest and least developed country in Asia, the minimum wage in Myanmar is US$ 1.25 per day, thus making it an attractive place for foreign countries to have their products manufactured at a minimum price. Another factor, obviously constituting a human rights issue, is the continued use of children and trafficked people in the labour force.[20] As such, working conditions are very poor, especially in the garment and textile sector. Often, factories have no health and safety regulations or HR policies. However, considering the rapid political and economic developments in the country, there is a chance that these factors may soon change, thus enabling the local manufacturers to become beneficiaries themselves.

Tourism

Since the beginning of the political changes, Myanmar has experienced a boom in tourism. People from all over the world are eager to visit and explore this 'Far Eastern country' that for decades has been wrapped in a veil of mystique and isolation. The Burmese people are welcoming the tourists, and in Yangon and other big cities the citizens appear very open with regard to describing the past history of their country.

During the years of military rule, the country was visited by limited numbers of tourists, partly due to the numerous travel restrictions but also because of the ethical dilemmas arising from human-rights abuses, etc. This may explain why tourism has not been treated as an economic factor in the same way as in many other developing countries. However, the gradually increasing influx of tourists is expected to play an important role in the economic development. The question is, however, to what extent the country has the capacity to handle this sudden boom in tourism?[21] At present the country is still struggling with poor infrastructure and a low capacity to accommodate the many tourists. Furthermore, tourism

19. See http://www.bbc.co.uk/news/business-22776521.
20. See http://www.forbes.com/sites/connorconnect/2012/10/18/can-manufacturing-succeed-in-myanmar.
21. See http://observers.france24.com/content/20130821-booming-tourism-burma-golden-rock-profit.

Tourists thronging the Shwedagon temple complex (photo: Marie Ditlevsen)

industry is still hampered by a number of formalities and restrictions, first of all travel restrictions that limit the areas where tourists may visit.[22]

Another important question is, who will be the beneficiaries of this boom in tourism. Potentially, the local people have the opportunity to benefit from it, but in many cases it seems that state-controlled organizations, or the cronies, are harvesting much of the profits.[23] For example, cronies are expected to enter the hotel industry (see p. 362) but there is a risk (and fear) that only a small group of people will benefit from this, and hence that it may contribute to greater inequality. In other words, as is the case with all other economic resources in Myanmar, the country and its people will not benefit from the booming tourism unless tourism projects involve, and are economically beneficial for, local residents. As an example, the DFID-supported Business Innovation Facility Program seeks to implement pro-poor projects in the tourism sector (among

---

22. See http://www.elevenmyanmar.com/tourism/3147-myanmar-s-once-restricted-sites-attract-foreign-tourists.

23. See http://observers.france24.com/content/20130821-booming-tourism-burma-golden-rock-profit.

other sectors), with the purpose of including poor people in tourism businesses (hotels, restaurants, guided tours etc.).

Illegal drug trade

Historically, opium has been an important crop especially along the Chinese border in Kachin and Shan states, and generally it has constituted an important source of income for people in Myanmar (see also p. 150). Some of the most important purchasers of opium come from China, and while the drug can be traded and consumed just as raw opium, it is also used to make heroin. Another illegal drug that Myanmar is increasingly known for is methamphetamines, which is produced in the same area. For all of these drugs, Myanmar is one of the leading producers in the world and thus over many decades played an important role in the infamous, drug-trading 'Golden Triangle'.

Over the decades since independence, many different armed groups have financed their activities via drug trade, especially in the north of the country. Notable examples were remnants of Kuomintang forces escaping the Chinese communist victory in 1949, the Mong Tai Army of opium warlord Khun Sa and the United Wa State Army (see 'Ethnic armed groups', p. 165ff.). The Tatmadaw has also been deeply involved in the drug trade. During the military period, the trade in opium and amphetamines was an important income source for the Tatmadaw. Today, while its economic involvement seems to be levelling off as a result of a national attempt to end the trade and reduce drug addiction in the population, in non-ceasefire areas it is still using the trade to control local militias and rebel groups for whom the production and sale of drugs are the basis of their livelihood.[24]

Recent official moves against the drug industry have seen the flight of many poppy-growers and conversion of lands into other forms of cultivation like soybeans and palm oil. Even so, Myanmar remains the world's second largest opium producer after Afghanistan. According to the UN Office on Drugs and Crime, the production of opium rose by 26% from 2012 to 2013. Continued poverty and food insecurity appear to be the main reasons, while a rising demand in Asia for illicit drugs is also said to be fuelling this increase in the production and trading of opium.

---

24. See http://www.mmtimes.com/index.php/national-news/8750-palaung-group-accuses-tatmadaw-of-failing-to-control-drug-trade.html.

Another important reason is that in certain parts of the country the climate and soil quality makes it difficult for farmers to grow alternative crops. This for example is the case in Karenni State, where the Union of Karenni State Youth explains how their area is too dry for alternative crops to be grown (poppy plants can survive on limited amounts of water). Furthermore, the Karennis have become used to earning money from such a valuable crop.[25]

The UN calls for efforts to further address this issue and to promote alternative crop production and livelihood methods. This is a difficult task, however, as the opium trade is a lucrative, high-cash market, and families engaged in this business have made a living out of it for generations.[26] Furthermore, it appears that the Myanmar government is not making an adequate effort to address this issue, not least because of the military's continued involvement in the industry.[27]

In conclusion

Generally speaking, Myanmar has potentially the resources required to experience transformational economic development in the near future. However, a number of compromises are needed in order to exploit and benefit from these resources in a sustainable manner. On the one hand, the implementation of infrastructure, mining and agricultural projects – some based on joint ventures between foreign investors and local actors – are needed in order to improve Myanmar's economic situation. The development of these projects is at present most often managed by the state or the cronies, who have the capital as well as the required experience. On the other hand, however, the implementation of foreign investment-based projects may be challenged and resisted by the general population, if local residents are not included in the projects and their needs/rights not properly respected. And if only the state and the cronies are the major beneficiaries of the projects, there is a risk that social gaps will widen. Furthermore, in many areas Myanmar does not have the capacity to manage and structure the development projects and economic changes. This issue is particularly

25. See http://www.irrawaddy.org/burma/karenni-farmers-options-besides-opium-civil-society-groups.html.

26. See http://www.irrawaddy.org/burma/un-poverty-pushing-burma-opium-output-higher.html.

27. See http://www.nytimes.com/2012/05/14/world/asia/drug-surge-clouds-myanmar-reform-effort.html?pagewanted=all&_r=0.

relevant in regard to the booming tourism industry, to which a number of barriers, such as poor infrastructure, continued travel restrictions and insufficient accommodation, constitute challenges. The ongoing challenges in regard to Myanmar's economic fundamentals, briefly presented and discussed in this chapter, will be further elaborated later in an analysis of development challenges and environmental issues (p. 387ff.).

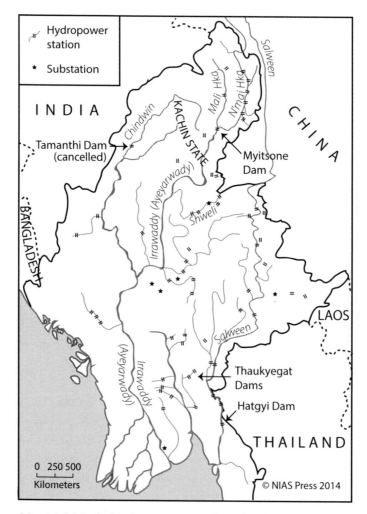

Map 10: Major hydroelectric projects, planned and actual

Based on a map in Earthrights International, 'China in Burma: The Increasing Investment of Chinese Multinational Corporations in Burma's Hydropower, Oil and Natural Gas, and Mining Sectors', 2008, by permission; updated and with non-Chinese projects added.

The Myitsone entanglement

The construction of the giant Myitsone Dam in eastern Kachin State has long provoked opposition from local people, Kachin separatists and environmentalists among others. Indeed, the dam issue seems to have been a factor behind the collapse of the Kachin ceasefire and outbreak of fighting in northern Myanmar in June 2011 (see p. 262ff.). Hence, when on 30 September 2011, President Thein Sein issued a decree halting construction of the dam, there was jubilation among its opponents and shocked disbelief among those with a stake in the project (not least the Chinese). However, construction work is only halted during the time of Thein Sein's government, i.e. until 2015; it is not cancelled and as such the dam issue is very much alive.

The dam site is located 3.2 kilometres below the confluence of the Mali River and the N'Mai River about 42 kilometres north of Myitkina, the capital of Kachin State (see Map 10, p. 356). The sources of both rivers are in the Himalayan glaciers north of Burma in the vicinity of 28° N.

The Myitsone Dam is part of the Confluence Region Hydropower Project (CRHP), which includes seven dams with a total installed capacity of 16,500 megawatts. The CRHP alone accounts for 41% of the total power capacity called for by a 30-year strategic energy plan for Myanmar outlined in 2001. This plan includes 64 hydropower plants. The dam project is controversial due to its enormous flood plain, environmental impact and location on the Sagaing fault line.

If the Myitsone Dam Project is completed as planned in 2017, it will be the fifteenth largest of its kind in the world. The dam, planned to be 1,310 meters long and 139.6 meters high, is being built by Burmese government contractors, led by Asia World, and the state-owned China Power Investment Corporation (CPI). It is estimated that it will provide up to 6,000 megawatts of electricity primarily for Yunnan, China.

On 16 June 2009, Burmese Ambassador Thein Lwin and CPI President Lu Qizhou signed a Memorandum of Agreement between the Department of Hydropower Implementation and CPI for the development, operation and transfer of hydropower projects in Maykha, Malikha and upstream of Irrawaddy-Myitsone River Basins. The official opening ceremony of the dam construction phase was held on December 21 that year.

The majority of total US$3.6 billion is supposed to be covered by CPI in a joint venture with Asia World, Suntac Technologies, the Myanmar Electrical Power Enterprise, and Kansai Electric Power Company. The Burmese government will presumably get 10% of the electricity generated and 15% of the project shares.

In December 2013, in a promotional campaign in response to halting of the dam project, Chinese authorities published the first 'social responsibility report' related to the Myitsone Dam project. The report from the Upstream Ayeyawady Confluence Basin Hydropower Co. (ACHC), largely owned by CPI, details 'tens of millions of dollars in investment to benefit the local people'. Burmese activists and opposition lawmakers slammed the report, calling it a piece of propaganda aimed at garnering support for an unpopular project that has left thousands of people displaced and polluted a vital waterway.

The report, which covers 2010–2012, says that the ACHC invested US$ 10 million to conduct an environment impact assessment, US$6.68 million for environment protection, $25 million to resettle displaced local residents, US$20 million to construct roads and bridges, US$564,000 on rice donations, and US$100,000 to assist agricultural production. CPI has constructed houses in two main resettlement villages. The homes appear sturdy on the outside, but residents say the builders opted for poor-quality wood. They also say that the villages experienced heavy flooding during the rainy season this year.

CPI's Yunnan subsidiary owns 80% of the shares in the ACHC, while Burma's Ministry of Electric Power owns 15% and Burmese conglomerate Asia World Co. owns 5%. According to Guo Gengliang, vice president and board director of the company, the ACHC has invested about 25 billion US dollars in the seven hydropower projects, with construction expected to last 15 years, followed by a 50-year operating period. The Myanmar government will gain about $54 billion in income by means of tax payments, free power and free shares, accounting for 60% of the total revenue of the Ayeyawady [Irrawaddy] projects, Guo Gengliang told *The Irrawaddy News*. He added that, after the concession period, hydropower assets totalling about $25 billion would be transferred to the Burma government, free of charge, for continuous operation.

In addition to courting the government, CPI has tried to win favour with Burma's main opposition party, the National League for Democracy (NLD), led by Aung San Suu Kyi. During 2013, members of the NLD visited China and reportedly 'learned' more about the hydropower projects. However, NLD members of parliament have also criticized the report, saying the Chinese company should have released more information earlier.

≤ FY

Local actors in the economy

While foreign investors and donors may make important contributions to the development of Myanmar, a number of local actors are also expected to play important roles in the economy.

The government/state

Potentially the Myanmar state could have an important role in economic development but this requires first of all the strengthening of various administrative capacities. As outlined in an earlier discussion on public administration (p. 65), the Myanmar economy has been bedevilled by corruption and mismanagement over a long period of time, and the government/state is only in the early stages of creating the administrative structure required to change this. Likewise, although it is implementing a number of economic reforms, the state still lacks the fundamental economic institutions required to manage internal economic affairs as well as to build up a well-functioning market economy. Hence, it remains a challenge for the government/state to function as a strong and influential player in economic development. (For more information, see the chapter by Sean Turnell, p. 369ff.)

Crony capitalists

A small group of about 15 business tycoons became successful during the period of military rule by being linked to and benefitting from the power of the military government. Today, these so-called 'cronies' have

Often said to be one of Myanmar's leading crony capitalists is the business tycoon Tay Za (photo courtesy The Irrawaddy*)*

interests in almost every sector of the Myanmar economy and now are positioning themselves as the indispensable middlemen between international investors flocking to the country and local power-holders concerned about foreign domination. (Nore information on this important economic group is on p. 362.)

The military

As discussed earlier (p. 78), the Tatmadaw retains significant entrenched power in the present constitution. Economically, it has a similarly entrenched position by running two of the most influential conglomerates in the country: Myanmar Economic Holdings and the Myanmar Economic Corporation (more details p. 382). Apart from this, the military has been deeply involved in the illegal drug trade. Today, this involvement is likely to level off but the military still uses the drug trade to control local militias and rebel groups in non-ceasefire areas for whom the production and trade in drugs is their main livelihood (see p. 354).

Local NGOs

NGOs and civil-society organizations were either banned or heavily restricted by the military regime, in order to prevent political unrest (see p. 87ff.). Today, with the welcoming of international NGOs and donors to support the development of Myanmar, they are mushrooming all over the country. This allows the general population to have a say in economic development but, perhaps more importantly, it is generating jobs. The role that local NGOs/civil-society organizations could potentially play was boosted in the wake of Cyclone Nargis in 2008. International NGOs and donors were not allowed to enter the areas affected by the cyclone, and in order to help the victims it was necessary to collaborate with local and national (often unofficial) NGOs/civil-society organizations that were able to reach the affected areas. Many of these collaborations continued, and today more and more of the local organizations exist and are building the skills, experience and contacts needed to have an impact on the economy.

Ethnic-minority companies

As noted above, some ethnic armed groups are involved in the drug trade; others finance their operations by controlling or feeding off other economic activities (the lumber business and mining of gemstones being well-known examples). Potentially, these and other, civilian-owned companies could have an important influence on improving living conditions in ethnic-minority areas. They are physically close to valuable natural resources, and by establishing small-scale, local companies there is a chance that the local population might benefit economically. As a result of ceasefire agreements, most ethnic-minority groups are now allowed to legally create their own businesses. However, for them to grow and benefit their local society, it may be necessary that they receive (economic) support from foreign investors; this may be an issue (see p. 387ff.).

Local traders

As a group, small-scale traders still play a significant role in the local economy and, at least in the short term, this is likely to continue. Until now, Muslims have had a significant influence in this group with their businesses often the targets of recent anti-Muslim violence (see also p. 279).

✍ MD

IN FOCUS

Crony capitalists

During the decades of military rule, much of the income generated from the country's valuable natural resources went to a few companies and individuals. Among these were two conglomerates run by the military; the private business interests of a fair few military officers also profited (see p. 382 for more details of these military interests). However, attracting the greatest attention is a small elite group of tycoons or oligarchs who were able to translate their personal links with the military into enormous riches for themselves.[1] Mostly engaged in construction, rubber, mining and logging, these crony capitalists (as they are generally known) were an indispensible part of the Myanmar economy by the time the military handed over power to a quasi-civilian government in 2011. As well, many cronies were involved in illegal trade (in opium, amphetamines, etc.) or trade that violated universal human rights, hence why most of them have been (and often still remain) on international sanctions lists.

Although most cronies grew wealthy under the military regime, they seem to be doing even better in the new open economy. Here, they have used their insider advantage to retain control of key sectors. Just as these crony capitalists appear in several places in this volume,[2] their interests extend to almost every sector of the Myanmar economy and beyond. For instance, besides controlling one of the country's top football clubs, the business tycoon Tay Za (see p. 360) is involved in agriculture and logging, mining, construction and property development, transportation (including a major domestic airline), hotels and tourism. Nor is he alone here. Moreover, with the country opening up and welcoming tourists, foreign investors, donors and NGOs, the cronies are expected to engage in the hotel trade, telecommunications and banking in particular.

---

1. As noted elsewhere (in Social Issues), it is estimated that currently 40 individuals in Myanmar have assets worth US$ 30 million or more. However, only about 15 of these are seen to be 'cronies'.
2. Not least in the chapters on social issues, economic reform, and development challenges and environmental issues.

While the cronies may have contributed to the impoverishment of the general population under the military rule, some of them have also used their wealth to establish development aid projects and companies that have become economically beneficial for the population in general. For example, when Cyclone Nargis struck the Delta region, Tay Za helped fund some of the relief work while the well-known Zaw Zaw set up the Ayeyarwady Foundation to support the victims of the disaster. Later, Zaw Zaw also supported the building of schools in various parts of the country.[3] Some people believe that such altruism merely attempts to improve reputations from being 'bad' to 'good' cronies (and thus removed from sanctions lists), just as their support for the democratic movements is calculated from what is beneficial to their own future business.

Regardless of their motivations, many cronies built up business expertise as well as considerable capital during the decades of military rule. They have also been adept at positioning themselves as the indispensable middlemen between international investors flocking to the country and local power-holders concerned about foreign domination. In contrast, the government is struggling with limited economic resources and low state capacity. This means that the country is dependent on other actors to finance its development, not least the improvement of its infrastructure. But, in order to avoid foreign domination of the giant, long-term projects that are needed, it is necessary that national, private-sector companies are involved.[4] For these reasons, despite their bad reputation, the ethical dilemma that they pose and the risk that they will end up dominating the economy, the cronies are considered important players in the future economic development of Myanmar. The current government (and President Thein Sein in particular) may have distanced itself from the cronies but the opposition NLD and Aung San Suu Kyi have essentially decided to 'forgive' them thus securing their involvement in economic development and benefitting from their business expertise and capital.

✍ MD

---

3.   *Irrawaddy News Magazine*, 28 January 2013: http://www.irrawaddy.org/archives/25311.

4.   *Myanmar Times*, 29 July 2013: http://www.mmtimes.com/index.php/opinion/7630-bringing-in-the-big-boys-why-myanmar-needs-its-cronies.html.

What does political change in Burma offer migrant workers in Thailand?

The Burmese diaspora is vast both in size and in its global extent, with maybe two million overseas Burmese found in Thailand, 500,000 in Malaysia and 100,000 in the U.S. As described elsewhere in this volume, many educated Burmese have returned home since 2011, often to become engaged in politics, the media, NGOs or business. But for the vast bulk of Burmese still living in Thailand, the situation is quite different.

The number of Burmese migrant workers in Thailand has been growing since the 1970s. They are found in a range of sectors including agriculture, fisheries, construction, domestic service and industry. However, since the Thai government embarked on a policy of decentralizing manufacturing industry in the 1990s, employment of Burmese workers in manufacturing industries on the Thai–Burma border, particularly in the area around Mae Sot, has accelerated rapidly. Estimates of Burmese workers employed in the Thai economy range from two to three million, with up to 300,000 working in the border factories and workshops making ready-made garments and sportswear for export as well as in a number of other sectors that also supply the domestic market, including shoes and mosquito nets. Much of this industrial activity is located in Tak province though there are also concentrations in central Thailand and in outlying Kanchanaburi province. Accurate data on the employment of Burmese migrant workers is difficult to come by because of the liminal legality that has characterized the Thai government's regulation of these migrants, meaning that up to 50 per cent of this work force remains undocumented.

In 1996, the Thai government introduced a system of registering migrant workers who do not have official work permits from the three

Unregistered migrant workers waiting to be employed at a garment Thai factory. Whenever there is a vacancy, the manager will come out of the factory and hire workers from among those waiting outside. Some workers wait for days to be employed. Some finally give up and move to wait outside another factory, only to be informed later that work was offered at the first factory just after she left. It is tough being a migrant worker (photo: Kyoko Kusakabe and Ruth Pearson)

neighbouring countries – Laos, Burma and Cambodia. Since that time, the registration system has changed almost every year and, with the exception of a brief period in 2004 when migrants could register independently, all other registration schemes tied migrant workers to a specific employer who was required to provide an official guarantee of employment for each worker in order for them to be registered. This has made the position of migrant workers weak, since it restricted their choice of workplace; if they changed the employer, their registration was nullified unless it could be transferred to the new employer – a rare occurrence. Mobility was limited to the location of employment/ registration. Women workers, the majority in the garment factories, faced losing their jobs and their registration if they became pregnant and had to stop working. Some provinces prohibited migrant workers from riding motorbikes or having meetings with more than five people. Migrant workers are forbidden to form independent unions in Thailand and cannot hold office in Thai unions. Constraints on collective activity and gatherings made any kind of organizing very difficult for migrant workers' organizations. This form of control of migrant workers from neighbouring countries thus offers Thailand access to a cheap labour force without having to offer these foreign workers any form of social security or safety net that is available to local workers.

Since 2009, a system of national verification and temporary passports has replaced the registration system, and all migrant workers from the three countries – Burma, Cambodia and Laos – were required to obtain documents from their place of origin in order to apply for a temporary passport. Burmese migrant workers were very suspicious of this new system, fearing that the authorities could trace their families back home and impose additional taxation or constraints on them. Those workers from ethnic groups that were in open conflict with the regime were often not able to get their nationality verified. Even without such fears, the complications and costs of obtaining the required documents, which often had to be undertaken by agents, were prohibitively high. The nationality verification system allows the Burmese government to have better control over the migrant movement. However, such a complicated system has discouraged workers to go through the system and, after 2009, most of the workers in border towns like Mae Sot ceased to be in the formal system and continued to work without any documents. In November 2013, the Burmese government announced that it would issue permanent travel passports to its citizens that would be valid for travel anywhere outside its borders (depending on visa constraints). However, for the majority of Burmese workers currently resident in Thailand who do not hold valid citizenship cards and/or household registration documents from their home country, returning to Burma to obtain these documents would be a too costly and risky process.

With the release of Aung San Suu Kyi in November 2010, Burma has gone through a series of economic and political reforms, opening up its economy to the outside world. US Secretary of State Hilary Clinton visited the country in December 2011, ending more than 15 years of US economic sanctions against Burma. Burma is the chair of ASEAN in 2014, and will be part of the ASEAN Economic Community (AEC) from 2015. The opening of the economy has meant a rapid rise in the amount of foreign direct investment into Burma, with more than USD 1.8 billion announced between April and August 2013, compared with

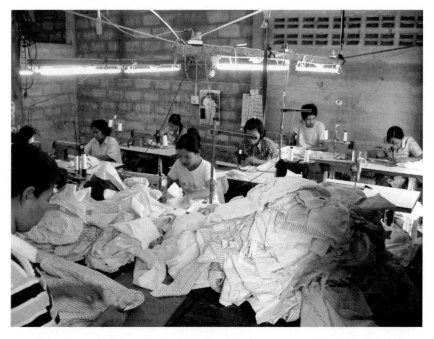

Unregistered women workers in a factory in Kanchanaburi Province (photo: Kyoko Kusakabe and Ruth Pearson)

USD 1.4 billion for the whole of 2012.[1] Several industrial zones within the country are now under development, which in time might offer employment to Burmese workers currently employed in Thailand.

On the other hand, wages are still low in Burma. Thailand has increased its minimum wage to 300 baht per day, while in Burma the wage can be half of that amount. Chantavanich (2012) noted that, in the Dawei Deep Seaport Project, the Italian–Thai Development Co. was offering a daily wage of 7,000 kyat (around 300 baht) to less-skilled workers whereas local subcontractors, who were hiring most of the labour, were only paying 4000 kyats.

Although there are increasing obstacles for migrant workers based in Thailand, not least because of the strict (and changing) nationality verification procedure in place, and in spite of the prospect of more employment opportunities in Burma in the future, it is hard to imagine that current migrant workers in Thailand will rush back to Burma to work there. Most Burmese migrant workers retain a clear sense of

---

1. See http://www.reuters.com/article/2013/09/20/myanmar-investment-idUSL3N0H-G0L420130920 (accessed on 31 October 2013).

national identity, have maintained extensive kinship links and express the intention to return to their own country in the long run. However, few are actively considering leaving Thailand in the foreseeable future. Many migrant workers have lived in Thailand for over a decade, and have formed and raised families in that country. Even though the economic – and therefore employment – prospects in Burma are improving, wages and working conditions are still inferior, and they are not yet convinced of Burma's long term political stability. Many of the families and communities of migrant workers, particularly those from non-Burman ethnic minorities, have experienced different forms of state oppression in recent decades – including armed conflict, forced labour, forced relocation, sexual and political violence and corruption. The vast majority of these workers are classified as semi- or unskilled, and so will not benefit from the proposals to allow free mobility of labour under the AEC (ASEAN Economic Community) for highly skilled and professional workers. As such, it is likely that the position of Burmese migrant workers in Thailand will remain precarious and vulnerable for many years to come.

References

Chantavanich, Supang (2012) 'Myanmar migrants to Thailand and implication to Myanmar Development', *Policy review series on Myanmar Economy*, No. 07, October, Bangkok Research Center, IDE-JETRO.

Pearson, Ruth and Kyoko Kusakabe (2012) *Thailand's Hidden Workforce: Burmese Migrant Women Factory Workers*. London, Zed Books.

✍ KK/RP

Burma's economy and the struggle for reform

Sean Turnell

In a nationally televised address in June 2012, Burma's President, Thein Sein, declared the goal of tripling the country's per capita GDP within five years. An audacious and almost certainly unrealistic objective, the President's call nevertheless captured something of the current zeitgeist with respect to Burma. Off limits to most investors for 50 years, Burma has become a 'must see' destination for the denizens of corporate boardrooms throughout the world. The final of Southeast Asia's tiger economies, so it goes, is awakening from its long hibernation.

The economic fundamentals supporting the current excitement about Burma's potential are both real, and imagined. Since taking of-fice in March 2011, President Thein Sein's administration has indeed embarked upon a series of reforms that have had a material effect on the country. Yet, much also remains undone. Burma's state continues to absorb far too much of the country's real and financial resources, while institutions and laws remain mostly ill-conducive to those necessary to genuinely turn the economy around. Enthusiasm is certainly warranted on Burma's economic possibilities, but sober reflection on the country's realities must accompany the exuberance.

In this chapter we briefly outline Burma's economy and its prospects. Beginning with an outline of the significant reforms that have been im-plemented under Thein Sein's administration, we move on to examine the lifting of international sanctions on Burma, and its improving eco-nomic circumstances more broadly. This is followed by a brief analysis of the economic context into which these changes are pitched, and the remaining obstacles and dilemmas that must be resolved if Burma is truly to follow the path to transformational growth and development.

Economic reform

The most important reforms that have taken place in Burma since the installation of Thein Sein's government in 2011 have taken place in the political, rather than the economic realm. Incomplete and imperfect as the former as yet are, Burma's political reforms have transformed international sentiment towards the country. Timed coincidentally with a desperate 'quest for yield' amongst international investors (amidst the on-going global financial crisis), it is perhaps not surprising that perceptions of Burma's emergence as a place of opportunity have such currency. However, some significant *economic* reforms have also taken place, to which we now turn.

'Floating' the Kyat

By far the most significant of the economic reforms enacted by the government of Thein Sein has been the decision, in April 2012, to reform Burma's exchange rate regime by allowing the country's currency, the *kyat,* to be determined via a 'managed float'.[1] Burma's previous dual exchange rate system, under which there prevailed an 'official' rate that set the *kyat* at a wildly unrealistic K 6 : US$ 1, against an unofficial market rate that mostly fluctuated around K 1,000 : US$ 1, was perhaps the most obvious symbol of the country's economic eccentricities. Under the new arrangements, an 'auction' is held each morning amongst 11 of Burma's banks to determine a reference rate that is more or less the free market rate for the *kyat* against the US dollar, the Euro and the Singapore dollar. Once set, other banks and money-changers can then exchange the *kyat* within a band of +/-0.8 % above or below the reference rate.

The decision to effectively float the *kyat* was symbolically an important one as noted, containing within it a hint that henceforth economic policy-making in Burma might be conducted along more rational and systematic lines. Perhaps even more important, however, is that it was a decision that brings with it the simultaneous hope that Burma's hitherto dire fiscal circumstances might at last be being addressed. Prior to the float, Burma's military regime had used the dual exchange rate to effectively expropriate the country's earnings from the export of natural gas (more on which below) by recording them in the public accounts at

---

1.   See "Central Bank to Strike New Exchange Rate for the Kyat', *Reuters,* March 21, 2012, http://www.bangkokpost.com/lite/topstories/285244/central-bank-to-strike-newexchange-rate-for-the-kyat, (accessed on 21 September 2013).

the moribund official exchange rate, rather than according to their true purchasing power as converted at the market rate.[2] With the old fixed rate of the *kyat* now abandoned in favour of the managed float, Burma's gas earnings (which flow through the state-owned Myanmar Oil and Gas Enterprise, MOGE) are now potentially convertible at a rate that can make a substantial difference to the country's fiscal circumstances. This has subsequently happened, with Burma's budget for 2012/13 (as well as the projections for 2013/14) including a contribution from MOGE consistent with its earnings being translated at the managed float exchange rate.[3]

Financial sector reform

Burma does not currently have a properly functioning financial system. Transformational reforms to the sector, via a new *Financial Institutions of Myanmar Law* are under consideration, but are not yet in promulgated. Two reforms that have taken place, however, have come in the form of new laws designed to establish in Burma a credible and independent central bank, and; in formalizing and legalizing microfinance via an eponymous law.

Burma's new central bank law

Burma's new central bank law (Central Bank of Myanmar Law, CBML, *Pyidaungsu Hluttaw Law No.16/2013*) came into effect in July 2013.[4] Replacing an ineffective law of the same name decreed in 1990, the objective of this new legislation is to grant greater policy-making independence to Burma's central bank. Hitherto the Central Bank of Myanmar (CBM) had been little more than a money printing outfit whose remit was more or less confined to the funding of Burma's chronic budget deficits. In granting this independence the CBML contains a number of measures, the most important of which include:

---

2. For the background on this, see Sean Turnell, 'Burma's Insatiable State', *Asian Survey*, vol. XLVIII, no. 6, November–December 2008, pp. 958–976.
3. Budget data here is based upon an official announcement of the Burmese Government on 2 February, 2012. See 'Myanmar plans jump in health, education spending', *Reuters*, 2 February 2012, http://in.reuters.com/article/2012/02/02/myanmar-economy-idINDEE8110DW20120202, accessed 30 August 2013).
4. An English translation of the law can be found at the website of the US Chamber of Commerce, http://www.uschamber.com/sites/default/files/international/files/Myanmar%20Central%20Bank%20Law.pdf, (accessed 14 October 2013).

- Promoting the status of CBM Governor to the equivalent of a Minister of Cabinet (along the way re-locating it outside the Ministry of Finance, within which it had been simply a division);
- Founding a nine-member decision-making board that comprises four representatives from the CBM itself (the Governor and three newly-created Deputy Governors) and five outside 'experts'. Such board members, as well as the Governor and Deputies, cannot be removed except for a Presidential determination that they are 'incapable of discharging their duties';
- The CBM is no longer permitted to buy primary issues of government bonds, or to otherwise directly lend to the government, in the absence parliamentary approval. Government bonds can be purchased from other banks, and from the general public, but without the authorization of parliament this can only be done through (at present non-existent) secondary-securities markets;
- In modern central banking practice, transparency and accountability is meant to be the natural accompaniment of independence. Under the new CBML, Burma's central bank is compelled to submit reports on monetary conditions to the parliament at least twice a year, and to publish quarterly reports on monetary developments.

All of this is an improvement over the old monetary order, but the provisions of the CBML do not yet allow the verdict that Burma now has a truly independent central bank. The CBM is no longer able to directly fund Burma's budget deficits without the say of parliament, but such approval might be presumed by a political party (or coalition of parties) that held the executive offices as well as a parliamentary majority. As noted, the CBM is also still able to purchase government securities from other state-owned banks. At present these banks are large purchasers of government debt. Of course, finally all will depend on the capacity of future governments to finance their spending by selling bonds to the public, borrowing from offshore and from private banks, and (most important of all) creating the fiscal circumstances (spending restraint and adequate taxation) that do not create the temptation for 'money printing'.

A new Microfinance Law
Burma's new Microfinance Law (*Pyidaungsu Hluttaw Law* no. 13, 30 November 2011) at last grants legal recognition and authorization to

the operation of microfinance institutions (MFIs). This was something long called for by Burma's MFIs, which were hitherto vulnerable to the fluctuating standings of their sponsoring NGOs. Less welcome to the MFIs, however, are clauses of this law that fix the interest rates that they can charge on loans and must pay on deposits, arguably at rates that will make financial sustainability difficult. On this score, however, much will depend upon prevailing inflation rates in Burma, and macro-economic conditions more broadly. Burma has several dozen MFIs, but one (operated by the US NGO, 'PACT', on behalf of the United Nations Development Programme, UNDP) dominates the sector. An MFI with around 450,000 members and 120 branches in 27 townships, it is a very large institution, even by global standards.[5] Since the promulgation of the Microfinance Law some 130 or so MFIs have been authorized – at once both an optimistic sign, but also a phenomenon prompting worries about possible future over-saturation in the sector.

Foreign Investment Law convolutions
Domestic legislation with respect to foreign investment is a key, often decisive, component of a country's relative attractiveness as a destination for international capital. But this is especially important for a transition country such as Burma, within which policy on this front has historically been unwelcoming and restrictive.

Signed into law by President Thein Sein in November 2012 is a new Foreign Investment Law (*Pyidaungsu Hluttaw Law No. 21/2012*, FIL) that is designed to make Burma a more attractive destination to investors abroad.[6] This new law grants foreign investors the right to hold long leases on land (greatly restricted hitherto), to enjoy a five-year profits tax 'holiday' and other tax concessions, and a guarantee against the nationalization of their businesses (a necessary, if not sufficient step given Burma's long history of state expropriation).

So far, so good. But Burma's new FIL is also reflective of the country's continuing divisions. Specifically, the law became heavily influenced by

---

5. For this, and other comparative data on Burma's microfinance sector, see Duflos, E., Li Ren and Li Yan Chen, *Microfinance in Myanmar: Sector Assessment,* January 2013, International Finance Corporation, http://www.cgap.org/sites/default/files/Microfinance%20in%20Myanmar%20Sector%20Assessment.pdf, (accessed on 14 October 2013).

6. The official English translation of the FIL can be found at the website of Burma's Directorate of Investment and Company Administration, www.dica.gov.mm, (accessed 12 October 2013).

interests of Burma's 'crony' conglomerates, whose rise to dominance over key areas of the economy has been a significant development over the last decade. With interests that extend to almost every sector, such cronies (as they are routinely called throughout Burma) are likely to feel the threat of foreign competition most acutely. Accordingly, and despite the liberal elements of the new FIL noted, other key clauses limit the role of foreign investors in a host of sectors, including retail trade, agricultural processing, fisheries, and many light industries and services. Other sections apply restrictions on the employment of even skilled foreign personnel, impose minimum capital requirements on foreign investors, and require that some projects can only proceed with Burmese joint-venture partners.

New land tenure laws

One of the most impenetrable barriers to the improvement of Burma's agricultural sector is the fact that all rural land is formally owned by the State. Individuals are eligible for 30-year inheritable *use* rights, with such rights determined by village-level land committees, but for most of the last five decades land could not be legally *and* voluntarily transferred between unrelated individuals. This also meant that land could not be used as collateral on loans. More broadly, the lack of land title denies the Burmese cultivator the incentive, and security, to invest or otherwise improve their holdings.

In late 2011 two new land laws were introduced before the Burmese parliament. Ostensibly designed to rectify some of the problems noted above, the Farmland Act (*Pyidaungsu Hluttaw Law No. 11/2012*) and the Vacant, Fallow and Virgin Lands Act (*Pyidaungsu Hluttaw Law No. 10/2012*) have, in practice, delivered nothing of the sort.[7] Continuing to contain provisions that deny farmers the right to decide for themselves 'what, when and how' to produce, their most important clauses seem to simply ensure the rights of a new executive body (headed by the Minister for Agriculture and Irrigation) to make what amounts to 'eminent domain' determinations that have been used to transfer land

---

7.   Official English translations of both of these laws are available at the Online Burma Library, http://www.burmalibrary.org/show.php?cat=1200, (accessed 11 October 2013). For a comprehensive overview of the laws, see the Food Security Working Groups, Land Core Group, 'Legal Review of Recently Enacted Farmland Law and Vacant, Fallow and Virgin Lands Management Law', November 2012, www.rightsandresources.org/documents/files/doc_5404.pdf

from small farmers to agricultural corporations. In the wake of their promulgation, millions of acres of land have been effectively confiscated from small holders in this way, and their titles reassigned (too often with little or no compensation) to such local and foreign investors.[8]

Recognizing the problem, in mid-2012 Burma's parliament established a 'Farmland Investigation Commission' to investigate 'land-grabbing', past and present. Quickly inundated with over 500 separate complaints involving over 250,000 acres of farmland, the Commission submitted a preliminary report to the parliament in March 2013.[9] The report found (unsurprisingly) that much of the land confiscations involved the military directly, as well as businesses connected to it, and recommended that all 'undeveloped lands' so affected be 'returned to their owners or handed over to the state'. For those cases in which the land had subsequently been developed or transformed, 'affected farmers should receive adequate compensation' from acquirers. The Commission continues to work, and while some compensation has been paid, the broader issue of land seizures continues to fester. Scarcely a day passes in Burma today without a protest somewhere in the country over unresolved land claims.[10]

Sanctions are lifted

The reforms begun by Thein Sein's government have not gone unrewarded by the countries that hitherto imposed sanctions on Burma's ruling military regimes. Anxious to reward the reforms, bolster the reformers, provide incentives for further reform – and, no doubt, to advantage their own business constituencies – countries such as Australia, Canada, members of the EU, as well as the United States, have all lifted sanctions completely or in large measure across 2012–13.

Of course, given its global import, as well as the fact that it was the most comprehensive 'sanctioner', the sanctions easing by the United States properly captured much attention. In May 2012 the US sus-

---

8. See Kyaw Kyaw, 'Land Reform is Key to Burma's Future', *The Diplomat*, 25 August 2012, http://thediplomat.com/2012/08/25/land-reform-key-to-burmas-future/ (accessed 30 August 2013).

9. For this, and subsequent citations from the report, see 'Military Involved in Massive Land Grabs: Parliamentary Report', *The Irrawaddy*, 5 March 2013, http://www.irrawaddy.org/archives/28506

10. For just one example, see Esther Htusan, 'Myanmar Farmers Find Little Relief from Land Grabs', 11 October 2013, Associated Press, http://bigstory.ap.org/article/myanmar-farmers-find-little-relief-land-grabs (accessed 14 October 2013).

pended two especially significant sanctions measures: an investment ban in place since 1997 (imposed by the Clinton Administration), and the ban on the export of US financial services to Burmese entities and nationals (imposed under the 2003 'Burmese Freedom and Democracy Act' [BFDA], and the 2008 'Tom Lantos Block Burmese JADE Act').[11] Remaining is the maintenance of a 'Specially Designated Names' list of individuals deemed (amongst other things) to be complicit in the commission of human rights abuses in Burma, and/or the provision of Burmese arms to North Korea.

The economy as context

The reforms outlined above are not pitched against a blank slate, of course, but onto an economy that has long performed far below potential. Although a country richly endowed with natural resources, abundant reserves of natural gas, ample water for irrigation and for hydropower, highly productive alluvial soils for the growing of crops, as well as favourable demographics, Burma remains the poorest country in Southeast Asia. GDP in 2013 is around US$ 59 billion, less than 15 % that of Thailand, Burma's historical peer.[12] Per capita GDP is less than US$ 1,000, placing the country substantially behind Vietnam, and even Bangladesh. Cambodia, Laos and Nepal.

The cause of this poverty is, simply and surely unarguably, the chronic economic mismanagement of the military regimes that ruled Burma for over fifty years. As we have seen, Burma's current government has attempted, so far fitfully and incompletely, to turn the country's economy around via economic reform. Understandably, however, the task is a steep one, not least since Burma remains without many of the institutions fundamental to the functioning of a market economy. A non-exhaustive list of these missing elements includes:

---

11. For full details of these sanctions relaxations, and the Acts originally authorizing them, see Michael Martin, 'U.S. Sanctions on Burma', *Congressional Research Service, Report for the 113th Congress,* 13 January 2013. Certain reporting requirements, however, are imposed on US investors in Burma still. US companies and individuals investing more than US$ 500,000, and all who partner with MOGE, must submit annual reports of their activities, and their implications with respect to human rights, labour rights, and some other issues, to the US State Department.

12. GDP estimates derived from International Monetary Fund 2013, *Myanmar: 2013 Article IV Consultation,* IMF Country Report No. 13/250, online at http://www.imf.org/external/pubs/ft/scr/2013/cr13250.pdf, (accessed on 14 October 2013).

- a political-economy effectively without the rule of law or sound property rights;
- critical shortages of human and institutional capacities in government and policy-making bodies;
- degraded infrastructure and public services from years of distorted priorities and neglect;
- a bloated military apparatus that continues to absorb the largest share of government spending;
- an industrial structure dominated by inefficient state-owned enterprises and politically-connected conglomerates;
- foreign debt arrears;
- conflict in ethnic minority areas that excludes large swathes of the country from regular commerce; and
- a large underground economy that includes substantial criminal activity.

Of course, reforming the above involves politics as much as economics in the narrow sense. Such reforms, and notwithstanding the developments noted elsewhere, are not yet apparent in Burma.

Beyond these fundamentals, various sectoral and policy issues shape Burma's economy today, and will determine what is both necessary and possible with respect to reform. In the below we review the most salient of these.

Fiscal affairs

Burma's budgetary position has dramatically improved across 2012/13, mainly due to the appropriate accounting of the country's foreign exchange gas earnings (as discussed above). Nevertheless, the country continues to run a large budget deficit which, according to the government's own projections for 2013/14, will be around 5% of GDP.[13] For a country such as Burma a funding gap of this size is not remarkable, but the way it is currently financed raises extra concerns. In the absence of an adequately functioning taxation system (taxes account for the lowest portion of GDP of any ASEAN country), or a substantial bond market and other fiscal accoutrements routine elsewhere, Burma's government

---

13. See 'Thein Sein Urges Budget to be Approved', 13 March 2013, *Mizzima News, http://www.mizzima.com/news/inside-burma/9046-thein-sein-urges-budget-to-be-approved.html*, (accessed 14 March 2013).

continues to rely on borrowing from the central bank to fund itself. Such 'printing money' (as it is popularly known) has long undermined trust in the *kyat*, and fuels Burma's high inflation rate. Currently estimated at around 6 % per annum, the latter is amongst the highest in the region.[14] Bringing with it certain transaction costs and other inefficiencies, Burma's high relative inflation rates also exacerbate the country's falling competitiveness from a rising *real* exchange rate for the *kyat* in recent times (more on which below).

Trade

In recent years Burma has enjoyed a healthy trade outlook. Surpluses have been the norm, while the rising imports of the last two years primarily reflect increasing imports of capital equipment in line with rising investor optimism. Table 1 below reveals this seemingly robust situation, and the accumulation of foreign reserves that it has delivered.

Table 1: Burma's trade balance ($US million)

	2007/08	2008/09	2009/10	2010/11	2011/12	2012/13
Exports	6,402	6,732	7,507	8,960	9,136	8,977
Imports	3,075	4,160	4,052	6,300	9,035	9,069
Foreign exchange reserves	4,040	5,105	6,050	6,600	7,000	7,600

Source: Myanmar Central Statistical Organization, https://www.mnped.gov.mm/index.php?option=com_content&view=article&id=95&Itemid=112&lang=en, (accessed October 10, 2013).

The reason for this structural reversal of Burma's export fortunes has been the aforementioned emergence of the country as a significant exporter of natural gas. To date this gas has been exclusively exported to Thailand, but from July 2013 gas volumes of similar magnitudes have started to be piped through Burma (from the so-called 'Shwe' fields in the Bay of Bengal) to China's Yunnan Province.[15]

Beyond gas, beans and pulse exports have been the encouraging story of Burmese trade in recent years – a success narrative that is due largely

---

14. Burma's average rate of inflation across 2000–2009 was double that of the next worst performer in the region (Sri Lanka). See International Monetary Fund 2013, *Myanmar: 2013 Article IV Consultation*, IMF Country Report No. 13/250, *op. cit.*

15. For a general background on the gas sector in Burma, see A. Kolås, 'Burma in the balance: The geopolitics of gas', *Strategic Analysis*, vol. 31, no. 4, 2010, pp. 625–643.

to the previous military regime's inattention to the sector, allowing some enterprising agricultural firms to identify and meet demand for these commodities from India. Teak and hardwood exports from Burma likewise yield significant revenues, but at substantial environmental and social cost. Burma's rice exports, a shadow of the time when Burma was the world's largest rice exporter, are overwhelmingly made up of low-priced 'broken rice' shipped to various African countries. Burma's once vibrant rice-export sector is greatly hampered by a number of hurdles, but especially on-and-off government prohibitions against private sector exports, a lack of access to finance, and degraded port infrastructure that makes the loading of large volumes of rice difficult.

Table 2: Exports: selected categories and totals ($US million)

Category	2007/08	2008/09	2009/10	2010/11	2011/12	2012/13
Gas	2,520.7	2,362.9	2,882.5	2,324.5	3,502.5	3666.1
Beans and pulses	627.9	932.3	920.4	741.7	986.1	961.7
Teak and hardwoods	538.4	489.1	489.2	550.1	604.6	579.5
Garments	282.7	289.8	280.7	350.0	497.5	695.4
Rice	102.5	202.2	252.9	182.0	267.2	544.1
Fish and seafood	193.0	264.0	271.1	262.1	442.8	567.5
TOTAL	6,402.1	6,732.3	7,507.1	8,960.0	9,135.6	8,977.0

Source: Myanmar Central Statistical Organization, https://www.mnped.gov.mm/index.php?option=com_content&view=article&id=95&Itemid=112&lang=en, (accessed October 10, 2013).

Under the new government of Thein Sein, the most notable reform enacted in the area of foreign trade has been the abolition of the Trade Council,[16] which hitherto controlled trade through its highly restrictive export and import licensing procedures – and replacing it with the Trade and Investment Supervision Committee (TISC). The latter has proved more liberal than its predecessor, and far quicker to make decisions. That said, the continuing maintenance of the import and export licensing system remains a major irritant to the 'normalization' of Burma's trade.

---

16. A body that had been chaired by former military regime Vice Chairman, Maung Aye, and subsequently Burma's former Vice President, Tin Aung Myint Oo. Under both, the Trade Council was a vehicle for restriction, and no little corruption.

Agriculture

Famously once the 'rice bowl' of South and Southeast Asia, Burma's agricultural output has long been suppressed by poor and intrusive policy-making, a chronic lack of credit, inadequate and degraded infrastructure, and an absence of secure land title and property rights. These woes, which have resulted in Burma slipping down the league tables in the trade of foodstuffs and commodities that it used to dominate, are the drivers of the dire poverty that is characteristic of the lives of the country's (majority) rural population.

Under the Presidency of Thein Sein there has been much talk of reform in agriculture. The first of the 'national workshops' (*Rural Development and Poverty Alleviation*, May 2011) that have been such a feature of the economic reform narrative in Burma was devoted to agriculture.[17] This came up with a number of objectives, mostly centred upon increasing productivity through improvements to rural infrastructure, access to affordable inputs, and expanded credit availability (with an emphasis upon microfinance). Other fora devoted to agriculture, sponsored by various multilateral institutions and agencies, have taken up similar themes across 2011–12.

Yet, and notwithstanding this emblematic primacy, the record of reforms actually implemented in Burma's agricultural sector is, as yet, meagre. As noted above, a microfinance law was passed in November 2011, but this has done little to bring about its extension into the more critical need for *institutional* rural finance.

Wholesale reform of agriculture in Burma is urgently needed, beginning with the removal of the market distortions that continue to bedevil the sector. Especially significant in this regard are the various export restrictions, production controls, and procurement orders that linger from the previous military regime. Burma's success as an exporter of beans and pulses in recent years demonstrates that its farmers and traders can respond vigorously to market signals. The trade in beans and pulses was liberalized a decade ago, in great contrast to the heavy hand of state intervention in most other commodities.

However, lifting the restrictions and limitations on trade, while necessary, will not be *sufficient* to re-establish Burma's degraded agricultural

---

17. Details of the workshop are provided at the website of Burma's embassy in Geneva, see http://missions.itu.int/~myanmar/11nlm/jun/n110621.htm, (accessed on 10 October 2013).

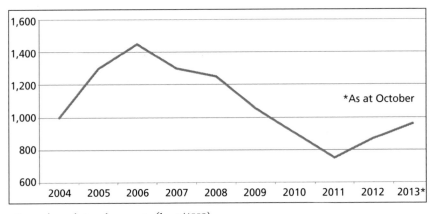

Burma's market exchange rate (kyat/$US)

sector. Under Burma's past military regimes the countryside was chronically neglected. Rural infrastructure is in a particularly parlous state, and
many villages are without viable roads to connect them to national (or
even local) markets. Fertilizer is unavailable in many areas, irrigation
systems are often silted up, seeds, pesticides, pumps and other apparatus
are largely absent, and fuel is often beyond financial reach. Market liberalization will solve some of these chronic problems, but substantial public expenditure and investment, especially on roads, bridges, irrigation,
as well as on power generation and distribution, seems unavoidable.

A volatile real exchange rate

The dominant trend in the market value of the *kyat* over the decades has
been relentlessly downward. Nevertheless, over the last few years it has
perversely been a *rising kyat* that has caused the most angst. From a low
of around K 1,450 : US$ 1 as recently as 2006, the *kyat* has appreciated
by around 40 % in nominal terms (and, taking into account inflation,
around 80% in real terms).

The rising value of the market exchange rate of the *kyat* across
2010–2012 caused much distress in a number of key export sectors in
Burma, whose representatives argue that they have become uncompeti-
tive as a consequence. In a survey of affiliated organizations conducted
by the Union of Myanmar Federation of Chambers of Commerce and
Industry (UMFCCI), various industry sectors were asked to nominate
the maximum value of the *kyat* that they could live with, and stay profit-
able at. With the exception of the rice and beans and pulse exporters,

none said that they could survive a rate below K 900 : US\$ 1.[18] Across 2013 the value of the *kyat* has been steadily depreciating again, but the anxieties created by its earlier rise (and continuing volatility) remain.

Military and crony companies

One of the most remarked-upon developments in the latter years of Burma's then-ruling SPDC regime was the increasing dominance of the economy by the military, and by a handful of elite business figures – universally known throughout Burma as the 'cronies' – attached to them (fuller details p. 362). In terms of the military itself, this dominance was manifested in various ways, but not least via two giant military corporations designed to enhance the economic objectives of Burma's military complex. These two giant corporations, the Union of Myanmar Economic Holdings Limited (UMEH, which is primarily concerned with trading, light industry and some mining activities), and the Myanmar Economic Corporation (MEC, which has specialized in heavy and strategically important industry), are the vehicles both for substantial 'off-budget' funding for the military, as well as the provision of income for serving and former military officers. Under the SPDC, both UMEH and MEC enjoyed what were effectively monopoly concessions over a range of activities (exclusive licences to import fuel, vehicles, cigarettes and other strong cash-flow items), as well as exemptions from tax and other government imposts.

In 2013 the grip of UMEH and MEC on lucrative streams of economic 'rents' remains undiminished in aggregate terms, even if their relative predominance in a range of areas has diminished. As for the so-called 'cronies', the picture is mixed for individual actors, but collectively there can be little doubt that they will remain a force in Burma's political economy. Of course, in this sense their role may turn out to be little different (for good or ill) to similar elite and 'connected' business groups elsewhere in Southeast Asia. Individually, however, the strategy of Burma's elite business figures has differed markedly. Some seemingly remain wedded to mine still-lucrative 'rents' in mining, infrastructure, forestry and other extractive sectors; while others are actively divesting

---

18. Now legally trading (within Burma), the daily exchange rate of the *kyat* is widely quoted. See, for instance, the foreign currency website, http://www.xe.com/currency/mmk-burmese-kyat?r=8, from which this latest rate of the *kyat* (K 860 : US\$ 1) is sourced. UMFCCI survey results privately provided to the author – the results are also consistent with the authors discussions with various Burmese businesses.

from controversial activities, and re-fashioning themselves as entre-preneurs in the services sector especially. Whether the latter can then become pillars of Burma's economic transformation is a question as important as it is perhaps imponderable yet.

Conclusion

The arrival of Burma's nominally civilian government in March 2011 has been the trigger for a series of reforms that have transformed the country's politics and international relations. Progress towards eco-nomic reform has also been made across this period, but thus far it is insufficient to deliver the transformational changes required to turn Burma's economy around. At present the contest between the forces of reform, and those that seek to protect existing arrangements, appears inconclusive. Upon it, however, depends Burma's future, and its ability to achieve the economic growth and development long postponed.

Foreign investors

Myanmar is experiencing an investment boom never experienced before in the country. For instance, in just five months in mid-2013, foreign direct investment (FDI) projects worth US$ 1.8 billion were approved. Compared to US$ 1.4 billion for all of 2012, this was a major leap forward for business sectors in Myanmar.[1]

In June 2013, as 14 enterprises from Thailand (US$ 379 million), Singapore (US$ 23.6 million), Britain (US$ 15.8 million), China (US$ 4.1 million) and India (US$ 9.6 million) were given permission to invest in the production and hotel sectors, foreign investment in Myanmar reached more than US$ 42 billion from 32 different coun-tries. Not only was a new investment total reached but also the type of investments approved marked a change from an earlier focus on invest-

---

1. See http://www.reuters.com/article/2013/09/20/myanmar-investment-idUSL3N0H-G0L420130920. The heightened interest in Myanmar as an investment destination can be seen in many ways. For instance, since the beginning of 2012 the Singapore/Malaysia-based Centre for Management Technology has held a broad range of sector-specific sum-mits in Myanmar that have attracted over 3,000 delegates from more than 50 countries. See http://www.cmtevents.com/aboutevent.aspx?ev=130941.

ment in oil, gas, mining and hydroelectric power to a broader focus on the development potential of other sectors as well.[2]

The oil and gas sector still accounts for one-third of FDI in Myanmar.[3] However, several multinational corporations have taken the first steps to invest in other sectors. As examples can be mentioned the pioneers Google, Unilever, Coca Cola, MasterCard, and Ford. The world's biggest brands are leading the way and behind them awaits a queue of smaller companies hoping to get a share.[4] Along with Coca-Cola other beverage companies such as Carlsberg, Heineken and Pepsi have started investing in Myanmar. The same goes for the car industry where, after Ford initiated investment in the sector, Nissan and Mitsubishi have followed suit. However, with a few cautious multinationals waiting to see how the market develops, many smaller companies are holding back as there are too many barriers and constraints in Myanmar to a successful investment.[5]

The government is planning to establish several special economic zones (SEZ), a concept that will provide investors with favourable policies on customs, labour and utilities inside the zones for a limited period. The zones are essential for attracting foreign investment in areas where the existing infrastructure is too weak to support the investment. The most promising of the zones is the Thilawa SEZ outside of Yangon, funded by large Japanese companies with the support of their government. Attracting much publicity, but a rather more doubtful proposition, is the port of Dawei SEZ, which is backed (on and off) by the Thai government.[6]

Most foreign investment comes from the major Asian countries and especially China and Thailand. While there have not been that many European or American companies competing for investment opportunities, international interest in Myanmar is spreading fast.

≤ JL

---

2. See http://www.ibtimes.com/myanmar-foreign-investment-reached-42-billion-32-countries-production-hotel-sectors-favored-june
3. See http://www.adb.org/news/myanmar-plans-electricity-expansion-assistance-adb-japan.
4. See http://www.bbc.co.uk/news/world-asia-22685263
5. See http://www.bbc.co.uk/news/world-asia-22685263
6. Ibid.

Investment issues

The high potential for growth and development has attracted new investment to Myanmar. The government is managing and facilitating trade and foreign direct investment (FDI) by removing the structural impediments but there is still a long way to go. In addition, it is working to develop social and physical infrastructure, introduce legal and institutional frameworks, and to develop the financial sector.

Both the government and the opposition in Myanmar have called for 'responsible investment'. Even so, foreign investment is badly needed to accelerate economic growth in the country. The government thus urges foreign investors not to wait until conditions inside the country are more stable but instead to make sure that their initial investment is as sound as possible (though this can be difficult in an environment where there is a lack of trustworthy information).[1] In short, foreign investors play an important role because there is a need to maintain the momentum for reform and a need for good practice from leading foreign investors.

However, there are many challenges facing foreign investors. Besides a lack of qualified human resources, in general the state needs the capacity to respond swiftly to investors' needs. For instance, there is clearly a need for a major reform of government administration (see p. 65), also that local officials are granted more authority to make more effective decisions. There are many political uncertainties as well, not least related to the recent communal violence in Rakhine State and in the centre of the country, the forthcoming elections in 2015 and the ongoing position of the military.

For companies actually setting up inside Myanmar, some of the challenges are very concrete and tangible. Myanmar's basic infrastructure is lacking (though improving for instance in telecommunications), there is a need for better roads and other transportation networks, and it is difficult for companies to get access to land. In addition to this, most of the country suffers from a poor and erratic electricity supply. Furthermore, Myanmar has Southeast Asia's highest office rental rates

---

1. See http://www.bloomberg.com/news/2013-09-21/myanmar-needs-responsible-investments-to-develop-suu-kyi-says.html.

due to a lack of business facilities in the biggest cities and control of the real-estate sector by crony capitalists.

Cronyism is at the heart of another problem facing foreign investors: the common requirement to have a local partner. While many sectors lack Burmese companies that can function as local partners, in other areas like banking, insurance and the media, there is a lack of a level playing field; existing crony capitalists hold a dominant position and see foreign investors as a threat. That said, in wide areas of the economy these cronies do play an important intermediary role between outside investors and power-holders concerned about excessive foreign influence in the country's affairs. (See also 'Crony capitalists', p. 362ff.)

Furthermore, corruption and facilitation payments are highlighted as risks for foreign investors. Also the effective rule of law is currently lacking. Securing a legal framework for investment is crucial for foreign investors because they need to be sure that they will not lose their investments. This is perhaps not an unreasonable fear given Myanmar's long history of state expropriation and often bad business practices.

           ✍ JL

New infrastructure needs to be in the right place – the motorways in and around Naypyidaw tend to be empty of traffic (photo: Marie Ditlevsen)

Development challenges and environmental issues

Marie Ditlevsen

In recent years Myanmar has seen a significant increase in economic activity. In part, but not only, this has been due to the country's emerging from isolation and receiving considerable new foreign investment. Nonetheless, Myanmar faces major development challenges and already the environmental repercussions of economic growth are a matter of concern.

Development challenges

Without doubt, Myanmar is experiencing a positive development in a number of areas. Most notably, the economic situation has improved remarkably during the past couple of years as a result of moving towards a market-oriented economy, the lifting of sanctions, and foreign aid and investment. According to the UNDP the country has experienced a downward trend of the overall poverty incidence dropping by about 6% between 2005 and 2010.[1]

In regard to the Millennium Development Goals 2015, Myanmar has made progress in areas such as the food poverty incidence, the under-5 mortality rate, the maternal mortality rate, and sanitation.[2] Furthermore, as pointed out earlier in 'Social issues' (p. 121ff.), the government is now prioritizing and hence allocating more resources to health and education, two sectors that suffered significantly during the period of the former military regime. Thus, generally speaking, living conditions for the people of Myanmar are slowly improving.

1. UNDP Poverty Profile, 2009–2010: http://www.mm.undp.org/ihlca/01_Poverty_ Profile/PDFs/03%20Poverty%20Profile_Poverty%20and%20Inequality.pdf
2. Asian Development Bank (2012); Millennium Development Goals, the MDG Data Report 2009–2010: http://www.mm.undp.org/ihlca/03_mdg-data/.

However, Myanmar's progress in reaching the MDGs still lags behind that of its ASEAN neighbours, particularly in the area of health. The country is still characterized as a Least Developed Country, with 25% of its people living below the poverty line, and the pace of development appears to be slow.

The slow progress of development is rooted in a number of different factors, some of which are related to social issues as described earlier. A number of major actors are involved in the development process: the Myanmar government, the opposition party NLD, local NGOs and civil-society groups, the 'cronies' as well as international investors and organizations including INGOs and donors. In other words, the development process is based on and affected by a number of quite different stakeholders, each having their own interests and needs.

Some of the most important challenges are presented and discussed below. The focus will be on international donors and investors, INGOs and local policy makers, and on their roles and challenges in the development of Myanmar.

Lack of capacity in the Myanmar government/state

In September 2013, President Thein Sein pointed out that 'without political stability economic development cannot be realized and without socioeconomic development political stability cannot be achieved, because politics and economy are interrelated.'[3] This appears to encapsulate the root cause, and dilemma, of Myanmar's development challenges. The question is what the new, quasi-civilian government can do to address this issue.

After the military coup in 1962, the Myanmar state gradually developed into a "weak state", and for almost half a century it was economically dependent on the military, the Tatmadaw.[4] During this period of time, the state was unable to perform primary state functions such as managing the economy and public services like health and education, and ensuring public order and security.

Thus, the economic and social development of Myanmar, a country once among the wealthiest in Southeast Asia, slowly degraded and eventually came to a standstill. Despite this situation of a state lacking

---

3. 'Burma's reform remains fruitless as a general rule', Asian Tribune, 28 September 2013: http://www.asiantribune.com/node/64776.
4. Robert H. Taylor: *The State in Myanmar*. London: Hurst & Company, 2009, p. 449.

the resources to get the country back on track, the majority of INGOs and foreign donors seeking to support the country were for a long time rejected (this is covered in greater detail later in this volume – see chapter on donors and INGOs, p. 406ff.).

Since the political changes in 2010–11 the situation is gradually changing, and the Myanmar state is in the process of growing stronger, partly as a result of foreign investment and support. But the limited state capacity remains a continued challenge for speeding up the pace of development.[5]

A large number of reforms have been launched but due to the limited state capacity uncertainties remain regarding the implementation and sustainability of the reforms. The Asian Tribune is among the critics arguing that the reform process is slow and fruitless,[6] and according to a McKinsey Global Institute Report from 2013, there are still uncertainties regarding the progress and maintenance of the reforms.[7] This uncertainty makes important actors, such as foreign investors, donors, and the private sector, hesitant to make long-term commitments in Myanmar.

It is important to note, however, that the implementation of economic and political reforms in Myanmar is a demanding and complex task, especially for a new government with limited capacity.[8] According to the Asian Development Bank, the limited capacity of the government is based on a number of determining factors, such as a weak macroeconomic management, and an underdeveloped financial sector.[9] Hence, until the state 'rebuilds' itself, including the economic and financial systems, it is dependent on foreign support.

The question is, however, to what extent foreign donors/investors are willing to engage with and support the Myanmar state? And what are the major challenges?

Ethnic and sectarian conflicts, human rights violations

Two important issues may have a negative impact on the willingness of foreign donors and investors to engage with Myanmar. These are the ethnic tensions, most notably those taking place in Kachin State, and the

---

5. McKinsey Global Institute (2013): 107.
6. 'Burma's reform remains fruitless as a general rule', Asian Tribune, 28 September 2013: http://www.asiantribune.com/node/64776.
7. McKinsey Global Institute (2013): 12.
8. Ibid.: 105.
9. Asian Development Bank (2012)..

sectarian unrest between Buddhists and Muslims in Rakhine State that has since spread to lowland areas in the centre of the country.

The government appears to have difficulties in controlling the conflicts, and when seeking to do so it often results in human rights violations. Meanwhile, Human Rights Watch reports: 'The Burmese military continues to engage in extrajudicial killings, attacks on civilians, forced labor, torture, pillage, and use of antipersonnel landmines'.[10] While such violations appear to be particularly widespread in Kachin State, Shan State also has been seriously affected, at least until the end of 2013. From Rakhine State there are similar reports of human rights violations, these mostly directed against the ethnic Rohingyas, who are being discriminated against even by law.[11] Apart from the human rights violations carried out in the ethnic minority areas, it is estimated that a large number of political activists are still imprisoned and, in spite of Myanmar signing a UN agreement to halt recruitment of child soldiers, there are still cases of this.[12]

The continued violation of human rights, in spite of reforms intending to change this practice, could constitute a serious challenge to the development of Myanmar as international donors, investors and INGOs will be reluctant to engage and support the country.

Until now, because of its appreciation and encouragement of the positive political and developmental changes, the international community has continued to lift sanctions, and thus 'accepted' the on-going violations of human rights in certain areas. However, in the longer run this may change, especially if the conflict in Kachin State intensifies and the sectarian unrest in Rakhine State spreads further.[13]

Foreign investors and donors are already hesitant about engaging in long-term commitments/investments,[14] and with continued ethnic/sectarian unrest, this uncertainty may increase. The international community has eased the sanctions against Myanmar, but a number of foreign actors such as the European Union have only suspended the sanctions

---

10. Burma News International (2013): 15; Human Rights Watch (2013b).
11. Human Rights Watch (2013a).
12. Human Rights Watch (2013b).
13. Burma News International (2013): 15.
14. McKinsey Global Institute (2013): 107.

for a limited period of time, hence enabling a swift reimplementation of the sanctions if necessary.[15]

It is important to note that, apart from its difficulties in controlling the conflicts, the government of President Thein Sein has similar difficulties in controlling military actions. As was the case during almost half a century of military rule, the government is still dependent, even economically, on the military. On several occasions, the military has ignored instructions from the president. For example, the Tatmadaw once ignored the president's instructions not to attack the KIA in Kachin State,[16] and during the conflict in Rakhine State there appears to have been similar discrepancy between the words of the president and the actions of the military.[17] In other words, reforms and promises by the new quasi-civilian government may be overridden by the military, which continues to have strong tentacles to the old ruling elite. According to the Asian Tribune, this issue needs to be addressed in order to create a society that is ethically suited for international development aid. In other words, President Thein Sein's first priority should be to 'tame the military'.[18]

Business (relations) at risk

For foreigners, including investors and INGOs, it is difficult, if not impossible, to obtain permission to enter the conflict areas, KIA-controlled areas in Kachin State being an example.[19] Firstly, these restrictions can prevent people in need from receiving vital support, and secondly they may prove to be a barrier to the development of potentially important business partnerships between foreign investors and ethnic groups.

As part of an earlier ceasefire process carried out in the late 1980s and early 1990s, ethnic groups were given the right to become 'legally involved in logging, mining, import and export, transportation, and a number of other businesses',[20] thus enabling them to participate in the

---

15. Human Rights Watch (2013b).
16. Burma News International (2013): 17; 'Thein Sein Cannot Control Army, Shan Rebels Say', The Irrawaddy News, 3 July 2013: http://www.irrawaddy.org/ceasefire/thein-sein-cannot-control-army-shan-rebels-say.html.
17. 'Muslim victims say police aided Thandwe attackers', Irrawaddy News Magazine, 7 Oct. 2013: http://www.irrawaddy.org/burma/muslim-victims-say-police-aided-thandwe-attackers.html.
18. 'Burma's reform remains fruitless as a general rule', Asian Tribune, 28 September 2013: http://www.asiantribune.com/node/64776.
19. Human Rights Watch (2013b).
20. Keenan (2013): 1.

development of the country. According to the briefing paper, 'Recent ceasefire agreements have also resulted in similar incentives being made and a number of armed ethnic groups have taken the opportunity to create their own companies.'[21]

The development of companies by ethnic groups could help ease the burden on local communties. However, the government and international donor community still need to provide support through the transition period.[22] Such partnering with foreign actors would provide the ethnic groups with an opportunity to build business capacity and improve their chances of accessing not only capital but also technology, best practices, etc., thus helping them compete both nationally and internationally.[23] From the perspective of the foreign actors, it is vital to gain access to the ethnic areas, as the majority of natural resources (and hence potential business projects) are located in the conflict zones.[24]

Due to the continued ethnic and sectarian conflicts, however, the basis for developing business partnerships with foreign investors appears uncertain and it remains a major challenge for the business development in the country.

The (potential) role of the cronies

Apart from including the ethnic groups in the business development, the Myanmar cronies (see p. 362) could possibly play a role in the development of the country. As previously described, the government is struggling with limited economic resources and a weak state capacity, which means that the country will have to rely on other actors (such as foreign donors and investors) to finance the major investments in the country, first of all the improvement of the infrastructure. However, in order to avoid foreign domination in long-term projects, it is necessary that national, private-sector companies become involved in such projects.[25] The cronies, having the financial strength and experience required to develop large-scale infrastructure projects, may come to play an important role for the development of the country.

---

21. Ibid.: 2.
22. Ibid.,: 3.
23. McKinsey Global Institute (2013): 110.
24. Burma News International (2013): 18.
25. 'Why Myanmar needs its "cronies"', *Myanmar Times*, 29 July 2013: http://www.mmtimes.com/index.php/opinion/7630-bringing-in-the-big-boys-why-myanmar-needs-its-cronies.html.

Officially, President Thein Sein is distancing himself and the government from the influence of cronies. Some of them were deeply involved in the corruption devastating the economy of Myanmar during the period of military rule, and some are therefore still on the US sanctions list. Hence, it puts the government in an ethical dilemma, but according to the *Myanmar Times*, this distancing may of pure economic necessity prove difficult in the longer run.[26]

It is interesting to note that Aung San Suu Kyi and the NLD have showed signs of openness towards the cronies, emphasizing the need for all potential actors to come together in developing the country.[27] The question is, however, whether the international donors and INGOs would be willing to do the same.

Environmental issues

The economic development of Myanmar should be viewed in the light of long-term sustainability and specifically in relation to the impact on the environment. Dam construction for energy production, oil and gas extraction, mining and deforestation are commercial activities that may have a negative effect on the environment. Deforestation in particular is seriously affecting the areas where logging is taking place.[28] In addition to these development-related activities, climate change may in the longer term have an impact on the environment and the living conditions, first of all of the people living in the lowland areas.

Due to Myanmar's long isolation, much of the country's natural wealth remains largely untapped.[29] However, increasing poverty during the period of military rule, exacerbated by global sanctions, combined with increasing and largely unrestricted commercial exploitations of the natural resources have led to environmentally destructive activities, first of all in the natural forests.

The exploitation of the natural teak forests has resulted in an increasing speed of forest loss. FAO has estimated a 19% decrease in total forest

---

26. Ibid.
27. 'Suu Kyi's party accepts crony donations in reform-era Myanmar', Reuters, 17 Jan. 2013: http://www.reuters.com/article/2013/01/17/us-myanmar-suukyi-idUSBRE90G0C820130117.
28. Burma Environmental Working Group (2011).
29. See www.ethicaltraveler.org/201/09/burma-new-environmental-challenges-and-opportunities.

Cleared hilltop in Shan State near the Chinese border, 2004; the nearby village is home to rice and opium farmers (photo courtesy of EPA/Barbara Walton)

area from 1990 to 2010.[30] At the same time there has been a rather dramatic change in the structure of the remaining forests. The forest category 'closed forest' has decreased from 78% in 1990 to 42% in 2010. This decrease indicates that a large part of the forests have been logged during the past 20 years.

Much of the exploitation was done by the military government, but according to the Forest Department, the major acceleration in logging coincided with the opening of the forestry sector for the private sector (in 1988). From that time, the government sold logging concessions to Thai logging companies, and in 2007–08 timber was the fourth most important export commodity.

The most serious destruction from logging has occurred in the ethnic areas along the borders with China and Thailand. These logging activities in the ethnic border areas were intensified as a consequence of the ceasefire agreements that allowed the ethnic groups to be involved in commercial activities.[31] Hence, while the recent ceasefire agreements, reintroducing these rights, could potentially benefit the economic and social develop-

---

30. FAO (2010).
31. Burma Environmental Working Group (2011). For instance, after signing a ceasefire with the regime in 1989, the New Democratic Army-Kachin of eastern Kachin State became heavily involved in the local cross-border timber trade (see p. 168).

ment of the country (as previously emphasized), this would very likely have a devastating impact on the environment in the ethnic areas.

The deforestation has an impact not only on the forests as a timber resource, but also as a secondary effect on the environment and on the living conditions of the people and the communities living in the forest areas. Logging has in some areas proved to be directly responsible for floods, soil erosion and landslides, and widespread loss of forests is affecting the ecosystems that the local people rely upon for their livelihoods and cultural practices. There is a great danger this may also affect Myanmar's unique wildlife, left undisturbed in the decades of isolation.

Unrestricted exploitation of the teak forests is considered one of the most pressing environmental issues in Myanmar. The opening up for foreign investors in the forestry sector may even result in increased pressure on the forest resources and potentially accelerate the negative impact on the environment – unless new regulations controlling the forest operations are being implemented and enforced.

Climate change is another important issue, first of all in the vulnerable and heavy populated lowland areas that are exposed to floods or damage by cyclones. Much of the mangrove forest in the coastal areas have been removed primarily to gain extra land for rice farming, but shrimp farming along the coast is seen as the leading cause of mangrove deforestation in recent times. The consequence of the removal of the mangrove is that the lowland areas are more exposed to cyclone damage, as the coastline is lacking a protective forest buffer zone.

In the longer term climate change and a potential rise in sea level may put the low-lying coastal areas at risk, especially during cyclones and floods. Sea level rise may eventually cause the displacement of thousands of people from the densely populated and fertile plains and coastal communities. The Berlin-based climate watchdog, Germanwatch, ranked Myanmar as the second worst country affected by extreme weather events caused by climate change from 1990 to 2008.[32] Poor countries like Myanmar are considered particularly vulnerable to climate risks. They are usually hit much harder than rich countries despite the fact that absolute monetary damages are often much higher in the rich countries.[33]

---

32. Sven Harmeling, Germanwatch, 'Global Climate Change Index 2010'. www.germanwatch. org/klima/cri2010.pdf
33. Burma Environmental Working Group (2011).

References

Asian Development Bank (2012) *Myanmar in Transition: Opportunities and Challenges.* Manila: ADB Publishing.

Burma Environmental Working Group (2011) *Burma's Environment: People, Problems, Policies.* Chiang Mai: Wanida Press.

Burma News International (2013) *Deciphering Myanmar's Peace Process – a Reference Guide, 2013.* Chiang Mai: Wanida Press.

FAO (2010) 'Global Forest Resource Assessment', Myanmar report.

Human Rights Watch (2013a) 'Burma: Revoke 'Two-Child Policy' For Rohingya: Coerced Birth Control Reflects Broader Persecution of Muslim Minority', 28 May: http://www.hrw.org/news/2013/05/28/burma-revoke-two-child-policy-rohingya.

——— (2013b) *World Report 2013*: http://www.hrw.org/world-report/2013/country-chapters/burma.

Keenan, Paul (2013) 'Business opportunities and armed ethnic groups. Yangon: Burma Centre for Ethnic Studies, Briefing Paper no. 17, September.

McKinsey Global Institute (2013) 'Myanmar's moment: Unique opportunities, major challenges': http://www.mckinsey.com/insights/asia-pacific/myanmars_moment.

Village in the Delta: still in the process of rebuilding their houses after Nargis (photo: Marie Ditlevsen)

Cyclone Nargis

Myanmar is geographically located in a region that is frequently affected by cyclones and typhoons (during the monsoon season in particular), but the country had never experienced a natural disaster of the magnitude of Cyclone Nargis, which struck the country on 2 May 2008, and it was neither resilient enough nor prepared to cope with the consequences. With devastating force, Nargis swept through the Ayeyarwady Delta region with wind speeds up to 200 km per hour at landfall, causing widespread flooding, destroying approximately 2,000 villages, and killing 138,000 people or more.[1] The former capital, Yangon, was also affected.

In the Delta area, villages are located at just above high-tide level; it is thus an area at serious risk from tropical storms. The region was previously known for its high agricultural production and was once considered to be the 'rice-bowl' of Asia. However, this situation deteriorated during the years of military rule and by 2008 the area was impoverished and vulnerable.[2] Moreover, the military government failed to warn the Delta population of the approaching cyclone and, when it struck, the government was very slow in responding to the vast humanitarian disaster and providing sufficient aid to its victims.[3]

Despite this desperate situation the government did not allow foreign aid agencies to enter the Delta, or the country, until 2–3 weeks after the disaster. In the meantime, local people and NGOs, with limited resources and capacity, made an effort to bring aid to the Delta. By the time that foreign aid agencies were allowed to enter, the situation was extremely severe and tense. In the heavily affected areas corpses were floating in the rivers, literally blocking the way for boats, and the survivors had lost their homes and livestock. In areas considered less affected by the cyclone, aid (mainly for reconstruction) was not received until 4–5 months after the disaster.[4]

The Cyclone Nargis had a devastating impact on the Delta, affecting the lives of approximately 2.4 million people, and the slow response by

1. WFP, News, Cyclone Nargis: two months later: http://www.wfp.org/stories/cyclone-nargis-two-months-later
2. Burma Campaign UK, Cyclone Nargis: http://www.burmacampaign.org.uk/index.php/burma/about-burma/about-burma/cyclone-nargis-main
3. *The Guardian*, 16 July 2013: http://www.theguardian.com/global-development-professionals-network/2013/jul/16/cyclone-nargis-burma-disaster-relief-aid?CMP=twt_gu
4. Marie Ditlevsen: 'Strengthening civil society in Myanmar – the influence of political reforms'. Master's thesis, Roskilde University, 2013.

Dwellings in the Delta; it is very obvious how high the tide can go and hence how vulnerable the people can be if the area is hit by another cyclone (photo: Marie Ditlevsen)

the military government demonstrated a lack of willingness or capacity to protect and help its own people. The inadequacy of the official response did have one positive result, however; it meant that civil society and even the local economy grew stronger.[5] In the critical situation just after the cyclone struck, local actors from different levels of society came together and worked for a common cause; very often these movements resulted in the development of more structured local NGOs and coalitions of groups at the national level.[6] Furthermore, when foreign aid was eventually allowed into the affected areas, the foreign agencies gradually gained more ground in the country, partly because they partnered with now-strengthened civil society actors. Moreover, after having delivered the most basic disaster relief, many foreign aid agencies continued operating in the Delta, focusing on improving the livelihoods of villagers while at the same time making the construction of villages more resilient to future natural disasters.[7]

Thus, while many thousands of people died and most survivors lost family members, homes and livestock, in the longer term Cyclone Nargis may have resulted in improving living conditions in the Delta. Today, six years after the cyclone struck, the physical damage is no longer visible. The only 'remnants' are wooden signs put up on the riverbanks in front of villages, indicating which foreign aid agency is supporting that particular village. Many aid agencies are still present, focused on improving the livelihood of the villagers.[8]

5. *New York Times*, 21 October 2008: http://query.nytimes.com/gst/fullpage.html?res=9A04E2DD143FF932A15753C1A96E9C8B63&ref=cyclonenargis
6. Ditlevsen: 'Strengthening civil society in Myanmar'.
7. *New York Times*, 21 October 2008.
8. Ditlevsen: 'Strengthening civil society in Myanmar'.

Foreign aid to Myanmar

Marie Ditlevsen

The increasing poverty, human rights violations and health issues that gradually unfolded during military rule attracted the attention of the international community. However, although both bilateral and multilateral donors showed interest in supporting the Myanmar people, the political situation and the violations of human rights made the support ethically sensitive, and many countries opposed providing aid to Myanmar under the military regime.[1] After the student uprisings in 1988 and the repression by the regime, a number of countries – mostly from the west – imposed economic sanctions and restrictions on the collaboration with the regime, thus de facto freezing direct support to the country.

The ethical dilemma of the donors during the time of military rule raised many questions. What kind of assistance could be provided to Myanmar? How could the Myanmar people be supported without the military regime benefitting? Furthermore, to what extent could donors (and INGOs) cooperate directly with the military regime?[2]

The military regime was restrictive in allowing foreign donors to operate in the country, and development organizations often found themselves restricted, controlled and under surveillance in the implementation and performing of development projects (for more details, see p. 406ff.). The majority of the donors weren't given permission to start operating in the country until the beginning of the 1990s, and they were only allowed to implement projects focusing on neutral, i.e. non-political, issues like health, education and income generation.[3]

---

1. International Crisis Group (2006): 4.
2. Fink (2009): 265.
3. Fink, *Living Silence in Burma*, p. 265.

Events like the student uprising in 1988,[4] the Buddhist monk's upris-ing ('Saffron Revolution') in 2007,[5] and Cyclone Nargis in 2008[6] were significant in shaping the attitude of donors to the country. The brutal repression of the 1988, which led to sanctions and the freezing of aid, is probably the most significant of these events, as it has had a crucial impact on the amounts of development assistance received. In 2006 the overall development assistance to Myanmar was among the lowest in the world at less than $3 per capita per year.[7]

The Nargis disaster in 2008 demonstrated to the world that the regime was not capable of handling the consequences of the cyclone and the human catastrophe, and relief aid was gradually allowed in. This opening-up for foreign assistance has since resulted in an increase of foreign aid through a number of development projects. While the primary objective of aid has been to support the economic and social development (health in particular), a secondary objective has been to encourage the democratic process.[8] After the political changes the sanc-tions have gradually been lifted, and since 2011 there has been a further increase in foreign aid to the country.

In the following sections, the most important donors to Myanmar, from independence in 1948 until today, are presented and discussed briefly. Due to limited space, the numerous INGOs and civil-society groups responsible of implementing the development projects will not be elaborated on. For wider aspects of the international engagement with Myanmar, see 'International actors' (p. 109ff.) and various contri-butions to the economic section of this volume (e.g. 'Foreign investors', p. 383ff.).

---

4. During the student uprising in 1988, which developed on university campuses and took place in Yangon (and Mandalay), hundreds of young protestors were killed by the military. The student protests aimed to introduce democracy into Myanmar. For more details, see 'The 8888 generation' on p. 69.

5. In 2007 monks in their traditional saffron-coloured robes walked the streets of Yangon, and other big cities, officially protesting against the rising fuel prices. Fuller details on p. 307ff.

6. Cyclone Nargis entered the Ayeyarwady Delta region on 2 May 2008, killing more than 100,000 people and devastating the entire area, including parts of Yangon. See p. 397ff.

7. International Crisis Group (2006): 4.

8. Fink (2009): 257.

Japan

Japan has been one of the most important and influential donors, providing the largest amounts of bilateral as well as multilateral development assistance to Myanmar. From the establishment of diplomatic relations in 1954 until 1990, Japanese development assistance to Myanmar 'represented one of the largest worldwide of the Japanese ODA programs annually'. While the purpose of Japanese assistance was to support and stabilize Myanmar economically and socially, at the same time this assistance may have been the reason why the military government was able to stay in power during periods of economic hardship – whether or not this was in the interests of Japan.[9]

After the second military coup in 1988, which crushed the student uprising, Japan initially followed suit with most other donor countries and froze its (bilateral) development assistance. However, in 1989 Japan formally recognized the new military government, and continued its assistance – although reduced to smaller and less significant amounts that directly targeted people in need.[10] Hence, although Japan wished to see democracy restored in Myanmar, the country did not go as far as many other countries in imposing sanctions on Myanmar. Apart from the long-term relationship between the countries, a possible explanation may be that Japan was concerned about losing political and economic access to Myanmar.[11]

Japan was one of the first countries to fully endorse the democratic reforms, for example by writing off nearly $2 billion of debt in 2013, and today Japan plans to resume supporting Myanmar through significant bilateral assistance. Hence, according to the Democratic Voice of Burma, 'A delegation of Japanese MPs met [in September 2013] with President Thein Sein in Naypyidaw, where they hashed out plans to boost development assistance for Burma's woefully neglected health care system.'[12] Apart from health issues, Japan is also planning on help-

---

9.   Steinberg (1990): 51.
10. Seekins (1992): 246. In his lengthier study, *Burma and Japan Since 1940* (NIAS Press, 2007), Seekins explores the enduring relationship between the countries dating from prior to the Japanese invasion.
11. Fink (2009): 256.
12. 'Burma and Japan to boost development ties', Democratic Voice of Burma, 6 September 2013: https://www.dvb.no/news/burma-and-japan-to-boost-development-ties/32304.

ing the country expand its electricity supply, which is among the lowest in Southeast Asia.[13]

United States (USAID)

The United States signed the first US–Burma Economic Cooperation Agreement in 1950. Through this agreement, USAID initially focused on providing supplies and technical training to improve agriculture, schools and hospitals. While the USAID Mission in Myanmar closed as a consequence of the military coup in 1962, the US and Myanmar nevertheless continued cooperating in the years following the coup, and new development projects were implemented and carried out. The 1988 student uprising, however, resulted in the US halting all economic support and withdrawing all personnel from the country.[14]

It was not until 1998 that the USAID, through international organizations like the World Health Organization (WHO), the Food and Agriculture Organization (FAO) and a number of INGOs, resumed its work in Myanmar, this time with a special focus on combating health issues like HIV/AIDS, TB and Malaria.[15] However, the US government maintained and indeed tightened its sanctions against Myanmar and, until the beginning of the political changes from 2011, the US refused to provide significant amounts of bilateral aid to Myanmar.[16]

Today the US has restored full diplomatic relations, re-established a USAID mission in the country, and eased financial and investment sanctions – with the exception of a few remaining sanctions on the 'cronies'. In November 2012, President Obama visited Myanmar, firstly in order to demonstrate support and encouragement for the political reform process, and secondly to discuss human rights. With regard to bilateral development assistance, the US has eased the ban on exports of financial services to Myanmar, thus enabling bilateral support and assistance from USAID and other institutions to resume.[17]

---

13. Asian Development Bank, 30 September 2013: http://www.adb.org/news/myanmar-plans-electricity-expansion-assistance-adb-japan
14. USAID, History: http://www.usaid.gov/burma/history
15. Ibid.
16. International Crisis Group (2006): 4.
17. US Department of State, 'US relations with Burma': http://www.state.gov/r/pa/ei/bgn/35910.htm.

The EU

While the US maintained a steadfast position regarding economic sanctions and freezing of bilateral assistance, the EU chose to loosen up and change its anti-aid policy at the beginning of the 2000s. In spite of also having been part of the movement suspending most development assistance since 1988, the EU took the first step towards resuming work in Myanmar in 2002, by committing a large-scale bilateral and European Commission funding in support of HIV/AIDS programmes.[18]

Later, in 2005, the European Commission, supported by Australia plus Denmark, the Netherlands, Norway, Sweden and the United Kingdom, established the Three Diseases (3D) Fund. The 3D Fund, which was renewed in 2012, is a multi-donor consortium that 'aims to reduce the human suffering caused by HIV and AIDS, Tuberculosis and Malaria in Myanmar'.[19]

Apart from the 3D Fund, the EU is also a member of LIFT (the Livelihood and Food Security Trust Fund), which is a consortium with roughly the same member countries as the 3D Fund. The objective of LIFT is to achieve the first Millennium Development Goal: 'Eradicate extreme poverty and hunger by 2015'.[20]

As such, due to the 3D Fund, LIFT and other initiatives, the EU has a comprehensive development assistance portfolio in Myanmar today.

The United Nations

Of the most influential multilateral donors, the United Nations has been present in Myanmar since independence in 1948. The UN covers many different development aspects through a multitude of programmes, organizations and funds. For example, the UNDP (United Nations Development Program) has introduced poverty-alleviation pro-grammes, particularly in rural areas, the WFP (World Food Program) has provided food to the Muslim Rohingya families in the Rakhine State and to survivors of Cyclone Nargis in the Ayeyarwady Delta region, and

---

18. International Crisis Group (2006): 3.
19. Three Diseases Fund: http://www.3dfund.org/; also International Crisis Group (2006): 4.
20. Ministry of Finance Japan, Report on 'Myanmar Donor Profiles', March 2012, p. 6: http://www.mof.go.jp/about_mof/councils/customs_foreign_exchange/sub-foreign_exchange/proceedings/material/gai240625/03.pdf. New members are New Zealand and Switzerland; Norway is not a LIFT member.

UNICEF has worked to expand immunization coverage in rural areas and to supply vaccines. The International Labour Organization has been similarly active in the country, working to eliminate the continued, although reduced, use of forced labour.[21]

As has been the case with the majority of donors and INGOs, the UN has been challenged by the political situation in the country. In connection with politically sensitive programmes, UN personnel (special rapporteurs etc.) have been banned. However, by working under a special mandate from the Executive Board, which 'focuses activities at programs with grassroots level impact in the areas of basic health, training and education, HIV/AIDS, the environment and food security', the UN can operate more freely than other foreign actors.[22]

Other major donors

While the UK is member of both the 3D Fund and LIFT, it has also played a major role in the provision of development assistance to Myanmar through DFID (Department for International Development), which leads the UK's work to end extreme poverty.[23]

One of the largest donors to Myanmar is Australia, with large amounts of its assistance delivered through the UN. According to a report on Myanmar donor profiles, by the Japanese Ministry of Finance, Australia's aid to Myanmar has increased by 65% since 2009–10.[24]

Foreign aid today and in the future

Since 2008, and in particular since the political reforms in 2010–11, it has undoubtedly become easier for foreign donors and INGOs to operate in Myanmar. The new quasi-civilian government, and President Thein Sein in particular, has broken the spell of isolation and is now welcoming foreign development assistance. The assistance is much needed, as the country is suffering from almost half a century of neglect, particularly within the areas of health and education, and thus far the

21. Fink (2009): 261. See also United Nations Development Program (UNDP), Myanmar: http://www.mm.undp.org/UN_in_myanmar.html.
22. United Nations Development Program Myanmar, HDI Fast Facts: http://www.mm.undp.org/HDI/HDI-FASTFACT.html.
23. Gov. UK, Department for International Development: https://www.gov.uk/government/organisations/department-for-international-development.
24. Ministry of Finance (2012): 6.

government alone does not have the capacity required to improve the situation.

Furthermore, the development assistance is gradually changing in character. Once largely consisting of humanitarian aid and service delivery, it is now focusing more on longer-term development work, including livelihood and capacity building for civil society.[25] Hence, from being completely neutral and non-political, for example improving access to health services and sanitation, foreign development assistance is now encouraging and strengthening civil-society groups to take part in their own development.

This freedom of action was unheard of before the democratic changes, but today the Myanmar people have officially the right to express their own opinions in order to improve their living conditions. This new situation makes it easier for foreign donors and INGOs to operate in the country, and the inflow of foreign aid has been significant since the political changes. The question is, however, to what extent Myanmar will have the skills and capacity to absorb this aid to the benefit of its people.

References

Fink, Christina (2009) *Living Silence in Burma – surviving under military rule.* Chiang Mai: Silkworm Books. Second edition.

International Crisis Group (2006) 'Myanmar: New Threats to Humanitarian Aid'. Asia Briefing no. 58. Yangon/Brussels, 8 December 2006.

Ministry of Finance (2012), 'Myanmar Donor Profiles'. Tokyo.

Seekins. Donald M. (1992) 'Japan's Aid Relations with Military Regimes in Burma, 1962–1991: The Kokunaika Process'. *Asian Survey*, Vol. 32, No. 3.

Steinberg, David I. (1990) 'Japanese Economic Assistance to Burma: Aid in the "Tarenagashi" Manner?' *Crossroads*, Vol. 5, No. 2.

---

25. Ibid.: 7.

Opportunities and challenges for donors and INGOs operating in Myanmar

Jonas Nøddekær and Marie Ditlevsen

*Recent political developments in Myanmar have made it easier for interna-
tional NGOs (INGOs) and donors to operate inside the country. Even so,
the situation is not easy (as recently seen with the threatened expulsion of
Médecins Sans Frontières from Rakhine State). In this chapter, the overall
concerns and considerations of the INGOs, exemplified by Dan Church Aid,
will be discussed by Jonas Nøddekær. Thereafter, the impact that the reform
process has on local people/civil society and consequently how working relations and conditions for INGOs (exemplified by ActionAid Myanmar) are
affected in the Burmese context will be discussed by Marie Ditlevsen.*

During the past almost 50 years of military rule, INGOs and international donors have been restricted in engaging with Myanmar – for
several reasons. Firstly, because of the Myanmar government's fear of
political interference from outside, and secondly because engaging with
Myanmar was by many countries considered ethically reprehensible
due to the violation of human rights.[1]

Since the political changes in 2010–11, Myanmar has gradually opened
up to the outside world, allowing INGOs and international donors to enter
and contribute to the development of the country. For the INGOs it has
become easier to obtain permission to access rural areas, which are usually
most severely affected by poverty and natural disasters. Furthermore, the
implementation of the political reforms is expected to create a basis for the
Burmese people to regain basic human rights like freedom of expression
and assembly, and hence pave the way for cooperation between INGOs
and civilians.

---

1. Ware (2012): 6, 12.

Despite these positive changes, however, the Myanmar context is still very sensitive, and a number of challenges have to be taken into consideration when implementing development projects in the country. In the following sections this issue will be elaborated by viewing the situation from the perspective of international donors/INGOs operating in Myanmar, as well as from the perspective of local people involved in the work of the INGOs.

The donor/INGO perspective

DanChurchAid (DCA) has had a long relationship with civil-society organizations in Myanmar. However, it was not until after Cyclone Nargis hit the Irrawaddy Delta in 2008 and claimed an estimated 150,000 lives that DCA decided to open an office in Myanmar to support the emergency and rehabilitation work.

Political developments in Myanmar have been rapid since 2008, taking the international community by surprise. For donors and International organizations such as DanChurchAid it has therefore been crucial to adjust and at times completely change strategies and programme activities, as new and unforeseen opportunities emerged. An on-going and in-built analysis of the context, of relevant stakeholders, and of power relations have been very important instruments to make sure that donors, UN organizations and international stakeholders respond with the proper programmes and activities responding to the changes.

In 2013, DCA approved a new five-year country programme and the following is a brief snapshot of the context analysis and strategic considerations that form an integrated part of the final country programme document.

The government of Myanmar has begun a programme of substantial reform in a range of social and economic areas. However, deep unresolved conflicts remain within Myanmar society, as evidenced by the recent violence in Rakhine State and the ongoing conflict in Kachin State. While new ceasefires have been made with most non-state armed groups, the move to political dialogue has been slower than expected. One key issue for many people in ceasefire areas is their unclear citizenship status and deep-rooted mistrust. Myanmar's complex and restrictive citizenship law presents some barriers but the main obstacles are practical and related to national identity cards. On another level, an improved security situation yet with unclear local governance has left ceasefire areas vulnerable to an unregulated and potentially exploitative private sector. This is especially important given the weak overall legal framework related to the environment – though this may change with the passing of a new environmental law. Finally, while communities can benefit from the decrease in violence, it also raises a new set of social tensions.

Myanmar's current legal and policy environment gives inadequate attention to the rights of women. The country's isolation from international and regional norms also presents a barrier to addressing these legal and policy issues. As with gender, the deep underlying ethnic mistrust is at the core of issues faced by conflict-affected populations. And while intended to be a positive influence, international aid has the potential to exacerbate these issues and undermine civil society – particularly by adding new resources into fragile systems where some may benefit more than others. Finally, limited systems of accountability for armed groups and the private sector present a barrier for addressing key problems for conflict-affected populations.

Myanmar's lack of wider democratization at both the national and local level presents an ongoing barrier to addressing key problems. In the new Myanmar context, there are few established 'rules' or institutions for how citizens can interact with the state, meaning that there is some unpredictability on both sides.

Civil-society action in Myanmar has become more specialized and at the same time diverse. Hence, while maintaining flexibility, donors will also need to define new areas of work and new forms of partnership. Examples of such new types of partnership can be found in the Southeast, where DanChurchAid's mine-awareness activities have proven to be a useful vehicle for building trust and relationships with new potential 'active citizenship' partners. This trust building through mine awareness not only includes local communities but also the national government, formerly rival non-state actors, faith-based organizations, school organizations and community-based organizations (CBOs). Furthermore, DanChurchAid has seen that creating 'bridges' within civil society, increasing understanding of the ceasefire economy, promoting women in peace building and providing an independent critique of the aid system are emerging as areas of opportunity in the coming years.

In the face of immense challenges and difficulties it should be appreciated that international recognition of agriculture is a key to poverty reduction, as is a focus on small-scale farmers in climate-change adaptation and mitigation. There is now widespread use of the rights-based approach and recognized links between food security and disaster risk reduction.

The political transition in Myanmar offers opportunities for civil society to engage with government while the devolution of power allows agencies to influence practices at the local level. These reforms are being rewarded with the progressive lifting of sanctions by Western countries. Greater freedom of speech is opening up opportunities for awareness raising and organization over rights among rural communities. Registration of international and local civil-society organizations will eventually allow these to claim their rights also with respect to the government.

Market-orientation of the economy has the potential to enhance efficiencies and, with civil-society influence, improve the marketing opportunities for small farmers. Consistent economic growth is enabling more budgetary support for social sector and even stronger economic growth is possible with Myanmar's abundance of natural resources, diverse agricultural base, access to the sea and strategic location between China and India.

Large-scale industrial development projects being negotiated or already under construction have the potential of providing much-needed job opportunities, and socio-economic programmes associated with these developments could boost development in the area, if designed and implemented in consultation with communities.

The ongoing peace process has drastically reduced the level of violence, it has improved access to fields and could soon enable isolated communities to receive assistance and services and gain entry to markets as restrictions on movement are being relaxed both into and out of government- and non-government-held areas. The Myanmar Peace Committee, the Myanmar Peace Centre and the Myanmar Peace Support Initiative should facilitate and coordinate assistance to conflict-affected communities and provide opportunities for civil society to influence the manner by which this assistance is decided upon and delivered.

A very important aspect of this assistance is the plight of the c. 125,000 refugees who for the past 30 years have lived in camps just across the border in neighbouring Thailand. The primary challenge remains to create conditions that will support sustainable voluntary return of refugees and displaced people. Until now, returns of refugees to Myanmar have been very low. The recorded decrease of some 9% in refugee camp population from August 2012 to August 2013 was mostly caused by relocation to third countries and not by return to Myanmar. Many refugees lost their land and homes inside Myanmar and often feel that they have nothing to return to.

Repatriation of up to 400,000 displaced persons in southeast Myanmar will present challenges and opportunities for agencies to monitor and facilitate a safe and dignified process of repatriation. Sustainability of these movements will depend on the livelihood opportunities available in the places of settlement that, to some extent, depends on the role and assistance provided by the non-government sector.

Compassion exhibited by people in Myanmar – effectively the social safety net of the nation – can be recognized and built upon by CBOs provided it is not exploited or overburdened. Existing state and religious structures can also provide effective mechanisms by which food assistance can be organized, provided that discriminatory distribution practices are monitored and controlled.

The uncertain nature of the reform process (the perspective of local actors)

The uncertainty regarding the reform process, particularly in regard to the local actors with whom international donors and INGOs cooperate, is briefly addressed above. In the following section this issue is further elaborated through a case study conducted in late 2012 at a civil-society project in the Ayeyarwady Delta region, an area southwest of Yangon, reached after an 8-hour boat-trip. Viewed from the perspective of local actors, the reform process and its influence on INGO's opportunities and challenges will be discussed.[2]

The empirical data from the study constitutes a number of in-depth interviews with different actors in the project: INGO staff, local NGO staff and villagers. The objective of the study was to explore what influence the political reforms have had on the local people and hence on the opportunities and challenges for INGOs when operating in the Burmese context.

When implementing development projects, it is essential for an INGO to establish partnerships across different levels of local actors, such as

---

2. This section draws extensively on Ditlevsen (2013). The interviewee responses quoted below are all from this source.

government officials, civil-society organizations and the villagers, in order to apply a context-sensitive approach. However, while it may have become easier for INGOs to obtain permission to access rural areas in need, cooperating with local actors involved in the project can still be demanding. An important reason is the uncertainties and complex nature of the political reforms.

The issue of 'unwritten rules'

During half a century of repression and isolation, the activities of local NGOs and in particular INGOs were severely restricted. The political reforms now being implemented are intended to loosen these restrictions. The reforms however should be viewed with caution as the underlying legislation has generally not been changed and the risk of breaking these rules of law, which are often broadly worded and thus subject to interpretation, is therefore still present.[3]

This uncertainty applies particularly for laws and regulations limiting people's freedom and rights. For example, the case study discovered that while it is now more or less acceptable to talk about the democratic changes, the NLD and Aung San Suu Kyi, it appears to be unacceptable (at least in villages in rural areas) to criticize the former government. Hence, in the villages included in the case study, there are obviously still some 'unwritten rules' or feelings of uncertainty that limit the freedom of expression.

The issue of 'unwritten rules' was less evident during an interview in Yangon but a sense of uncertainty was still apparent. At the beginning of the interview, two female project managers from a local NGO operating in the Delta enthusiastically reported: 'Now the door is open. Now we can open our mouths, and not just our ears.' This positive attitude, confirming the media's reporting of change and openness, however, changed during the interview: 'We got the president and everything is changing. But still some [things are] left. A lot of things left ... not changing yet.' The reason for this slow process may be that some reforms have yet to be implemented or that some laws have been only partially changed.

In the rural villages in the Ayeyarwady Delta it is difficult to determine whether, or to what extent, the reforms have actually reached the villages. Only a few villagers were open-minded and talkative, explaining that

---

3. 'Myanmar Frees Group of Dissenters', *New York Times*, 24 April 2013: http://www.nytimes.com/2013/04/24/world/asia/myanmar-frees-group-of-dissenters.html.

'before, like two years ago, when you listened to the radio you wouldn't hear anything about it. But now that the political situation is changing, everything is open and … you can say whatever you want or whatever you need.' While this openness appeared to be rather an exceptional case, it nevertheless suggests that the reform on freedom of expression at least had reached this village. Likewise the reform on freedom of assembly, allowing people to organize in (non-political) groups, appeared to have reached the majority of the villages. According to a local villager, 'it has become easier to participate in a group, and two years ago it wasn't like that'.

In other villages, however, this atmosphere of openness did not seem to exist in the same way. A local villager, who made a living from rice farming, explained how a military-controlled rice-farming company was exploiting the entire rice-farming business, making life challenging for the rice-farmers. He wrapped up this criticism about the government by explaining that he still could not talk about such things outside, with other people. In the case study, this farmer was the only villager directly criticizing the government.

The relationship between local actors and the government

According to a project coordinator, the government used to be very 'far away' from the community and not involving local actors/civil society in state affairs. Now 'the government, civil society and non-state actors are trying to understand each other'. In her narrative, the civil society–state relationship has developed from a structure marked by a distinct gap between civil society and the state to a structure in which the two spheres are more dependent on each other. Ideally, this situation would make it easier for the INGOs, who are now focusing increasingly on the strengthening of civil society.

In spite of this intended change in relationship, however, there appears to be a barrier when it comes to being able to *influence* the authorities. When asked whether this is possible, a project manager replied: 'We do not like to influence them [township authorities]. The township authority mindset is not changed … even though the high level [government] has changed already.' In other words, while the government is now open for change, the township authorities operating between government and the villages are still living by the old structures. Hence, it appears that the township level constitutes an obstacle to the penetration of the political reforms, and thus to INGOs operating in the villages.

As such, despite the fact that INGOs are gradually being allowed to operate in the rural areas, it is apparently still difficult for INGO staff, as well as local NGO staff, to access these areas. It appears that the authorities (especially township authorities) are suspicious of foreigners entering their areas and villages of responsibility, and it is likely that the INGO staff will be kept under surveillance by the authorities or local police throughout the visit.

Furthermore, obviously it has not been in the nature of the Burmese people to engage with the authorities. According to a project coordinator, 'civil society normally organizes themselves and work alone ... and normally they never relate with the government'. Hence, although the overall intention is to implement changes in the country, this may be difficult to achieve in reality due to the fact that the 'beneficiaries' (villagers) still follow former authority structures in which civilians are not supposed to *influence* the authorities.

This issue was confirmed during interviews with villagers, where it was emphasized that 'you can only cooperate with them [authorities]; you cannot influence them'. In other words, the political reforms are not (yet) able to change the old military top-down structures in which the Burmese people have been controlled by the authorities, an aspect that may constitute a barrier for INGOs implementing (bottom-up) projects at grass-root level. This argument is supported by Anthony Ware, who believes that residues of 'ancient political values reverberate within contemporary Burmese politics',[4] and the contemporary Burmese society is strongly influenced by the past military structures.

This issue can also be traced in the working conditions of both local NGOs and INGOs. To be accepted and allowed to operate as an NGO, an official registration granted by the government (Ministry of Home Affairs) is required. However, despite the fact that officially this registration has become easier to obtain, it is apparently very expensive and the process of obtaining it is bureaucratic and time consuming. According to an INGO staffer, it 'creates another problem for local NGOs. The registration fee is about 600 dollars and the local NGOs do not want to spend this money.'

Hence, despite the fact that the Myanmar government is now officially encouraging and supporting local civil-society organizations/NGOs to

---

4. Ware (2012): 85.

develop, remaining rules and practices hamper this process and allow the government to stay in control. This situation poses a challenge for INGOs, especially when requiring that local cooperating NGOs are officially registered.

Slow change of mindset

Overall, on the surface, or at national level, the political changes are visible. People feel liberated, and they initially express a positive attitude towards the political changes and reforms. However, there appears to be a geographical difference. While people living in the cities are experiencing the reforms, the impression from the villages in the Ayeyarwady Delta area was that, apart from a few cases, the villagers were either unaware of the reforms or not particularly comfortable discussing them. Furthermore, the people expressed that real changes have not yet materialized.

One reason for the slow implementation of the reforms may be that the Burmese people still have not adapted their mindsets and behaviour to the new situation. After the many years of command-driven, top-down procedures, it is difficult to change the mindsets not only of the villagers but also of the authorities. It appears that part of the society is still 'stuck in the old structure' hence making it difficult to achieve a more collaborative and equal relationship with the INGOs.

Another reason for a slow implementation in the villages could be that, in spite of reforms, the basic laws have not been changed. This creates uncertainty and a potential fear of breaking the underlying rules and regulations. This uncertainty concerning the reforms, together with an apparently continued surveillance by the authorities, may still constitute an obstacle or a delaying factor for INGOs implementing development projects in the country.

References

Ditlevsen, Marie (2013) 'Strengthening civil society in Myanmar – the influence of political reforms'. Master's thesis, Roskilde University.

Ware, A. (2012) *Context-sensitive Development*. Sterling, VA: Stylish Publishing.

PART FOUR

The way ahead

Whither Burma?

Flemming Ytzen and Mikael Gravers

Political developments in Burma/Myanmar since 2011 have raised enormous expectations inside the country as well as in the international community. Finally, this tormented country seems to be moving towards some kind of political normalcy, away from isolation and xenophobia.

The single dominant question that permeates every debate on Burma's future is about what the military will do. The government has released hundreds of political prisoners, relaxed parts of the media censorship, drafted dozens of new laws and, notably, it has allowed the first elections since 1990. Where to go next?

Amidst the optimism, caution is needed to make appropriate judgments. The reform process has been a top-down affair from the start, carried by two leaders, President Thein Sein and Nobel Laureate Aung San Suu Kyi. Obviously, reforms need to be anchored in institutions and, first and foremost, the constitution. The military's role in government is inconsistent with true democracy and the rule of law. The constitution will need to be changed to make it subject to civilian leadership.

However, it seems unlikely that the military will allow substantial changes of the constitution before the elections in 2015. Three contentious articles – 59(f) preventing Aung San Suu Kyi from standing for president, 109(b) reserving 25% of the seats in parliament for the military, and 436 stating that a change to the constitution needs the endorsement of more than 75% of representatives – are likely to be maintained by the military.

Aung San Suu Kyi and the 1988 students are currently campaigning in support of a revision and a reduced influence of the army, while the USDP is mobilizing against this action. The Election Commission has warned Aung San Suu Kyi that she should not challenge the army and that she 'is speaking outside the constitution', which she has sworn to defend. U Thein Sein has warned that a change in the constitution may lead to unrest in Burma, i.e. that the army use the fear of instability and their own role in maintaining order as an argument against a change. Some Burma watchers argue that it is the strategy of the Tatmadaw to maintain the status quo until Aung San Suu Kyi is too old to stand for president or gives up the idea.

Even if the NLD leader were permitted to run for president, the result would not be a foregone conclusion. In a recent poll, the USDP was seen as a competent party by 84% of respondents. The party obviously has support in the population. Moreover, although 64% wanted a change to the constitution, only 35% were for more autonomy for the ethnic states. Thus, the outcome of the 2015 elections may not be a landslide victory for the NLD, which by some observers is seen as having a relatively weak organization.

What the people of Burma/Myanmar has experienced is a military government shifting power from one generation of officers to another and taking limited reform steps by consolidating their power at home and abroad to increase their legitimacy to govern. Reforms are limited precisely because they are intended to be that way. President Thein Sein may be a genuine reformer but many in the military do not truly want to shift to a civilian democracy. Instead, they want to consolidate its existing power by removing some of the obstacles of direct ruling-by-force. This could be called rule-by-proxy while keeping the fortunes.

Many in the military remain distrustful of civilian politics. This, together with fears about instability at a time of major political change, means that the military is not yet ready to give up the constitutional prerogatives that ensure, through guaranteed legislative representation, that it has a veto on changes to the constitution as well as control of key security ministries.

Those guarantees have given the military elite the confidence to allow a major liberalization of politics and the economy, even when many of the changes impact on its interests. Its proportion of the government budget has been significantly reduced while the huge military-owned conglomerates have lost some lucrative monopolies and other economic privileges.

With the country heading for crucial elections in 2015, its future is fraught with uncertainties. A fully-fledged, western-style democracy is

Peace talks between the ethnic Nationwide Ceasefire Coordination Team and government Union Peacemaking Working Committee in Yangon, April 2014 (photo: Lian Sakhong)

unrealistic. On a more optimistic note, the reform process has unleashed societal forces that have given life to a civil society on an unprecedented scale. The media has become more vibrant and given space for lively debates about how political power and vested interests should be reshaped.

However, there are other urgent issues and challenges. One is the nationwide ceasefire with the ethnic armed organizations. The negotiations continue and involve military representatives as well as parliamentarians. The government and the military have for the first time agreed to include the term 'federalism' in the draft text. The negotiation process, though, has slowed down and the negotiating teams have reached the real stumbling blocks.

First, the ethnic nationalities' idea of a federal constitution includes having a federal army. The Tatmadaw does not like the idea of a federal union and equates it with fragmentation. Hence, while the term is now included, it is still uncertain if the army will agree to genuine intra-state power sharing. Further, the army still demands that all ethnic armed groups respect the constitution and that they integrate into the Tatmadaw. For the ethnic armed groups this is tantamount to a surrender.

Moreover, fighting continues in Kachin State and has spread to the Shan States where the Ta'ang National Liberation front, allied with the Kachin, has been on the offensive. The situation in other parts of Shan State seems unstable as the Restoration Council of Shan States proclaims that it will continue armed struggle while the United Wa State Army seems very little involved in the peace process. Meanwhile, the Kachin are now negotiating separately with the government in order to find a solution. The army, on the other hand, says that it is merely defending itself.

The *second* issue in relation to the ethnic armed groups is the question of laws. The government/army demand that the groups adhere to 'existing laws' under the ceasefire. That means they will still be illegal organizations – as seen in a recent case where Shan leaders of Shan National League for Democracy will be prosecuted under the Unlawful Associations Act. They can end up in jail for five years. There are many other legal issues that have to be dealt with such as the widespread land grabbing and civil rights in general. The problem of Internally Displaced Persons is not something from the past but a growing one.

The *third* issue is the renewed xenophobic nationalism. It has not only been evident in the anti-Muslim campaign and drafting of inter-faith marriage laws but was also a major factor during the census where ethnic groups complained about the categories used in the registration and identification. This issue is highly explosive, also for the NLD, in the coming election campaign and moderate rhetoric will be needed by all parties. If ethno-national differences overpower the electoral process, renewed violence may be a dreadful outcome.

Finally, a crucial issue is the disarming and demilitarization of Burma, an issue rarely discussed. The Tatmadaw and the ethnic armed organizations find that their weaponry is a natural part of their political authority and power. They cannot yet imagine a time without weapons and argue that defensive and protective measures are necessary to uphold their claims and rights. Thus, a post-ceasefire scenario may need international help in peacekeeping during a demobilization as well as a development project to support the livelihood of former combatants.[1]

---

1. On the peace process, see recent reports referenced below.

What can the outside world expect?

During the coming decade, Burma/Myanmar may start to resemble its neighbour Thailand. It will undoubtedly be more prosperous and more unequal. The landscape of political forces and economic power-holders will be more fractured as elected politicians continue their struggle to make institutions more responsible and transparent.

The period of transition from an almost totalitarian rule to a 'disciplined' democracy is a precarious time of uncertainty and potential instability. Nationalism, xenophobia, fear and mistrust in all relations combined with decades of widespread violence have accumulated a huge amount of imagined and real incompatibilities between the many parties to the conflicts in Burma. A ceasefire agreement is not the same as peace but is an instrument of conflict management. Thus, a continuous dialogue and monitoring of the agreement in order to prevent misunderstandings during setbacks, and preventing minor clashes and disagreements from exploding, is of outmost importance to all parties. Thereafter, patience in political negotiations as well as trust building embedded in progress of the talks may contribute to a stabilization of the situation. The gradual devolution of the military-dominated system, as well as a gradual disarming of combatants, is only possible when all parties have trust in and adhere to a mutually agreed form of democracy within the state of Burma/Myanmar.

References

The Irrawaddy (2014) 'Norway-backed Burma Peace Project Set to Continue', 23 May: http://www.irrawaddy.org/burma/norway-backed-burma-peace-project-set-continue.html.

Johnson, Chris and Michael Lidauer (2014) 'Testing Ceasefires, Building Trust: Myanmar Peace Support Initiative Operational Review': http://nis-foundation.org/project-highlights/publications/testing-ceasefires-building-trust/.

Legal Aid Network (2014) 'Potential Peace in Burma or Regional Instability?': http://www.kaladanpress.org/index.php/scholar-column-mainmenu-36/burma/4524-potential-for-peace-in-burma-or-regional-instability.html.

Myanmar Peace Support Initiative (2014) 'Lessons Learned from MPSI Work Supporting the Peace Process in Myanmar: March 2012-March 2014': http://www.burmalibrary.org/docs17/MPSI_Lessons_Learned_Paper-March_2014-en-red.pdf.

APPENDIX ONE

Historical landmarks

1824–26	First Anglo–Burman war; annexation of Tenasserim and Arakan.
1852	Second Anglo–Burman War. Annexation of Lower Burma including Rangoon.
1885–86	Final British annexation of Burma and deportation of King Thibaw. A long 'pacification' campaign against several Burmese rebellions often led by former monks.
1906	Young Men's Buddhist Association formed. The beginning of Burmese nationalism and the independence struggle.
1920	General Council of Buddhist Associations is founded and country-wide, nationalist organizations formed.
1922	Frontier area administered directly by the governor. Shan States in a federation.
1923	Dyarchy. The British administration of Burma is split from India.
1930–31	Burma hit by the Depression. A rebellion led by former monk Hsaya San breaks out.
1937	Parliamentary government of PM Ba Maw formed with limited powers. The Karen obtain 12 communal seats.
1942	Japanese occupation. Many ethnic groups support the British in the jungle war that follows. Aung San and his 30 *Thakin* ('master') comrades return from Japan and join the invasion with their Burma Independence Army (later Burma National Army).
1944	Formation of Anti-Fascist Peoples Freedom League (AFPFL) lead by Aung San.
1946, 1947	The Panglong Conferences and Panglong Agreement between Aung San and Shan, Kachin and Chin on their

future self-determination, an agreement never materialized in the 1947 constitution.

1947	Aung San and eight of his ministers, including his elder brother, are assassinated. His political adversary U Saw hanged for the murders.
1948	Independence. U Nu becomes prime minister. Start of insurrections by Karenni and some other ethnic groups, elements of the People's Volunteer Organization (former soldiers), and the Communist Party of Burma.
1949	Start of insurrection by the Karen National Union.
1956	Sixth World Buddhist Council held in Rangoon.
1958	Start of fragmented insurrections in Shan State.
1961	Buddhism becomes the state religion under PM U Nu. Start of Kachin insurrection.
1962	Military coup by General Ne Win. U Nu and other politicians jailed. Rule by Nationalist Revolutionary Council. Eviction of missionaries, ban on horse racing and other Western 'vices', and the use of English language; censorship of media.
1964	Nationalization of many businesses.
1970	U Nu in exile in Thailand and working with ethnic opposition. United National Liberation Front founded.
1971	Burma Socialist Programme Party (BSPP) holds its first congress.
1974	Second constitution. Riots after the funeral of UN General Secretary U Thant.
1988	8.8.88 Rebellion. Ne Win resigns from the BSPP, which is dissolved. Military coup and formation of State Law and Order Restoration Council (SLORC). Aung San Suu Kyi (ASSK) forms the National League for Democracy (NLD).
1989	Communist Party of Burma dissolved. 'Myanmar' is promulgated as the official name for Burma.
1990	General election, with 81% of seats won by the NLD. Army ignores the results.

1997	SLORC replaced by State Peace and Development Council (SPDC).
2002	Ne Win and his family arrested for planning a coup. Ne Win dies.
2005–06	Capital moved to Naipyidaw ('the abode of kings') in central Burma.
2007	'Saffron Revolution'. Young monks protest against economic, social and moral decline.
2008	Cyclone Nargis kills 150,000 in the Irrawaddy Delta. The new constitution approved in a flawed referendum.
2010	Elections, boycotted by NLD, and later release of ASSK.
2011	Nominally civilian government under Thein Sein sworn in. Beginning of reform process prompting a high-profile visit by Hilary Clinton.
2012	Ceasefires with some separatist groups but ethnic violence erupts in Rakhine State. In by-elections, ASSK and the NLD win 44 seats. Reforms gather pace. Visits by many foreign dignitaries, easing of international sanctions and offers of aid.
2013	Reforms continue amid a flood of foreign aid and investment. Fighting intensifies in Kachin State and anti-Muslim violence spreads outside Rakhine State but work also progresses towards reaching a national ceasefire.
2014	Tensions are high as the country's first census in three decades is carried out. Despite ongoing fighting in the north of the country, progress is made on achieving a nationwide ceasefire.

List of Organizations

Note: Organizations marked by an asterisk (*) are defunct.

AA Arakan Army

AAPP	Assistance Association for Political Prisoners (Burma)
ABSDF	All Burma Students Democratic Front
*AFPFL	Anti-Fascist People's Freedom League
ALA	Arakan Liberation Army (military wing of ALP)
ALP	Arakan Liberation Party (a.k.a. Rakhine State Liberation Party)
AMRDP	All Mon Region Democracy Party
ANC	Arakan National Council
ARIF	Arakan Rohingya Islamic Front
ARNO	Arakan Rohingya National Organization
ASEAN	Association of South East Asian Nations
*BCP	Burma Communist Party
*BSSP	Burma Socialist Programme Party
CNA	Chin National Army (military wing of CNF)
CNF	Chin National Front
CNP	Chin National Party
CPB	See BCP
*DKBA	Democratic Karen Buddhist Army
DKBA-5	Democratic Karen Benevolent Army
IMA	Itihadul Mozahidin of Arakan
KA	Karenni Army (military wing of KNPP)
*KDA	Kachin Defense Army
KDP	Karen Democratic Party
KIA	Kachin Independence Army (military wing of KIO)

KIO	Kachin Independence Organization
KKO	Klo Htoo Baw Karen Organization (political wing of DKBA-5)
*KMT	Kuomintang
KNA	Karen National Association
KNLA	Karen National Liberation Army (military wing of KNU)
KNLP	Kayan New Land Party
KNP	Karen National Party
KNPLF	Karenni National People's Liberation Front
KNPP	Karenni National Progressive Party
KNU	Karen National Union
KPC	KNU/KNLA Peace Council
KPP	Karen People's Party
KSDDP	Karen State Democracy and Development Party
*KPF	Karen Peace Force
LDU	Lahu Democratic Union
MDUF	Myeik-Dawei United Front
MNDAA	Myanmar National Democratic Alliance Army
MNLA	Mon National Liberation Army (military wing of NMSP)
*MTA	Mong Tai Army
NCGUB	National Coalition Government of the Union of Burma
NDAA	National Democratic Alliance Army-Eastern Shan State
*NDA-K	New Democratic Army-Kachin
NDF	National Democratic Force
NLD	National League for Democracy
NMSP	New Mon State Party
NSCN-K	National Socialist Council of Nagaland – Khaplang
NUP	National Unity Party
*PA	People's Army (military wing of the BCP)
PNLA	Pa-O National Liberation Army (military wing of PNLO)
PNLO	Pa-O National Liberation Organization

PNO	Pa-O National Organization
*PPLO	Pa-O People's Liberation Organization
PSDP	Phloung-Sgaw (Phalon-Sawaw) Democratic Party
*PSLA	Palaung State Liberation Army (military wing of PSLO)
PSLF	Palaung State Liberation Front (political wing of TNLA)
*PSLO	Palaung State Liberation Organization
RCSS	Restoration Council of Shan State
*RNDP	Rakhine Nationalities Development Party
RNP	Rakhine National Party
*RPF	Rohingya Patriotic Front
*RLO	Rohingya Liberation Organization
RSO	Rohingya Solidarity Organization
*SLORC	State Law and Order Restoration Council
*SPDC	State Peace and Development Council
SNDP	Shan Nationalities Democratic Party
*SNPLO	Shan State Nationalities People's Liberation Organization
SSA-S	Shan State Army-South (military wing of RCSS)
SSA-N	Shan State Army-North (military wing of SSPP)
*SSNA	Shan State National Army
SSPP	Shan State Progress Party
*SURA	Shan United Revolutionary Army
TNLA	Ta'ang National Liberation Army
*USDC	Union Solidarity and Development Council
USDP	Union Solidarity and Development Party
UWSA	United Wa State Army
UWSP	United Wa State Party (political wing of UWSA)
WNA	Wa National Army (military wing of WNO)
WNO	Wa National Organization
WNUP	Wa National Unity Party
ZRA	Zomi Reunification Army (military wing of ZRO)
ZRO	Zomi Reunification Organization

Further Reading

A vast literature exists on all aspects of Burma/Myanmar. The following list is aimed at readers of this volume (though obviously this is guesswork), added considerations being if the book is topical and easily available. For a detailed bibliography, see Andrew Selth, 'Burma (Myanmar) since the 1988 uprising: a select bibliography', Griffith University, 2012: http://www.burmalibrary.org/docs14/Selth-Burma-Bibliography2012-red.pdf.

Allen, Louis (2000 [1984]) *Burma: The Longest War 1941–45*. London: Phoenix.

Aung San Suu Kyi (1991) *Freedom from Fear: And Other Writings*. London: Penguin.

——, *Letters From Burma*. London: Penguin, 2010 (1997)

Aung Thwin, Matrii (2011) *The Return of the Galon King: History, Law, and Rebellion in Colonial Burma*. Athens, OH: Ohio University.

Aung Thwin, Michael and Matrii Aung Thwin (2012) *A History of Myanmar Since Ancient Times: Traditions and Transformations*. London: Reaktion Books.

Butwell, Richard (1963) *U Nu of Burma*. Stanford: Stanford University Press.

Callahan, Mary P. (2003) *Making Enemies: War and State Building in Burma*. Ithaca: Cornell University Press.

Charney, Michael W. (2009) *A History of Modern Burma*. Cambridge: Cambridge University Press.

Fink, Christina (2011) *Living Silence: Burma under Military Rule*. Chiang Mai: Silkworm Books.

Gibson, R.M. and Wenhua Chen (2011) *The Secret Army: Chiang Kai-shek and the Drug Warlords of the Golden Triangle*. Singapore: John Wiley.

Gravers, Mikael (ed.) (2007) *Exploring Ethnic Diversity in Burma*. Copenhagen: NIAS Press.

Harriden, Jessica (2012) *The Authority of Influence: Women and Power in Burmese History*. Copenhagen: NIAS Press.

Holliday, Ian (2011) *Burma Redux: Global Justice and the Quest for Political Reform in Myanmar*. Hong Kong: University of Hong Kong Press.

Ikeya, Chie (2011) *Refiguring Women, Colonialism, and Modernity in Burma.* Honolulu: University of Hawai'i Press.

Kuijper, Elke and Ashin Kovida (eds), *Burma Voices: People of Burma in Their Own Words.* Mae Sot, Thailand: Project Printing 2012.

Lintner, Bertil (1989) *Outrage: Burma's Struggle for Democracy.* Hong Kong: Review Publishing Company Limited.

————— (1994) *Burma in Revolt: Opium and Insurgency since 1948.* Boulder: Westview Press & Bangkok: White Lotus.

————— (2011) *Aung San Suu Kyi and Burma's Struggle for Democracy.* Chiang Mai: Silkworm Books.

MacLean, Rory (2012 [1998]) *Under the Dragon: A Journey Through Burma.* London: I B Tauris.

Myanmar Peace Monitor (2014) *Deciphering Myanmar's Peace Process: A Reference Guide 2014,* Chiang Mai: Burma News International: http://www.mmpeacemonitor.org/images/pdf/deciphering_myanmar_peace_process_2014.pdf.

Naw, Angelene (2001) *Aung San and the Struggle for Burmese Independence.* Chiang Mai: Silkworm Books and Copenhagen: NIAS Press.

Orwell, George (2001 [1934]) *Burmese Days.* London: Penguin Modern Classics.

Popham, Peter (2011) *The Lady and the Peacock: The Life of Aung San Suu Kyi.* London: Rider Books.

Rogers, Benedict (2010) *Than Shwe: Unmasking Burma's Tyrant.* Chiang Mai: Silkworm Books.

————— (2012) *Burma: A Nation at the Crossroads.* London, Rider Books.

Sadan, Mandy (2013) *Being and Becoming Kachin: Histories Beyond the State in the Borderworlds of Burma.* Oxford: Oxford University Press/British Academy.

Schober, Juliane (2011) *Modern Buddhist Conjunctures in Myanmar: Cultural Narratives, Colonial Legacies, and Civil Society.* Honolulu: University of Hawai'i Press.

Seekins (2006) Donald M., *Historical Dictionary of Burma (Myanmar).* Lanham, MA: Scarecrow Press.

Selth, Andrew (2002) *Burma's Armed Forces: Power Without Glory.* Norwalk, CT: EastBridge.

Silverstein, Josef (1993) *The Political Legacy of Aung San.* Ithaca: Cornell University Southeast Asia Program, revised edition.

Smith, Martin (1999) *Burma: Insurgency and the Politics of Ethnicity.* London: Zed Books, revised and updated edition.

South, Ashley (2003) *Mon Nationalism and Civil War in Burma. The Golden Sheldrake.* London: Routledge.

———(2008) *Ethnic Politics in Burma: States of Conflict.* London: Routledge.

Steinberg, David I. (2001) *Burma: The State of Myanmar.* Washington, DC: Georgetown University Press.

——— (2010) *Burma/Myanmar: What Everyone Needs to Know.* New York: Oxford University Press.

Steinberg, David I. and Hongwei Fan (2012) *Modern China–Myanmar Relations: Dilemmas of Mutual Dependence.* Copenhagen: NIAS Press.

Thant Myint-U (2001) *The Making of Modern Burma.* Cambridge: Cambridge University Press.

——— (2006) *The River of Lost Footsteps: Histories of Burma.* New York: Farrar, Straus and Giroux.

Taylor, Robert H. (2009) *The State in Myanmar.* London: Hurst & Company.

Turnell, Sean (2009) *Fiery Dragons: Banks, Moneylenders and Microfinance in Burma.* Copenhagen: NIAS Press.

Index

8888
  generation 69–71. *See also* Min Ko
    Naing
  movement/uprising 54, 58, 67,
    69–70, 89, 171, 177, 272, 400
969 movement 56, 67, 314–18.
  See also anti-Muslim violence;
  Buddhism; nationalism;
  Rohingya; Wirathu; xenophobia

ActionAid Myanmar 406. *See also*
  INGOs
activism/activists 9, 237, 247, 335,
  358
  arrest/imprisonment 44; ~ and
    release 33
  Buddhist. *See* 969 movement; anti-
    colonial movement; Saffron
    Revolution
  civil society 91, 92, 230–31
  exiled groups 40, 232, 234, 241,
    242, 243,
  peace 232, 233
  political/pro-democracy 72, 219,
    231, 232, 390
  student 232, 273
  women 90, 137, 138, 233
AFPFL (Anti-Fascist Peoples
    Freedom League) 63, 165, 182,
    184, 302, 333, 400. *See also* Aung
    San; U Nu
agriculture 341–44, 380–81, 408
  aid for 358, 402, 408–09. *See also*
    FAO
  British development of 145–46
  Burma as rice-bowl of Asia 342,
    379, 380, 397
  investment in 374

most important economic sector
  344
  see also land-grabbing; land tenure
Akha (ethnic group) 156, 158, 169.
  See also NDAA
alms-giving 66, 279, 289, 320
  rejected 308. *See also* Saffron
    Revolution
amphetamines. *See* drug trade
Amyotha Hluttaw. *See* Hlutataw
ana (authority) 46, 64. *See also awza*;
  power and leadership
Anglo-Burman wars 143, 422. *See
  also* colonial legacy
animists 123, 157–59 *passim*, 175,
  176, 181, 187, 188, 279, 281–83
  passim
Anglican Church 88, 279, 203, 204,
  280. *See also* Christianity
anti-colonial movement 62, 180,
  286, 298–99, 301
  in Ceylon and India 298, 318–19
  monks and 298, 313
  see also Aung San; nationalism;
    xenophobia
Anti-Fascist Peoples Freedom
  League. *See* AFPFL
anti-Muslim
  activities 67, 314, 317–18, 420
  movement. *See* 969 movement
  sentiments 160, 313, 319, 334, 336
  violence 21, 56, 84, 146, 160, 301,
    310, 314–16, 361, 424. *See also*
    communal violence; violence
Arakan (former kingdom/province)
  310, 311, 325, 326
  British conquest 328, 422
  Burmese conquest 310, 333

communal violence in. *See* communal violence
first Muslims in 280, 310, 311, 325
colonial period 325, 332–32, 335; Bengali immigration during ~ 325
State. *See* Rakhine State
armed forces/army. *See* military
ASEAN 41, 114, 368, 377, 388
economic interests 349. *See also* foreign investment
Myanmar chair of in 2014 103, 248, 366
Aung Min, U 206, 230, 266, 268–69, 276. *See also* nationwide ceasefire agreement: negotiations
Aung San 1, 146, 302
assassination 1, 49, 183, 423
as father of ASSK 70, 96, 106, 290
nationalist ideology 147, 302
as nationalist leader 49, 147, 165, 422. *See also* AFPFL; BCP
negotiations on independence 147, 176, 183, 185, 422–23
supports Japanese in WWII 62, 147, 176, 181, 301, 422; ~ switches to British 62, 147, 182
Aung San Suu Kyi (ASSK) 28, 49–52, 56, 106, 135, 291, 363
on Buddhism 67, 289–92
as daughter of Aung San 70, 96, 106, 290
as democracy icon 27, 29, 51, 102, 106, 118, 130, 135
elected to parliament 51, 106
entry into politics 69, 70
house arrest 27, 28, 49, 50; freed from ~ 1, 20, 50, 218
running for president 21, 26, 52, 317; eligibility for ~ 50, 59, 60, 380, 417–18. *See also* constitution
on Rohingyas 312, 316, 336–337
and Thein Sein 21, 25, 26, 59, 417
see also NLD
awza (influence) 46. *See also* ana; power and leadership

Ayeyarwady (Irrawaddy)
delta 124, 125, 132, 145, 155, 165, 174, 182, 235, 280, 300, 357, 363, 410, 411, 414. *See also* agriculture
devastated by Nargis. *See* Cyclone Nargis
Region 80, 124
river 96, 98, 145, 231, 263

Ba Maw, Prime Minister 113, 147, 422
Bamar. *See* Burman
Baptists 280. *See also* Christianity
BCP (Burma Communist Party) 64, 98, 109, 165, 168–70, 223, 270, 423
BGF (Border Guard Force) 55, 153, 164–71 *passim*, 189, 193, 206–12 *passim*, 261, 265, 271, 273. *See also* EAGs; military
Bo Mya (KNU leader) 106, 190, 204–05
Border Guard Force. *See* BGF
British rule
conquest. *See* Anglo-Burman wars
resistance to 145, 179–81, 296–301. *See also* anti-colonial movement; *min laùng*
use of ethnic groups 145, 163, 178–81, 285–86
see also colonial legacy
Buddhism 56, 57, 63, 66, 67, 131, 155–59 *passim*, 171, 175, 179, 180, 187–89, 263, 279–320 *passim*, 328, 423
of ASSK 67, 289–92
in civil society 199, 280, 295. *See also* Buddhist: schools
constitutional recognition 66, 279, 283, 293
'in danger' 296, 300, 308, 309, 313, 319
importance/presence 66, 123, 280, 293, 295. *See also* alms-giving
and the military 67, 294, 302–09

and nationalism 57, 111, 179–81, 294, 298–302, 310–19, 331–32. *See also* 969; anti-colonial movement; nationalism; Wirathu

and non-violence 290, 295, 308. *See also* violence

organization. *See* Sangha; State Sangha Nayaka Committee

and state power 144, 178–79, 295–96, 302–06

vinaya rules 297, 299, 301, 304, 306

see also monks; pagodas; Sangha

Burma Independence Army (BIA) 176, 181–82, 301, 326, 422. *See also* Aung San; World War II

Burma Socialist Program Party (BSPP) 60, 70, 88, 186, 422, 423. *See also* Ne Win

Burman (Bamar, ethnic group) 2, 31, 56, 63, 64, 78, 79, 87, 88, 91, 122, 131, 143–46, 147, 149, 155, 157–59, 165, 171, 174, 176–86, 189, 190, 192, 223, 229–33, 237, 245, 247, 254, 260, 278, 280, 284, 300, 311–13, 319, 320, 328–35, 368, 422

business(es) 160

big ~ 311, 342; ~ interests 60

businessmen 35, 67, 125, 139, 185, 207, 258, 324, 382. *See also* cronies

Chinese 96, 262, 270–71, 351

in conflict zones 211–13, 216, 225, 248, 391–92

of ethnic armed groups 165, 169, 190, 192–93, 209–10, 361, 391–92

facilities, lack of 386. *See also* infrastructure

foreign 36, 71, 110–19 *passim*, 198, 208, 211, 317, 351, 384, 391; attack on ~ 96, 146, 373, 423

local 211, 333, 343–44, 361, 382

interests 67, 212

military involvement in 67, 262, 264, 362, 375, 382, 412. *See also* military

Muslim 313, 361

networks 71

opportunities 209

partnerships 71, 211, 262, 374, 386, 391–92. *See also* joint ventures

and peace process 226, 267

regulation 248

see also investment; sanctions

CBOs (community-based organizations) 86, 237, 408. *See also* civil society; NGOs

ceasefire negotiations. *See* nationwide ceasefire agreement

ceasefire(s) 152, 164, 209, 239, 251–52, 421

argument if political settlement first 152, 193

Kachin. *See* Kachin conflict

limited by lack of political solution 152

nationwide. *See* nationwide ceasefire agreement

preliminary ~ since 2011 43, 164, 168–173, 224–25, 251, 275. *See also* KNU

separate ~ with military regime 152, 164, 166–171, 224, 229, 391

census (2014) 121, 154, 155, 229, 235, 424

concerns of ethnic minorities 236, 420

disputes 121

exclusion of Rohingya category 155, 311, 329

first since 1983 21, 154, 269

Kachin boycott 154, 269–70, 278

preliminary counting by ethnic groups 154

political sensitivity of 78, 420

results 78, 154

Central Bank of Myanmar 371

chettiars. *See* moneylenders

child soldiers 45, 261, 390

Chin (ethnic group) 60, 79, 122, 124,
    145, 149, 157, 159, 172, 175,
    178, 179, 183, 219, 220, 273,
    274, 280, 334, 422, 425
Chin National Front 172, 273, 274
China 33, 55, 89, 95–119 *passim*,
    150, 160–62, 165, 169, 256, 258,
    262, 263, 267, 270–74 *passim*,
    347, 348, 350, 351, 354, 357,
    359, 384, 394, 409
    businesses 96, 262, 270–71, 351
    energy pipelines to 98, 104, 111,
        348, 350. *See also* energy sector;
        pipeline
    investments by. *See* investment
    and Kachin conflict 266, 270–72
    and Myitsone dam 96, 103, 107,
        111, 151, 231, 265, 357, 358
    strategic interests 95–111 *passim*
    see also BCP; Yunnan
Chinese (ethnicity). *See* Kokang;
    Sino-Burmese
Chinese Nationalist troops. *See* KMT
Christianity 144, 167, 176, 178, 180,
    181, 280, 283, 285, 288. *See also*
    Anglican Church; Baptists
Christians 145, 178, 181, 184, 190,
    220, 296, 319
citizenship 146, 148, 149, 162, 163,
    228, 311, 323, 324, 326–31, 334,
    336, 366, 407, 408
    ~ Act 148, 330
    see also ethnicity; *tai yin tha*
civil society
    defining 86
    development of 87–94 *passim*
    important role of Buddhism 199,
        280, 295
    and peace process 204–07, 223–49
        passim. See also peace process
civil-society groups 36, 81, 83, 89,
    137, 201, 210, 211, 341, 388,
    400, 405, 409
    Christian 91, 230
    criticism of EAGs 242
    freedom of manoeuvre 91, 230; ~
        restricted 360, 413–14

greater political engagement 231
    and INGOs 201, 405, 407,
        410–11. *See also* INGOs
    lack of coordination 201
    need for patronage and protection.
        See patron–client relations
    position boosted after Nargis 361
    provision of health care 78, 127; ~
        and education 78
    on Thai border 91–92, 234,
        240–41
    traditional 127
    see also CBOs; Cyclone Nargis;
        NGOs
climate change 295, 393, 395, 409.
    See also environmental issues
colonialism 46, 121, 122, 183–84,
    280, 285–86, 288
    and Buddhism 144, 178–81, 294,
        298
    economic transformation 145–46,
        163
    divide-and-rule policy 145, 154,
        178–81, 275
    ethnic divisions 145, 149, 159,
        175, 310–13, 325–26
    legacy 130, 143–48
    see also anti-colonial movement;
        British rule
communal violence 21, 87, 142,
    160, 175, 224, 238, 247, 282,
    310–316, 323–37 *passim*, 385,
    407, 420, 424
    during WWII 182, 325–26
    see also anti-Muslim: violence;
        Rakhine State; Rohingya;
        violence
community-based organizations. *See*
    CBOs
constitution
    1948 183
    2008 27, 29, 30, 34, 35, 36, 37, 40,
        44, 45, 88, 96, 100, 101, 106,
        137, 149, 150, 152, 153, 183,
        184, 185, 190, 224, 227, 229,
        250, 268, 271, 273, 278, 280,
        283, 286, 293, 304, 306, 315,
        317, 319, 329, 334, 335, 360

citizenship and ethnicity. *See* citizenship
difficulty in amending 52–84 *passim*, 417–20 *passim*
place of Buddhism 66, 279, 283, 293
reserved status for military 30–36 *passim*
see also state and government
cronies (tycoons) 34, 64, 67, 71, 125, 126, 341, 351, 353, 359–63 *passim*, 386, 392–93
conglomerates 342, 362, 374, 382
and illegal trade 362
on sanctions lists 126
see also Tay Za; Zaw Zaw
culture 96, 111, 122–23, 131, 138, 144, 149–55, 159, 161–62, 185, 235, 279–80, 297, 320, 329. *See also* Burman; ethnic minorities/nationalities
Cyclone Nargis. *See* Nargis

dams. *See* hydropower projects
Danu (ethnic group) 79, 80, 156, 159
Dawei
    ethnic group 156–57, 171
    town/region (Tavoy) 115, 151, 367, 384. *See also* Tanintharyi
deforestation 221, 346, 393–95. *See also* forests
democracy 2, 43–45, 91, 95, 130, 147, 230, 417
    democratization 36, 55, 87, 102, 175, 318, 408
    'disciplined' 36, 421
    prospects for 27–29, 36, 417–21
    roadmap to 73, 101, 267
Democratic Karen Benevolent Army. *See* DKBA-5
Democratic Karen Buddhist Army. *See* DKBA
Democratic Voice of Burma. *See* DVB; media
development
    challenges 387–93. *See also* foreign aid; NGOs; INGOs

economic 48, 133, 208, 213, 246, 254, 336, 340–44 *passim*, 347, 352, 355, 359, 361, 363, 388, 393
    programmes 113, 116
    projects 88, 153, 192, 200, 209–11, 295, 340–42, 350, 355, 388, 399, 400, 402, 407, 409, 410, 414, 420
    social 133, 388, 400
dhammaraja (righteous ruler) 289, 295–302 *passim*, 308. *See also* ASSK: on Buddhism; Buddhism: and state power
DKBA (Democratic Karen Buddhist Army) 164, 171, 209–10, 212, 315
    becomes BGF 171, 206
    defection of 5th Brigade. *See* DKBA-5
    as government proxy 189
    splits from/attacks KNU 188–89
DKBA-5 (Democratic Karen Benevolent Army) 164, 171, 190, 193, 212
    alliance with KNU 207, 211
    splits from DKBA 171, 189
    see also KKO
donors. *See* foreign donors
drug trade 153, 161, 264, 291, 354–55
    amphetamines (*yaa baa*) 150, 168, 169, 354, 362
    EAGs and 64, 165–70, 193, 360–61. *See also* MNDAA; NDAA; UWSA 153, 169
    military involvement 360
    opium and heroin production 150–51, 354–55
    suppression 115, 290
    see also Golden Triangle
DVB (Democratic Voice of Burma) 26, 41

EAGs (ethnic armed groups)
    alliances 152–54, 275. *See also* NCCT; UNFC

business interests 165, 169, 190,
192–93, 209–10, 361, 391–92,
394
ceasefires with government/mili-
tary regime. *See* ceasefire(s)
incorporation into Border Guard
Force. *See* BGF
list of 165–72
local criticism of 242
mistrust of government/military
154, 177, 190–93, 202, 214,
228, 278, 312, 408, 421
economic
development 48, 208, 213, 246, 254,
336, 340–44 *passim*, 347, 352,
355, 359, 361, 363, 388, 393
interests 64, 106, 112, 226
growth 36, 126, 127, 383, 385,
387, 409
policies 6, 161, 342, 370
socio- ~ programmes 409
reforms. *See* reforms: economic
sanctions. *See* sanctions
education 64, 78–79, 91, 131–33,
137, 139, 145–46, 190, 200,
208, 227, 230, 236, 240, 245–46,
255, 257, 287–88, 310–11, 319,
387–88, 399, 404
curriculum 131, 255
quality of 131–33
system 131, 132, 133, 255,
elections
1960 63, 203, 334
1990 28, 49–50, 70, 117, 232, 423
2010 19, 25, 47, 54, 58–60, 72–73,
89, 100, 190, 224, 259–60, 334,
424
2015 30–32, 34, 36, 53, 74–75,
226, 229, 248, 317, 318, 385,
417–18
April 2012 by-election 9, 27, 29,
51, 59, 60, 73, 75, 82
electoral system 36, 59, 74, 82, 84
2010 election laws 50
presidential eligibility 50, 59, 60,
380, 417–18
elites 7, 93, 146, 147, 185, 216, 225,
230–40 *passim*, 264, 285–86,

362, 382, 391, 418. *See also* cronies; social structure
energy sector 348–51
environmental issues 345, 393–398.
See also climate change; deforestation
ethnic conflicts 39, 92, 119, 145, 173,
175, 198, 199, 209, 226, 241,
257, 319. *See also* ceasefire(s);
communal violence; federalism;
peace process
ethnic minorities/nationalities 26,
43, 45, 48, 51, 58, 63, 65, 78, 90,
110, 121, 122, 145, 147, 148,
151–55, 178, 182, 183, 190, 193,
200, 202, 208, 228, 235, 257,
262, 267, 268, 274, 276, 278,
281, 284, 304, 317, 366, 391,
392, 394, 396, 420, 422, 423
armed organizations. *See* EAGs
political parties 31, 60–61, 186,
205–07, 226, 239, 246, 248,
329, 333, 334
recognized 'national races' 78, 149,
160, 311, 328, 330, 334
umbrella groups 152–54, 275. *See
also* ENC; UNFC
see also Akha; Chin; Danu; Dawei;
Kachin; Kayah; Kayan; Karen;
Kokang; Lahu; Mon; Naga; Pa-
o; Palaung; Rakhine; Rohingya;
Shan; Wa
Ethnic Nationalities Council (ENC)
152
ethnicity 31, 154, 173, 175, 177, 178,
189, 233, 337
European Union 33, 116–17, 390
exchange rate (kyat) 370–71, 378,
381–82
exiles 2, 29, 92, 102, 135, 240, 241;
~ returning home 217–22, 232,
241. *See also* 8888 generation;
activism

FAA (Frontier Area Administration)
182–84

FAO (Food and Agriculture Organization) 393, 402
federalism 64, 79, 182–84, 419
  army 64, 153, 193, 267, 268, 419
  state 36, 46, 150, 152–53, 190, 250, 267–69, 419
  see also constitution; military; Panglong Agreement
foreign donors 389, 392, 399, 405
Foreign Investment Law 198, 348, 373
forests 97, 221, 264
  forestry sector 145, 344–47, 382, 394–95
  logging of 125, 151, 193, 209, 211, 216, 262, 269, 345, 362, 391–95 passim
  teak 124, 143, 344–45, 379, 393–95
  threat to 151. See also environmental issues
  see also deforestation
freedom
  of association 42, 207, 234, 420
  of expression 42, 217, 232, 406, 411, 412
Frontier Area Administration. See FAA
Furnivall, J.S. 146–47

GDP (gross domestic product) 126, 131, 369, 376, 377
Golden Triangle 151, 161, 169, 354. See also drug trade
government
  difficulty in controlling Tatmadaw 53, 55, 153, 266, 277, 391
  military regime. See SLORC; SPDC
  quasi-civilian 25, 38, 46, 55, 61, 121, 341, 388, 391, 404; transition to ~ 46, 61; reasons for ~ 38, 55
  see also state and government
Gun Maw, Major-General (KIA) 266–69 passim, 276, 277

Hat Gyi Dam 151, 210, 211, 356
health 8, 12, 33, 64, 66, 78–79, 121, 126–29, 131, 133, 202, 227, 240, 244–45, 248, 257, 280, 283, 352, 387–88, 399, 401–05 passim. See also HIV/AIDS
health-care system 126, 127, 131, 401
heroin. See drug trade
Hinduism 123, 279, 283, 324. See also religion
HIV/AIDS 9, 18, 128–30, 295, 402–04
Hluttaw (legislature)
  Amyotha ~ (upper house) 58, 75, 77. See also government; parliament
  Pyidaungsu ~ (national assembly) 61, 75–76, 78, 81–83. See also government; parliament
  Pyithu Hlutataw (lower house) 58, 75–77. See also Shwe Mann
  Region/State assemblies 58, 61, 75–76, 78, 79
  see also state and government
Hpa-an 191, 192, 205, 209, 210, 275, 276
hpòun (karmic power) 178, 180, 296, 300, 303
  ~ gyi, (designation) 296
  kan- ~ (karmic power) 296
  see also power and leadership
hydropower projects 99, 356–59, 376
  Chinese 151, 209, 210, 211, 265, 350, 357. See also Myitsone Dam
  see also Ayeyarwady River; energy; Hat Gyi Dam; infrastructure; Salween River; Tamanthi Dam

IDPs (internally displaced people) 10, 159, 199, 223, 256, 259. See also refugees
India 40, 49, 98, 103, 104, 105, 106, 108, 111, 112, 143, 145, 150, 157, 159, 162, 163, 172, 178,

179, 182, 256, 263, 270, 298, 10, 313, 318, 328, 332, 350, 379, 383, 409
Indians 145–46, 155, 160, 162–63, 326
infrastructure 98, 104, 115, 145, 208, 210, 213, 342, 348, 350–52, 355, 356, 377, 379–82, 384, 385, 392. *See also* hydropower projects
INGOs (international NGOs) 129–30, 133, 199–202, 212–13, 388–91, 393, 399–414 *passim*
bottom-up projects 413
project implementation 198–202, 350, 355
see also civil-society groups; development; foreign aid; NGOs
Interfaith Marriage Bill 137, 318, 327, 420. *See also* Islam: intermarriage
internally displaced people. *See* IDPs
international
actors 109–19, 203. *See also* ASEAN; China; European Union; India; Japan; Thailand; United States
donors. *See* foreign donors
NGOs. *See* INGOs
investment 36, 71, 107, 108, 112–15, 118, 119, 133, 138, 191, 198, 199, 208, 209, 213, 341, 342, 348, 350, 355, 358, 366, 373, 376, 379, 381–90, 392, 402, 424
Irrawaddy delta, Region and river. *See* Ayeyarwady
Irrawaddy, The (news organization) 26
Islam 123, 283, 333
communities 160–61, 280–82, 311–313, 324–25, 390
history 160–61, 280–81, 324–26, 335
intermarriage 312–18 *passim*, 331. *See also* Interfaith Marriage Bill
militant 312–13, 323, 335–337
see also anti-Muslim; mosques; Muslims; Rohingya; schools

Japan 62, 106, 112, 113, 114, 401. *See also* World War II
Jinghpaw (Kachin sub-group) 150, 162, 263, 270, 285
joint ventures 348, 351, 355
judiciary 33, 34, 59, 76, 77. *See also* government

Kachin (ethnic group) 79, 157, 166–68, 175, 263–64
and Christianity 145, 167, 280, 287, 288
cross-border linkages 150, 263, 285–86
recruitment in colonial forces 145, 178, 286–87
see also Jinghpaw
Kachin conflict
breakdown of ceasefire 20, 44, 224, 265, 357
effect on peace process 247
Chinese intervention 21, 167, 224, 266, 270–72
media coverage 232–33
peace talks 167, 265, 266–69
role/attitude of Tatmadaw 21, 53, 55, 167, 224, 227, 265–70, 277–78, 391, 420
spreads to northern Shan State 269, 278, 420. *See also* TNLA
see also IDPs; refugees
Kachin Independence Army. *See* KIA
Kachin Independence Organization. *See* KIO
Kachin State 80, 153, 236
census-taking blocked. *See* census
natural wealth 346. *See also* natural resources
ongoing conflict in. *See* Kachin conflict
separatist struggle 150, 164, 166–67, 175, 186, 423. *See also* Kachin conflict; KIO
see also Myitsone Dam
kala ('foreigner', 'black') 179, 297, 310, 313, 332. *See also* xenophobia
kan-hpòun. See hpòun

Karen (ethnic group) 79, 122, 155–56, 171, 174–77,
Animist 187
Buddhist 155, 171, 175, 178, 187–88, 280
Christian 155, 171, 175, 178, 181
nationalism 181, 184–86. *See also* nationalism
recruitment in colonial forces 145, 178–81
separatist struggle 164, 171, 175, 185–87, 203–04; origins of ~ 183–85
Karen Affairs Committee 192
Karen National Association (KNA) 181, 184
Karen National Defence Organization. *See* KNDO
Karen National Union. *See* KNU
Karen National Liberation Army. *See* KNLA
Karen Peace Council 190
Karen (Kayin) State 151–55 *passim*, 174, 176, 185–86, 190–212 *passim*, 235, 312, 315, 327
Karen State Peace Committee 204
Karen Unity and Peace Committee 192, 205
Karen Youth Organization 184
Karenni (ethnic group). *See* Kayah
Karenni National People's Liberation Front. *See* KNPLF
Karenni National Progressive Party. *See* KNPP
Karenni Army 170, 225, 261, 274. See *also* EAGs; KNPP
Karenni (Kayah) State 55, 80, 145, 153, 157, 158, 159, 170, 175, 183, 186, 355
Kayah (Karenni, ethnic group) 79, 122, 150, 156, 158, 159, 170, 174–75, 183, 240, 251, 257, 280, 423
Kayah State. *See* Karenni State
Kayan 156, 159, 170, 175
Kayan New Land Party 164, 170

Kayin, as name for Karen people 154, 159, 174. *See also* Karen
Kayin People's Party 191
Kayin State. *See* Karen State
Khin Maung Win. *See* media
Khin Nyunt, Lt.-Gen. 38, 100, 101, 205, 306
Khun Sa (opium warlord) 169, 354
KIA (Kachin Independence Army) 166–67
cooperation with TNLA 275
defection of NDA-K and KDA 168
ongoing conflict with Tatmadaw. *See* Kachin conflict
KIO (Kachin Independence Organization) 166, 262, 270
alliances 168, 272–75
Christian linkage 167, 270, 288
and civil-society organizations 236–37
denies access to census enumerators 269–70. *See also* census
economic activities 262, 264
KKO (Klo Htoo Baw Karen Organization) 190, 193. *See also* DKBA-5
KMT (Kuomintang) 117, 161, 166, 169, 170, 354. *See also* drug trade
KNDO (Karen National Defence Organization) 185, 186, 216
KNLA (Karen National Liberation Army) 164, 171, 176, 177, 185–91 *passim*, 207, 211, 212, 215, 235, 261. *See also* KNU
KNPLF (Karenni National People's Liberation Front) 164, 165, 170
KNPP (Karenni National Progressive Party) 170, 251, 261, 274
KNU (Karen National Union) 164, 171, 261
breaks ranks with other ethnic groups 191, 275–76
ceasefire with government 177, 198, 205, 235
Christian leadership 185; Buddhist dissatisfaction with ~ 187–88

and civil-society organizations 201, 205, 235
defection of DKBA 171, 177, 187–88
divisions 186–94 *passim*,
driven out of Myanmar 171, 177, 188–89
origins 176, 185
see also Karen; KNLA; peace process
Ko Ko Hlaing (dissident) 29
Kokang
  autonomous region 55, 79, 80
  ethnic group 156, 158, 161, 273
  '~ Incident' 55, 100, 168, 169, 274
  see also drug trade; Golden Triangle; MNDAA; Sino-Burmese
Korea. *See* North Korea; South Korea
Kuomintang. *See* KMT
kyat. *See* exchange rate

Lahu (ethnic group) 156, 158, 169, 183
Laiza 13, 17, 265, 345
  KIO/KIA HQ 15, 231, 265, 269, 270
  meeting 152–53, 192, 253, 267–69 *passim*, 276. *See also* NCCT
land
  grabbing 34, 151, 153, 194, 210, 211, 216, 342, 343, 374–75, 420
  tenure 342, 344, 374–75
  see also agriculture
Lashio 98, 282
leadership. *See* power and leadership
Least Developed Country, Myanmar classified as 124, 352, 388
logging. *See* forests
lokiya (mundane world) 300, 302
lokuttara (spiritual domain) 300. *See also* Buddhism
longyi 122, 123

Maha Thamada ('elected king') 294, 295, 300, 303. *See also* Buddhism: and state power

malaria 128, 402, 403
manufacturing 210, 351–52, 364, 368
MEC (Myanmar Economic Corporation) 54, 63, 360, 382
media 32–33, 39–42, 44, 139, 233, 245, 386, 419
  2013 Press Law 40
  censorship 20, 24, 32–33, 39, 40, 42, 44, 232, 417, 423
  Electronics Transactions Law 40
  Khin Maung Win on the ~ 41–42
  international 40, 67, 323
  Printers and Publishers Registration Act 40
  run by exiled groups 40
  see also Irrawaddy; Mizzima; social media
metta sutta (sermon on loving kindness) 307
middle class 36, 136, 232. *See also* social structure
microfinance 139, 342, 344, 371, 372, 373, 380
military
  attempt to control Buddhism 67, 294, 302–09. *See also* State Sangha Nayaka Committee
  business activities 67, 262, 264, 362, 375, 382, 412. *See also* MEC; UMEH
  hostility to idea of federal army 153, 193, 268, 419. *See also* federalism
  ongoing conflict with KIA and TNLA. *See* Kachin conflict
  power of 44, 54, 359; ~ esp. on ethnic issues 277
  as protector of the Union 62, 63
  special status 30–36 *passim*
Millennium Development Goals 2015 387
Min Aung Hlaing, Snr Gen. (C-in-C, Tatmadaw) 55–56, 83, 84, 103, 153, 191, 268, 275–78. *See also* military; National Defence and Security Council

Min Ko Naing (Paw U Tun) 70–71.
    See also 8888 generation
mining 125, 209, 211, 212, 216, 231,
    264, 267, 294, 346–48, 355, 361,
    362, 382, 384, 391, 393
Ministry of Home Affairs 79, 413
mìn laùng ('imminent ruler', rebel)
    179, 296–304 *passim. See also*
    British rule: resistance to
MNDAA (Myanmar National
    Democratic Alliance Army) 164,
    168, 169, 274. *See also* EAGs;
    Kokang
MNLA (Mon National Liberation
    Army) 164, 171, 175, 225,
Mon 251, 255, 316
    armed groups. *See* MNLA
    and census 154
    ethnic group 122, 155–56, 235–36,
        280, 284, 326
    history 176, 179
    political parties 60. *See also* NMSP
    State 79, 80, 155, 157, 205, 238,
        314
Mon National Liberation Army. *See*
    MNLA
monks 180, 204, 279, 327
    and nationalism. *See* nationalism
    political engagement 283, 293–
        320; unease about ~ 67, 299,
        308–09
    resistance to British. *See* anti-co-
        lonial movement; British rule:
        resistance to
    and violence 297, 299, 301
    see also Buddhism; Sangha; Sri
        Lanka
moneylenders (*chettiars*) 145–46,
    163, 299. *See also* Indians
Mongla group. *See* NDAA
mosques 123, 161, 279, 281, 303,
    312–15, 327. *See* anti-Muslim;
    Muslims
MPC (Myanmar Peace Centre) 206,
    232, 245, 266, 276, 409. *See also*
    peace process

MPSI (Myanmar Peace Support
    Initiative) 230, 238, 251, 409. *See
    also* peace process
Muslims 160–61, 179, 280–82, 304,
    311–315, 334, 361, 390
    conflicts with Buddhists 111, 163,
    violence against. *See* anti-Muslim:
        violence
    see also Islam; Rohingya
Mutu Say Poe, Gen. (KNU) 191,
    266, 275. *See also* KNU; peace
    process
Myaing Gyi Ngu monastery 187,
    188, 306. *See also* Thuzana, U
Myanmar, as official name of country
    2, 423
Myanmar Army. *See* military
Myanmar Economic Corporation.
    See MEC
Myanmar Economic Holdings. *See*
    UMEH
Myanmar Peace Centre. *See* MPC
Myanmar Peace Support Initiative.
    See MPSI
Myitkyina 98, 266–68 *passim*, 277,
    282
Myitsone Dam 20, 96, 103, 107, 111,
    151, 231, 265, 340, 356–59. *See
    also* hydropower projects

Naga
    autonomous zone (Nagaland) 78,
        80, 104
    ethnic group 156, 159
    insurgency 104, 164, 172. *See also*
        EAGs
Nargis, Cyclone 47, 73, 89–91,
    230–31, 290, 295, 361, 363,
    397–98, 400, 403, 407
National Defence and Security
    Council 27, 56, 62, 77–78, 268.
    See also state and government
National Democratic Alliance Army-
    Eastern Shan State. *See* NDAA
National Democratic Force. *See* NDF

National League for Democracy. *See* NLD

National Unity Party. *See* NUP

nationwide ceasefire agreement 152, 193, 262, 278, 419
  EAG conditions for 152, 267–68,
  EAG negotiating team formed. *See* NCCT
  negotiations for 21, 252–53. *See also* Aung Min
  vs separate agreements 152, 275–76
  see also EAGs; peace process

Nationwide Ceasefire Coordination Team. *See* NCCT

nationalism 111, 131, 147, 160
  Buddhism and 57, 111, 179–81, 294, 298–302, 310–19, 331–32. *See also* 969; anti-colonial movement; Buddhism; Wirathu
  ethno- ~ 173–77 *passim*, 286–88
  xenophobic 160, 310–19 *passim*, 420. *See also* xenophobia

natural resources 64, 124, 143, 208, 209, 211, 213, 225, 226, 231, 242, 246, 269, 271, 341, 346–47, 361, 362, 376, 392, 393, 409. *See also* deforestation; energy sector; environmental issues; mining sector

Naw Zipporah Sein (KNU) 138, 191

Naypyidaw 10, 29, 30, 82, 108, 121, 297, 305, 386
  national capital moved to 10, 19
  see also government; Hluttaw

NCCT (Nationwide Ceasefire Coordination Team) 152, 166–72 *passim*, 253, 419. *See also* EAGs; Laiza: meeting; nationwide ceasefire agreement; peace process

New Mon State Party. *See* NMSP

Ne Win, General 60, 162, 305
  1962 coup 63, 117, 167, 186, 203, 304

1988 events and fall from power 49, 70, 72, 423. *See also* 8888: movement/uprising
  and Buddhism 67, 304–05
  caretaker government 67, 203, 304, 326
  dies under house arrest 38, 55, 424
  economic nationalism 146, 161, 163, 326
  one of Aung San's Thakins 148
  regime of 40, 63, 70, 305
  see also BSPP

NDAA (National Democratic Alliance Army-Eastern Shan State) 164, 168–69, 224, 272, 274. *See also* Akha; drug trade; Golden Triangle; EAGs

NDF (National Democratic Force) 19, 59, 60, 61

NGOs (non-governmental organizations)
  local 129, 201, 202, 212, 213, 240, 340, 360–61, 388, 398, 410, 411, 413
  international. *See* INGOs
  see also CBOs, civil society; civil-society groups

NLD (National League for Democracy) 25, 49, 53, 58–60, 70, 73, 91, 117, 231, 359, 420, 423. *See also* Aung San Suu Kyi; political parties

NMSP (New Mon State Party) 171, 236, 251, 255, 274,

non-state armed groups. *See* BCP; EAGs; KMT

North Korea 53, 95, 99–100, 102, 108, 119, 376

NSAG (non-state armed groups). *See* BCP; EAGs; KMT

nuns, Buddhist 9, 66, 279, 295. *See also* Sangha

NUP (National Unity Party) 59, 60, 61

Obama, President Barack 21, 102, 402. *See also* United States

Oktama, U (rebel monk) 297
Ottama, U (nationalist monk) 298,
    299, 301
opium. *See* drug trade

Pa-o 61, 183
    armed groups 170, 175, 225. *See
        also* EAGs; PNLO
    autonomous zone 79–80,
    ethnic group 156–57, 170, 174–75
    separatist struggle 164, 170, 175.
        See also EAGs; peace process
pagodas 178, 188–89, 279, 283, 288,
    296, 297, 302, 305
    renovation by military 305
    Sule 3, 4, 313
    see also Buddhism; Shwedagon
Palaung 275
    armed groups 164, 168. *See also*
        EAGs; TNLA
    ethnic group 156, 158, 175
    separatist struggle 164, 168, 175
Panglong Agreement 153, 183, 184,
    193, 422. *See also* federalism
Panglong Conference 176, 182–84,
    268, 422
parami (moral perfection) 295, 301,
    303, 309. *See also* Buddhism: and
    state power; power and leader-
    ship: moral
parliament. *See* Hluttaw
patron–client relations 47, 65, 67, 91,
    145, 179, 189, 234, 240
pattam nikaujjana (rejecting alms)
    307. *See also* Saffron Revolution
peace process
    business involvement in 226, 267
    effect of Kachin conflict on 247
    government and 20, 44, 167,
        191–92, 226, 275–76. See also
        ceasefire(s)
    lack of grassroots participation 207
    need to consider economic factors
        213
    need to engage political parties in
        248

peace-building 152, 202–04,
    223–48 *passim*, 250, 252, 254
    religious leaders and 203
    Tatmadaw and 55, 167, 266, 277,
        391. *See also* military
Phloung-Sgaw (Phalon-Sawaw)
    Democratic Party 60, 190
pipelines 98–99, 104–05, 111,
    348–50
PNLO (Pa-O National Liberation
    Organization) 164, 170. *See also*
    EAGs; Pa-o
political parties 25, 52, 57–61, 72,
    82, 183, 374
    ethnic minority parties 31, 60–61,
        186, 205–07, 226, 239, 246,
        248, 329, 333, 334
    male domination of 137
    and peace process 248
    see also NLD; USDP
political reforms. *See* reforms: political
population 61, 66, 78, 121–24,
    154–59, 162–63, 174, 178, 328,
    343, 344. *See also* census; ethnic-
    ity; religion; social issues
poverty 28, 116, 124, 132, 199, 208,
    210, 319, 320, 336, 341, 348,
    354, 376, 380, 387, 388, 393,
    399, 403, 404, 406, 408
    alleviation 116, 380, 403,
    ~ line 124, 132, 388
    see also social structure
power and leadership
    authority vs influence. *See ana;
        awza*
    karmic/spiritual. *See hpoùn*
    moral 46, 289, 290, 295, 303, 309;
        ~ vs immoral 289, 290. *See also
        parami*
    royal 144, 295–96
    see also state and government
presidency. *See* state and government
press. *See* media
Pyinya Thami, U (Karen monk) 204

quasi-civilian government. *See* gov-
    ernment

Rakhine (ethnic group) 79, 171–72, 235, 280, 310, 311
  armed groups 168, 170–71, 225, 273, 333
Rakhine State 80, 124, 238, 328
  communal violence in 21, 24, 224, 247, 282, 310–12, 314–16, 323–37 *passim*, 385. *See also* communal violence
  ethnic parties 329, 333, 334
  separatist struggle 164, 171–72
  see also Arakan; Rohingya
Rangoon. *See* Yangon
rape 44, 138, 194, 256, 260–61, 305, 323, 327
reforms
  economic 20, 73, 198, 213, 226, 359, 370–75, 376, 380, 383
  political 20, 73, 112, 198, 206, 213, 245, 340, 342, 344, 366, 370, 389, 402, 406, 410–414 *passim*
refugees 43, 55, 92, 100, 114–15, 161, 187, 189, 194, 199, 211, 223–24, 242–43, 256–57, 259, 311, 327, 335, 409–10. *See also* IDPs
Regions 75–81, 226. *See also* state and government; States
religion 33, 63, 67, 122, 123, 137, 150, 173, 178, 180, 181, 189, 194, 235, 263, 279, 281, 283–86, 293, 296, 302, 304, 306, 312–14, 318–20, 337, 423. *See also* animism; Buddhism, Christianity; Islam
Rohingya 155, 257, 310, 311, 324, 328
  armed groups 164, 172, 336
  ASSK on 312, 316, 336–337
  denied citizenship 148, 149, 329–31, 337; ~ and regarded as illegal immigrants 294, 332; ~ but rejected by Bangladesh 311
  identity excluded from 2014 census 155, 311, 329
  international condemnation of treatment 124, 280, 326, 332
  origins 310, 324–25, 328–29
  two-child policy 124, 331

violence between ~ and Rakhine 21, 24, 224, 247, 282, 310–12, 314–16, 323–37 *passim*, 385. *See also* communal violence

Saffron Revolution 3, 4, 19, 49, 55, 67, 89, 230, 291, 294, 305, 306, 307–10, 318, 424
Sakhong, Lian H. 217–22, 252
Salween
  area 176, 179
  river 151, 188, 209, 210, 263. *See also* Hat Gyi Dam; hydropower projects
sanctions 21, 33, 45, 74, 97–99, 109, 112, 116–19, 124, 126, 311, 340, 341, 351, 362, 363, 366, 369, 375, 376, 387, 390, 391, 393, 399–403, 409, 424
Sangha 66–67
  importance/presence 66, 123, 280, 293, 295. *See also* alms-giving
  involvement in anti-colonial movement 296–99
  military attempts to control 67, 294, 302–09
  organization 67, 88, 422. *See also* State Sangha Nayaka Committee
  traditional role 144, 178–79, 296–98; loss of ~ 298
  see also Buddhism; monks; nuns; Sri Lanka
Saw Ba U Gyi (Karen leader) 186, 189, 190, 191, 203
schools 9, 132, 189, 200, 265, 363, 402
  Buddhist 9, 66, 144, 280, 295, 302, 319
  Christian 145
  closure of 131
  dhamma 319
  government 9, 88
  Islamic 312
  Mon 255
  use of minority languages in 88, 149, 246, 255
  see also education; universities

Shan (ethnic group, Tai Yai) 79, 115, 122, 155, 159, 168–70, 235, 257, 273, 280; '~ National Race' 175
Shan State 79–80, 124, 153, 155–159, 238, 390, 420
  2014 census 154
  armed groups 20, 225, 164–70 *passim*, 275. *See also* EAGs; SSA-S; SSA-N; TNLA; UWSA
  centre of drug trade 161, 354. *See also* drug trade; MNDAA; NDAA; UWSA
  natural wealth 346, 394. *See also* natural resources
  ongoing fighting in northern ~ 20–21, 84, 225, 262, 269, 278, 420. *See also* SSA-N; TNLA
  separatist struggle 150, 164, 168–70, 175, 423; origins of ~ 183–84, 186, 304, 422–23
Shan State Army, South. *See* SSA-S
Shan State Army, North. *See* SSA-N
Shan State National Army 170
Shwe Mann (speaker) 34–35, 37, 52–53, 57, 58, 62, 81, 82, 84
Shwe pipelines 98–99, 104–05, 111, 348–50
Shwedagon Pagoda 3, 4, 69, 143, 147, 155, 305, 313, 320
Sino-Burmese (ethnicity) 107, 108, 160, 162, 163, 270, 277
SLORC (State Law and Order Restoration Council) 54, 58, 63, 70, 72, 89, 423
social development 133, 388, 400. *See also* development
social issues 3, 121–33 *passim*. *See also* education; ethnicity; health; HIV/AIDS; population; poverty; social structure
social media 57, 232
social structure 7, 93, 124–26. *See also* cronies; elites; middle class; poverty; social issues
South Korea 36, 100, 349, 350

SPDC (State Peace and Development Council) 25, 47, 52, 54, 63, 72
Sri Lanka 298, 302, 318–19, 378. *See also* Buddhism: and nationalism
SSA-S (Shan State Army, South) 169, 261, 266, 274, 275, 427. *See also* drug trade; EAGs; Shan
SSA-N (Shan State Army, North) 152, 153, 168, 273, 274. *See also* EAGs; Shan
state and government
  apex of power. *See* National Defence and Security Council
  legislature. *See* Hluttaw
  presidency 59–60, 74–77
  separation of powers 73, 74, 76, 77
  special status of the military 30–36 *passim*
  see also constitution; electoral system; federalism; judiciary; Regions; States
State Sangha Nayaka Committee 67, 294, 304–05, 317. *See also* Buddhism: organization
State Law and Order Restoration Council. *See* SLORC
State Peace and Development Council. *See* SPDC
States 75–81, 226. *See also* Regions; state and government
Stevenson, Noel 182–83. *See also* FAA; Panglong Conference
students 1988. *See* 8888 generation; activism
surveillance 231, 309, 399, 413, 414

Ta'ang National Liberation Army (Palaung). *See* TNLA
Tamanthi Dam 21, 356. *See also* hydropower projects; India
Tanintharyi (Tenasserim) 80, 171, 1 85, 205, 215–16, 238, 422. *See also* Dawei
Tatmadaw. *See* military

Tay Za 267, 360, 362, 363. *See also* cronies

tai yin tha ('original people') 148, 160, 311. *See also* citizenship; ethnicity

teak wood. *See* forests

tea money 47, 63, 65. *See also* corruption

Thailand 40, 92, 104, 114, 115, 150, 151, 153, 187, 189, 199, 210, 217. 224, 234, 236, 239, 240, 242, 243, 244, 256, 257, 258, 259, 260, 263, 270, 274, 309, 314, 348, 351, 364, 365, 366, 367, 368, 376, 378, 383, 384, 394, 409, 421

Than Shwe (former junta leader) 10, 33–34, 38, 54–55, 89, 190, 305, 306

thanaka 123

Thibaw, King 143, 296, 298, 422. *See also* Anglo-Burman wars

Thein Sein, U (president) 28, 37, 47–49, 363, 404
 and 2015 election 21, 26. *See also* constitution; elections
 and Aung San Suu Kyi 21, 25, 26, 59, 417
 control of military 55, 167, 266, 277, 391
 forms quasi-civilian government 20, 26
 and peace process 20, 44, 167, 191–92, 226, 275–76. See also ceasefire(s); peace process
 reformist programme 37, 49, 55, 118, 226, 369, 379, 418
 suspends construction of Myitsone Dam 20, 95, 100, 103, 107, 357

Three Diseases Fund (3D Fund) 403

Thuzana, U 187–90, 306. *See also* DKBA

TNLA (Ta'ang National Liberation Army) 164, 164, 168, 275, 278. *See also* KIA; Palaung

tourism 341, 352, 353, 354, 356, 362

tuberculosis (TB) 402

two-child policy 124

U Nu, Prime Minister 63, 176, 183, 301–04, 326, 333, 423

UEC (Union Election Commission) 76, 82

UMEH (Union of Myanmar Economic Holdings) 63, 347, 360, 382

UNFC (United Nationalities Federal Council) 152, 153, 166–72 *passim*, 193, 267, 272, 274, 276. *See also* NCCT; peace process

United Wa State Army/Party. *See* UWSA

'Union' vs 'Federation' 183. *See also* constitution; federalism; military: as protector of the Union; Panglong Conference; state and government

Union Election Commission. *See* UEC

Union of Myanmar Economic Holdings. *See* UMEH

Union of Myanmar Federation of Chambers of Commerce and Industry (UMFCCI) 381

Union Solidarity Development Association/Party. *See* USDA; USDP

universities 131, 133, 137, 146, 277, 288, 307, 400. *See also* education

USDA (Union Solidarity Development Association) 50, 57, 58, 89

USDP (Union Solidarity Development Party) 30, 47, 53, 54, 57–58, 59, 75, 81–84, 89, 334, 417, 419

UWSA (United Wa State Army) 55, 153, 164, 165, 169, 170, 273–74
 Chinese links 169
 and drug trade 150, 354. *See also* drug trade
 and peace process 153, 274, 420
 see also Wa

violence 34, 45, 56, 110, 112, 175,
177, 178, 233, 308–09, 312, 368
against women 135, 138, 256,
260–61. *See also* rape
anti-Muslim 21, 56, 84, 146, 160,
301, 310, 314–16, 361, 424
communal. *See* communal violence

Wa (ethnic group) 156, 158, 175,
183, 224, 271. *See also* UWSA
wildlife 395. *See also* environmental
issues
Wirathu, U (Ashin) 56–57, 310,
314–18
women 44, 135–39, 207, 236–37,
239, 251, 301, 365, 408. See also
activism; Interfaith Marriage
Bill; nuns; rape; violence

World War II 112, 177, 181–82, 184,
286, 325–26

wunthanu athin (nationalist organization) 298–300. *See also* nationalism

xenophobia 111, 160, 162, 163, 310,
313, 319, 417, 420, 421. *See also*
anti-Muslim; *kala*; nationalism

yaa baa (amphetamines). *See* drug
trade
Yangon (Rangoon) 3–12, 70, 96,
121, 146, 218, 303, 312, 352,
422, 423
capital moves to Naypyiday 10, 19
an Indian city 146, 163
Yunnan 97, 98, 105, 150, 155, 157,
158, 159, 160, 161, 162, 166,
168, 263, 265, 266, 270, 271,
281, 285, 357, 358, 378. *See also*
China

Zaw Zaw 263. *See also* cronies